THE
BEST PLAYS OF 1919-20

AND THE

YEAR BOOK OF THE DRAMA
IN AMERICA

Edited by

BURNS MANTLE

BOSTON

SMALL, MAYNARD & COMPANY

PUBLISHERS

CONTENTS

INTRODUCTION

The drama, and more particularly the theater, has been somewhat neglected in the annual reviews covering the artistic achievements of the year. The drama, at least, as it refers particularly to the " regular " theatrical season. Notice is frequently taken of the various forward movements, and the work of interested amateur and semi-amateur organizations. Those interested specifically in the Little Theater movement, for example, have been kept well informed of the activities and achievements of its sponsors. But there is still something to be said for the theater season that, for all its regularity and its admitted commercialism, still plays an important part in the lives of the people.

The purpose of this volume, therefore, is to fill another of those long-felt wants of which, it pleases authors to assume, the public is never conscious until the want is supplied. The aim has been to cover, as completely and as accurately as possible, the activities of the theatrical season in New York, the theory being that by so doing we cover at least the physical source of supply of the drama in America. There are, it is true, a number of productions of new plays made each season outside of New York, particularly in Chicago and Boston, and a scattering few in other cities. These are no less important than the productions made in New York, but it happens that in nine cases out of ten they are preliminary showings of plays intended later for the New York market, and, being worthy, they invariably reach New York within a season of their production. We feel, therefore, that every drama entitled to inclusion in this record is shown in New York some months ahead of the time it is ready to be submitted to the country at large, and it is the theater followers of the country at large whom we seek to serve.

The body of the book contains excerpts, or descriptive synopses, of the ten best plays of the year. For the selection of these particular plays no more is claimed than that they represent the best judgment of the editor, variously confirmed by the public's indorsement. The intention frankly has been to compromise between the popular success, as representing the choice of the people who support the theater, and the success with sufficient claim to literary distinction of text or theme to justify its publication. As frequently has been pointed out, there are many plays that read well which do not " act," as the players phrase the description, and many a success that " acts." usually by reason of the popularity and skill of the players engaged, becomes the sheerest piffle when submitted to the test of type. Therefore a sanely considered compromise of some sort is necessary to balance the selection.

If we seem to have favored the American drama and the native dramatist, it has been without prejudice. However, in making a choice between a play of foreign and one of native authorship, other things being equal. we have not hesitated to give the native dramatist the benefit of his proud countryman's interest in his success. We were, for instance, momentarily in doubt as to whether we should take W. Somerset Maugham's immensely amusing and cleverly written English comedy, " Too Many Husbands," or Salisbury Field's equally bright, but perhaps a shade less ingenious American comedy, " Wedding Bells." The fact that of the two the Englishman's comedy seemed to us quite a bit the more dependent upon the cleverness of the English actors who played it, helped in the decision, but we daresay had the Englishman written " Wedding

Bells " and the American " Too Many Husbands " we should have taken the latter play.

We have included " The Jest," which, technically, belongs with the productions of 1918–19, having been produced in the late spring of 1919, first, because it represents one of the outstanding dramatic successes of the last decade, and, second, because though it was first produced a year ago it achieved its greatest success when its run was resumed at the beginning of last season.

There can be little doubt as to the others. John Drinkwater's " Abraham Lincoln " is easily the most inspiring dramatic success of our time. Being a chronicle play, and divided into episodes with but a thread of continuity, it is one of those plays that is much more impressive in the acting than in the reading, and we have therefore reduced it to the descriptive synopsis form in the hope of thus more clearly visualizing the action.

Eugene O'Neill's " Beyond the Horizon " is likewise one of the fine achievements of the theater, for a duplication of which I believe American theatrical historians will search vainly. We, at least, recall no serious drama of native authorship to be compared with it in the quality of its observant philosophy, its homely and truthful characterization, its gripping theme, its inexorable logic. It won for Mr. O'Neill the Pulitzer prize of $1,000 as " the best play of the year."

James Forbes' " The Famous Mrs. Fair " is of lighter weight, but it, too, has the advantage of a soundly fashioned foundation of character, and that holding human quality that differentiates the real from the superficial and artificial drama.

Booth Tarkington's " Clarence " has been classified by one of its reviewers as the " finest light comedy ever written by an American." While personally we consider this praise somewhat extravagant, holding "Clarence" to be a cleverly written and amusing play, but verging too closely upon farce, and swinging too wide of plausibility, to be accepted seriously as representing the native drama at its best, we feel it is easily entitled to its place in this list of entertainments.

St. John Ervine's "Jane Clegg" is, to us, a perfect sample of the domestic drama at its best, a keenly analytical observation of character, with neither a forced scene nor a wasted speech in its three acts. Zoe Akins' "Declassee" may truthfully be described, we believe, as the best imitation in style of the Pinero drawing-room drama that any American playwright has thus far achieved, which may be said without discredit to Miss Akins. When an imitation so closely approaches the work of a master it honors the imitator as greatly as it flatters the model.

Of the lighter comedies selected, George Middleton and Guy Bolton's "Adam and Eva" is wholesomely and characteristically American; a comedy drama with a touch of satire and a serious thought bracing its comedy theme, and "Mamma's Affair," which won for Rachel Barton Butler a $500 prize offered by Producer Oliver Morosco, and for Professor George Baker's Harvard playwrights such additional fame as attaches to the production of a reasonably popular play written by a graduate of "English 47," is a light but clever satire. And so the list is completed.

As for the remainder of the book's contents they are intended as a comprehensive record of the season as a whole. Though we consider that the theater year proper begins in August and is ended by the first of the succeeding June we have included in this record such summer productions as were made in June and July and continued playing during the fall months. It is a compilation, we believe, that has not previously been attempted in so complete a form, and it is hoped in succeeding volumes to amplify and improve upon it. As a work of reference we hope the Year Book will prove of interest to those whose pleasure it is to keep in close touch with the theater and of some value to those whose work demands such a reference constantly within reach. In compiling the list of advance bookings for the season of 1920–21 we are grateful for the assistance of Mr. Victor Leighton and Mr. Jules Murry.

B. M.

Forest Hills, L. I.,
June 15, 1920.

THE BEST PLAYS OF 1919-20

THE BEST PLAYS OF 1919-1920

THE SEASON IN REVIEW

FOR five weeks following the August opening of the theatrical season of 1919-20 the actors' strike halted, and also enlivened, the drama's progress. The Actors' Equity Association, which had for some years been gaining in strength and importance, issued what amounted to an ultimatum regarding certain reforms that its members had voted should be put into effect. These included extra pay for extra performances, eight performances to constitute a week's work, pay for rehearsals over a stipulated number necessary to the staging of a production, and full pay for those pre-holiday weeks, the week before Christmas and Holy Week, when for years it had been a common custom either to lay the company off without pay or play and pay half salaries. The actors demanded pay when they played. There were other minor problems involved, but these were the main contentions. The actors agreed to submit the issues to arbitration, but the managers refused the offer, saying that inasmuch as the Actors' Equity had allied itself with the American Federation of Labor it had become in effect a labor organization, subject to the dictation of the supreme council of the laborites, and could not therefore speak for itself as exclusively an association of actors.

For the first weeks of the strike neither side made much headway. The managers completed their own organization, agreed to an assessment of a heavy fine if any of them should violate his promise to refuse to engage members of the Equity Association or should otherwise compromise with the enemy, and the actors took readily to the familiar methods of winning strikes, first by " walking out " of the theaters and later by picketing the houses that were "unfair." The managers financed their fight by heavy contributions to a war fund, and the actors supplemented contributions and assessments by giving all-star Equity Benefits, which were hugely successful.

The sympathy of the public appeared to be largely with the actors. The same qualities that had endeared them to playgoing thousands placed them somewhat in the position of personal friends who were seemingly being unjustly treated, and this public sympathy did much to strengthen their position.

Toward the end of the trouble a rival organization known as the Actors' Fidelity Association sprung into being. It was financed largely by George M. Cohan, who being both actor and manager, had sided with the managers and against his old associates of the Equity. The Fidelity attracted to its side some hundreds of those who were opposed to joining with the American Federation of Labor, feeling that art and labor had little in common. But by the time the Fidelity (the " Fidos " its members were called by their rivals) was established the Equity had the fight well in hand and finally, during the first week of September, at a meeting of representatives of the Producing Managers' Association and the Actors' Equity Association, with their respective attorneys, a compromise was reached and the strike declared off.

It was, in the official announcements, a " peace without victory," with both sides reasonably satisfied, but most of the jollifying was done by the actors. There was surprising little bitterness and no attempted reprisals following the settlement. The Equity form of contract was agreed upon and within a few weeks the arbitration committees of the two contending organizations had settled amicably several thousand individual cases submitted for adjustment. The membership of the Equity Association was practically tripled by spring, and, thanks partly to the theatrical prosperity that followed, the managers appeared satisfied with the outcome.

Following the strike there was a rush of new plays. By the end of the second week twenty-eight companies had reorganized and were playing in the Broadway theaters. This number was rapidly added to until by October the full quota of approximately fifty musical and dramatic attractions were playing, a majority of them to huge audiences.

These included the exceptionally popular " Lightnin' " and " East is West," the first of which began its run in August, 1918, and the latter in December, 1918, continuing, with the exception of the time lost during the strike, through the summer and the succeeding season. This gave " Lightnin' " the record for the longest continuous run in the history of New York theaters. It had been played for over 800 performances and was still popular when this record was compiled, while " East Is West " had passed the 600 mark and was still pressing forward.

In the September list also were " Friendly Enemies," " The Better 'Ole," " The Royal Vagabond," " The Ziegfeld Follies of 1919," the Hippodrome's " Happy Days," " Adam and Eva," " A Voice in the Dark," " The Crimson Alibi," " Clarence," " Civilian Clothes," " Moonlight and Honeysuckle," " The Five Million," " Scandal," " Greenwich Village Follies," and " The Gold Diggers." " Friendly Enemies " and " The Better 'Ole " were hold-overs from the previous season and " Scandal " had been brought on from Chicago, where it had already achieved something of a record. This play ran through the season in New York, as also did "Adam and Eva," "Clarence" and "The Gold Diggers." The others, with a considerable number of less popular attractions, enjoyed average runs of two, three or four months and were then sent on tour.

October added "The Storm," "Declassee," "Apple Blossoms," "Too Many Husbands," "His Honor Abe Potash," "The Little Whopper," "On the Hiring Line," "Buddies," and the Winter Garden's "Passing Show of 1919." In Zoe Akins' "Declassee" Ethel Barrymore scored the most pronounced of her recent triumphs, and Booth Tarkington, who, in collaboration with Harry Leon Wilson, had failed earlier in the season with "Up From Nowhere," was credited with having written in "Clarence" one of the best of American light comedies. Both these plays ran the season out, as also did "Buddies" and "The Passing Show," while "Apple Blossoms" achieved a creditable record of 236 performances. It was during October that E. H. Sothern and Julia Marlowe returned to the stage for another season's tour, playing "Hamlet," "Twelfth Night" and "The Shrew." They were highly successful.

The November contributions were only thirteen in number. By this time the available theaters were mostly occupied with paying attractions. The most notable of the thirteen were the musical comedy, James Montgomery's "Irene," David Belasco's production of his own and George Scarborough's "The Son-Daughter," both of which continued through till spring, and Salisbury Field's "Wedding Bells," which ran for 168 performances. Others included Billie Burke's return from a year in the cinema with Somerset Maugham's "Caesar's Wife," an interesting but not popular Irish drama, Lenox Robinson's "The Lost Leader," and a production by the Theater Guild of

William Dean Howells' "The Rise of Silas Lapham."

Counting out the Sundays there were nearly enough plays produced in December to provide a new play a night. Twenty-two productions were made. These included the long-heralded "Aphrodite," "One Night in Rome," "My Lady Friends," "Monsieur Beaucaire," "Abraham Lincoln," "For the Defense," "The Sign on the Door," "The Famous Mrs. Fair," and Elsie Janis' war-time revue. John Drinkwater's "Abraham Lincoln" immediately took its place as the dramatic sensation of the year. Hartley Manners' "One Night in Rome" brought Laurette Taylor back to a public with which she is immensely popular, but failed to duplicate the success of her previous offerings. James Forbes' "The Famous Mrs. Fair" was credited with being by far the best of the post-war plays. "Monsieur Beaucaire" duplicated in New York something of the success it previously had enjoyed in London, and Channing Pollock's "The Sign on the Door" was accepted as the most stirring of the season's melodramas. There were also fourteen special matinee performances of Gorky's "Night Lodging" during the month.

During the mid-season weeks of January there were another fifteen plays produced but of the fifteen only four were successful in meeting the test of 100 performances or more. And that is the test Broadway applies. If an attraction continues to play, without undue forcing, for twelve or thirteen weeks it is reasonably to be credited with being a success and may confidently be sent into the hinterland with the indorsement of the capital. But if it falls below that it usually is silently listed with the failures or quasi-failures.

The four that came through the January fire were " The Purple Mask," " The Acquittal," " Mamma's

Affair," " The Passion Flower," and a revue, " As
You Were." Leo Ditrichstein's staging of and appearance in " The Purple Mask," an adaptation from
the French made by the English actor, Matheson
Lang, helped that old-fashioned mystery romance considerably. " The Acquittal " represented, technically,
the best performance of melodrama the season dis-
closed and established Rita Weiman, the author, as a
playwright with a promising future. " The Passion
Flower," as translated by John Garrett Underhill from
the Spanish of Jacinto Benevente, a somewhat turgid
but intimately revealing domestic drama, reintroduced
Nance O'Neill, the tragic actress, to the Broadway
stage after a considerable absence. " Mamma's Affair," Rachel Barton Butler's Harvard prize play,
created a considerable stir among discriminating playgoers, and " As You Were," following the usual form
of the modern revue, revealed so surprising a beauty
in setting as to win an enthusiastic press indorsement
for its producer, a newcomer to the field named John
Murray Anderson.

The plays that fell below the Broadway test for one
reason or another included a reverent but somewhat
artificial rewriting of the Christ story with the Passion Play of Oberammergau used as a background.
This was called " The Light of the World," and was
elaborately staged. Attributed in the program to the
authorship of one " Pierre Saisson," it was later acknowledged by its real authors, George Middleton and
Guy Bolton, who previously had been successful with
" Adam and Eva " and the season before with " Polly
With a Past." Thirty-one performances at the Lyric
Theater and it was gone There was also a fine performance of Tolstoi's " The Power of Darkness "
given by the Theater Guild, staged by Emmanuel
Reicher, with his son, Frank Reicher, prominently cast
as " Daddy " Akim. Grace George came forward with

her second play of the year. " She Would and She Did " having failed her she offered " The ' Ruined ' Lady," a sprightly light comedy written by Frances Nordstrom of the varieties which, though it played for less than a month in New York, proceeded to Chicago and became there one of the marked successes of the season. Otis Skinner, electing to devote another season to the romantic drama, and also to the type of Italian character he had played with popular successs in Booth Tarkington's " Mister Antonio," presented a play called " Pietro," of which Maude Durbin Skinner, his wife, was part author, and Jules Eckert Goodman the other part. It achieved forty-one performances at the Criterion Theater and then went bravely in search of box-office receipts in the West. A well-acted and more than reasonably interesting melodrama of the month was one called " Big Game," but the play-going public would have none of it and probably by this time it has been made over into a scenario for the screen.

February was an interesting month for several reasons. For one Maxine Elliott, after having played most successfully through the West with William Faversham in "Lord and Lady Algy," determined upon a starring tour of her own, and presented a play by William Hulburt called " Trimmed in Scarlet " at the theater bearing her name. Miss Elliott was an entire success, commanding the usual chorus of superlatives in praise of her beauty's preservation, but the play was weak and the actress decided to withdraw it after two weeks. Miss Elliott was followed at the same theater by John Drew, who also had been absent from the local stage for a matter of two years. Mr. Drew's play was Rupert Hughes' " The Cat-bird," a pleasantly entertaining little comedy that presented the star as a middle-aged entomologist. But it, too, failed to achieve a popularity sufficient to keep it playing longer than a month. Near the end of February the Theater Guild presented its second St. John Ervine play, "Jane Clegg." Elsie Ferguson, after three years devoted to motion pictures, returned to the stage as the heroine of Arnold Bennett's "Sacred and Profane Love," and Lionel Barrymore, eager to re-establish himself as an independent star, following his joint-starring engagement with his brother John, in "The Jest," appeared in Eugene Brieux' "The Letter of the Law." Miss Ferguson and Mr. Barrymore were welcomed with considerable enthusiasm, but the plays in which they appeared caused no particular excitement. The Ervine drama, however, kept the Theater Guild busy, and happy, the rest of the season. February also saw Rachel Crothers' determined effort to show those defiant managers who had insisted her drama, "He and She," was not one to pay its way, that they were wrong. When it had been done previousy, notably as "The Herfords," it had not been properly cast, insisted the author, nor was the temper of the times so well suited to the understanding of its theme. So she produced "He and She" herself, and likewise herself played the heroine. It was a good performance of a sincerely and well written play, but the public was less responsive than was hoped for and after twenty-eight performances the courageous author acknowledged herself beaten and withdrew her play. "The Wonderful Thing," with Jeanne Eagels playing what was frequently referred to as a "French Peg-o'-my Heart," and "The Night Boat," a Charles B. Dillingham musical play, were other successful productions of the month.

March was distinguished by the production of "The Tragedy of Richard III," which brought John Barrymore forward in his first Shakespearean role. This was a triumphant occasion for all concerned, including Arthur Hopkins, the producer, and Robert Edmund Jones, who designed scenery and costumes. Not only did young Mr. Barrymore surprise and delight the most loyal of his admirers, but he convinced the doubters finally that he is possessed of great gifts of histrionism. Within comparatively few weeks he mastered the reading of verse and so improved his voice control as to add immeasurably to the beauty of his reading. There was no tinge of that flippant colloquialism the modern actor so frequently assumes to mask his inability to read blank verse, nor anything resembling a pompous imitation of the booming rhetorical school of old. A similarly sound and satisfying compromise was effected in the playing of the scenes, with the result that the Barrymore " Richard " immediately took its place as a notable achievement of the theater rather than merely the personal success of a favorite actor. Unfortunately, in the midst of his triumph. and while the audiences were still crowding the theater to its capacity, Mr. Barrymore felt himself upon the verge of a nervous breakdown and decided that he must rest. In addition to rehearsing and helping to superintend the production of " Richard," he had also been posing for the picture of " Dr. Jekyll and Mr. Hyde," and the strain had proved too severe. Therefore the engagement was halted and Mr. Barrymore spent the spring and summer in recuperating his wasted strength.

In March also came Theda Bara with " The Blue Flame," thus giving a touch of variety to the drama of the day. Miss Bara, having achieved an international reputation as the most alluring, or at least the most effective, of those sinuous villainesses of the screen known as " vamps," was considered a good investment, a " sure-fire " investment, in fact, as a legitimate star, if the proper play could be found for her. " The Blue Flame " seemed just the right vehicle. The story was of a young agnostic who believed that he. as well as

God, could create life, and who tried it with the body of his fiancee, after she had been killed by lightning, only to discover that while he had restored the beat of the pulse he had been unable to supply the lady with a soul. The play was produced, and the curiosity to see it in certain eastern cities, notably Boston, was so great that frequently riots were threatened. New York, however, laughed openly at the rather preposterous dialogue and the wildly melodramatic situations, and so, after forty-eight performances " The Blue Flame " was sent on tour, where it prospered exceedingly.

This was the month in which Percy Mackaye's " ballad-drama," " George Washington," was played for sixteen performances and withdrawn. Designed originally as a masque to be performed in the open, and on festival occasions, it did not lend itself gracefully to reshaping for the theater. Furthermore it was brought into direct contrast with the impressively staged " Abraham Lincoln," and the comparison was entirely against it. Walter Hampden, who had played the titular role, revived " Hamlet," in which role he he had scored a distinct success the previous season. There was also a revival of the " Medea " of Euripides, given at the Garrick Theater by Maurice Browne and Ellen Van Volkenburg, and two melodramas inspired by the prevalent interest in things spiritual. These were " The Hole in the Wall " and " The Ouija Board," both interesting, but the latter rather the more wierd and thrilling of the two.

Not much happened during April worthy of review. There was an elaborate revival of the twenty-year-old " Florodora," with a new sextette of beauties and an old sextette dressed as were the original six. It was a worthy and also a successful revival. Ed Wynn, the comedian who, because of his activities in the actors' strike, had earned the undying enmity of his employers, came to town with a " Carnival " which he personally had organized and staged to provide himself with a job. His venture was entirely successful and promises to join the hardy annuals in the revue class. A musical version of Catherine Chisholm Cushing's Scotch comedy, " Kitty MacKaye," called " Lassie," was offered in April and popularly received, and there was a second revival of Gorky's " Night Lodging " which continued for a fortnight.

May is usually a month of summer shows and dramatic revivals — the summer shows hoping to gain such headway during the remaining weeks of reasonably cool weather that they may continue through June and July, and the dramatic revivals offering managers with idle and expensive actors on their hands, to whom they have guaranteed salaries for a certain number of weeks, a chance to utilize their services. This year, however, there was but one revival, and that a modernized version by Zoe Akins of " Forget-me-not," called " Foot-loose." Arthur Richman's romantic comedy, " Not So Long Ago," placed back in the New York of the early 70s, proved a placid but agreeable entertainment, and there was one promising musical comedy in " Honey Girl," which is a musicalized version of the comedy drama, " Checkers," popular fifteen years ago. Another drama with a spiritualistic theme was Anne Crawford Flexner's " All Soul's Eve," in which the spirit of a dead mother returns and takes possession of the body of an Irish nurse, the better to watch over a sick child.

A fine season in many ways. A remarkable season in that it has been witness to the breaking of several records of one kind or another. The quality of the plays, speaking generally. averages much higher than it has in any season we remember in which there has been an equal number of new plays offered. The fact that there have been more long runs than ever before

is not particularly significant, being traceable directly
to the prosperity prevailing.   It is significant, however,
that there were a greater number of plays produced
by independent producers, as distinguished from the
organized and, in a sense, commercially allied producers, than ever before.   This, first because there was
a quantity of " outside money," war profits and the
like, in search of theatrical investments ; and, second,
because the prevailing prosperity, having lessened the
chances of failure, served to buck up the courage of
the timid little fellow with a play to present and a
small bank-roll with which to negotiate the debut.
Many of these independents have been successful, and
as in almost every instance they have brought with
them new ideas, new courage and expanding ambi-
tions their influence on the future of the drama is
quite sure to be felt.

   In this connection we are reminded of the charge
that the theater is gradually being taken over by the
motion picture interests, a charge which created some
little excitement during the winter when it was discovered that one big picture concern had secured control
of three or four New York theaters with the intention
of producing plays therein which later would be turned
into moving pictures.   In this way it was " movie
money " that financed Ethel Barrymore's season in
" Declassee," and John D. Williams' ventures with
" Beyond the Horizon " and " For the Defense," not to
mention half a dozen others.   The fear of some is that
plays will be chosen hereafter not on their merits as
drama but rather because of their possible future value
as screen plays.   It is a little early to judge the effect
the closer linking of the screen and stage will have on
the drama, but personally, considering what we know of
the influences bearing upon the selection and production of plays in the past, we cannot work up much
excitement over the threatened invasion.   And as this

happens to be the first year in which the distrusted cinema magnates have taken a hand in producing plays, and also the best season we have enjoyed in years in the general quality of the productions made, we will have to wait a more convincing proof than any we have so far been shown before believing the new influence is working great harm to the theater.

Statistically, also, it proved a most interesting season. There were produced in New York approximately 150 new plays, dramatic and musical. Of these there were six with more than 300 performances each to its credit, fourteen with over 200, and 26 that passed the 100 performance division.

"ABRAHAM LINCOLN"

An American Chronicle Play in Six Episodes

By John Drinkwater

WITH some slight misgiving on the part of both the English author, John Drinkwater, and the American producer, William Harris, Jr., " Abraham Lincoln " was first presented at the Cort Theater, New York, on Dec. 15, 1919. Much had been written in a jocular vein of the courage, not to say " nerve," required by an English poet who would attempt to write an historical drama on so intimately American a theme as that supplied by the life and character of Lincoln, and there were many in the audience that opening night of a mind defiantly to oppose any indorsement of the proceedings. As frequently happens, however, those who came to scoff remained to applaud. By the time the third episode had been reached the success of the premier was assured and the triumph of the play freely predicted.

We naturally are inclined to feel that the restaging the play received on this side of the Atlantic, had something to do with its local success. Lester Lonergan, who directed the rehearsals, no doubt did a great deal to clear the action and the text of such foreign atmosphere and incidental detail as were said to have been made sport of by those Americans who had seen the play in London. Also the outstanding success of Frank McGlynn, the actor engaged for the titular rôle, and who not only contributed a fine performance but who is a perfect physical selection for the "type," unquestionably helped greatly with the success. But there is something more deeply significant than can be accounted for by these material aids back of the success of "Abraham Lincoln," something that can perhaps best be described as a spiritual quality so fine, so universally human, so holding that the recital strikes a note of exaltation like unto that inspired by a passion play. It is a quality that was felt in England, both in Birmingham, where the play was first presented by the Repertory company of which the author is director, and later in London, as quickly as it was in America.

"'Abraham Lincoln' was performed in London at an obscure and ugly theater in a distant suburb by an unknown management with a cast which did not contain the name of a single player of reputation," St. John Ervine has written for the *North American Review*. "There was not an actor in the cast with sufficient popularity to draw sixpence into the theater. The scenic effects were so slight as to be negligible. There was no orchestra. . . . And yet the play was an enormous success.

It also is an enormous success in New York, and will be an enormous success on tour for years to come. Because it is truly a great play. A synopsis is appended:

EPISODE I

It is early evening. In the parlor of Abraham Lincoln's home in Springfield, Ill., in the spring of 1861, two of Lincoln's neighbors sit before a grate fire quietly smoking. They are Mr. Stone and Mr. Cuffney, and, having heard that the Republican Convention in Chicago has agreed to extend to their old friend an invitation to be the party's nominee for the office of President of the United States, they have come to wish him well and to express the hope that he will accept.

Lincoln enters the room unannounced. The pockets of his long coat are stuffed with papers, and the old hat is perched uncertainly above his high forehead. His clean-shaven, angular face is serious, as with the weight of the pending decision, but the lines are smoothed away in a gentle smile of greeting for the old friends and the wife.

They have come, the visitors explain, to be the first to congratulate him. And they are humbled by the thought of his being chosen to " be one of the great ones of the earth." It makes the chosen one humble, too, Lincoln agrees. It is not an office a man would seek nor accept, with times what they are — but for that inner conviction that shapes the destinies of men . . . They drink a health —" to Abraham Lincoln and the United States "— and he joins them " to the hope of honest friends . . ."

The delegation is shown in. Its members are William Tucker, merchant; Henry Hind, attorney; Elias Price, preacher; James Macintosh, editor. Mr. Tucker is the chairman, and, it may be, a little conscious of the honor. He, and his fellow delegates, have been sent to tender to Mr. Lincoln an invitation to become the Republican Party nominee for the office of President of the United States, and because of an existing split in the ranks of the Democratic Party, the election of the Republican nominee is practically a certainty.

Have they considered his disqualifications, as well as his qualifications? Lincoln demands. There are some things, some characteristic peculiarities, it may be, that Washington society may not approve. There are, too, Seward and Hook; they are men of great experience, and they are ambitious . . .

There will be many serious questions of policy to be determined, and he is a stubborn man, Lincoln continues. If it should transpire that the South should claim the right to secede, or to go farther than it has gone with slavery, and the decision should rest with him, he would have everybody's mind clear as to his attitude. If there must be resistance he will stand inexorably for that decision. . . .

Knowing, then, his position on the greatest of the problems his administration will likely be called upon to face; that under no circumstances will he recede from his stand against slavery; that, because of what he knows and of what he had seen when he was a boy in New Orleans, he has taken oath, if ever he has a chance to hit slavery he will hit it hard, they still have no other conditions to make?

They assure him again that they have none. Their invitation is still the same and there is not one among them who is not proud to bear it to him. Then, he will accept. He calls to Susan to show the gentlemen in to Mrs. Lincoln, and as they leave the room he stands silent for a moment. Slowly his eyes turn to the map of the United States hanging upon the wall. Steadily, anxiously he gazes upon it, spreading his great arms as though to embrace the country in charge of whose destinies he is shortly to be placed. Then, turning to the center table, he kneels beside it. His head is bowed and his face is buried in his hands in an attitude of prayer as the curtain falls.

EPISODE II

It is ten months later. In Secretary of State Seward's room in Washington, Johnson White and Caleb Jennings, commissioners representing the Confederate States of the South, are meeting with the Secretary in some hope that he may help them to avert the calamity of civil war which threatens. They know, they tell Seward, as all the South knows, that he is the one member of the cabinet most likely to understand clearly the situation.

The Secretary replies that he is not unconscious of

their intended compliment, but he cannot go farther than that. Seven of the southern states have declared an intention of seceding from the Union; President Lincoln, with the indorsement of his cabinet, feels that such action must inevitably lead to the decline of America.

Still, the commissioners insist, there is a chance for compromise. If the government will order the withdrawal of the garrison from Fort Sumter the South will agree to take no further action at present, and South Carolina will quite likely be willing to lead the other seceding states in a reconsideration of their intention to break with the Union. . . . Certainly, though the President is firm in his decisions, even to the point of stubbornness, it is not unreasonable to hope that he might listen to the advice of the most able man among his advisers.

Before the commissioners can gracefully withdraw President Lincoln enters the room. He is bearded, now, and already the strain of his great responsibilities are beginning to show in the lines of his face. Jennings and White seek to continue their exit, but Lincoln asks them to remain. He would like to talk with them for five minutes, if they will be so kind —

Seward explains that the gentlemen from the South have come in the hope of sounding such " moderating influences " as may be brought to bear on the situation. The President is equally hopeful that they have brought " moderating influences " with them. It would, perhaps, have been in better taste if they had appealed directly to the government, but — what is it they have to suggest?

Jennings repeats the proposition that the forces at Fort Sumter be withdrawn, and that the South be, in a measure, assured of its right to independent action, whatever the question involved.

The President replies that such a compromise is impossible. They may believe that they have an honest case, but they have not. The South is much more deeply interested in putting the stamp of national approval on slavery than it is in establishing its rights of secession, and that shall never be. It knows that abolition is a possibility, if not a probability of the future, and seeks by forcing its right to secede to make abolition impossible. . . . Let them understand, too, and that clearly, that the issue of civil war rests with the South. So long as it remains loyal to the Union it will be privileged to fight for slavery by all constitutional means, and extend its foundations if it can. But if it seeks the disruption of the Union by insisting upon its right to destroy the Union, then shall the burden of war rest with it. Let them send that message to the men of the South, and let them beg, by all the bonds of affection that should hold a united people together, that they order Beauregard's withdrawal before it is too late. A special wire shall be placed at their service to facilitate the transmission of their message.

A messenger who had ridden straight from Major Anderson at Fort Sumter arrives. He brings the news that the fort can be held for no more than three days without provisions or reinforcements. Within three days the decision must be for war, unless the South's commissioners succeed in convincing their people. A vain hope. Already the reply has come from the South that they will not give way. Nor do they leave any opening for further discussion. Quickly the President summons the cabinet — Salmon P. Chase, Montgomery Blair, Simon Cameron, Caleb Smith, Burnet Hook (the one fictitious character in the play) and Gideon Welles. Solemnly the President states the situation to them. The government faces the gravest crisis in its history. either the order must be to hold Sumter or —

Would it not be wise to withdraw altogether, queries Hook; to give the South a chance at suggesting compromise, and to plead military necessity, if need be, as an excuse for the move? To which the President replies that in his opinion to do anything that would suggest temporizing then would be fundamentally to admit the South's claim to its right of independent action. And if that question be not met now, it would have to be met soon. To withdraw might postpone war, it could not conceivably prevent it. . . . To do all that could be done to hold Sumter would be to notify the world of the government's intention to defend a clean cause; they were not the aggressors, but the aggressed; in their hands they held a sacred trust; their duty was to defend it. . . . The question is for the provisioning of Fort Sumter: The President, Chase and Blair vote aye. . . . For the withdrawal of Major Anderson's troops: Seward, Smith, Hook, Welles and Cameron.

For a moment the silence is profound. Then the President speaks. The responsibility of over-riding the decision of the cabinet may devolve upon him. It is he Congress and the country will hold responsible. In the event of his taking that action should he receive any of their resignations? Again there is silence. The meeting is dismissed. . . . The messenger is summoned and bidden to return immediately to Major Anderson. Lincoln's decision has been made. The first shipment of provisions for the relief of the fort will go forward that evening!

EPISODE III

Nearly two years later, in a small reception room in the White House. A Mrs. Goliath Blow has called. She has come to reassure herself that the dear President is not growing weary of the war and that he will not think of lessening his firmness until the awful South is thoroughly beaten. Mrs. Blow is the wife of a war profiteer.

A Mrs. Otherly is announced. She is in mourning.

She has lost a son at the front. Still, as Mrs. Blow points out, they must all expect to make sacrifices. Conditions are terrible, what with the price of everything advancing. She and Goliath have been actually compelled to cut down several of their subscriptions.

The President enters the room. His face is drawn; his eyes are tired. Yes, he has news. The Union forces have won a victory, with a loss of 800 men to the enemy's 2,700 — thirty-five hundred casualties! What a whimsical way to look at it, observes Mrs. Blow — when only the 800 Federals really matter.

Mrs. Otherly begs the President's permission to ask him a question? Must the war go on? Isn't there some way of stopping it?

Such a foolish question would never have occurred to Mrs. Blow. She admits it.

Yet, agrees Lincoln, it is a right question. For two years he has put it daily to himself. In two years war has become a bitterness to him almost past the enduring. But he can see no other way. The justice of the cause for which the North is fighting has not been changed. War is wrong; has always been wrong; always will be wrong. But so long as men are weak, and foolish and jealous, wars will continue. None can outstrip the world. There is an instinct to which men are beholden that bids them resist aggression. Wrong it may be, but there it is. Gradually it may be overcome by clear thinking. To have said that there should be no war, because war was an evil thing, would have settled nothing. It is a great responsibility to decide so grave a question, but all he could do, all any man could do, was to uphold and to defend the truth as he saw it.

Mrs. Blow agrees perfectly. Just as Goliath had said, those Southern brutes must be taught a lesson. Perhaps, suggests the President, he could get Goliath a commission, seeing he is only 38. The idea is quite

silly to Mrs. Blow.   Goliath is needed at home.   He
has so many government contracts to look after.   But
she will be glad to tell him what the President has said,
especially about those people who want to stop wars.
Of course she is sorry for Mrs. Otherly, but why make
matters worse by thinking that way about them?   She
does hope the dear President will not think of weak-
ening.

As she turns to go she offers the President her hand,
which he does not take, but he speaks plainly.   He
would have her know that he is ashamed of her and
of all her kind; of all who, without sacrifice of any
kind, go about talking of destroying the South and
preaching revenge and destruction and hatred.   The
people of the South are mistaken, but they are honestly mistaken and in, to them, a great cause.   It is
people like her that dishonor the cause for which the
North is fighting.   And as she leaves, too completely
squelched to reply, the President summons Susan and
bids her be careful the next time Mrs. Blow calls.   He
fears she may meet with an accident.

President Lincoln has sent for William Custis, an
aged negro preacher.   The old man was born a slave,
but gaining his freedom in later years, acquired some
education and has spent his life working for his people.
It is to him that the President first intimates his intention of signing the Proclamation of Emancipation.
For long he has considered it.   Now his decision has
been made.   Slavery shall be abolished.

In the street below is heard the tramp of marching
soldiers, and as they pass the window they can be heard
singing in chorus: " John Brown's body lies a moul-
d'ring in the grave."

EPISODE IV

A few days later there is a meeting of the cabinet at
Washington.   Caleb Smith is gone and Simon Came-

ron has been succeeded by Edwin M. Stanton, as Secretary of War. The others are Seward, Chase, Blair, Welles and Hook. They arrange themselves at the table while awaiting the arrival of the President. The talk is of the summons for this special meeting. Stanton explains that there is special news from the front. McClellan has just defeated Lee at Antietam. It is the greatest victory the Union forces have yet scored and will probably mark the turning point of the war.

It is Hook's opinion that this is probably the time the President will select to bring up his Emancipation Proclamation again. And he (Hook) is unalterably opposed to it. What does it mean, anyway? As he understands the situation, the North is fighting to preserve the integrity of the Union. Now the President talks as though emancipation were the only thing that concerned him.

Seward corrects him. The President has always held the preservation of the Union as the paramount issue of the war, but there has never been any question of his feeling regarding slavery. Had he not said:

" If I could save the Union without freeing any slaves, I would do it; and if I could save it by freeing all the slaves I would do it; and if I could save it by freeing some and leaving others alone, I would also do that. My paramount object in this struggle is to save the union."

The President comes. Apparently he is in fine spirits, but almost afraid to admit it, even to himself. It has been so long since there was good news to report. In his hand he carries a small book, and now, as though to compose his own thoughts as well as those of his associates, he begs permission to read it. Hook sneers, and Stanton moves uneasily in his seat. Here is a special meeting of the cabinet called to consider the greatest victory of the war and the President asks permission to read a book! The others settled in their chairs as Lincoln proceeds to regale them with Artemus Ward's " High Handed Outrage at Utica." . . .

The meeting proceeds. McClellan, Seward assumes, is in pursuit of Lee, which leads the President, with the suggestion of a smile, to intimate that his Secretary of State is something of an optimist. But, if McClellan is not in pursuit of ·Lee, he agrees, he will send Grant after him. But, interposes, Blair. Grant drinks. To which the President replies that if he knew Grant's brand he would send a barrel to some of his other generals. Drink or not, Grant wins victories.

Hook, growing restless, not to say disgusted, at this levity, would like to know if there is any other business to be considered. There is. And it is then the President produces his proclamation. The moment has arrived, he believes, for its issuance. To refresh their memories he reads it to them again:

" It is proclaimed that on the first day of January in the year of our Lord one thousand, eight hundred and sixty-three, all persons held as slaves within any state, the people whereof shall then be in rebellion against the United States, shall be then, thenceforward, and forever free."

Hook is immediately on his feet with a protest. Any such proclamation should not be issued before victory is sure. To put it forward now would cause dissension when unity was most needed. But the President is firm. He has for months considered with great earnestness the responsibility of issuing the proclamation. Once he had given way to them when they had thought it not the proper time to issue it. But now he is convinced the hour has arrived. . . .

Stanton, Chase and Hook are for delay. Let the

present business of preserving the Union be given all attention. But the President's mind is made up, and as he repeats the significant words, " Shall be thenceforward and forever free," he affixes his signature to the proclamation.

There is a moment's silence and then the members of the cabinet quietly withdraw. Seward, Blair and Welles shake the President's hand; the others merely bow. As Hook is leaving the President calls him back. As he had once had an understanding with another member of his ministry he now purposes to face Hook with the plain facts of his intriguing disloyalty. Hook, Lincoln knows, is ambitious and envious. He tells him so. Hook is frank enough to admit that he is opposed to the President's policy and to his " lack of firmness." He would have him definitely declare what shall be the punishment of the rebels after the war. The President answers that he refuses to permit the war to become a " blood-feud "; the government will defeat treason, but in place of punishing it with severity it will meet it with conciliation; such may be a policy of weakness to Hook, but it is to him a policy of faith and compassion.

As his anger mounts the accused minister offers to resign his post — and Lincoln accepts his resignation. Hook angrily departs, begging to be excused from the formality of shaking hands. Over the face of the President spreads a look of great pity, and of great weariness. He asks that his secretary be sent to him. When Hay arrives he bids him read a passage from Shakespeare's " The Tempest "— a favorite passage, beginning: " Our revels now are ended; these, our actors, as I foretold you, were all spirits, and are melted into air, thin air; " and ending: " We are such stuff as dreams are made on, and our little life is rounded with a sleep." The curtain falls.

EPISODE V

It is an April evening in 1865.   In a farmhouse near
Appomattox, General Grant, as Commander-in-Chief
of the Union forces, has made his headquarters.   He
is smoking and occasionally he takes a drink of
whiskey.

He is awaiting word from General Meade, in command of the field forces that have General Robert E.
Lee's Confederate Army practically surrounded.   It is,
so far as Grant can see, only a matter of hours before
Lee will be forced to surrender.   Lee is a great man,
but he cannot conquer the unconquerable.

An orderly announces the arrival of President Lincoln.   The President's visit is unexpected, but, as he
explains to Grant, he grew anxious and could not keep
away.   Now he hears with a great sigh of relief that
the end is seemingly near.   When it comes they " must
be merciful."

. . . .

The night passes.   At 6 o'clock an orderly sent with
a cup of coffee for the President finds him still sleeping soundly, his long body stretched between two chairs.
A discreet rattling of dishes arouses him.   Slowly, and
a little painfully, he pulls himself together.

A moment later General Grant arrives to report that
word has come from General Meade.   Lee had asked
for an armistice at 4 o'clock.   There is a moment's
silence as the two men look at each other.   The end
has come, and yet, though for four long years " life has
been but the hope of this moment," how simple is its
coming!   Gravely the President extends his hand to
his Commander-in-Chief.   Grant has served the country well; he has made the President's work possible.
But, replies Grant, he could not have succeeded if the
President had not believed in him.

Soon General Meade arrives to confirm the report of

the surrender. After a word or two with Grant —
and an order that there shall be no hanging or shooting
of the conquered rebels; that the worst that shall happen to them is that they shall be frightened out of the
country — Lincoln is gone, on his way back to the
capital.

General Lee arrives. A war-weary man, and a
beaten one, but of dignified bearing and punctiliously
groomed. He returns the salute of his conqueror and
there is an exchange of compliments. General Grant
submits the terms upon which surrender will be accepted. They are "magnanimous," General Lee
agrees, but he would like to make one submission.
The officers have been allowed to keep their horses.
Could the same privilege be extended the cavalry troop-
ers? Their horses also are their own. Grant understands. Horses will be needed on the farms. It shall
be as Lee wishes. A moment's pause and the gallant
Southerner unbuckles his sword and offers it to his
conqueror. Grant bids him return it to his scabbard.
It has but one rightful place. They shake hands and
gravely salute each other. As Lee turns toward the
door the curtain falls.

EPISODE VI

In the lounge of Ford's Theater, outside the President's box, the night of a gala performance of "Our
American Cousin," April 14, 1865, there are gossiping
groups of spectators. Through the doors of the box
President Lincoln and Secretary Stanton can be seen
talking together. Near them are Mrs. Lincoln and
another lady and an officer.

An act of the play has been finished. There is the
sound of applause from the auditorium. The orchestra plays patriotic airs. Suddenly there are cries of
"Lincoln!" "The President!" "Speech!" The
gossips stop to listen. The President rises slowly in

his place and holds up his hand.   There is immediate
silence.   The President speaks. . . .

" After four dark and difficult years we have achieved
the great purpose for which we set out.   General Lee's
surrender to General Grant leaves but one Confederate
force in the field.   The end is immediate and certain.
. . . The task of reconciliation, of setting order where
there is now confusion, of bringing about a settlement
at once just and merciful, and of directing the life of a
reunited country into prosperous channels of good will
and generosity, will demand all our wisdom, all our
loyalty.   It is the proudest hope of my life that I may
be of some service in this work. . . . Whatever it may
be it can be but little in return for all the kindness and
forbearance that I have received.   With malice toward none, with charity for all, it is for us to resolve
that this nation, under God, shall have a new birth of
freedom; and that government of the people, by the
people, for the people shall not perish from the earth."

The cheering dies away.   A call boy announces the
last act.   The doors of the boxes are closed.   The
three raps of the stage manager are heard and the play
is resumed.   Suddenly from the entrance at the left
John Wilkes Booth appears.   He edges his way
stealthily toward the center box.   Arrived there he
uncovers the hand hidden beneath his cloak, exposing
the revolver he carries.   Pulling open the door of the
box he fires, slams the door to and hurries away.   The
door opens and an officer dashes out in pursuit of
Booth.   Mrs. Lincoln is seen kneeling by the side of
the President.   A doctor is hurriedly summoned.   A
crowd of spectators from the other boxes and from the
auditorium begins to gather.   There is a buzz of muffled conversation, of exclamations of grief and of horror.   Suddenly a hush falls upon the crowd as Secre-

tary Stanton steps from the box. He raises his hand.
" Now he belongs to the ages," he says.   The sobbing
of the crowd grows gradually in volume.   The curtain
falls.

"BEYOND THE HORIZON"

An American Tragedy in Three Acts

By Eugene O'Neill

BEING one of those serious dramas with which the commercial theater hesitates to ally itself, on the theory that American playgoers do not like serious plays, " Beyond the Horizon " was first presented at a special matinee performance at the Morosco Theatre on Feb. 2, 1920 — partly as an experiment on the part of John D. Williams, the producer, and partly to quiet the pleading of Richard Bennett, the actor, who, having read the play, insistently demanded a chance to play the chief male rôle. The reviewers of the press hailed the new play with enthusiasm, and the matinees grew so steadily in popularity that when the Morosco Theatre was no longer available the attraction was moved to the Criterion, on Feb. 23. Finally the Little Theatre was secured and on March 9 the play began a " regular " engagement there that continued until spring. By that time there were many who were willing to accept this first long play from Eugene O'Neill's pen as representing the closest approach any native author has yet made to *the* great American play so long and so hopefully looked for.

" Beyond the Horizon " is the tragedy of a dreamer who lacked the courage to live his dream. Robert Mayo, son of James and Kate Mayo, born on a New England farm, but with no love of the soil, has grown up a frail youth to whom the mysterious far places of the world beckon alluringly. The opening scene of the play finds him as he is about to set out on his first

journey beyond the blue hills that encircle his home.
" The hushed twilight of a day in May is just beginning.   The horizon hills are still rimmed by a faint line
of flame, and the sky above them glows with the crimson flush of the sunset.   At the rise of the curtain
Robert Mayo is discovered.   He is a tall, slender
young man of 23.   There is a touch of the poet about
him expressed in his high forehead and wide, dark
eyes.   His features are delicate and refined, leaning to
weakness in the mouth and chin.   He is reading a book
by the fading sunset light."

Here his brother, Andrew, finds him.   Andrew is
four years older and an opposite type to Robert —
" husky, sun-bronzed, handsome in a large-featured,
manly way — a son of the soil, intelligent in a shrewd
way, but with nothing of the intellectual about him."
There is a deep brotherly sympathy between the two.
They discuss Robert's sailing on his Uncle Dick's ship,
the *Sunda*, next day.   The appeal of the " far off and
the unknown, the mystery and spell of the East . . .
the joy of wandering on and on in quest of the secret
that is hidden just over there beyond the horizon,"
does not appeal particularly to Andrew, but he's glad,
for Robert's sake, that he is going.   Presently another
subject is touched upon lightly between them — that of
Ruth Atkins.   They have lived neighbor to Ruth practically all their lives.   Both brothers have been — still
are, in fact — in love with her, but she has appeared
to favor Andrew, and they have accepted her decision
as final.   " We can't help those things, Rob," suggests
Andrew ; and they both understand.

But later, when Ruth finds Robert still gazing in-
tently at the sunset, the situation changes.   " She is a
healthy, blonde, out-of-door girl of 20, with a graceful,
slender figure, and undeniably pretty. . . . Her small,
regular features are marked by a certain strength, an
underlying stubborn fixity of purpose hidden in the

frankly appealing charm of her fresh youthfulness."

It is a little difficult for Ruth to understand why Robert is going away — and not so very easy for her to explain why she can't understand. " Oh, Rob, why *do* you want to go? " she demands, finally, in a desperation born of her own unhappiness; ". . . it seems such a shame."

" I could hardly back out now," he explains, a little puzzled; " even if I wanted to. And I'll be forgotten before you know it."

" You won't," she cries. " I'll never forget! . . ."

ROBERT — (*moodily*). I doubt if you'll understand. It's difficult to explain, even to myself. It's more an instinctive longing that won't stand dissection . . . I can remember being conscious of it first when I was only a kid — you haven't forgotten what a sickly specimen I was then, in those days, have you?

RUTH — (*with a shudder*). They're past. Let's not think about them.

ROBERT — You'll have to understand. Well — in those days, when Ma was fixing meals, she used to get me out of the way by pushing my chair to the west window and telling me to look out and be quiet. That wasn't hard. I guess I was always quiet in those days. . . . So I used to stare out over the fields to the hills — out there — (*pointing to the horizon*) and start dreaming — someone had told me the sea was beyond those hills — and I used to wonder what the sea was like — and try to form a picture of it in my mind's eye. And other times my eyes would follow this road winding off into the distance — towards the hills — as if it, too, was searching for the sea. And I'd promise myself that when I grew up and was strong — I'd follow this road — and it and I would find the sea together. You see — my making this trip is only keeping that promise of long ago.

RUTH — Yes.

ROBERT — Those were the only happy moments of my life then, Ruth — dreaming there at the window. I got to know all the different kinds of sunsets by heart that took place over there — beyond the horizon. So gradually I came to believe that all the wonders of the world happened on the other side of those hills. Beyond them was the home of the good fairies who performed beautiful miracles. I believed in fairies then — Perhaps I still do. Anyway in those days they were real enough — sometimes — I could actually hear them calling to me to come out and play — dance with them down the road in the dusk in a game of hide and seek to find out where the sun was hiding. . . . Then I would start crying because I couldn't go and Ma would think I was in pain — That's why I'm going now, I suppose. For I can still hear them calling — Do you understand me, Ruth?

RUTH — Yes.

ROBERT — You feel it then?

RUTH — Yes — yes I do! (*Unconsciously she snuggles close against his side — his arm steals abou her waist as if he weren't aware of the action*) Oh — Rob how could I help feeling it? You tell things so beautifully!

ROBERT — So you see when Uncle Dick said I could go to sea with him I was overjoyed at the prospect — then I suddenly awoke to the truth — the thing I wanted most was right here — you mustn't mind my telling you this, Ruth — it can't make any difference now and I realize how impossible my staying here is, and I understand and I'm happy for Andy's sake and yours. You see — the revelation of my own love opened my eyes to the love of you and Andy.

RUTH — (*breaking out stormily*). I don't — I don't love Andy — I don't! . . . Whatever put such a fool notion into your head? (*She throws her arms about his neck*) Oh Rob — don't go away — please — you mustn't now. You can't — I won't let you — it'd break my — my heart!

Robert — Do you mean that — that you love me?

Ruth — Yes —yes— of course, I do — what'd you s'pose? You stupid thing! I've loved you right along.

Robert — But you and Andy were always together!

Ruth — Because you never seemed to want to go any place with me. You were always reading an old book and not paying any attention to me. I was too proud to let you see I cared because I thought the year you had away to college had made you stuck-up, and you thought yourself too educated to waste any time on me.

Robert — And I was thinking — What fools we've both been!

The revelation of Ruth's love for him changes all Robert's plans. " I think love must have been the secret — the secret that called to me over the world's rim," he confesses to the now radiant girl. But the prospect of breaking the news to the folks is not a pleasant one. Still, it must be done.

The scene changes to the sitting room of the Mayo farmhouse about 9 o'clock the same night. " The atmosphere is one of the orderly comfort of a simple, hard-earned prosperity, enjoyed and maintained by the family as a unit." Father and Mother Mayo, and Uncle Dick are gathered around the center table. Andrew sits glumly at one side. The evening meal has been recently finished, Robert has gone to take Ruth and her mother home — rather to the surprise of the family, that task usually falling to Andrew. The family discussion is of " Robbie's " going away; of the good it will do him and the void it will leave in the family circle. Suddenly Andrew remembers the unfinished evening chores and leaves them, which gives

Mrs. Mayo a chance to free her mind of a troubling thought.

MRS. MAYO — Did you notice, James, how queer everyone was at supper? Robert seemed stirred up about something and Ruth was so flustered and giggly — and Andy sat there dumb — looking as if he'd lost his best friend — and all of them only nibbled their food.

MAYO — Guess they was all thinkin' about to-morrow, same as us.

MRS. MAYO — No — I'm afraid something's happened — something else.

MAYO — You mean —'bout Ruth?

MRS. MAYO — Yes.

MAYO — I hope her and Andy ain't had a serious fallin' out. I always sorter hoped they'd hitch up together sooner or later. What d' you say, Dick? Don't you think them two'd pair up well?

SCOTT — A sweet, wholesome couple, they'd make.

MAYO — It'd be a good thing for Andy in more ways than one. I ain't what you'd call calculatin' generally, and I b'lieve in lettin' young folks run their affairs to suit themselves, but there's advantages for both o' them in this match you can't overlook in reason. The Atkins' farm is right next to our'n. Jined together they'd make a jim-dandy of a place, with plenty of room to work in. And being a widder with only a daughter, and laid up all the time to boot, Mrs. Atkins can't do nothin' with the place as it ought to be done. Her hired help just goes along as they please, in spite of her everlastin' complainin' at 'em. She needs a first-class farmer to take hold o' things — and Andy's just the one.

MRS. MAYO — I don't think Ruth loves Andy.

MAYO — You don't? Well — maybe a woman's eyes is sharper in such things, but they're always together. And if she don't love him now, she'll likely come round in time.. . . You seem mighty fixed in your opinion, Katey. How d'you know?

MRS. MAYO. It's just what I feel.

Then Robert comes, " smilingly happy and humming a song to himself." An " undercurrent of nervous uneasiness manifests itself in his bearing," but he knows the story of his changed plans must be told, and is determined to have it over with. During the recital Andrew enters the room quietly and listens. Robert is so taken up with his story of the " something very wonderful and beautiful — something I did not take into consideration previously because I hadn't dared to hope that such happiness could ever come to me," that he does not notice Andrew.

MAYO. Let's get to the point, son.

ROBERT — Well — the point is this, Pa — I'm not going. I mean I can't go to-morrow with Uncle Dick — or at any other time either.

MAYO — Seems to me it's a pretty late hour in the day for you to be upsettin' all your plans so sudden. What is this foolishness you're talkin' of?

ROBERT — Ruth told me this evening that — she loved me. It changed things a lot because I thought she loved someone else. So you see I couldn't go away now — even if I wanted too.

MRS. MAYO — Of course not! . . . I knew it! I was just telling your father when you came in — and, oh, Robbie, I'm so happy you're not going!

ROBERT — I knew you'd be glad, Ma.

MAYO — Well — I'll be damned! You do beat all for gettin' folks mind all tangled up, Robert. And Ruth, too! Whatever got into her of a sudden? Why, I was thinkin'—

MRS. MAYO — Never mind what you were thinking, James. It wouldn't be any use telling us that now.

And what you were hoping for turns out just the same, doesn't it?

MAYO — Yes — I suppose you're right, Katey. But how'd it ever come about! It do beat anything I ever heard.

The family congratulations follow. Even Andrew comes forward, a little awkwardly but with frank sincerity, to wish his brother luck. Only Uncle Dick is seriously disturbed by the announcement that Robert has changed his mind. What's he goin' to do with that sta'b'd cabin he fixed up, an' the special grub he stocked up with, not to mention the new mattress and sheets and bookcases he had put in so's the boy might be comfortable? Like as not his crew'll " suspicion it was a woman " he'd planned to ship along, and that she give him the go-by at the last minute. Gawd A'mighty! That was a disturbin' thought.

But Andrew plans to ease Uncle Dick's fears. As suddenly as Robert has decided to stay on and help run the farm Andrew decides to take his place in Uncle Dick's ship. To the Mayo family this decision is even more astonishing than the other. Particularly to Father Mayo, who had long since learned to lean on Andrew as his right hand man, to think of him as a Mayo born an' bred, who would live an' die on the old farm. " What's come over you so sudden, Andy? " the old man demands, fairly stunned by the turn things have taken. " You know's well as I do that it wouldn't be fair for you to run off at a moment's notice right now when we're up to our necks in hard work."

ANDREW — You can easily get a man to do my work.

MAYO — It sounds strange to hear you, Andy, that I always thought had good sense, talkin' crazy like that. Get a man to do your work! — you aint been

workin' here for no hire, Andy, that you kin give me
your notice to quit like you've done. The farm is
your'n as well as mine. You've always worked on it
with that understanding — and what you're sayin' you
intend doin' is just skulkin' out o' your rightful responsibility.

ANDREW — I feel I oughtn't to miss this chance to
go out into the world and see things — and — I want
to go.

MAYO — (*with bitter scorn*). So — you want to go
out into the world and see things! . . . You're a liar,
Andy Mayo — and a mean one to boot!

MRS. MAYO — James!

ROBERT — Pa!

MAYO — I never thought I'd live to see the day when
a son o' mine'd look me in the face and tell me a bare-
faced lie!

MRS. MAYO — James!

ROBERT — Pa!

SCOTT — Steady there, Jim!

MAYO — Keep out of this — all of you. He's a liar
and he knows it. You're runnin' away 'cause you're
put out and riled 'cause your own brother's got Ruth
'stead of you, and —

ANDREW — Stop — Pa! I won't stand hearing that
— not even from you!

MAYO — It's the truth — and you know it.

MRS. MAYO — Sh-h-h!

ANDREW — You're wrong, Pa — it isn't the truth.
I don't love Ruth — I never loved her — and the
thought of such a thing never entered my head.

MAYO — Hump! You're pilin' lie on lie!

ANDREW — I don't care — I've done my share of
work here. I've earned my right to quit when I want
to.

ROBERT — Andy — don't! You're only making it
worse.

ANDREW — I'm sick and tired of the whole damn business. I hate the farm and every inch of ground in it. I'm sick of digging in the dirt and sweating in the sun like a slave without getting a word of thanks for it. I'm through — through for good and all — and if Uncle Dick won't take me on his ship — I'll find another. I'll get away somewhere — somehow.

MRS. MAYO — Don't you answer him, James. He doesn't know what he's saying to you. Don't say a word to him 'till he's in his right sense, again. Please, James, don't —

MAYO — (*to* ANDREW). You dare to — you dare to speak like that to me! You talk like that 'bout this farm — the Mayo farm — where you was born — you — you (*clenching his fist and advancing threateningly*) You damned whelp!

MRS. MAYO — James!

SCOTT — Easy there, Jim!

ROBERT — (*throwing himself between them*). Stop! Are you mad?

MAYO — (*to Andrew*). And you can go — tomorrow morning — and, by God — don't come back! Don't dare come back — by God — not while I'm living — or I'll — I'll —

Trembling over his muttered threat Mayo makes his way toward the stairway leading to his sleeping room. Only the echoing clamp, clamp of his heavy boots is heard in answer to Mrs. Mayo's pleading that he take back what he said to Andy.

Nothing can alter Andrew's determination to go, and Uncle Dick is willing to take him, though he's not the one to want to be a party to any family trouble. So it is planned that Robert shall drive them down to the harbor early in the morning, before the elder Mayos are stirring. Robert is shaken by the thought of what has happened, but Andrew is philosophical.

ANDREW — Buck up, Rob. It ain't any use crying over spilt milk — and it'll all turn out for the best — let's hope. It couldn't be helped — what's happened.

ROBERT — But it's a lie, Andy, a lie!

ANDREW — Of course, it's a lie. You know it and I know it — but that's all *ought* to know it.

ROBERT — God! It's terrible! I feel so guilty — to think that I should be the cause of your suffering after we've been such pals all our lives. If I could have foreseen what'd happen I'd never have said a word to Ruth. Honest I wouldn't have, Andy.

ANDREW — I know you wouldn't and that would have been worse, for Ruth would've suffered then. . . . It's best as it is. One of us had to stand the gaff and it happened to be me — that's all. Pa'll see how I felt — after a time.

ROBERT — Andy! Oh, I wish I could tell you half I feel of how fine you are —

ANDREW — I guess Ruth's got a right to have who she likes.

Andrew blows out the oil lamp and shuts off the drafts in the stove. " In the shadowy darkness the dark figures of the two boys can be seen groping their way toward the doorway in the rear as the curtain falls."

ACT II

There is a lapse of three years between the first and second acts. It is now the afternoon of a hot, sun-baked day in midsummer. The scene is unchanged, save in atmosphere. In the sitting room of the Mayo farmhouse " little significant details give evidence of carelessness, of inefficiency, of an industry gone to seed."

Mrs. Mayo and Ruth's mother, Mrs. Atkins (" a thin, pale-faced, unintelligent looking woman of about 48, with hard, bright eyes; a victim of partial paralysis for many years, condemned to be pushed from day to day of her life in a wheel chair, she has developed the selfish, irritable nature of the chronic invalid; ") are discussing the most recent of the problems that has arisen to confront Robert and Ruth, and their little girl, Mary, now 2 years old.

MRS. ATKINS — What I was sayin' was that since Robert's been in charge things have been goin' down hill steady. Robert don't let on to you what's happenin' and you'd never see it yourself if 'twas under your nose. But — thank the Lord — Ruth still comes to me once in a while. Do you know what Ruth told me last night? But I forgot, she said not to tell you till he — still, I think you've got a right to know, and it's my duty not to let such things go on behind your back.

MRS. MAYO — You can tell me if you want to.

MRS. ATKINS — Ruth was almost crazy about it. Robert told her he'd have to mortgage the farm — said he didn't know how he'd pull through 'till harvest without it, and he can't get money any other way. Now — what do you think of your Robert?

MRS. MAYO — If it has to be —

MRS. ATKINS — You don't mean to say you're goin' to sign away your farm, Kate Mayo — after me warnin' you?

MRS. MAYO — I'll do what Robbie says is needful.

MRS. ATKINS — Well — of all the foolishness! — Well — it's your farm — not mine — as usual I've nothing to say.

There is a hope in the minds of all the family — Andrew is coming back. It may be, as the mother hopes, that he will have tired of travel and will be ready to settle down and take charge of things. Not much has been heard from Andrew. He has been made head officer of Uncle Dick Scott's boat, but neither Robert nor his mother, and least of all Ruth, believes that he will care to continue his seafaring life. " That foolin' on ships is all right for a spell," avers Mrs. Atkins; " but he must be right sick of it by this time."

Mrs. Mayo — I wonder if he's — He used to be so fine-looking and strong. Three years! It seems more like three hundred. Oh — if James could only have lived till he came back — and forgiven him!

Mrs. Atkins — He never would have — not James Mayo. Didn't he keep his heart hardened against him till the last in spite of all you and Robert done to soften him?

Mrs. Mayo — Don't you dare say that! . . . Oh, I know deep down in his heart he forgave Andy, though he was too stubborn ever to own up to it. It was that brought on his death — breaking his heart just on account of his stubborn pride.

Mrs. Atkins — (the whining cry of the child sounds from the kitchen). It was the will of God! Drat that young one! Seems as if she cries all the time on purpose to set a body's nerves on edge.

Mrs. Mayo — It's the heat upsets her. Mary doesn't feel any too well these days, poor little child.

Mrs. Atkins — She gets it right from her Pa — bein' sickly all the time. You can't deny Robert was always ailin' as a child. It was a crazy mistake for them two to get married. I argued against it all the time, but Ruth was so spelled with Robert's wild poetry notions she wouldn't listen to sense. Andy was the one who would have been the match for her.

Mrs. Mayo — I've often thought since it might have been better the other way. But Ruth and Robbie seem so happy together.

MRS. ATKINS — It was God's work — not mine — thank goodness. And His will be done.

But Ruth and Robert are not happy. Nor have they been for some time, though they have made an effort to hide their real feelings. " Ruth has aged appreciably. Her face has lost its youth and its freshness. There is a trace in her expression of something hard and spiteful." She resents Robert's lack of order, his being always late to his meals; her care of the child has made them both peevish and irritable. She resents little Mary's preference for her father. On this particularly disagreeable day she hates everything and everybody. The sight of Robert calmly reading a book after she has been sweltering in the kitchen to keep his dinner warm for him makes her furious.

RUTH — For heaven's sake — put down that old book! Don't you see your dinner's getting cold?

ROBERT — The food is lucky to be able to get cold this weather.

RUTH — You've got work that's got to be done.

ROBERT — Yes — I was forgetting that.

RUTH — Work you'll never get done by reading books all the time.

ROBERT — Why do you resent the pleasure I get out of reading? Is it because — ?

RUTH — Because I'm too stupid to understand them, I s'pose you were going to say.

ROBERT — It certainly looks — No — no. . . . Oh, Ruth — why must we quarrel like this? Why do you make me say things I don't mean? Why can't we pull together? We used to.

RUTH — I do the best I know how.

ROBERT — I know you do. But let's both of us try to do better. We can improve — say a word of en-

couragement once in a while when things go wrong,
even if it is my fault. You know the odds I've been
up against since Pa died. I'm not a farmer. I've
never claimed to be one. But there's nothing else I can
do under the circumstances — and I've got to pull
things through somehow. With your help I can do it.
With you against me — So *you* promise that — and
I'll promise to be here when the clock strikes — and
anything else you tell me to. Is it a bargain?

RUTH — I s'pose so.

The truce does not continue long. Soon the discussion veers again to its most common subject — that of
Robert's incompetence and the general deterioration
that has followed his management of things. But
again there is that hope in Andrew's return. " Andy'll
know what to do in a minute," declares Robert.
" Though I doubt if he'll want to settle down to a
humdrum farm life — after all he's been through."

RUTH — Andy's not like you — he likes the farm.

ROBERT — God! The things he's seen and experi-
enced! Think of the places he's been. All the wonderful far places I used to dream about. What a trip!
God —how I envy him.

RUTH — I s'pose you're sorry now you didn't go?

ROBERT —(*too occupied with his own thoughts to
hear her*). Oh — those cursed hills — how I've grown
to hate the sight of them! They're like the walls of a
narrow prison yard shutting me in from all the freedom and wonder of life. Sometimes I think if it
wasn't for you, Ruth, and — little Mary — I'd walk
down the road with just one desire in my heart — to
put the whole rim of the world between me and those
hills and be able to breathe freely once more. (*He
sighs.*) There I go — dreaming again —

RUTH — Well — you're not the only one!

ROBERT — And Andy — who's had the chance — what has he got out of it? His letters read like the diary of a farmer! "We're in Singapore now. It's a dirty hole of a place and hotter than hell. Two of the crew are down with fever and we're short handed on the work. I'll be damn glad when we sail again, although tacking back and forth in these blistering seas is a rotten job too!" . . . That's the way he summed up his impressions of the East.

RUTH — You needn't make fun of Andy.

ROBERT — When I think — but what's the use — I wasn't making fun of Andy personally.

RUTH — You was too — making fun of him! And I ain't going to stand for it! You ought to be ashamed of yourself! A fine one to talk about anyone else — after the way you've ruined everything with your lazy loafing —

ROBERT — Stop that kind of talk, do you hear?

RUTH — You findin' fault — you're jealous! Jealous because he's made a man of himself while you're nothing but a — but a —

ROBERT — Ruth! Ruth! You'll be sorry for talking like that.

RUTH — I won't! I'm only saying what I've been thinking for years.

ROBERT — Ruth! You can't mean that!

RUTH — Well — what do you think — living with a man like you. You think you're so much better than other folks, with your college education, where you never learned a thing. I s'pose you think I ought to be proud to be your wife — a poor ignorant thing like me! But I'm not. I hate it. I hate the sight of you. Oh, if I'd only known! If I could have seen how you were in your true self — I'd have killed myself before I'd have married you! I was sorry for it before we'd been together a month.

ROBERT — And now — I'm finding out what — what

a — a creature I've been living with! It isn't that I haven't guessed how mean and small you are — but I've kept on telling myself that I must be wrong — mistaken —

RUTH — You said you'd go out on the road if it wasn't for Mary and me. Well — you can go — and the sooner the better! I don't care! I'll be glad to get rid of you! The farm'll be better off too. There's a curse on it ever since you took hold. So go! Go and be a tramp like you've always wanted. It's all you're good for. I can get along without you, don't you worry. Andy's coming back — he'll attend to things like they should be. He'll show what a man can do! We don't need you. Andy's coming!

ROBERT — What do you mean! What are you thinking of? What's in your evil mind? Do you — you — mean —

RUTH — Yes, I do. I'd say it if you was to kill me! I love Andy. I do! I do! I always loved him. And he loves me! He loves me! I know he does. He always did! And you know he did, too! So go! Go — if you want to!

ROBERT — You — you —

(*He stands glaring at her as she leans back, supporting herself by the table, gasping for breath. A loud frightened whimper sounds from the awakened child in the bedroom. It continues. The man and woman stand looking at one another in horror, the extent of their terrible quarrel suddenly brought to them. A pause. The noise of a horse and carriage comes from the road before the house. The two, suddenly struck by the same premonition, listen to it breathlessly, as to a sound heard in a dream. It stops. They hear Andy's voice from the road shouting a long hail —" Ahoy there!"*)

RUTH —(*With a strangled cry of joy*). Andy!

Andy! (*She rushes and grabs the knob of the screen door, about to fling it open.*)

ROBERT —(*In a voice of command that forces obedience*). Stop! (*He goes to the door and gently pushes the trembling Ruth away from it. The child's crying rises to a louder pitch.*) I'll meet Andy! You'd better go in to Mary, Ruth!

" There is something in his eyes that makes her turn and walk slowly into the bedroom." Robert opens the door and walks out to meet Andy as the curtain falls.

The scene changes to the top of a hill on the farm. It is 11 o'clock next day. From the hill there is a distant view of the sea. It is a favorite retreat of Robert Mayo's. He is there now, with little Mary. " His face is pale and haggard, his expression one of utter despondency." Mary can't understand why her father doesn't feel like playing with her, and she is quite distressed when he suggests that perhaps if he were to go away she wouldn't mind so very much — especially if her Uncle Andy were to stay on. But Mary is ever so positive she doesn't want her dada to go away — ever. He has to promise her he won't to quiet her.

Andy finds them there — after he has been over the farm with Ruth and learned something, though not all, of how things stand. He does not suspect, for one thing, that Ruth and Robert have quarreled, or that Ruth, in her secret heart, is hoping that some arrangement can be made whereby he and not Robert will stay on — with her and Mary. But Andrew is full of his own plans — which are to get back to Buenos Aires and into the grain business, as soon as he can straighten out affairs at home a little and get Robert and the farm started right again. Still, the subject of Ruth must be discussed sooner or later, however reluctant the brothers may be to bring it up.

ANDREW — You've forgotten all about what — caused me to go, haven't you, Rob? I was a slushier damn fool in those days than you were. But it was an act of Providence I did go. It opened my eyes to how I'd been fooling myself. Why, I'd forgotten all about — that — before I'd been at sea six months.

ROBERT — You're speaking of Ruth?

ANDREW — Yes. I didn't want you to get false notions in your head, or I wouldn't say anything. I'm telling you the truth when I say I'd forgotten long ago. It don't sound well for me, getting over things so easy, but I guess it never really amounted to more than a kid idea, I was letting rule me. I'm certain now I never was in love — I was getting fun out of thinking I was — and being a hero to myself. There! Gosh — I'm glad that's off my chest. I've been feeling sort of awkward ever since I've been home, thinking of what you two might think. You've got it all straight now, haven't you, Rob?

ROBERT — Yes, Andy.

ANDREW — And I'll tell Ruth too, if I can get up the nerve. She must feel kind of funny having me round — after what used to be — and not knowing how I feel about it.

ROBERT — Perhaps — for her sake — you'd better not tell her.

ANDREW — For her sake? Oh, you mean she wouldn't want to be reminded of my foolishness? Still I think it'd be worse if —

ROBERT — Do as you please, Andy — but for God's sake, let's not talk about it!

It is on the hilltop that, a little later, Ruth and Andy have their first confidential chat. Ruth has taken a holiday from the kitchen in honor of Andrew's visit, and put on her white dress. " She looks pretty, flushed and full of life "— until she, too, hears of Andrew's plans to go away again.   Then all the joy of her new-born hope dies out of her face.

RUTH — Oh, Andy, you can't go!   Why, we've all thought — we've all been hoping and praying you was coming home to stay, to settle down on the farm and see to things.   You must not go!   Think of how your Ma'll take on if you go — and how the farm'll be ruined if you leave it to Rob to look after.   You can see that.

ANDREW — Rob hasn't done so bad.   When I get a man to direct things the farm'll be safe enough.

RUTH — But your Ma — think of her.

ANDREW — She's used to me being away.   She won't object when she knows it's best for her and all of us for me to go.   You ask Rob.   In a couple of years down there I'll make my pile — see if I don't! And then I'll come back and settle down and turn this farm into the crackiest place in the whole State.   In the meantime, I can help you both from down there. . . . I tell you, Ruth, I'm going to make good right from the minute I land, if working hard and a determination to get on can do it — and I *know* they can. You ought to be able to understand what I feel.

RUTH — Yes — I s'pose I ought.

ANDREW — I felt sure you'd see — and wait till Rob tells you about —

RUTH — What did he tell you — about me?

ANDREW — Tell?   About you?   Why. nothing.

RUTH — Are you telling me the truth, Andy Mayo? Didn't he say — I —

ANDREW — No — he didn't mention you — I can remember.   Why?   What made you think he did?

RUTH — Oh, I wish I could tell if you're lying or not.

ANDREW — What're you talking about?   I didn't

use to lie to you, did I? And what in the name of God is there to lie for?

RUTH — Are you sure — will you swear — it isn't the reason? — the same reason that made you go last time that's driving you away again? 'Cause if it is — I was going to say — you mustn't go on that account.

ANDREW — Oh, is that what you're driving at? Well — you needn't worry about that no more.

RUTH — Andy! Please!

ANDREW — Let me finish that now I've started. It'll help clear things up. I don't want you to think once a fool always a fool and be upset all the time I'm here on my fool account. I want you to believe I put all that silly nonsense back of me a long time ago — and now — it seems — well — as if you'd always been my sister, that's what, Ruth.

RUTH — For God's sake, Andy — won't you please stop talking?

ANDREW — Seems if I put my foot in it whenever I open my mouth to-day. Rob shut me up with almost the same words when I tried speaking to him about it.

RUTH — You told him — what you've told me?

ANDREW — Why, sure — why not?

RUTH — Oh, my God!

ANDREW — Why? Shouldn't I have?

RUTH — Oh, I don't care what you do! I don't care! Leave me alone.

The return of Captain Dick Scott puts an end to the interview — and to the happiness of everyone concerned, except Andrew. Uncle Dick has heard of a great chance for Andrew in the village — a ship is sailing next day for the Argentine and is in need of a second officer. Andy can have the berth, if he'll take it. Andrew doesn't know just what to do. He doesn't like to start right off again, just as he's got home — but there is the chance, and there mightn't be another for six months. Besides, the quicker he goes the quicker he'll be back again, and in a position to help them with the money he is going to make in the grain business. So he decides to go.

"Andrew and the captain leave. Ruth puts Mary on the ground and hides her face in her hands. Her shoulders shake as if she were sobbing. Robert stares at her with a grim, somber expression. 'Daddie, Mama's cryin', Daddie,' wails Mary. 'No, she isn't, little girl,' her father assures her, in a voice he endeavors to keep from being harsh. 'The sun hurts her eyes, that's all.' . . . Ruth wipes her eyes quickly. 'Come on, Mary; I'll get your dinner for you.' She walks out, her eyes fixed on the ground, the skipping Mary tugging at her hand. Robert waits a moment for them to get ahead and then slowly follows."

ACT III

Five years have passed. The scene is again the sitting room of the farmhouse, " about 6 o'clock in the morning of a day toward the end of October. It is not yet dawn. . . . The room, seen by the light of the shadeless oil lamp with a smoky chimney which stands on the table, presents an appearance of decay, of dissolution. . . . The whole atmosphere of the room, contrasted with that of former years, is one of an habitual poverty too hopelessly resigned to be any longer ashamed or even conscious of itself."

" At the rise of the curtain Ruth is discovered sitting by the stove, with hands outstretched to the warmth as if the air in the room were damp and cold. . . . She has aged horribly. Her pale, deeply lined face has the stony lack of expression of one to whom nothing more can ever happen, whose capacity for emotion has been exhausted. When she speaks her voice is without timbre, low and monotonous."

Ruth's mother, huddled in her wheel chair, is asleep at the other side of the stove. They have been sitting up all night, waiting for Andrew, who, having arrived in New York from the Argentine, and learned that Robert is seriously ill, has wired that he is bringing a specialist to see his brother.

" A moment later Robert appears in the doorway of his bedroom, leaning weakly against it for support. His hair is long and unkempt, his face and body emaciated. There are bright patches of crimson over his cheek bones and his eyes are burning with fever."

The irritability that accompanies a long illness has seized him. He is embittered and ironical in his references to himself, to Ruth, to Andrew. They are in a conspiracy to make him out sicker than he is. He has no faith in doctors. Pleurisy is not consumption — and he is suffering from an attack of pleurisy. Nothing more. His thoughts are rambling and detached. Yet in his lucid moments he realizes the situation clearly. "I'll be frank, Ruth," he confesses at such a moment; "I've been an utter failure, and I've dragged you with me. I couldn't blame you in all justice for hating me."

RUTH —(*without feeling*). I don't hate you. It's been my fault too, I s'pose.

ROBERT — No. You couldn't help loving — Andy.

RUTH —(*dully*). I don't love anyone.

ROBERT — You needn't deny it. It doesn't matter. (*After a pause — with a tender smile.*) Do you know, Ruth, what I've been dreaming back there in the dark? It may sound silly of me, but — I was planning our future when I get well. . . . After all, why shouldn't we have a future? We're young yet. If we can only shake off the curse of this farm! It's the farm that's ruined our lives, damn it! And now that Andy's coming back — I'm going to sink my foolish pride, Ruth! I'll borrow the money from him to give us a start in the city. We'll go where people live instead of stagnating, and start all over again. (*Confidently*) I won't be the failure there that I've been here, Ruth. You won't need to be ashamed of me there. I'll prove to you the reading I've done can be put to some use. (*Vaguely*) I'll write, or something of that sort. I've always wanted to write. (*Pleadingly*) You'll want to do that, won't you, Ruth?

RUTH —(*dully*). There's Ma.

ROBERT — She can come with us.

RUTH — She wouldn't.

ROBERT —(*angrily*). So that's your answer! You're lying, Ruth! You mother's just an excuse. You want to stay here. You think that because Andy's coming back that — (*He chokes and has an attack of coughing.*)

RUTH — What's the matter? I'll go with you, Rob. I don't care for Andy like you think. Stop that coughing, for goodness sake! It's awful bad for you. (*She soothes him in dull tones*) I'll go with you to the city — soon's you're well again. Honest, I will, Rob; I promise! Do you feel better now?

ROBERT — Yes. Then you *will* go, Ruth?

RUTH — Yes.

ROBERT —(*excitedly*). We'll make a new start, Ruth — just you and I. Life owes us some happiness after what we've been through. It must! Otherwise our suffering would be meaningless — and that is unthinkable.

RUTH — Yes, yes, of course, Rob, but you mustn't —

ROBERT — Oh, don't be afraid! I feel completely well, really I do — now that I can hope again. Oh. if you knew how glorious it feels to have something to look forward to — not just a dream, but something

tangible, something already within our grasp! **Can't**
you feel the thrill of it, too — the vision of a **new life**
opening up after all the horrible years?

RUTH — Yes, yes, but do be —

ROBERT — Nonsense! I won't be careful. I'm getting back all my strength. (*He gets lightly to his
feet*) See! I feel light as a feather. (*He walks to
her chair and bends down to kiss her smilingly*) One
kiss — the first in years, isn't it? — to greet the **dawn**
of a new life together.

RUTH —(*submitting to his kiss — worriedly*). Sit
down, Rob, for goodness' sake!

ROBERT — I won't sit down. You're silly to **worry.**
Listen. All our suffering has been a test through
which we had to pass to prove ourselves worthy of a
finer realization. (*Exultingly*) And we did **pass**
through it! It hasn't broken us! And now the **dream**
is to come true! Don't you see?

RUTH —(*looking at him with frightened eyes as if
she thought he had gone mad*). Yes, Rob, I see; but
won't you go back to bed now and rest?

ROBERT — No. I'm going to see the sun rise. **It's**
an augury of good fortune.

But his false strength fails him and soon he is **willing**
to go back to his bed. The frightened Ruth **wakens**
Mrs. Atkins. She needs company. A great fear has
suddenly possessed her — that Rob is "kind of mad."
Soon Andrew comes, bringing with him the **specialist**
from the city. Together they hurry to Robert's **room.**
When Andrew re-enters he realizes for the first **time**
something of what has been happening in his absence.
" His face is drawn in a shocked expression of **great**
grief. He sighs heavily, staring mournfully in **front**
of him." Ruth is watching him.

ANDREW —(*in a harsh vocie*).   How long has this been going on?

RUTH — You mean — how long has he been sick?

ANDREW — Of course!   What else?

RUTH — It was last summer he had a bad spell first, but he's been ailin' ever since Mary died — eight months ago.

ANDREW — Why didn't you let me know — cable me?   Do you want him to die, all of you?   I'm damned if it doesn't look that way!   (*His voice breaking*)   Poor old chap!   To be sick in this out-of-the-way hole without anyone to attend to him but a country quack!   It's a damned shame!

RUTH — I wanted to send you word once, but he only got mad when I told him.   He was too proud to ask anything, he said.

ANDREW — Proud?   To ask *me?*   I can't understand the way you've acted.   Didn't you see how sick he was getting?   Couldn't you realize — why, I nearly dropped in my tracks when I saw him!   He looks — terrible!   I suppose you're so used to the idea of his being delicate that you took his sickness as a matter of course.   God, if I'd only known!

RUTH —(*without emotion*).   A letter takes so long to get where you were — and we couldn't afford to telegraph.   We owed everyone already, and I couldn't ask Ma.   She'd been giving me money out of her savings for the last two years till she hadn't much left.   Don't say anything to Rob about it.   I never told him.   He'd only be mad at me if he knew.   But I had to, because — God knows how we'd have got on if I hadn't.

ANDREW — You mean to say —   (*His eyes seem to take in the poverty-stricken appearance of the room for the first time*)   You sent that telegram to me collect.   Was it because —   (*Ruth nods silently*)   Good God!

And all this time I've been — why, I've had everything! . . . But — I can't get it through my head.
Why? Why? What has happened? How did it
ever come about? Tell me!

RUTH —(*dully*). There's nothing much to tell.
Things kept getting worse, that's all — and Rob didn't
seem to care.

ANDREW — But has'nt he been working the farm?

RUTH — He never took any interest since way back
when your Ma died. After that he got men to take
charge, and they nearly all cheated him — he couldn't
tell — and left one after another. And then there'd
be times when there was no one to see to it, when he'd
be looking to hire someone new. And the hands
wouldn't stay. It was hard to get them. They didn't
want to work here, and as soon as they'd get a chance
to work some other place they'd leave. Then after
Mary died he didn't pay no heed to anything any more
— just stayed indoors and took to reading books again.
So I had to ask Ma if she wouldn't help us some.

ANDREW —(*surprised and horrified*). Why, damn
it, this is frightful! Rob must be mad not to have let
me know. Too proud to ask help of me! It's an
insane idea! It's crazy! And for Rob, of all people,
to feel that way! What's the matter with him, in
God's name? He didn't appear to have changed when
I was talking to him a second ago. He seemed the
same old Rob — only very sick physically. (*A sudden, horrible suspicion entering his mind*) Ruth!
Tell me the truth. His mind hasn't gone back on him,
has it?

RUTH —(*dully*). I don't know. Mary's dying
broke him up terrible — but he's used to her being gone
by this, I spose.

ANDREW — Do you mean to say you're used to it?

RUTH — There's a time comes — when you don't
mind any more — anything.

ANDREW — (*with great sympathy*). I'm sorry I talked the way I did just now, Ruth — if I seemed to blame you. I didn't realize — The sight of Rob lying in bed there, so gone to pieces — it made me furious at everyone. Forgive me, Ruth.

RUTH — There's nothing to forgive. It doesn't matter.

Dr. Fawcett's diagnosis is not encouraging. Ruth receives it dully. She had known what to suspect. But Andrew refuses to give up hope. There must be something that can be done —

FAWCETT —(*calmly*). I am concerned only with facts, my dear sir, and this is one of them. Your brother has not long to live — perhaps a few days, perhaps only a few hours. I would not dare to venture a prediction on that score. It is a marvel that he is alive at this moment. My examination revealed that both of his lungs are terribly affected. A hemorrhage, resulting from any exertion or merely through the unaided progress of the disease itself, will undoubtedly prove fatal.

ANDREW —(*brokenly*). Good God! (*Ruth keeps her eyes fixed on her lap in a trance-like stare.*)

FAWCETT — I am sorry I have to tell you this, sorry my trip should prove to be of such little avail. If there was anything that could be done —

ANDREW — There isn't anything?

FAWCETT — I am afraid not. It is too late. Six months ago there might have —

ANDREW — But if we were to take him to the mountains — or to Arizona — or

FAWCETT — That might have prolonged his life six months ago. (*Andrews groans*) But now — (*He shrugs his soulders significantly*) I would only be raising a hope in you foredoomed to disappointment if

I encouraged any belief that a change of air could accomplish the impossible. He could not make a journey. The excitement, the effort required, would inevitably bring on the end.

ANDREW — Good heavens, you haven't told him this, have you, Doctor?

FAWCETT — No. I lied to him. I said a change of climate to the mountains, the desert, would bring about a cure. He laughed at that. He seemed to find it amusing for some reason or other. I am sure he knew I was lying. A clear foresight seems to come to people as near death as he is. One feels foolish lying to them; and yet one feels one ought to do it, I don't know why.

A part of the conversation Robert has overheard from the doorway of his room. The approach of death does not frighten him. He insists on coming again into the living room, and talking with them. " A dying man has some rights. hasn't he? " They fix a place for him by the fire.

ROBERT — Listen, Andy. You've asked me not to talk — and I won't after I've made my position clear. (*Slowly*) In the first place I know I'm dying. (*Ruth bows her head and covers her face with her hands. She remains like this all during the scene between the two brothers.*)

ANDREW — Rob! That isn't so!

ROBERT —(*wearily*). It *is* so! Don't lie to me. It's useless and it irritates me. After Ruth put me to bed before you came, I saw it clearly for the first time. (*Bitterly*) I'd been making plans for our future — Ruth's and mine — so it came hard at first — the realization. Then when the doctor examined me, I knew — although he tried to lie about it. And then to make sure I listened at the door to what he told you. So, for my sake, don't mock me with fairy tales about Arizona, or any such rot as that. Because I'm dying is no reason you should treat me as an imbecile or a coward. Now that I'm sure what's happening I can say Kismet to it with all my heart. It was only the silly uncertainty that hurt. (*There is a pause. Andrew looks around in impotent anguish, not knowing what to say. Robert regards him wtih an affectionate smile.*)

ANDREW —(*Finally blurts out*). It isn't foolish. You *have* got a chance. If you heard all the Doctor said that ought to prove it to you.

ROBERT —Oh, you mean when he spoke of the possibility of a miracle? (*Dryly*) The Doctor and I disagree on that point. I don't believe in miracles — in my case. Besides, I know more than any doctor on earth *could* know — because I feel what's coming.

From Andrew he hears the story of his brother's early successes and later failures in the grain business — failures that came through speculation. There's irony in that. " You — a farmer — to gamble in a wheat pit with scraps of paper," he says to Andrew. " There's a spiritual significance in that picture, Andy. I'm a failure, and Ruth's another — but we can both justly lay some of the blame for our stumbling on God. But you're the deepest-dyed failure of the three, Andy. . . . My brain is muddled. But part of what I mean is that your gambling with the thing you used to love to create proves how far astray you've gotten from the truth. So you'll be punished. You'll have to suffer to win back —" Again a spell of coughing stops him. When he has the strength his thought returns to Ruth — and the future.

ROBERT — I want you to promise me to do one thing, Andy, after —

Andrew — I'll promise anything, as God is my
Judge!

Robert — Remember, Andy, Ruth has suffered
double her share, and you haven't suffered at all. . . .
Only through contact with suffering, Andy, will you —
awaken. Listen. You must marry Ruth — afterwards.

Ruth — (*with a cry*). Rob!

Andrew — (*making signs for her to humor him —
gently*). You're tired out, Rob. You shouldn't have
talked so much. You better lie down and rest a while,
don't you think? We can talk later on.

Robert — Later on! You always were an optimist,
Andy! Yes, I'll go and rest a while. It must be near
sunrise, isn't it? It's getting grey out.

Andrew — Yes — pretty near. It's after six.

Robert — Pull the bed around so it'll face the window, will you, Andy? I can't sleep, but I'll rest and
forget if I can watch the rim of the hills and dream
of what is waiting beyond. And shut the door, Andy.
I want to be alone.

Andrew is puzzled by Robert's attitude toward him
and Ruth, and the request that they marry. He asks
Ruth if she knows just what is passing ·in Rob's
mind.

Ruth — He might be thinking of — something happened five years back, the time you came home from
the trip.

Andrew — What happened? What do you mean?

Ruth — (*dully*). It was the day you came. We
had a fight.

Andrew — A fight? What has that to do with
me?

Ruth — It was about you — in a way.

Andrew — About *me?*

RUTH — Yes, mostly. You see I'd found out I'd made a mistake about Rob soon after we were married — when it was too late.

ANDREW — Mistake? You mean — you found out you didn't love Rob?

RUTH — Yes.

ANDREW — Good God!

RUTH — And then I thought that when Mary came it'd be different, and I'd love him; but it didn't happen that way. And I couldn't bear with his blundering and book-reading — and I grew to hate him, almost.

ANDREW — Ruth!

RUTH — I couldn't help it. No woman could. It had to be because I loved someone else, I'd found out. (*She sighs wearily*) It can't do no harm to tell you now — when it's all past and gone — and dead. *You* were the one I really loved — only I didn't come to the knowledge of it 'til too late.

ANDREW — (*stunned*). Ruth! Do you know what you're saying?

RUTH — It was true — then. (*With sudden fierceness*) How could I help it? No woman could.

ANDREW — Then — you loved me — that time I came home?

RUTH — Yes.

ANDREW — But — couldn't you see — I didn't love you — that way?

RUTH — (*doggedly*). Yes — I saw then; but I'd known your real reason for leaving home the first time — everybody knew it — and for three years I'd been thinking —

ANDREW — That I loved you?

RUTH — Yes. Then that day on the hill you laughed about what a fool you'd been for loving me once — and I knew it was all over.

ANDREW — Good God, but I never thought — . . . And did Rob —

RUTH — That was what I'd started to tell. We'd had a fight just before you came and I got crazy mad — and I told him all I've told you.

ANDREW — You told Rob — you loved me?

RUTH — Yes.

ANDREW — (*shrinking away from her in horror*) You — you — you mad fool, you! How could you do such a thing?

RUTH — I couldn't help it. I'd got to the end of bearing things — without talking.

ANDREW — And the thought of the child — his child and yours — couldn't keep your mouth shut?

RUTH — I was crazy mad at him — when I told.

ANDREW — Then Rob must have known every moment I stayed here! And yet he never said or showed — God, how he must have suffered! Didn't you know how much he loved you?

RUTH — (*dully*). Yes. I knew he liked me.

ANDREW — Liked you! How can you talk in that cold tone — now — when he's dying! What kind of a woman are you? I'd never believe it was in you to be so — Couldn't you have kept silent — no matter what you felt or thought? Did you have to torture him? No wonder he's dying. I don't see how he's lived through it as long as he has. I couldn't. No. I'd have killed myself — or killed you.

RUTH — I wish he had — killed me.

ANDREW — And you've lived together for five years with this horrible secret between you?

RUTH — We've lived in the same house — not as man and wife.

ANDREW — But what does he feel about it now? Tell me! Does he still think —

RUTH — I don't know. We've never spoke a word about it since that day. Maybe, from the way he went on, he s'poses I care for you yet. Maybe that's one reason he said what he did.

ANDREW — But you don't. You can't. It's outrageous. It's stupid! You don't love me!

RUTH — I wouldn't know how to feel love, even if I tried, any more.

ANDREW — (*brutally*). And I don't love you, that's sure! . . . It's damnable such a thing should be between Rob and me — we that have been pals ever since we were born, almost. Why, I love Rob better'n anybody in the world and always did. There isn't a thing on God's green earth I wouldn't have done to keep trouble away from him. And now I have to be the very one. Its damnable! How am I going to face him again? What can I say to him now? (*He groans with anguished rage. After a pause*) He asked me to promise — what am I going to do?

RUTH — You can promise — so's it'll ease his mind — and not mean anything.

ANDREW — What? Lie to him now — when he's dying? Can you believe I'd descend as low as that? And there's no sense in my lying. He knows I don't love you. (*Determinedly*) No! It's *you* who'll have to do the lying, since it must be done. You're the cause of all this. You've got to! You've got a chance now to undo some of all the suffering you've brought on Rob. Go in to him! Tell him you never loved me — it was all a mistake. Tell him you only said so because you were mad and didn't know what you were saying, and you've been ashamed to own up to the truth before this. Tell him something, anything, that'll bring him peace and make him believe you've loved him all the time.

RUTH — It's no good. He wouldn't believe me.

ANDREW — You've got to make him believe you, do you hear? You've got to — now — hurry — you never know when it may be too late. For God's sake, Ruth! Don't you see you owe it to him? You'll never forgive yourself if you don't.

Ruth — I'll go. But it won't do any good. (Andrew's *eyes are fixed on her anxiously. She opens the
door and steps inside the room. She remains standing there for a minute. Then she calls in a frightened voice*) Rob! Where are you? Andy! Andy!
He's gone!

Andrew — (*rushing in to her. There is a pause
and then* Andrew *is heard*). God damn you! — You
never told him!

(The Curtain Falls)

"THE FAMOUS MRS. FAIR"

An American Drama in Four Acts

By James Forbes

"THE FAMOUS MRS. FAIR" was produced at the Henry Miller Theatre, December 22, 1919. It proved the most timely of the post-bellum dramas and easily the most entertaining, and was soon accepted as one of the season's successes. The Mrs. Fair of the title is representative of those American women who, being in a position to do so, plunged into war work early in 1915. "Nancy Fair," writes Mr. Forbes, "is the type of American woman who previous to the war found an outlet for the energies not spent in the care of her home and family. in society, women's clubs, charitable undertakings and outdoor sports. Unsuspected executive capacity so frequently inherited by American women from their fathers was called into play by the War and her success in organizing one of the first units of women to go overseas and its achievements under her direction during four years' service with the French Army has brought her admiration, honors, fame. She is devoted to her family and eager for the reunion with them, yet is restless, excited, and pathetically out of touch with their interests. Unknown to herself she is really less in tune with her family than with the women of her unit who adore her and with whom she has shared the dangers and the joys of war work. Her personality is vivid, her sense of humor keen, her disposition gay and affectionate and in a word she radiates charm."

Among her other activities Nancy Fair became an ambulance driver, and because she was fearless she achieved the Croix de Guerre and gained for herself much fame. When America entered the war her 19-year-old son, Alan, joined the American forces, took intensive training at Plattsburg and won his commission as a lieutenant. Her husband, Jeffrey, took a position as one of the " dollar-a-year patriots " at Washington, and the daughter, 16-year-old Sylvia, was left in charge of a housekeeper and such of the neighbors as remained at home.

At the beginning of the play, following the signing of the armistice, Mrs. Fair has returned to her Long Island home eager to resume her position as wife and mother. The occasion of her return is the cause of much family rejoicing. The children have decorated the living room in her honor, a conspicuous placard bearing the legend, " Welcome to Our Heroine." Now she has arrived and the family greetings are over. She is holding her daughter at arm's length, greedily, proudly drinking in her youthful freshness and beauty through eyes misty with tears of joy. And Sylvia is as happy as she. " Oh, Mother," she cries, " you look so young ! "

NANCY — Nobody ever had a nicer daughter.

ALAN — They've got to go some to tie you, mother — eh, Dad?

FAIR — I'll say it.

NANCY — Such compliments from my family. You're not getting me in a good humor so that you can spring something on me?

ALAN — How does it seem to be home, Mother?

NANCY — If Sylvia won't be shocked at my language, I'll confess I'm having a pippin' of a time.

ALAN — You are going to find it awfully flat.

NANCY — What do you mean?

FAIR — Yes, I'd like to know what he means.

SYLVIA — Alan! The idea! She didn't find it flat when she was here the last time!

ALAN — Mother was busy getting money for her unit and she was going back. Take it from me, I've been through it. You're going to miss the something — I don't know what it is — but life over there gets you. You know that, Mother. You'll find yourself thinking more about the people you left over there, than your old friends here.

SYLVIA — You won't get bored at home, will you, Mother?

NANCY — Alan, be quiet!

SYLVIA — You won't will you, Mother?

NANCY — What are you worrying about, dear?

SYLVIA — But you won't, will you?

NANCY — No! No! No! You silly goose! (NANCY *has taken* SYLVIA's *face in her hands. She kisses her between each "no" and at the end of the speech. Then sits down and draws* SYLVIA *down beside her*).

FAIR — (*to* ALAN). What are you trying to be? A kill-joy? (*To* NANCY) It's good to see you over there, Nancy. We missed you, eh Sylvia?

SYLVIA — And you missed us, didn't you, Mother?

ALAN — When she had the time to think about you. But you didn't have the time —

FAIR — Say, will you let your mother speak for herself?

ALAN — Just the same, I'm right, aren't I, Mother?

NANCY — Perhaps — in a way. But I had lots of time to be lonesome for all of you. . . .

With the family greetings over, the talk turns to the neighborhood gossip and the family activities during Nancy's absence. Sylvia, she learns, has been thrown a great deal with Angy Brice, an attractive little widow who lives next door. Jeffrey, too, had taken a neighborly, not to say a fatherly, interest in Angy as one with whom he might legitimately pass a few of his lonesome evenings. Alan, who is secretly engaged to Peggy Gibbs the sister of his " buddie," a sensible little stenographer, has decided not to go back to Yale and is seriously thinking of " going in for mining."

In the midst of these revelations a small, white cloud appears on the horizon of the Fair family's happiness. Dudley Gillette, the manager of a lecture bureau, has called and left a contract for Nancy to sign. Alan doesn't think for a moment that his mother will be interested in it, and the elder Fair, though he thinks Nancy would be the best judge of that, is inclined to treat the matter as a joke, a lofty masculine attitude that Mrs. Fair rather resents. " Well, Mr. Jeffrey Fair," she says, " there is nothing funny about the money he offers me. Alan, what's a hundred times $300? "

ALAN — $30,000.

NANCY — Help!

FAIR — Oh, it's a fake.

SYLVIA — Mother, you couldn't lecture. You don't know how.

NANCY — Oh, don't I, miss? I gave a little talk one night to the boys on the boat and they assured me that I was a " riot."

FAIR — What did you talk about?

NANCY — My experiences.

SYLVIA — Did you like doing it?

NANCY — It was rather fun. Of course if I did it here it wouldn't be for the money.

FAIR — But, Nancy, you're not going to do it here.

ALAN — That contract calls for a coast-to-coast tour.

NANCY — I've never been to California.

FAIR — Why, you haven't been home for more than

twenty minutes. You're surely not contemplating going away again? (NANCY *is silent*) Nancy, what are you thinking about?

NANCY — I was just thinking that $30,000 would do a lot of reconstructing —

ALAN — She's back in France! What did I tell you?

FAIR — This home could do with a little " reconstructing."

NANCY — Oh, come now, Jeff. After what I heard you can't tell me that you need anything.

SYLVIA — We need you, Mother, awfully.

NANCY — Well, my lamb, you are going to have me.

FAIR — The question is, for how long?

NANCY — It's a wise wife who keeps her husband guessing. Come along, Sylvia, and watch Mother get the glad hand from the help.

Though they do not take the lecture proposition seriously both the father and son are worried by it. The father is convinced that to oppose Nancy would be the worst thing they could do. Alan admits the logic of this decision but warns his father that he had better prepare for the day when " mother takes a look around and says : ' France never was like this.' "

" And when that cold gray morning arrives," he adds, " don't be too busy to make life very damned interesting for mother." " That's a pretty tall order for a man without any gold lace on his chest," replies Fair, " but I'll do my darndest."

Nancy's own state of mind if further unsettled by the reports she gets from the other members of her unit, who have squeezed themselves again into their uniforms and are now come to welcome their beloved leader home.

NANCY — Now girls tell me and tell me true. How

does it feel to be at home? (*No one speaks*)   Don't everybody shriek with joy at once!

MRS. WYNNE — Seems to me I've been home a million years.

MRS. PERRIN — After a couple of days with my kiddies, I sighed for the peace and quiet of an air raid.

MRS. BROWN — You're in luck to have them.   I've been driven to card indexing my hens!

MRS. CONVERSE — I wish you'd come over and card index my Swede cook!

MRS. WELLS — I must confess that after I had kissed my old man and all the grandchildren — they looked sort of strange to me.

NANCY — Girls, this sounds awful.   Possibly Alan was right.   He said I would find it flat.

MRS. WYNNE — After being on the hop skip and jump for four years, it's the very devil to sit around " Bla."

MRS. PERRIN — Have you any plans?

NANCY — I had thought of buying all the clothes in New York, seeing all the shows, playing around with my family.

MRS. CONVERSE — We've done all that.   And then what?

NANCY — Why, eh —

MRS. PERRIN — Exactly.   " Why, eh —"

MRS. BROWN — You see, Nancy — now we have time to burn and no matches.

NANCY — What are all the other war workers doing?

MRS. BROWN — Kicking about being demobilized.

NANCY — It's a burning shame that Washington couldn't have used all this organized talent.

Nancy, pinning on her croix de guerre, prepares to meet a small army of reporters arrived to interview her. "You're not going to see them?" expostulates her husband. "Not if you don't wish it," replies Nancy. But at a warning glance from Alan his father withdraws his objection. As Nancy retires Fair turns to Alan.

"Can you beat it — *my* wife!"

"That's not your wife, dad," Alan answers, "that's Major Fair."

ACT II

A month elapses. Nancy has not signed Gillette's contract, but she has delivered her first lecture, as an experiment, and enjoyed the taste of fame and the thrill it gave her. On the lawn outside the Fair home the newspaper and magazine boys are waiting to photograph her. Everybody is excited and overjoyed at her success — everybody excepting her husband and her son. Sylvia, who has been reading reports of her mother's début as a lecturer, is puzzled by the attitude of these two.

SYLVIA — Oh! Have you seen the afternoon papers?

FAIR — We have.

SYLVIA — (*first to* ALAN *then* JEFFREY). Aren't they wonderful? (FAIR *and* ALAN *are silent*) Aren't they wonderful? Oh, I think that you are both as mean as you can be about Mother! I should think you'd be proud of her!

FAIR — We were.

SYLVIA — Why aren't you now? Everybody crazy about her last night and neither of you so much as congratulated her.

ALAN — I couldn't get near her.

SYLVIA — You didn't try very hard. And, Daddy, you left us flat and went home with Angy Brice.

FAIR — Angy was feeling seedy.

SYLVIA — Humph! May be, sometimes I think Angy doesn't like Mother.

ALAN — Just finding that out?

FAIR — Nonsense, children, she admires her enormously.

SYLVIA — You might have waited and said something nice to Mother this morning.

ALAN — We had a foursome on and she wasn't up.

FAIR — Oh, enough people will make a fuss over her.

SYLVIA — I don't see why you two hate the " fuss," everyone makes over Mother. She can't help being celebrated and having people chase after her. You see just as much of her as I do. I don't mind but you, Alan, act so funny. (*Tearfully*) Nothing's the same as I thought it would be when Mother came home. I don't know what's the matter. (*She cries.*)

FAIR — Why, Sylvia, Alan and I wouldn't do anything to worry you for the world, would we?

ALAN — Certainly not.

SYLVIA — Then why aren't you both nicer to Mother?

FAIR — Oh come on now, don't cry. Don't you know your old Daddy wouldn't hurt you? Pick your spot and I'll lie down and let you walk on me. (SYLVIA *smiles*) That's better.

SYLVIA — Don't you want to come out and get in the muss?

FAIR — Who's out there?

SYLVIA — Bridget Wynne and the others.

FAIR — No I saw all of them yesterday.

SYLVIA — Now, Daddy. you're not going to be nasty about these photographs.

FAIR — Not a yap out of me. . . . (*After* SYLVIA *has gone*) Gosh I'd like to come into this place just once and not find that bunch of women here. A man would have more privacy in the Grand Central Depot.

ALAN — You said it.   Whenever mother *is* at home this house looks like a Clubwomen's Old Home week.

FAIR — Wouldn't you think after four years together, they'd be tired of each other?

ALAN — And the line of flattery they hand out and mother lapping it up like a cat does cream.

FAIR — I know.   Even a woman as level headed as your mother will soon believe she's the greatest thing in the world.

ALAN — Why don't you take her away out of it all?

FAIR — She's booked up a month ahead.   Banquets, receptions, although I thought she'd been given one by everybody from the mayor down to the Conductorette's Union.

ALAN — And they have almost worn out that Croix de Guerre passing it around from hand to hand.

FAIR — Yes, and what are you going to do about it?

ALAN — Why did you let her start?

FAIR — Who told me to keep her busy?

ALAN — I did — I did.   I wasn't counting on the endurance of women.   If I had hit a gait like Mother's —

FAIR — She hasn't rested a day since she arrived.

ALAN — It's a wonder to me that she hasn't had a nervous breakdown.

FAIR — Son, the only thing that makes a woman have a nervous breakdown nowadays is having to stay at home.

Affairs in the Fair home are proceeding slowly but surely from bad to worse.   The men folk would discourage Nancy's signing the lecture contract, if they knew how.   Alan advises his father frankly to " tie

a can to Gillette," but Fair is too wise to do that.
" I haven't lived with your mother all these years
without realizing that if you want her to do something tell her she can't," he explains. Gillette, of
course, is pulling every wire to induce Mrs. Fair to
sign, and incidentally he is making love to Sylvia.
Angy Brice, too, taking advantage of the situation, is
keenly sympathetic and ever so eager to do all that
she can to help Mr. Fair accept the threatened desertion of Nancy philosophically. Alan's problem concerns Peggy Gibbs. He has decided to announce their
engagement, though Peggy begs him not to. " Let
your mother get to know me first," she begs. " If
you thrust me at her it may prejudice her." Also
she refuses to marry any man who expects to live on
the money his father has given him. Alan proudly
squelches this objection by announcing that he has a
job. He is to work for the man who was his top
sergeant and get $30 a week.

ALAN — Look here. I postponed our marriage to
wait for a family reunion that didn't reune. Then
I had to wait until I got a job. Well, I have one.
Now it's up to you. If you don't want to marry me,
say so.

PEGGY — I do, Alan. You know I do. But I want
your father and mother to approve. There is a chance
they mightn't like me.

ALAN — You're not marrying them.

Their tiff is interrupted by the return of Fair. Thus
he is the first to be told of the engagement.

ALAN — You see, Dad, Peggy is my " buddy's "
sister.

FAIR — Yes?

PEGGY — Oh, Alan, let us be frank. (*To* FAIR)

It annoys him when I say it but I'm not of your class.
I'm a stenographer.

ALAN — She's a private secretary.

FAIR — What is the difference?

PEGGY — Twenty dollars a week, sir.

FAIR — Thank you. I deserved that.

ALAN — Well, Dad, are you for me or " agin " me?

FAIR — That depends.

ALAN — On what?

PEGGY — On me. You can't expect your father to
give a snap judgment on a person he has just met.
Suppose you leave us together so that we can have a
little talk.

FAIR — A very good idea.

ALAN — (to PEGGY). Don't be nervous. dear.
Dad's aces. (To FAIR) Now, Dad, no heavy father
stuff. (ALAN exits.)

FAIR — Well, Miss Gibbs?

PEGGY — To begin with, Mr. Fair, my family and
I are, socially speaking, a total loss.

FAIR — In what way?

PEGGY — My father is the village postman. My
brother is now in the Detective Bureau but was a
policeman.

FAIR — I see.

PEGGY — Yes, I thought you would. My mother
does her own work but the weekly washing is sent
out.

FAIR — Very interesting, especially that bit about
the laundry.

PEGGY — I graduated from high school, then went
to Brown's Business College. I am now employed at
forty dollars a week as a private secretary in the office
of a firm of lawyers, O'Brien and Rosenweber.

FAIR — I know of them.

PEGGY — I am twenty-three years old, quite healthy,
am supposed to have a good disposition. Oh, there is

one thing more. I'm a suffragette and while I am not militant, I do parade. I believe that is all.

FAIR — And you have Thursdays off? My dear Miss Gibbs, I'm not interviewing you as a prospective servant but as a possible daughter-in-law.

PEGGY — Well, you wanted to know about me, didn't you?

FAIR — You suggested the interview. I appreciate that it's a very difficult one for you. It isn't exactly easy for me. Yet, if I didn't learn something of the girl my son wishes to marry, I would be failing in my duty as a father, wouldn't I?

PEGGY — Yes.

FAIR — Why are you so on the defensive?

PEGGY — Possibly because I'm a little afraid.

FAIR — Surely not of me? Unless you're marrying Alan for —

PEGGY — For money and this sort of thing! No! Not that I wouldn't like it and enjoy it but only if Alan earned it. And he will in time. He's made a start. He has a job.

FAIR — Why didn't he come to me for a position?

PEGGY — Oh, Mr. Fair, please don't help him. That would spoil all my plans.

FAIR — How?

PEGGY — It's better for him to be entirely on his own.

FAIR — Why?

PEGGY — The dear boy is full of the brotherhood of man — he got that from the trenches — and if he is going to keep it, it's necessary for him to live simply for a time at least!

FAIR — Sounds to me like a very serious courtship.

PEGGY — Is anything more serious than marriage? I'm scared to death of it.

FAIR — Why?

PEGGY — I have to give up a great deal of my liberty

and I want to be sure it's worth it. Oh dear, life and what to do with it and Alan's problem and mine seem so much simpler on our back verandah.

After his talk with Peggy, Fair is quite convinced that she is a proper mate for his son. "If I were Alan and you were you," he confesses, "I'd marry you and say damn the families." But Nancy, returning from the club, is both surprised and hurt that she should not have been the first to be consulted in the serious matter of her son's matrimonial intentions.

NANCY — (*to* FAIR). How long have you known of this engagement?

FAIR — Not until to-day.

NANCY — And did you welcome her with outstretched arms at once?

FAIR — Frankly, I was surprised, but after I had had a talk with her —

NANCY — Exactly. You had an opportunity to judge of her before you gave your approval, but I am expected.to give at once, the son I've loved, watched over, prayed for, to a girl of whom I know nothing.

FAIR — I told you I vouched for her.

NANCY — What's that to me? He's my son too.

FAIR — That's jealousy talking.

NANCY — Is it strange that I should be jealous? Isn't it hard for any mother just at first to give her son to another woman? If Alan had had any right feeling for me he would have told me tenderly, tactfully, that he loved some one else more than me. Instead he let you thrust the fact at me. I don't know what I have ever done that he should have told you, even Sylvia, before me; made me feel like an outsider.

FAIR — Who is to blame for that? You put yourself outside your home. You can't hope to receive

Alan's confidence if you are never here to get it.
You can't go on neglecting your family —

NANCY — What? I give up everybody and everything belonging to me and endure privations, horrors,
because I think it's my greatest duty and then I am
neglecting my family! My family seems to have gotten along very well without me and ever since I came
home you and Alan have resented everything I've
done.

FAIR — We don't approve of what you've been doing.

NANCY — Approve? Must I secure the approval of
my husband and my son for what I think best to do?

FAIR — Your desire to appear in public, for instance?

NANCY — If you had been overseas and had been
urged to appear in public would you have had to ask
my approval? No. It would have been the perfectly
natural thing for you to do.

FAIR — It's not the same thing.

NANCY — Because I'm a woman. Well, this war
has settled one thing definitely. A woman's work
counts for just as much as a man's and she is entitled
to all the rewards it brings her.

FAIR — You've done your duty by your country, but,
by God, you're capitalizing it.

NANCY — Jeffrey!

FAIR — Ever since you've been home you've thought
of everything but your duty to your family. All you
think of is your appearance at public functions, getting your name and photograph in print. Can you
deny that you are eager to sign this contract so that
you can make a triumphant tour of the country telling
the great American public how you helped win the
war? Well, you'll put an end to all this publicity.
You'll stop all these ridiculous lectures. You'll tear

up that contract.   You'll give up this tour and remain
here where you belong.

NANCY — And why must I do all this?   Why must
I remain here where I belong?

FAIR — Because I am your husband and I forbid
you to go!

That little word " forbid "— a fighting word with the
true feminist — settled it.   " Nancy watches Jeffrey
for a few seconds, then goes around the table, sits, and
signs the contract."

ACT III

True to her liberty-loving principles, Mrs. Fair went
a-touring, and took her daughter with her.   But after
a month of it Sylvia returned suddenly to her father.
" I can understand just what happened," Fair explains
to Alan, who feared that Sylvia had quarreled with
Nancy; " her mother was entertained a great deal.
That was part of the game of being ' the famous Mrs.
Fair.'   It wasn't possible to include Sylvia in all of
the functions.   Naturally, she was bored.   So she
came home."   With Sylvia home Fair took rooms in
an apartment in New York, because he suspected it
would be lonesome for her in the country without her
mother.   Also he reverted to his former custom of
looking to Angy Brice to help him fill in his dull evenings.   Alan and Peggy have married, and, save for
their regret over Mrs. Fair's attitude, are ideally
happy.

And now, three months later, Nancy is home from
her first tour prepared to spend a few days with
her family before she starts out again.   She is not
particularly happy over the situation as she finds
it.   She is ready and eager to " make up " with Alan

and Peggy, and she is not inclined to take seriously
Jeffrey's developing grouch.   But she is worried, not
to say shocked, at the change she notes in Sylvia.   At
their first meeting Nancy seeks to discover the causes
for this change.   "Well, darling," she says, the moment she and Sylvia are alone, pulling her "baby"
down into the chair with her; "glad to have your
mother home again?"

SYLVIA — Believe me, I am.
NANCY — Why do you wear your hair like that?
SYLVIA — Everyone in my crowd does.
NANCY — Come and sit down.   I want to know all
you've been doing.
SYLVIA — I wrote to you.
NANCY — Not so often lately.
SYLVIA — With somethin' doin' every minute, I
didn't have the time. . . . My, I've missed this.
NANCY — So have I, dear.   Now begin at the be-
ginning.
SYLVIA — Let's skip the beginning — it was horrid.
NANCY — In what way, dear?
SYLVIA — I was so lonesome.
NANCY — As soon as I knew that you were to be at
this hotel instead of at home, I wired Bridget Wynne.
Didn't she look you up?
SYLVIA — Oh, all the women came once.   Mrs.
Wynne gave me a luncheon and a box party and asked
all the girls in our set.   It was a perfect lemon.
NANCY — How?
SYLVIA — For all the attention they paid me I might
as well not have been there.
NANCY — Why should they be rude to you?
SYLVIA — They didn't mean to be.   I didn't know
all the little intimate things they talked about.   One
girl's mother was doing this for her and another one's
mother was doing that — Anyway, I felt like an out-

sider in what should have been my own crowd.   When I got home, I just bawled my head off and Daddy said we wouldn't bother with any of them again.   But it was pretty awful, especially as I didn't have Angy to fall back on.

NANCY — No?

SYLVIA — Daddy said you didn't like me to be intimate with her.

NANCY — I see.   Haven't you seen Alan and Peggy?

SYLVIA — It's terribly dull at their flat.   They're so crazy about each other that half the time they don't know you're around.

NANCY — Didn't father go about with you?

SYLVIA — Oh yes.   Daddy's a darling, but he is old. Gillie's been my lifesaver.

NANCY — Who is Gillie?

SYLVIA — Mr. Gillette!   He took me to tea one day at a dancing place and introduced me to his friends and when he found I liked them he said: " Sylvia this old town is yours.   We'll take it all apart and see what makes it tick."

NANCY — That doesn't sound like Mr. Gillette.

SYLVIA — Oh, he put on his grand manners with you.   You don't know the real Gillie.

NANCY — No, I don't believe I do.   Who are these friends?

SYLVIA — I don't know.   Just New Yorkers.

NANCY — Has your father met them?

SYLVIA — Oh yes.

NANCY — Has he gone around with you?

SYLVIA — Not to the lively parties.

NANCY — My dear!   Who chaperones you?

SYLVIA — A woman pal of Dudley's.

NANCY — Is she a married woman?

SYLVIA — Is she?   Three times.

NANCY — How awful!

SYLVIA — She's terribly nice.   You must know her.

So sweet to me. Takes me motoring in the **park al**-most every afternoon.

NANCY — Where did you meet her, dear?

SYLVIA — At a party at the Drowsy Saint.

NANCY — Where's that?

SYLVIA — It's a new freak place in the Village!

NANCY — Who took you *there?*

SYLVIA — Gillie. He's a sweetie lamb and so gener-ous. He spends money like water.

NANCY — He doesn't make love to you?

SYLVIA — No — but I guess he'd like to.

NANCY — Darling, you mustn't say such things. It isn't nice.

SYLVIA — Why not?

NANCY — Well, nice nice girls don't, that's all.

SYLVIA — (*sitting up*). What else don't they do?

NANCY — Well, dear, they don't go to the places you've been going, and they don't rouge or wear hats from Francine's.

SYLVIA — All the women in my crowd do.

NANCY — Then I think you're going with the wrong crowd.

SYLVIA — How do you know? You've never seen any of them. They may not belong, but they know how to be kind.

NANCY — Sylvia, I'm sorry. I don't mean to criti-cize —

SYLVIA — (*testily*). But you are. Daddy's the only one that never finds fault with me. He's the only one that loves me, really.

NANCY — It isn't always kind to allow you to just do as you please. Oh, my dear, don't say that to me.

SYLVIA — Doesn't everyone else in this family do as they please?

After her talk with Sylvia the light begins to break in

upon Nancy Fair. By the time Gillette calls she has reached a definite decision concerning her next tour. Her manager comes, all smiles and compliments, and with a sly wink or two for Sylvia.

GILLETTE — Good evening, Mrs. Fair. It's a very great pleasure to see you again.

SYLVIA — Well, Mother, when you're through with Gillie have them page me in the lounge. I'll go down and hear a little jazz.

NANCY — No Sylvia. You'll wait in my room, please. (NANCY *exits peevishly.*)

GILLETTE — Mrs. Fair, I must congratulate you on the success of your tour. It was phenomenal. I am proud to have had the *privilege* of presenting you to the American public. (NANCY *makes no reply*) I trust that you have found it agreeable to appear under my management? (NANCY *still stares into space*) I hope our association will continue. I've secured even better terms for the new tour.

NANCY — I am not going on another tour.

GILLETTE — You are not going on — but, Mrs. Fair, all the arrangements have been made. '

NANCY — They will have to be cancelled.

GILLETTE — But you agreed to it by letter. You phoned me to bring these contracts to-night.

NANCY — Things have occurred that have made me change my mind.

GILLETTE — Are you dissatisfied with me?

NANCY — No, but I can't go on.

GILLETTE — You can't mean that you are going to give up all your triumphs?

NANCY — Triumphs!

GILLETTE — But Mrs. Fair I am leaving to-night for Montreal to arrange for your appearance in Canada. The people in the east haven't heard you talk of your great work.

NANCY — Mr. Gillette, there is nothing that could induce me to talk of my great work again. I will be very much obliged if you will bring me an accounting to-morrow.

GILLETTE — To-morrow?

NANCY — Yes. I think there is about fifteen thousand dollars due.

GILLETTE — Why, I won't be able to make a settlement to-morrow. It will take the bookkeeper several days to make out the statement.

NANCY — Let me have it as soon as possible as I am going to reopen our house in the country. And now I believe Sylvia has some message for you — and I will send her in and you can say good-by to her.

GILLETTE — Good-bye?

NANCY — I think it wiser. Sylvia has been telling me of your kindness to her. I don't wish to seem ungrateful but I would rather you did not see her again, at least for the present.

GILLETTE — Are you insinuating that I am not good enough to associate with your daughter?

NANCY — I never insinuate, Mr. Gillette. If I must speak more plainly I will and I hope you will not resent it.

GILLETTE — Well —

NANCY — Sylvia's story of her friendship with you has made me realize that you and I have rather different standards as to the sort of associates and amusements that are suitable for a girl of her age and upbringing.

GILLETTE — She enjoyed the associates and the amusements.

NANCY — Probably, but I am sure that she will like much more the ones I intend to provide for her from now on. When may I expect the statement?

GILLETTE — The day after tomorrow.

NANCY — Good night, Mr. Gillette.

But it is not as easy as Nancy had hoped to turn Sylvia's thoughts away from Gillette. She sees the manager now as a martyr, and herself as the cause of his unhappiness, a state of mind that fits very well with the crafty " Gillie's " hastily made plans for the future. " Did mother say anything unkind to you? " Sylvia demands when she is alone with Gillette.

GILLETTE — Did she? She spoke plainly and hoped I wouldn't resent it. Me doing all I could to keep you from being lonely! A lot of thanks I got. Told me I wasn't good enough to associate with you. Well, if she objects to me, what's she going to say about your father and Angy Brice?

SYLVIA — Dudley! What do you mean?

GILLETTE — The minute your mother's wise she'll get a divorce.

SYLVIA — Divorce?

GILLETTE — Why, you poor kid, aren't you on to your father and Angy Brice? Everybody else in town is.

SYLVIA — Oh, I never thought my Daddy would go back on me.

GILLETTE — Your whole family's gone back on you. That selfish brother of yours having no time for anybody but his wife. Your mother leaving you alone for years at a stretch and your father running around with Angy Brice. A lot they care about you.

SYLVIA — Nobody wants me.

GILLETTE — I want you. I'm the only one that cares anything about you and I've been ordered to say good-by to you.

SYLVIA — Good-by?

GILLETTE — Yes, and you're going to be taken down to the country.

SYLVIA — I won't go.

GILLETTE — You'll have to go.   And you'll soon forget all about me.

SYLVIA — I won't.

GILLETTE — Oh, yes you will.

SYLVIA — I won't.

GILLETTE — No?   Then prove it.

SYLVIA — How?

GILLETTE — Come with me to Montreal to-night.

SYLVIA — Oh, Dudley!

GILLETTE — We'll be married as soon as we get there.

SYLVIA — I couldn't.   They'd never forgive me.

GILLETTE — Sure they will.   Didn't they forgive Alan?   Why they'll be on their knees to you and to me too.

SYLVIA — I don't know what to do.

GILLETTE — Oh, all right.   I might have known you wouldn't come through.   You pretend to care about me.   It's only a bluff.   Well, stay here where nobody wants you!   Good-bye.

SYLVIA — Oh, Dudley, please don't go.

GILLETTE — Well, what are you going to do about it?

SYLVIA — You're sure you really want me?

GILLETTE — Of course I want you.   (*Nervously*) We can't talk here.   Meet me downstairs in the lounge and we'll talk it over.   Now, you won't weaken?

Nancy returns to find Gillette alone.   He has said good-by to Sylvia, he explains, and she has gone to her room.   Reassured that she has this particular angle of the family problem in hand, Nancy is reminded of another phase when Angy Brice calls Jeffrey Fair on the telephone.   Nancy speaks to Jeffrey about this friendship of his.   Of course, she explains, she understands, but she is afraid others do not.   She has heard what people are saying, and some of her friends have been kind enough to write her. Frankly, her pride is hurt. Jeffrey naturally views the affair differently. Hasn't Nancy deliberately forsaken his bed and board — hasn't she —

FAIR — What right have you to object to anything I do?

NANCY — My right as your wife.

FAIR — Haven't you forfeited that right?

NANCY — How?

FAIR — If you prefer the public to your husband you mustn't kick at the price you have to pay.

NANCY — Meaning that I am not to protest if you choose to make me conspicuous by your attentions to that woman. Really, this is delicious. (*She laughs.*)

FAIR — Are you paying me the compliment of being jealous of me?

NANCY — Jealous of a man who doesn't want me?

FAIR — Oh, Nancy, you know damned well I want you. . . . You may not be jealous of me but I am of you and everything that concerns you. I'm jealous of your career because it took you away from me. . . . I tried to live up to our agreement. Hadn't I the right to expect that you'd live up to it, too? If it was my job to provide the home, wasn't it your job to take care of it? Had you the right, be honest Nancy, to go on this tour? You can't be married and be a free agent without making someone suffer. I am so damn sick of my life — as I'm living it now. But I don't want to keep you if you want to be free.

NANCY — I don't want to be free. Oh wait. I want to be honest with myself and with you. I couldn't go back to my life as I lived it four years ago. It isn't that I don't want my home. While I was in France there were glorious moments and honors and flattery, but there were nights when I was so sick of the horrors, the pain, the misery, that it seemed to

me if I couldn't put my head on your shoulder and
cry out the loneliness in my heart against yours I
couldn't go on. With death on every side I used to
worry for fear you weren't taking care of yourself.
They decorated me for bravery. They never knew
what a coward I was about you. Why on this tour
the nights when I had had a great success and while
people were crowding around me congratulating me,
I'd see some wife tuck her hand through her husband's
arm just as I had tucked mine so many times through
yours and she would trot away home with her man and
I would go to a lonely hotel room and think about you.
Then's when I would realize that success meant nothing if I had to give up you.

FAIR — Then, Nancy, I've got you again.

NANCY — Yes and hang on to me. If I ever try
to go away again, lock me up on bread and water.

But it is a short-lived reconciliation. Just as they
are planning to go back to the country, and Nancy is
radiant in thinking of all the things she will do to make
up to her unhappy family for having deserted them,
and of how she will win Sylvia back to her, Jeffrey,
intending only to reassure her that she has nothing
more to fear from Angy Brice's attractions for him,
confidently remarks that he has that very evening " dis-
charged all his obligations to her."

Nancy has never suspected there were " obligations ";
that Mrs. Brice has any real claim upon Jeffrey is news
to her — shocking news. Neither does Jeffrey's demand that she should " be big enough to understand "
satisfy her. She could forgive a great deal — but not
everything. If that is how matters stand there is nothing for her to do but to apply for a divorce.

NANCY — I refuse to listen to anything more. All
I want to know is are you going to try to keep me

against my will or must I make a scandal to get free?
. . . Surely you don't want to blacken the name of the
woman you are going to marry?

FAIR — I am not going to marry her. She knows
it. I'm not in love with her nor she with me. A sum
of money will console her.

NANCY — Your bargain with her has no interest
for me. You may make what use of your freedom
you choose. I mean to have mine.

FAIR — Very well. My lawyer knows the amount
of my income. You may have what you wish of it.

NANCY — I wouldn't take any of it were it not for
Sylvia.

FAIR — What do you mean? Sylvia?

NANCY — Do you think I would allow her to remain with you? Look what your neglect has made
of her. Through your carelessness Mr. Gillette has
been allowed to introduce her to a sort of life until she
is no more the child I sent home to you. Do you
think when I realize that you are responsible that I
would entrust her to you again? Never. Never!

FAIR — She's the biggest thing in my life. I'll never
let her go.

NANCY — She's the only thing in mine.

FAIR — And do you think I'm going to let you have
her?

NANCY — If you force me to do it I will tell the
truth about you.

FAIR — So that is your threat. She is in her room,
you say. Well, you tell her the truth about me and
let her decide.

ALAN — (*entering   excitedly*). Dad — Mother —
where is Sylvia?

NANCY — She is in her room.

ALAN — She is not — I saw right, it *was* Sylvia
in that taxi cab with Gillette. They drove away just
as we arrived.

PEGGY — I found this letter on Sylvia's dressing
table.

ALAN — For you, Dad.

FAIR —" Daddy I —

NANCY — Jeff — Jeff!

FAIR — She has decided — (*rushing to the phone*)
Give me police headquarters — for God's sake —
quick!

The curtain falls.

ACT IV

For two hours the search for Sylvia has gone on.
Peggy's brother, the detective, is taking a hand in it.
But so far no trace has been found, either of Sylvia
or Gillette. Peggy is with Nancy, trying to cheer
her.

PEGGY — We'll hear some good news soon now. . . .
Wouldn't you like a cup of tea? (NANCY *shakes her
head*) Not if I sent for the things and made it myself? I make very nice tea.

NANCY — I'm sure you do. But I couldn't.

PEGGY — Oh, Mrs. Fair, I wouldn't keep on reading
that letter.

NANCY — Oh, Peggy, I know it by heart. " I'm in
everybody's way. Nobody wants me. Dudley does,
so I'm going with him. . . . Sylvia." Oh my baby!

PEGGY — Please don't cry. Please.

NANCY — No. I mustn't. I musn't. Oh if I
could only do something!

PEGGY — There is nothing to do but wait.

NANCY — Oh Peggy tell me again that they'll find
her.

PEGGY — Of course they will. Now Mrs. Fair you
mustn't. Please don't cry. . . . The one thing I can't
understand is Sylvia's leaving her father. She would

never have gone if she hadn't felt that in some way he had turned against her. She might have left —

NANCY — You could understand her leaving me. I'm beginning to understand that. too. I'm beginning to see that he has more right to her than I have.

PEGGY — Oh, I don't mean that she doesn't love you, but the love Sylvia had for her father was wonderful.

NANCY — He had earned it.

In the face of this greater tragedy the Fairs forget their own quarrel. And though Jeffrey is bitter, he also is " big enough " to be kind. He lays the blame all upon Gillette, whom he is now convinced is not only trying to steal Sylvia away from them but is also seeking to avoid an investigation of his financial accounts with Mrs. Fair.

" Curse the day the swine came into my house! " he shouts, but Nancy's pathetic answering plea stops him.

" O, Jeff," she begs, " don't make me feel my responsibility for it all any more than I do. I can't bear it. I can't bear it! "

" I'm sorry, Nancy."

Suddenly Alan bursts into the room. " She's here! " he cries.

FAIR — Thank God! (NANCY *makes a rush for the door*. ALAN *stops her*.)

ALAN — Wait, Mother. What are you going to say to her? What are you going to do?

NANCY — Oh, Alan what would I do?

ALAN — I didn't know.

FAIR — Where did you find her?

ALAN — At 125th Street Station. They were on their way to Montreal.

FAIR — Where is he?

ALAN — I've taken care of him. He's —

NANCY — What does it matter where he is? All that matters is that she's here. Don't shut her outside. Alan, do you hear me? Let me go to her.

FAIR — Easy, Nancy, easy.

ALAN — All right, Mother, all right, but be careful, treat her very gently. (ALAN *goes to get* SYLVIA.)

NANCY — Jeffrey, I'm giving up my claims to her. She's yours. So be kind to her.

Alan brings Sylvia in. She is still defiant, and a little sullen. When her mother rushes toward her Sylvia stops her. Nancy is stunned. Peggy tries to save the situation by asking Sylvia if she will not sit down.

" I can take what everybody has to say, standing ! " Sylvia replies.

NANCY — Darling, don't be afraid.

SYLVIA — I'm not afraid.

NANCY — We're not going to scold you. We're not going to say anything.

SYLVIA — No? Well, I am.

Bitterly Sylvia denies their right to interfere with her affairs. Why did they " butt in "? Because they loved her? Humph, they acted like it. What right have they to suspect Dudley Gillette? They can't prove he is an embezzler, or that he meant her harm. She won't believe he has confessed. Her father is the first she will listen to.

FAIR — I am sorry, dear, that all this had to happen; that you feel we've all conspired to disgrace you, but we were only trying to protect you.

SYLVIA — Protect me? If you wanted to protect

me why wait? You knew that I was going about with him.

NANCY — But, Sylvia, your father didn't realize the sort of friends that Mr. Gillette was —

SYLVIA — He introduced me to the only friends he had. What do you know about them? You never met them.

FAIR — Sylvia, I forbid you to use that tone to your mother.

NANCY — Sylvia is right, Jeff. I judged them solely by what she told me of them.

SYLVIA — And while you were judging you passed sentence on Dudley too, didn't you? You forbade my best friend seeing me again.

FAIR — Your mother had every right to do that.

SYLVIA — She had no right to make him feel that he wasn't fit to associate with me, when she introduced him to me.

FAIR — She did not know that you were associating with him so intimately.

SYLVIA — No, she wasn't here, was she?

NANCY — No, Sylvia, I wasn't here.

FAIR — But I was. I'm to blame — I should have watched over you —

SYLVIA — But you didn't care what I was doing, where I was going, just so you were free to run around with Mrs. Brice.

NANCY — Sylvia, how dare you talk like that to your father?

ALAN — Haven't you any respect? Haven't you any feeling? Can't you see that you are hurting Father and Mother cruelly?

SYLVIA — Well, haven't they hurt me?

But she can't keep the tears back long, and with her tears comes her confession. She wanted to get away from them all — because they do not want her.

Her mother doesn't love her, or she would not have left her.   Her father doesn't love her — he loves Angy Brice.

SYLVIA — Everybody has known but us that he was going to get rid of mother and marry Angy. (*She looks at her mother, pointedly*) Mother, aren't you going to leave daddy?

NANCY — (*turning away from all the family*) No.

FAIR — Nancy!

SYLVIA — Why Dudley said — that's why I went with him.   I didn't know what would become of me when you separated.   I thought Daddy had gone back on me.

FAIR — Sylvia, I'll never go back on you, if you'll only —

NANCY — Jeff, don't make conditions.   We've both been wrong, we must be content with whatever Sylvia wants.

SYLVIA — I only want you all to want me.

NANCY — Oh, my dear, my dear.

With her daughter safe again in her arms, the problems of one ambitious feminist are, temporarily at least, solved for her.   It is Alan who has the tag of the play.

" Alan," demands Peggy. " where is Gillette? "

" In an ambulance," shouts that exultant youth.

"DECLASSEE"

A Drama in Three Acts

By Zoe Aikins

ETHEL BARRYMORE began her season at the Empire theater the evening of October 6th in "Declassee." Both star and play were acclaimed by the reviews and this verdict was generously indorsed by a public that continued to crowd the theater, until spring. "Declassee," though written by an American, Zoe Aikins, who was born in the Ozark Mountains of Missouri, is concerned principally with the adventures of a titled Englishwoman, Lady Helen Haden — married to the somewhat impossible Sir Bruce Haden, a butcher elevated to the knighthood by a king grateful for the commercial prestige he has helped to build for England. Lady Helen has lived a little recklessly in an effort to make life a trifle more endurable. She has flirted discreetly, as becomes a lady whose father was an earl, whose godmother was a queen of England, and whose line of ancestors stretches back a matter of several hundred years, and she has been extravagant. "She doesn't know," declares a friend of hers, "and will never learn — the difference between a pound and a shilling." "Oh," replies another, "she knows that a pound is something you give the head waiter and a shilling is something you give the taxi driver. Helen thinks that is what real money is for — to tip people with."

At the opening of the play, without preliminary warning, the audience is plunged into the very heart of a tense dramatic situation. Lady Helen has been entertaining friends at bridge. Sir Bruce, "a little bit drunk — and maybe a little bit jealous," has deliberately accused Edward Thayer, a young American, and the guest of Lady Helen, of having cheated at cards. During the polite uproar following, the friends of the Hadens have striven diplomatically to adjust the matter, that it may be smoothed over and anything resembling a scandal avoided. At the rise of the curtain diplomacy has succeeded to the extent of inducing both Lady Helen and Sir Bruce to return to the drawing room and continue the game. The accused Thayer, at the pleading of the others, has agreed to "smile and do his best."

This is the situation when Lady Helen enters.

"A faint smile is on her face, but she is pale and very grave under the ripple of amusement that plays over her." The still ugly Sir Bruce, she notices, has returned to the brandy decanter. Her effort is to put the company at ease. Her tone is gay, but her nerves are taut as she volunteers the information that she has been consulting Zellito, a fortune teller. "Dancing is her real job," Lady Helen explains. "Fortune telling is just a sort of gift. She doesn't do it unless she feels a special interest in you. It's enormously flattering to have her feel a special interest in one. It makes one feel so important, psychically — as if one had a destiny or something of the sort. Zellito thinks I have one but she wouldn't tell me what it was. Some sort of spectacular doom, I suppose — I wonder? I never believe doctors and I never believe lawyers,— but I always believe fortune-tellers."

SIR BRUCE — Yes, you would,— being one of the mad Varvicks.

LADY HELEN — The mad Varvicks will soon trouble the world no longer. (*Turning to* MRS. LESLIE *and*

EDWARD THAYER) I suppose you don't know about the mad Varvicks? There was once quite a lot of us, and now I'm the only one that's left. We were very gay about five hundred years ago. But even then we were a little mad, too, I suppose. And we kept on being gay and mad through some of the soberest days that England has ever known. Sometimes we lost our heads; sometimes we went to house parties in the tower; sometimes we hunted with the King and knew all the secrets of the Queen. But there never was a battle fought for England, by sea or land, in which some Varvick did not offer his gay mad life. Perhaps that's how we got the habit of dying. We've always died, I think we've rather liked dying,— just as we've always liked our ghosts and our debts and our hereditary gout and our scandals and our troubadours and our fortune-telling gypsies and even our white sheep. We do admit to an occasional white sheep in the family,— one every century or so. . . . And now — before we attempt to play again — (*She grows stern*) I think that my husband wishes to apologize to Mr. Thayer, before all of you, for what he said to Mr. Thayer, before all of you in this room a little while ago.

Sir Bruce protests. He had his suspicions. He still has them.

LADY HELEN — You accused one of my friends, a young man who is a stranger in this country, and who came to this house on my invitation, of trying to cheat you at cards. You cannot prove your statement — that he systematically looked over your shoulder, or your partner's; but on the other hand he cannot disprove it. It is one of those charges that it is infamously unfair to make because there is no way to get at the truth. But in this case, even if I had never seen Mr. Thayer before,— even if I did not know him impossible of such dishonesty,— I would insist, as I insist now, upon giving him the benefit of the very great doubt that your suspicions had any justification whatever —

SIR BRUCE — I tell you my *suspicions* —!

LADY HELEN — Wait a minute, Bruce! You were very headstrong a moment ago in calling this friend of mine a cheat and a liar, and ordering him from the house; and I know you well enough to know that the story would have got about, and he would have been done for — even if everyone else in this room had kept decently silent. . . . Oh, I know!

SIR BRUCE — Well, I let him stay, didn't I? There he is. I'm willing to say no more.

LADY HELEN — You — let — him stay! Because I would have left this house — just as surely as I'm standing here — if you had not retracted! And you didn't want that. God knows why — but you didn't. You —

SIR BRUCE — I tell you I'm willing to say no more — if you want to let the matter drop now. I know men who wouldn't let it drop. But I'm willing.

LADY HELEN — But I'm not,— not until you've said to Mr. Thayer that you apologize.

Sir Bruce apologizes, but not until Lady Helen has started to leave his house. Then he becomes abject. " I was wrong," he says, slightly overdoing his humbleness, " I'm very sorry. I apologize to Mr. Thayer: I apologize to my wife; and I apologize to you all. I'm not a very pleasant sort, I suppose, and — oh well, I apologize, and I hope that everyone realizes that I spoke hastily and unjustly, and that I'm very sorry."

" When I begin invoking the mad Varvicks for Bruce's benefit, you can always know that I'm a bit desperate," Lady Helen later explained to Lady Wildering. "It's the one thing that he still likes about me,— being a mad Varvick, I mean,— and of course he always pretends to scorn it."

LADY WILDERING — Of course.

LADY HELEN — But I think that he thinks I'm the maddest of the lot. We'd had some discussions earlier in the day — about a few bills that seemed particularly mad to him. Bruce believes in being extravagant economically. He's made a fine art of it. His apology was very pretty, I thought,— prettier than anyone could have hoped for, under the circumstances.

LADY WILDERING — Yes,— I think that he said just the right thing.

LADY HELEN — Thank God he did. It's not supremely jolly to be married to Bruce, but I don't know what I'd do if he threw me over, or I had to throw him over . . . ? Run a hat shop or something, I suppose,— though every time I've run anything — even a booth in a bazaar — I've managed in some mysterious way to be in debt to somebody as a result. No, I'd have no luck with hat shops and things of that sort. It would be easier to sell a pearl every day or two — until they were all gone —

CHARLOTTE — Yes? And then?

LADY HELEN — Then . . . ? I suppose I'd become declassee, in time . . . and the Queen wouldn't care whether I had a cold or not . . . I love that thing that Harry is always playing — only it's like — like rain and ghosts — and the moors in winter — and last year's styles — and photographs of one's self at seventeen. There's no doubt about it,— it's depressing."

Young Thayer is grateful, but still a little worried. He doesn't quite understand Lady Helen. "You were wonderful," he says to her. "If I didn't know better

I could almost have thought you really cared for me."

LADY HELEN — What I said in your behalf tonight I would have said, exactly as I told my husband, in behalf of any stranger in the same situation.

EDWARD — Oh!

LADY HELEN — But it wouldn't have meant so much to me, of course, if it had not been someone I cared for.

EDWARD — Look here — *do* you care for me?

LADY HELEN — You know.

EDWARD — I wish I did know.

LADY HELEN — If you don't know,— if you *really* don't know, why bother about it?

EDWARD — One shouldn't bother about it. You are right. After all, I'm just an incident in your life — just someone who happened to interest you for a month or so, one spring out of all the other springs. Last year it was someone else; and next year it will be another, and after that another —

LADY HELEN — So you don't mean to let yourself care one little bit more about me than you think I care about you, do you, Ned? (*He does not answer; she continues lightly*) You think you are just one of my caprices, don't you? (*He stilll does not answer; again her tone is light, but very tender*) I suppose, after all, there was someone whom you thought you cared for last spring — and the spring before? And surely there will be someone this time next year   ? And perhaps *that* someone will be the right one, and she'll have all the other springtimes, as well. I hope so. And I hope that she will have a very firm hand — for she will need it with you, my dear; and a very tender heart, for she will need that too; and a very wise head — you're not very wise yourself, you know . . . And I hope that she will be young and lovely and that you will be always very happy together, and very, very sad apart — as long as both of you live.

EDWARD — That's a strange way to talk.

LADY HELEN — Poor Ned! Hasn't anyone ever wanted you to be happy before?

EDWARD — Not anyone who pretended to be in love with me.

LADY HELEN — Love is something that not many of us know much about. I don't pretend to know myself — and I've never *pretended* to love you, Ned. . I'm afraid of the very word. *Love!* It's a word I've never used . . . to anyone . . .

EDWARD — But only a week ago . . . oh, I don't understand you.

LADY HELEN — My dear, you are stupid.

EDWARD — You wrote me such wonderful letters from the country. Is it stupid to think you cared for me when you wrote them?

LADY HELEN — No, I don't think the stupidest person would doubt that I cared for you when I wrote them. But let's not talk about what we feel or don't feel, to-night.

.   .   .   .

LADY HELEN — It isn't really important whether I care for you or not; or whether or not you care for me. If you were Tristan and I were Isolde, and we'd drunk a deathless love potion, there would be nothing that we could do about it . . . nothing! Don't smile. There are some things one can do nothing about. One is being born. One is love. And one is death. . . Oh, Tristan and Isolde could go into the wilderness for love, yes. . . But not you and I. At least not together. I don't know about you. You are younger; less sophisticated; not so restless, I hope, but you *are* selfish; and you are comfort-loving, just as I am. . . and, after all, there are no wildernesses any more, are there? So even if this feeling between us, this — shall I call it, like Juliet, " this bud of love "

should perhaps prove a beauteous flower, it could
bloom only to be trampled in the mire. I don't want
that. I'd rather break it now, with my own hands,
from its stem — and lay it away with the dream that I
had once.

EDWARD — I wish I could believe that, at least, you'd
like for things to be different, and we could begin all
over again together.

LADY HELEN — I don't know what I wish for myself. Ned. But my life is like water that has gone over
the dam and turned no mill wheels — there I am — not
— happy, but not unhappy as my days run on to the
sea, idly yet too swiftly, for I love living. But
you. . . I want something very fine for you — I want
to be so proud of you that there will be tears in my
eyes when I think of you.

The name of a certain Mrs. Leslie is mentioned
She is also a guest at the bridge party; an American,
too, of a type frequently encountered in American
colonies abroad. "One is always seeing them about
and meeting them, too," Lady Wildering explains.
"They are always living in hotels, always apparently on the wing; always good looking; always
beautifully dressed; always pleasure-seeking; their
friends are always people they've just met; they're
agreeable enough, frequently amusing; they never have
such things as husbands or relatives or children; and
they emerge from perfect obscurity, as detached from
any possible background as silhouettes cut from black
paper, and pasted on a blank page."

Mrs. Leslie has been Thayer's partner at bridge and
the young man thinks Lady Helen may, in a way,
resent his interest in her. But she denies the implica-
tion. "She's very pretty; she's amusing sometimes,
and she plays admirable bridge. I'm not jealous — but

I might like her better if I liked you less," her lady-ship admits.

The bridge games are resumed and the curtain is lowered to indicate the passage of an hour. When it rises, the drama reverts quickly to the tense mood of the earlier scene of accusation and apology. From the room in which she has been playing with Mrs. Leslie, Mr. Thayer and Harry Charteris, Lady Helen sweeps in " in so furious a rage that she wears the superb aspect of a violet goddess walking on wind." Thayer follows " helpless, humiliated and in despair." He, (with Mrs. Leslie) has been caught cheating a second time — and this time by Lady Helen herself. She turns on Thayer.

LADY HELEN — God knows why you should have done this a second time! You must be insane. Or — did you — did you think it all out very cleverly —? Did you think I was too blind and too stupid to detect your miserable signals? Or that I had such supreme *faith* in you that I wouldn't believe even the evidence of my own eyes? Or that I would be complacent because I had defended you an hour ago, and would find it humiliating to go to my husband and tell him that he was right and I was wrong? Or has dis-honesty become such a habit with you that you find it impossible not to cheat when you can? Is that it? You'd better go, Mrs. Leslie. Don't try to speak to me. Just go.

.   .   .   .

EDWARD — There's nothing I can say — now — ex-cept that I'm sorry.

LADY HELEN — You must say that to my husband.

EDWARD — To your husband!

LADY HELEN — Yes. He said it to you. You must say it to him.

EDWARD — You mean — to tell him?

LADY HELEN — Of course.

EDWARD — But why? You'll only put yourself in a hole. You'll only be admitting that you were wrong. And I won't ever come here again. I'll keep out of your way — but you can't — you can't tell him.

LADY HELEN — He was right. I was wrong. Of course I'll tell him. And I expect you to ask for his pardon before everyone that heard him ask for yours.

EDWARD — I won't. I tell you, I won't. You know what sort of man he is. He'll tell his story all over London. And it won't stop there. They'll know it in New York. It will ruin me for good and all. . . I am sorry. I'll never do it again. I needed the money. . . It didn't seem so awfully wrong to fake a bit — and win it from people who didn't need it, and who didn't care, as long as they were amused, whether they lost it, or not. And it got to be a habit — it got so I couldn't resist a chance — just as you said. But I'll never do it again. . . . Only, for God's sake, let me go — without the scandal that your husband will surely make. I — I'm not afraid of Charteris. He'll keep quiet if you ask him. But — life won't be worth living if everybody knows!

LADY HELEN — Is that all? Have you never heard of *fair play?* Well, turn about is fair play. It's my husband's turn now.

EDWARD — You don't dare.

LADY HELEN — I don't dare? Dare what? Admit that I was wrong and he was right?

EDWARD — You said tonight that if he kicked me out of this house, you'd go out of it too, forever. Very well; I say that if he kicks me out, you *will* go out of it too, forever. . . You don't get what I'm driving at, do you? I mean that I've got letters of yours — I've got them, right here. If you tell on me, I'll tell on you. If you're so damned keen on playing fair

with your brute of a husband — I'll play fair with
him too. . . You're willing to see me sent to the devil,
yes. But how about yourself?

Lady Helen's answer is to call her guests and her
husband. "I've something to tell you, all of you,"
she begins. "About Mr. Thayer. You were right,
Bruce — and I was quite, quite wrong. He —"
The curtain falls.

ACT II

There is a lapse of two years between the first and
second acts. Lady Helen and several of her friends
are in New York. Sir Bruce had ordered his wife out
of the house the night of the interrupted bridge party,
and divorced her a year later. The letters that Thayer
had turned over to him were his excuse, though he did
not introduce them as evidence.

In New York Lady Helen has become rather declassee, living by her wits and "going about with all
sorts of people." Society had taken her up when she
arrived, but had later dropped her. The sale of her
jewels "one by one" has provided for her maintenance, however, and permitted her to live true to her
own code of respectability. Edward Thayer has disappeared.

The Wilderings are on their way to Washington
Sir Emmett having been appointed to the post of ambassador. They are sitting now in the lounge of a
prominent New York hotel wondering what has become of Lady Helen and rather hoping they will
not meet her. "I should be seeing ghosts," says Sir
Emmett, "ghosts of the mad Varvicks racing their
phantom horses down the winds of eternity; swift
riders with plumes streaming and armor flashing; their
phantom hounds leaping before them; a great race —
warriors and courtiers and sportsmen riding into ob-

livion . . . and Helen following them — the last of their line, a ghost of to-morrow.   The Varvicks should have made a better ending."

" But Helen's an Englishwoman," declares one of the party, " and our own kind, and although she's done every damnable thing that a woman can do to cut herself adrift from us, there's nothing, nothing in the world that I wouldn't do for her, if it could do any good."

SIR EMMETT — But nothing can do any good.   It's just because she is an Englishwoman and our own kind that we must be stern with ourselves about her.   She had a great name, great traditions, great gifts, great charm; and in God's name, what has she done with them?   For her personal misfortunes one might be sorry — one is sorry, sorry beyond all words; but as an Englishman, as a representative of my king, I cannot forgive an Englishwoman for making, in a strange country, a sneer of her class, a joke of her rank, and a miserable adventure of her life."

And then Lady Helen walks in upon them.   She has invited a mixed group of her American friends to have tea with her — three Croatian acrobats she had met through Zellito, the fortune telling dancer; Rudolph Solomon, a distinguished and very rich American Jew, and Alice Vance, his musical comedy mistress.

The meeting with her English friends is quite exciting for Lady Helen, and a little sad.   They try to make her welcome, to include her again in their plans — but she knows how they must feel.   So she soon draws away from them and joins her own guests.

Soon they are gone too, all but Solomon.   And he, catching the meditative look in her eyes, grows serious.

"You are very child-like, Lady Helen," he says.

LADY HELEN — Is that why you are looking at me so sternly? Are you thinking that I've got my frock very soiled?

SOLOMON — I'm thinking that you've run very hard, and played very recklessly.

LADY HELEN — So I have. It's sometimes very difficult to realize that this is a serious world — and that life is something more than a hill-top in the sun, with an adventure lurking in every flower. There are so many things to make one smile; and the older one grows, and the more one is alone, the oftener one smiles to oneself. . . I don't say that they are always happy smiles — but just the fact of being alive is rather gay;

"For to admire and for to see,
For to behold the world so wide. . ."

Only an Englishman could have written that. Did you ever meet Kipling, by the way? He used to dine with us — (*She breaks off sharply*). Thank you for the set of Conrad's books. I love them. Do you know the South Sea Islands? We cruised among them all one winter. The stars are very wonderful. We lived on the yacht and put in at every port that took our fancy. You should do that some time — if only for the stars and the strange hushed nights.

  .   .   .   .

SOLOMON — I was thinking of a shooting star, Lady Helen,— a star that I saw once, fall from the sky, into that dark garden of water that lies between New York and the outer ocean. I was a newsboy, and I had sold all my papers; I was lying on the grass in Battery Park because it was better than going to the place that I called home. I was half asleep when I saw the lightning of the shooting star.

LADY HELEN — And now what are you thinking of?

SOLOMON — I was thinking that there are better things in life, even than cruising beneath the stars in the South Seas.

LADY HELEN — It's very beautiful — crusing beneath the stars in the South Seas. What is better?

SOLOMON — Purpose. . . The Progress of one's spirit upon a pilgrimage of achievement; the building of one's life after the plan of one's dreams. . When the grass of Battery Park was my bed, an earl was as legendary to me as the Santa Claus that drove his reindeers down the chimneys of fortunate children at Christmas time. An earl's daughter as remote as the furthest star in the darkness of the night. Yet here we are, Lady Helen,— you and I.

LADY HELEN — Yes, here we are; you and I. . .

SOLOMON — I suppose that I seem to you very conscious of all that I have got from life? Well, I *am* conscious of it. It's a great satisfaction to have got what one has wanted. And I've not stopped, you know, at getting money. I've gone on. I know the world, and its finest things,— its cities, its music, its literature, and all its games. I've thrust my hand into the past and touched history. In my house there are marbles and swords and fans — memoirs of popes and emperors and warriors, and queens and immortal courtesans. And I've touched the future, too. My money is building projects that will benefit generations not yet born.

LADY HELEN —It's power that you really wanted — and have got, isn't it?

SOLOMON — Power — and the flavor of life at its rarest; and to know that, there is one thing more that I must have — you! I want you!

LADY HELEN — But I'm no longer a sufficiently precious object for the golden cabinet of your very successful life.

SOLOMON — But I want you.

LADY HELEN — That's rather ambiguous.

SOLOMON — I want an ambiguous thing,— romance.

LADY HELEN — Oh, I see.

SOLOMON — I'd be very generous.

LADY HELEN — Alice Vance has not found you so.

SOLOMON — You are not Alice Vance. My first generosity to you would be in the nature of generosity to her. . .

LADY HELEN — It means nothing to you, at all, I suppose,— that she cares for you?

SOLOMON — If she does, I am sorry; but that's the usual tragedy of the heart, isn't it? Caring for someone who does not care for you?

LADY HELEN — I believe that it is — the usual tragedy of the heart — and one tragedy, more or less, in a world of tragedies, doesn't matter.

SOLOMON — We might go very far together — you and I.

LADY HELEN — And I'm not likely to go very far alone, I suppose?

SOLOMON — I don't know. I can't say. To me you seem singularly in need of someone to take care of you — to take care of you, devotedly. I don't want you to disappear into the darkness. And there is a certain sort of outer darkness from which I can save you, forever.

LADY HELEN — Poverty, you mean?

SOLOMON — Yes. You're quite wonderful now, Lady Helen — but there's " to-morrow and to-morrow and to-morrow. . ."

LADY HELEN — I know. And there's old age around the curve — and just one more pearl. (*She looks at the ring on her finger and laughs a little, uneasily*).
        .   .   .   .

Well — whatever is ahead for either of us, we have each found life a strange adventure, haven't we?

We've each come a long distance. The little newsboy
has come a long way from his bed on the grass in Battery Park, and the child who was christened Victoria
Helen Alice Alexandria Varvick has come a long way
from the arms of the queen who was her godmother.

SOLOMON — And no one knows how much farther
each of us has to go, Lady Helen " To-morrow and to-
morrow and to-morrow."

LADY HELEN—No, no one knows; but it's a part of
the adventure to keep one's courage, and not to care
too greatly how the wheel of fortune turns; for we
must all go from the game. empty-handed. at last; and
if we've played fairly I don't believe that we will mind,
really, when the moment comes to blow out our candles
and sleep.

SOLOMON — You mean —?

LADY HELEN — I mean, my friend, that I am going
to refuse your ambiguous offer and all that it might
lead to. And I really like you very much. And it's
a temptation, too, to think of the sheer decency of having enough money again for one's whims — which
seems so much more important, somehow, than one's
needs. But it isn't quite cricket, according to my topsy
turvy ethics, to take away a woman's lover — though
I suppose I wouldn't hesitate if you were her husband.
Alice loves you; and there's something about love —
true love — that's very touching, to me; something at
which even I cannot smile. . .

SOLOMON — You must have been very much in love
once.

LADY HELEN — I was.

SOLOMON — What happened?

LADY HELEN — I ran very hard and played very
recklessly, and fell down, and soiled my frock and cut
my hands and cried a little, and laughed a little.
That's all.

SOLOMON — Didn't he care for you?

LADY HELEN — Not the least bit in the world.

SOLOMON — And that was why —

LADY HELEN — Oh no; that wasn't why I ran hard
— and played recklessly. I knew, from the very beginning that he didn't care for me — at least, that it
was nothing to what I felt for him. So I made up
my mind to do what was best for him. . . I was married, you see. I had made up my mind never to see
him any more — just to be an influence, if I could, for
good, in his life.

SOLOMON —What happened? (*he lays his hand
on hers a moment*). Don't tell me if you'd rather not.

LADY HELEN — He cheated at cards. I couldn't
bear that.

SOLOMON — I understand. That ended it, of
course.

LADY HELEN — It should have, but it didn't.
That's all.

SOLOMON — How long ago did this happen?

LADY HELEN — So long ago that it's not real now.

With Solomon gone, Lady Helen calls for her
check — and asks for a pencil to sign it. There is
whispering among the waiters then, for there has been
an order that Lady Helen is not to be permitted to
sign any more checks. The head waiter explains, as
gently as he can, and she understands. Slowly she
slips a ring from her finger and, rolling up the check,
puts the ring around it. " I'll give this to you, Jean,"
she says —" and — will you give my waiter his tip for
me ? "

She had paid for her tea with her last pearl.

ACT III

The third act advances the story a week to the night
of Rudolph Solomon's party in his wonderful house,
the scene showing "a room straight out of the Italian

Renaissance," richly furnished with some of the price-less antiques of Solomon's collections. Lady Helen recognizes some of them — the King James' chair, for instance, that once stood in Varvick Hall, and in which the king sat for his portrait. And the Gainsborough portrait of her great great grandmother. " I'm always meeting my relatives on other people's walls," she explains, " and sometimes I have to be introduced to them — if they were sold off before my day, I mean — but not to Georgiana, Duchess of Staffordshire. She was our greatest favorite — we kept her as long as we could possibly afford her."

Ambassador and Lady Wildering are among the guests — Lady Helen suspects why. " We'd do anything for you, Helen," Lady Wildering agrees. " Besides, your friend is a very remarkable man. It's been very pleasant for us to meet him."

LADY HELEN — Oh, Edith dear — I understand what you're all about, bless you.   . It's a perfect conspiracy. You're determined to send my stock up so high that Rudolph Solomon will want to marry me — although he doesn't want to in the least. Don't deny it, Edith. Perhaps I will join the conspiracy myself. . . There's " to-morrow and to-morrow and to-morrow," to be got through with, somehow; and one must get used to the idea of the setting sun. . . This table came from the Palazzo Cavalli. . . The sun sets for cities and races too. Venice is in twilight now. And the families that were glorious when she was glorious are only the ghosts that haunt her lagoons . . I'm not very modern, I suppose. I love old things — things that one seems to share with time. . . It gives me a queer warm homesick feeling to see my great great grandmother's picture on that wall. (*She goes and draws back the curtains to look at the picture*) How young she was once — my great great grandmother! The sun never set for her. She fell from her horse, hunting, and died when she was thirty, soon after Gainsborough made her immortal.

LADY WILDERING — Where is Sargent's portrait of you?

LADY HELEN — It was sold. I believe that I'm hanging in the Louvre now. It's amusing, isn't it, how far and wide the winds of fate sometimes carry leaves from the same tree?

Rudolph Solomon in no way resents the conspiracy, even though he may suspect it. His desire for Helen has grown with his better acquaintance of her.

SOLOMON — I have thought of you, and you only, for months. I know you very well — better than anyone in the world knows you. You fascinated me from the moment I met you three years ago, in London — when you used to let me invite you to luncheon sometimes — and nearly always forgot to come — or — when you came — forgot my name. You never could remember whether it was David or Abraham or Solomon.

LADY HELEN — I have always been stupid about names.

SOLOMON — Particularly about your own. . . Oh, I know that if it were not so you would still be forgetting mine. But if mine were yours would you be as careless of it as you have been of your own?

LADY HELEN — If your name were mine? Are you asking me to marry you?

SOLOMON — I want to ask you to marry me. But — I'm very proud of my name, Helen. That may seem a little silly to one whose ancestors have written themselves down, generation after generation, in the history of England. But I *am* proud of it. And it hurts me to give it into the keeping of one who has already been so careless of the traditions and glories about her own — as you.

LADY HELEN — This is a strange wooing.

SOLOMON — Yes, it is a strange wooing, indeed. Strange for me. . . I'm not a sentimentalist. And I'm not a weakling. When I've thought of marriage at all I've thought of a mother for the children that I've hoped to have. Health and simple goodness and dignity — those were to be her indispensable characteristics. I've known women well enough to know that most of them determine their own fates according to their temperaments. But — what are you, anyway, Helen? A mother who never had a child? An artist without a talent? A courtesan born to the purple? What are you?

LADY HELEN — It doesn't matter.

SOLOMON — But it does matter! I love you. You belong here — in my house. I didn't know that I loved you until a week ago when I looked into your heart, and found another love there — the thing that cut you adrift, I suppose, and sent you all soiled and broken, to me. . . . Do you care for me? You will marry me?

LADY HELEN — I — I like you. I've great respect for you. What I might come to feel for you I don't know. I can see how life with you would be very easy — very easy and beautiful. And you know that — if you want to marry me — I should be mad if I refused.

SOLOMON — (*taking a string of pearls from his pocket*). You have been selling these, one by one. Put them on. (*He gives her the pearls and she bends her neck while he fastens them*).

LADY HELEN — Thanks. (*He holds her by the shoulders*).

SOLOMON — You *will* be good, won't you? You're

so reckless — like a wind.   But you will take care —
won't you?   And let all the old miserable gossip die?
LADY HELEN — I'll take care.   I promise.   I'll be
good.   I'll be quite a reformed chacter, Rudolph, if
you talk to me like that.

Then Edward Thayer comes back.   He had been in
South Africa since he left London, and he had prospered — prospered and reformed.   He is a little
startled to hear that Lady Helen is the guest of
honor at Mr. Solomon's party — and more surprised
to learn that she has agreed to marry his host.   They
do not meet at first, Thayer and Lady Helen.   She is
not even aware of his coming.   Not until after Solomon has learned, through Mrs. Leslie, that Thayer is
the man of the card-cheating episode, the man for
whom Lady Helen had confessed her love, the ghost
of which " still walked in her heart."   And he knows
his own romance is not to be after all.   He goes in
search of Lady Helen to explain.

SOLOMON — I am going to say something which
may seem strange to you.   I think it would be a mistake for us to go through with this marriage.   You
don't understand — but you will in a moment.   There
is someone else who can explain better than I.   Wait
here — (*He goes toward the door of the dining
room*).

LADY HELEN — Don't bother to explain, my friend.
It might be awkward; and it isn't necessary — I can
imagine so many more reasons than anyone could possibly tell me.   Good night.   I shall never be sorry for
those few intimate moments when I felt that I knew
a very remarkable person, very well indeed, and when
I had the very novel sensations of being safe, and at
peace.

SOLOMON — It is not always enough for a woman to

feel safe and at peace. Don't go. There is someone I want you to see. Please — wait here!

But Lady Helen doesn't wait. For a little she pauses to listen to the wild gypsy music they are playing in the next room for Zellito's dance. "Almost instantly she is alive with interest." She stops a servant who is passing champagne and drains a glass — and then a second. But suddenly she is weary and determines to leave. "Say to Mr. Solomon that I was very tired and did not wait to say good night. . . That's all, don't wait."

Lady Helen drinks her wine more slowly, thoughtfully, " as if finding the flavor an experience — but her eyes are a little frightened. Then she puts her glass down, and with a last lingering look about her leaves the room."

A moment later Edward Thayer, as though in search of someone, enters and finding no one there, turns back disappointed. A second later Lady Helen, her brilliant evening cloak over her shoulder, stands for a moment in the doorway to listen to the music — and then passes on.

.   .   .   .

It was Alice Vance who saw the accident. She was standing at the window trying vaguely to comprehend what Rudolph Solomon was saying — that he was not going to be married after all — and that she should be glad. The servant entered with his message. " I was to give you a message from her ladyship, sir," he said; " she wished me to say that she was tired and would not stay to say goodby."

Suddenly Alice Vance screamed and covered her face with her hands. From the window she had seen a woman — a woman in a brilliant evening wrap — knocked down by a swiftly moving taxi. It was Lady Helen Haden.

They brought her into the house, and did what they could to make her comfortable. "Don't worry about me," she pleaded with them. "I hope it's the end. It ought to be at any rate — it would be such a regular Varvick ending! One ought to have something in common with one's family — even if it's only one's death. . . . Draw that curtain a little wider, Charlotte dear, so that I may see my great grandmother — there — across the river."

Thus it was that Thayer found her. He came forward, tremblingly, and threw himself at her feet. She moved her arm, painfully, to let it rest on his hair. "Ned," she said, "I don't understand. . . Is it a dream, my dear? It must be a dream."

SOLOMON — You are not dreaming. He has come back.

LADY HELEN — Now I understand why you —

SOLOMON —He's come back — a man.

THAYER — Yes — I've come back — a man. I've wanted to thank you a million times. You did just the right thing — and oh, God! I don't dare to think of what I did to you!

LADY HELEN — Don't think — now. Tell me — more —?

THAYER — I went to South Africa — but it doesn't matter where I went or what I did. The only thing that matters is that you saved me. I've worked. I've been honest. I've made good — and I don't know what I would have been except for you. And I've been in torture whenever I've thought of you — and remembered what I'd done. . . I heard of you, now and then — and I came back to find you, if I could, and ask you if you'd forgive me — and marry me — and go back with me — (*She seems to bend her head. Solomon goes towards the doorway at the back.*)

SOLOMON — I will be — just outside.

THAYER — But it was because I thought it was the only decent thing I could do. You were right — when you said there'd be other springtimes, and maybe, one girl for all of them. I've found her now. I thought I hated all women for a while. Then I began to think how decent you'd been to me — even though you seemed so cruel that night. And before long you got sort of holy to me — like a sister or a good angel. Then I met the girl. Her name is Phyllis — isn't it pretty? Phyllis. . . You remember what you said about hoping that she and I would be very happy together and very sad apart as long as we lived? That's just how it is with us. But we'd made up our minds that we ought to be sad — if — if some of the things we'd heard were true — and you needed me. If I hadn't found you were going to marry Rudolph Solomon, you'd have never known about — her. But he told me —"

   .   .   .   .

Lady Helen did not hear that part of the speech concerning the new-found Phyllis. When they revived her from the fainting spell she only remembered that Ned had returned. "I got lost," she explained. "You came to find me, dear, and what else? I beg your pardon, but I didn't seem to hear the rest. It's too wonderful. . ."

THAYER — (*steadily*) I said that I had come to ask you to be my wife.

Again she sinks into brief unconsciousness. When she can speak again she turns to Solomon. "I see how life with you would have been very easy and very beautiful," she said. "I do, really; I was quite disappointed when you threw me over to-night. I didn't know it was because Ned had come back. And — Ned —"

THAYER — Yes.

LADY HELEN — Hold my hand. . . We're drifting out on the tide, together. Rather jolly — isn't it? . . . Where's the champagne? You'll have to hold it, I'm afraid, Ned. My arms have gone queer, too. . . Hold it high. It's a toast. To England! (*She drinks a little*) 'Oh to be in England — Now that April's here —' Only it isn't April — is it?

A SERVANT — The doctor is coming, sir. His car just stopped outside.

LADY HELEN — The doctor? It will be the first time I ever had one. I never was sick a day in my life. Ask Blossom. Oh Ned — (*A convulsion suddenly shakes her. She clings to him*) Just you — and my young great great grandmother, in her big hat — there — across the river. And the gay music! Everything else — is — going. It's like the theatre — when they turn out the lights —before the curtain rises — on the next act —"

The last of the " mad Varwicks " was at peace.

"JANE CLEGG"

A Domestic Drama in Three Acts

BY ST. JOHN ERVINE

THE Theatre Guild, following its success with St. John Ervine's "John Ferguson" the previous season, began the new year full of hope with a fine staging of John Masefield's tragedy, "The Faithful" (Oct. 13). An artistic but not a financial success resulted. Then they turned to a dramatization of William Dean Howells' "Silas Lapham" (Nov. 25), and this lingered uncertainly through several weeks. Their third production was Tolstoi's "Power of Darkness" (Jan. 19), which earned them many fine reviews, but little money, and finally they decided to try another play by St. John Ervine, his "Jane Clegg," which was first presented by Miss Horniman's company in Manchester, England, in 1913, and subsequently in London. This quiet little domestic drama, a perfect sample of its type, proved another popular success for the Guild and ran out the season. The first performance was given February 23, 1920.

The action of the play occurs in the living room of the Cleggs' house in a small English town. "Jane Clegg, a tall, dark woman, aged thirty-two, is seated at a large table, sewing. It is nearly nine o'clock, and, as the evening is chilly, a bright fire burns in the grate. The room has a cosy air, although it is furnished in the undistinguished manner characteristic of the homes of the lower middle class. A corner of the table is reserved for a meal for a late comer. Johnnie and

Jenny, aged ten and eight years respectively, are playing on a rug in front of the fire. . . Mrs. Clegg, the grandmother, is seated in a low rocking chair, her arms folded across her breast, idly watching them. She is a stout, coarse, and very sentimental woman and her voice has in it a continual note of querulousness. She glances at the clock and then speaks to her daughter-in-law."

MRS. CLEGG — I can't think wot's keepin' 'Enry.

JANE CLEGG — (*without looking up from her sewing*). Busy, I suppose.

MRS. CLEGG — 'E's always busy. I don't believe men are 'alf so busy as they make out they are! Besides I know 'Enry! I 'aven't 'ad the motherin' of 'im for nothink. 'E don't kill 'imself with work, 'Enry don't.

JANE CLEGG — (*in an undertone*). Oh, *hush*, mother, before the children.

MRS. CLEGG — Oh, I daresay they know all about 'im. Children knows more about their parents nowadays than their parents knows about them, from wot I can see of it.

JANE CLEGG — Henry's work keeps him out late. It isn't as if he had regular hours like other men. A traveller isn't like ordinary people.

MRS. CLEGG — No, that's true. It isn't a proper life for a man, not travellin' isn't. A married man, any'ow. They see too much. I don't believe in men seein' too much. It unsettles 'em.

JANE CLEGG — Oh, I don't know! Some men are born to be unsettled and some aren't. I suppose that's the way with everything.

MRS. CLEGG — You take things too calm, you do. I 'aven't any patience with you! Look at the way you took it when 'e went after that woman! . . .

JANE CLEGG — Oh, please, please!

Mrs. Clegg — I'd 'ave tore 'er 'air off. That was the least you could 'ave done.

With the children off to bed, and the tardy 'Enry still unaccounted for, the grandmother insists on continuing the discussion of Henry's past derelictions and Jane's lack of firmness with him. It is all very well for a wife to " make allowances." as Jane suggests, but there's a limit — and there must be some explanation.

Mrs. Clegg — I suppose you must be fond of 'im, or you wouldn't 'ave married 'im.

Jane Clegg — I was very fond of him.

Mrs. Clegg — But you're not now, eh?

Jane Clegg — (returning to her seat). Oh, I don't know about that. I suppose I'm as fond of him as any woman is of her husband after she's been married to him twelve years. It's a long time, isn't it?

Mrs. Clegg — 'Orrible!

Jane Clegg — Do you know why I didn't leave Henry when that happened? It was simply because I couldn't.

Mrs. Clegg — 'Ow du mean?

Jane Clegg — Isn't it simple enough? Johnny was four and Jenny was two. Henry had a good situation If I had left him, I should not have earned more than a pound a week at the best, and I couldn't have looked after the children and worked as well. I don't suppose I should have got work at all here. A woman who leaves her husband on moral grounds is treated as badly as a woman who runs away with another man.

Mrs. Clegg — Well, of course, it isn't right to leave your 'usband. Till death do you part, that's wot the Bible says. I wasn't 'intin' at anything of that sort I only suggested that you should be firm with 'im.

JANE CLEGG — Why shouldn't I leave him, if he isn't loyal?

MRS. CLEGG — Oh, my dear, 'ow can you ask such a question? Wotever would people say?

JANE CLEGG — Why shouldn't I leave him?

MRS. CLEGG — Because it isn't right, that's why.

JANE CLEGG — But why isn't it right?

MRS. CLEGG — You are a one for askin' questions! Nice thing it would be I'm sure if women started leavin' their 'usbands like that.

.   .   .   .   .   .

JANE CLEGG — I don't believe in putting up with things unless you can't help yourself. I couldn't help myself before, but I can now. Uncle Tom's money makes that possible.

MRS. CLEGG — That made 'im angry, that did. When you wouldn't let 'im 'ave the money to start for 'imself.

JANE CLEGG — You know quite well he'd have lost it all. He's a good traveller, but he couldn't control a business of his own. He's not that sort. I made up my mind when I got the money that I would spend it on Johnny and Jenny. I want to give them both a good chance. You know how fond Johnny is of playing with engines and making things. I want to spend the money on making an engineer of him, if that's what he wants to be.

.   .   .   .   .   .

JANE CLEGG — I never see anything or go anywhere. I have to cook and wash and nurse and mend and teach! . . . And then I'm not certain of Henry. That's what's so hard. I give him everything, and he isn't faithful.

MRS. CLEGG — 'E was always a man for women. There's a lot like that. They don't mean no 'arm, but some'ow they do it. I 'eard tell once of someone that

said it was silly of women to complain about things
like that, and mebbe 'e was right. They're not made
like us, men aren't. I never wanted but one man in
my life, but my 'usband, bless 'im, 'e was never satisfied. 'E used to say it near broke 'is 'eart to be a
Christian! 'E 'ad a great respect for Turks an'
foreigners. 'Enry takes after 'im. (*She pauses for
a moment*) I dunno! Men's a funny lot wotever
way you take 'em, an' it's my belief a wise woman
shuts 'er eyes to more'n 'alf wot goes on in the world.
She'd be un'appy if she didn't, an' it's no good bein'
un'appy.

JANE CLEGG — I'm not like that. I demand as
much as I give. It isn't fair to take all and give
nothing.

MRS. CLEGG — (*impatiently*).— But! . . .

JANE CLEGG — Oh, I know what you're going to
say. I don't care what men say or what anybody says;
Henry must give me as much as I give to him. That's
only decent.

MRS. CLEGG — Well, I'm sure I 'ope you get it.
There's few women does. Men is guilty sinners.
You can't get over that. If they ain't sinnin' one way,
they're sinnin' another, an' you can't stop 'em. The
Lord can't do it, an' it ain't likely you can.

The delayed Henry Clegg arrives at last. He is "a
middle-sized man, good-natured, genial, fairly handsome, though a little fleshy and somewhat weak looking. . . . Although he is superficially open and frank
there is about him an air of furtiveness, almost mean-
ness, and he will turn away quickly from a steady
look." He is full of excuses to explain his being late
and a little relieved to change the subject. A letter
has come for him, and he finds it an important letter
— one containing a check for a hundred and forty
pounds that should have been sent to the office of his

firm. "Somebody ought to get the sack for that," declares Henry. "If I wasn't honest, and was to hop 'round to the bank tomorrow morning and cash this — well, it 'ud be all umpydoodelum with some chap's job."

He hasn't much use for his employers, Henry hasn't. They drive a man something awful. "It's enough to make a chap turn Socialist." But he must put up with it. There isn't much chance of anything better turning up, and Jane hasn't indicated any intention of letting him have a bit of the money Uncle Tom left her. He could have done well with a bit of that money.

HENRY CLEGG — I could have doubled that money three times over. I could still do it. I heard today about something! . . . Look here, Jane, if you would let me have two hundred of it, I could pull off a good thing in about six months. Straight, I could.

JANE CLEGG — What could you pull off?

HENRY CLEGG — Well, I can't give many particulars about it, because I told the chap I wouldn't say a word to anyone, not even to you. He knew you'd come in for a bit of money, and he mentioned it himself. He naturally thought I could get the money easy enough. I didn't like to tell him you'd got it, and wouldn't let me have any of it. Makes a man look such a damned fool, that sort of thing. It's a bit of a spec at present, of course, and there's one or two after it. That's why he told me not to tell anyone.

MRS. CLEGG — I should think you could tell Jane. That's on'y nacherel, she bein' your wife.

HENRY CLEGG — No, I promised I wouldn't.

JANE CLEGG — Don't bother, Henry. I know you don't like breaking promises. Your friend won't get my money. I've made up my mind that I shall keep it for Johnny and Jenny.

HENRY CLEGG — (*with great fury*). There, you hear that, mother! That's the sort of a woman she is. Not a spark of love for me in her.

JANE CLEGG — You know, Henry! . . .

HENRY CLEGG — Don't talk to me. I don't want to hear what you've got to say.

The arrival of Mr. Munce to see Henry on a business matter of supreme importance (to Mr. Munce) sends the Clegg women to bed. Mr. Munce is a " bookie." Through him Mr. Clegg has been trying to raise a little money by speculating on the chances of certain horses to outrun certain other horses. Their business dealings, covering a considerable period, have left Henry Clegg in the bookmaker's debt in the sum of twenty-five pounds, and as the latter sees ruin and exposure staring him in the face unless within the week he meet all his outstanding obligations, he is of a mind to press Mr. Clegg, who has made and broken any number of promises to pay, for the money due. The fact that Mr. Munce is in possession of two facts concerned with Henry Clegg's private life — first, that his wife, Jane Clegg, has recently come into a sum of money, and, second, that he (*Henry*) has been frequently seen of late entertaining another young woman on the other side of the town — contributes to his determination to have his money or know the reason why.

MUNCE — What you done with your ole woman's money?

HENRY CLEGG — I tell you I haven't done anything with it!

MUNCE — Don't you tell me. I know. You bin spendin' it on that bit of skirt I saw you with this afternoon, that's what you bin doin', 'stead o' payin' your debts.

HENRY CLEGG — (*anxiously*). Don't shout, old man.

MUNCE — It's enough to make a chap shout ain't it? — Goin' an' bluein' all your money on a tart, an' you owes me twenty-five poun's. Twenty-five poun's. An' 'ere's me don't know where to turn for money.

HENRY CLEGG — I tell you I haven't spent it on her. Straight, I haven't. Look here, I may as well be honest with you. The girl you saw me with this afternoon, she's a friend of mine, see!

MUNCE — Yes, I thought so. Fine lookin' bit o' goods, too!

HENRY CLEGG — (*proudly*). Not bad, is she?

MUNCE — I s'pose your missus don't know about 'er, eih? Ho, ho, ho, ho!

HENRY CLEGG — Don't laugh so loud, old chap. My wife and me don't get on very well. You know!

MUNCE — (*sympathetically*). I know, old chap. Funny, ain't it, 'ow the one you're married to ain't 'alf so nice as the one you keep.

HENRY CLEGG — And you see, well, things haven't been going right with me lately. Of course, Kitty, that's her name, not my wife, the other one, she's always hard up! . . .

MUNCE — Just what I said, didden I? Spendin' all your blinkin' money on a tart 'stead o' payin' your debts of honour. Debts of honour, mind you! That's wot I call doin' the dirty!

HENRY CLEGG — I'm in rare old mess, that's wot I am. Kitty's bin to the doctor this mornin'! She's not sure! . . .

MUNCE — (*after a prolonged whistle*). Oh, ho! So's that's 'ow the land lays, is it? So 'elp me!

HENRY CLEGG — I don't know what the devil to do. There's you and Kitty . . . she'll want a bit of money to keep her mouth shut. If I could only raise a bit, I'd take her off to Canada or somewhere. I'm damned

fond of her, that's what I am.   I can't stick my wife.
She's hard, Munce, hard as hell.

MUNCE — I 'ope you won't do nothink rash, not
afore you've paid me my whack.

HENRY CLEGG — I haven't got the money to be rash.
I wish I had.

MUNCE — Well, I dunno.   Seems t' me I shall lose
what you owe me.   I shall 'ave to do somethink.   Absolute!   (*He gets up, twirls round on his foot, and
then sits down again*)   What I can't make out is,
what you done with your wife's money.

Clegg insists that he has done nothing with his wife's
money, because she has refused to give it to him,
which is a rare joke in Mr. Munce's estimation.   " A
clout aside the 'ead " is what he would use as an
argument if a wife of his dared take such a stand.
In any event he sees no reasonable excuse in that
argument for Clegg's not paying him.

MUNCE — No good talkin' like that.   You *got* to
get it, or there'll be trouble.   See!   I don't want to
be nasty, you know, but I could be nasty if I wanted
to, couldn't I?

HENRY CLEGG — Eh?

MUNCE — Your missus would be interested to 'ear
about Kitty an' the interestin' event, eih, woulden
she?

HENRY CLEGG — You wouldn't give me away, would
you?   I told you in confidence.

MUNCE — An' 'ow about my twenty-five quid, eih?
Mebbe she'd like to 'ear about that.   An' ole 'Arper,
'e'd be delighted to 'ear as 'ow 'is traveller owed a
bookie twenty-five quid, an' didden know 'ow to pay
it, eh?

HENRY CLEGG — You wouldn't do a dirty trick like
that, would you?

MUNCE — You pay me money, an' I won't. 'Ang it all, why should I consider you w'en you don't care a dam about me? I'll be ruined if 1 don't get the money this week, but you don't think about that. It's all you with you.

.   .   .   .

HENRY CLEGG — I'll do my best.

MUNCE — (holding out his hand). You'll 'ave to. I'm about desprit, an' that's the God's truth. 'Ere, buck up, ole chap. You'll be all right. She'll pay up right enough. You kiss 'er a bit; that'll put 'er in a good temper. You on'y got to treat 'em reasonable, an' they're all right. Give 'er a bit of a kiss now an' again, an' she'll be like a lamb. You bin runnin' too much after that Kitty, y' know, an' neglectin' your missus, an' o' course that gets their backs up. You got to yoomer 'em. 1 expec' it'll be all right. I woulden feel so perky about it, if I didden know she 'ad that money. Straight, I woulden! Goo'-night, ole chap. (*He shakes hands with* CLEGG.)

HENRY CLEGG — Good-night, old chap.

MUNCE — You be all right, you see! (*They go into the hall together,* CLEGG *opens the door, and* MUNCE *passes out*) Goo'-night, ole chap. Remember me to the missus!

HENRY CLEGG — Good-night! (*He shuts the street-door and returns to the sitting-room. He stands in front of the fire for a few moments in an undecided manner. He puts his hand in his pocket and takes out the cheque from Armstrong & Brown. He fingers it for a while, gazing abstractedly at the fire. Then he puts the cheque back into his pocket, turns down the lamps, and goes out of the room, shutting the door behind him.*)

Act II

Two days later Jane Clegg is again waiting for the family to gather for the evening meal, when Mr. Morrison calls. He is the cashier at Henry Clegg's place of employment and he has come in search of Clegg, who has not been at the office all day. Though Morrison is obviously evasive, his manner plainly indicates to Jane Clegg that something is wrong. She hurries the children through their meal and off to bed, before she seeks to get at the real reason for the cashier's call.

JANE CLEGG — Mr. Morrison, you know something about my husband!

MR. MORRISON — (*startled*). Oh, no, Mrs. Clegg; that is to say, I've really come to find out! . . .

JANE CLEGG — What is it?

MR. MORRISON — Well, the truth of the matter is, I'm afraid — mind you, I don't know! . . .

JANE CLEGG — Yes!

MRS. CLEGG — Is there anythink wrong?

MR. MORRISON — I'm afraid Clegg may have made a mistake. Of course, I don't know. That's why I came round, just to find out.

MRS. CLEGG — Mistake! Wot mistake!

JANE CLEGG — What kind of a mistake, Mr. Morrison?

MR. MORRISON — Well, you see, a cheque! . . .

JANE CLEGG — Yes?

MR. MORRISON — Of course, it may be a mistake, as I say, only it's odd.

MRS. CLEGG — I dunno wot you're talkin' about.

JANE CLEGG — Go on, Mr. Morrison, explain it all please.

MR. MORRISON — Well, you see a firm that owes us some money, rather a big amount, sent the cheque in after a lot of bother, and it appears they made it payable to Clegg and sent it to him at the office two or three days ago.

JANE CLEGG — Yes.

MRS. CLEGG — Yes, that's right. A boy brought the letter 'ere. I saw 'Enry openin' the letter meself. It was a cheque all right. You needn't be alarmed, Mr. Morrison. 'Enry'll 'ave it safe!

MR. MORRISON — That's just the point, Mrs. Clegg. You see he didn't say anything about it. I'm cashier. He ought to have told me. I sent a reminder to the firm, and last night they telephoned through to say they'd sent it, and explained what had happened. Of course, I thought it was odd Clegg hadn't said anything, or given me the cheque, only I thought he'd forgotten it, and I meant to ask him about it this morning. But he never turned up.

.   .   .   .

JANE CLEGG — How much is it, Mr. Morrison?

MR. MORRISON — I don't know quite. There's this cheque for one hundred and forty pounds, but there may be more.

MRS. CLEGG —'Ow can you say such things.

JANE CLEGG — Of course, Mr. Morrison, if what you say is true, the money will be repaid.

MRS. CLEGG — Of course, it will. I dessay 'Enry didn't mean to take the money, that is *if* 'e did take it, which I don't believe, not really take it, I mean, but if 'e did, *if* mind you, of course it'll be paid. 'E'd be the first to say that 'imself. 'Enry never done nothink under'and, not really under'and.

MR. MORRISON —(*to* JANE CLEGG). You see, Mrs. Clegg, all our staff is insured against accidents of this 'ort, and the difficulty is that the policy contains a clause to the effect that the defaulter must be prosecuted and convicted before the insurance companys pays up, otherwise there's no proof of embezzlement.

MRS. CLEGG — I've always 'eard them insurance companies was tricky.

MR. MORRISON — Of course, if the money is paid back, the insurance company won't want to prosecute. In fact, I don't suppose the guv'nor'll say anything about it. As a matter of fact, he doesn't know yet. I'm the only one that knows.

The turn of a key in the lock announces Clegg's return. He enters the room blithely enough, but at the sight of Morrison " he starts violently, then recovers himself a little and smiles feebly." His attempts at jocularity do not carry him far, however, nor do his attempts at explanation explain anything. He has the check, he says, and will return it in the morning, which satisfies neither his wife nor Mr. Morrison. Under their questioning he finally is forced to confess that he cashed the check. The revelation is followed by a painful silence, broken finally by the cashier.

MR. MORRISON — Of course, you know, this is very serious.

JANE CLEGG — (quickly). Mr. Morrison, you will remember your promise not to say anything about this to Mr. Harper. The money will be paid tomorrow. I'll see to that.

MR. MORRISON — I didn't make any promise, Mrs. Clegg. It's my duty to tell Mr. Harper. This may not be the only sum!

HENRY CLEGG — It is.

MR. MORRISON — And it may happen again. I must tell him, Mrs. Clegg.

MRS. CLEGG — But 'e'll lose 'is situation, if you do.

MR. MORRISON — I'm sorry. As I said, we've worked together a good many years, but I must do my duty.

Mrs. Clegg — You wouldn't see 'im disgraced, would you? Oh, Mr. Morrison, don't go an' do it! Think of 'is wife an' children. An' me, too. (*She weeps while she speaks*) I've lived 'ere all me life, an' no one 'as never bin able to say a word agin me, not no one. I've always kept meself respectable, wotever's 'appened, an' now! (*To her son*) Oh, 'Enry, tell 'im it ain't true. I'm an ole woman, an' I couldn't bear to die thinkin' you was in prison!

Henry Clegg — Prison?

Mrs. Clegg —'E says you'll be put in prison for this.

Mr. Morrison — Not if the money is repaid.

Jane Clegg — It will be repaid. (*She goes to* Mrs. Clegg) It will be all right, mother. The money will be paid. Mr. Morrison, must you tell Mr. Harper?

Mr. Morrison — I'm afraid so, Mrs. Clegg. I can't help it.

Mrs. Clegg — You can 'elp anythink if you want to!

Mr. Morrison — I've got myself to think of, and if the guv'nor found out! And there's the future. It might happen again.

Jane Clegg — Mr. Morrison, will you agree to this? Henry will resign his post with Mr. Harper, and we'll leave the town! . . .

Mrs. Clegg — Oh, no! . . .

Jane Clegg — We'll go to Canada or somewhere, where we can start afresh. The money shall be paid, and you shan't have any anxiety about the future. Will you agree to say nothing to Mr. Harper, if we do that?

Mr. Morrison — I don't want to appear hard!

Jane Clegg — Please, Mr. Morrison. You see, it isn't only Henry. There's Johnny and Jenny.

Mr. Morrison — Yes, I see that, of course.

Jane Clegg — I'd planned things for them, but!

. . . Oh, well, it can't be helped. You won't speak to
Mr. Harper about this, will you?

MR. MORRISON — (*after a short pause*). All right,
Mrs. Clegg, I won't!

The quarter hour following is a bad quarter hour
for Henry Clegg. Jane demands to know what he
has done with the money — and his excuse, if he has
any, for having taken it. Her insistence is not at all
wifely, the elder Mrs. Clegg insists. " 'H's your
'usband, Jane," she reproachfully reminds her daughter. But Jane is not to be swerved from her determination to know the truth. " If I'm to repay the
money he stole," she says, finally, " I must know what
he did with it."

HENRY CLEGG — All right. Look here, Jane, you'll
see me through this, won't you? They *could* put me
in jail, you know . . . I couldn't stand that! It's
Harper's own fault, blast him!

MRS. CLEGG — I knoo it was someone's fault!

HENRY CLEGG — (*to* JANE). It was like this, you
see! You know when they put me on that new round?

JANE — Yes.

HENRY CLEGG — Well, it's an expensive round to
work. You have to treat these damned shopkeepers
like lords before they'll give you an order. And I'm
only allowed a pound a week for expenses. I've spent
that in a day. Of course, I didn't tell you. I didn't
want to upset you, and I thought I should pull round
all right. So I should, only for the bad debts. It
was that did it. A man went smash and hadn't paid
a sou to us, and so old Harper made me responsible
for the whole bally lot. He's like that, the old screw.
Makes his travellers bear the bad debts. That was how
it began. I tried to make it up by horse-racing. You

know! Oh, it's a mug's game. I know that, but we're all mugs when we're in a hole. I was in a rotten hole, too. That fellow Munce who came in here the other night, he's a bookie. He was worrying me for money I owed him, and you wouldn't let me have any . . .

MRS. CLEGG — I knoo you was doin' wrong in not lettin' 'im 'ave it.

HENRY CLEGG — And then that cheque came. I didn't mean to take it really. It just came into my head. I thought I'd be able to make it up somehow.

JANE CLEGG — Why didn't you tell me about the bad debts?

HENRY CLEGG — What would have been the good? It was before your uncle left you that money.

JANE CLEGG — Why didn't you tell me then?

HENRY CLEGG — I'd started betting then, and I wasn't exactly proud of myself.

MRS. CLEGG — Jus' like 'is poor father was. 'E was proud, too.

HENRY CLEGG — Besides, I thought you'd be sure to let me have the money or some of it. It seemed natural somehow.

MRS. CLEGG — Any nice woman would 'ave let you 'ave it.

JANE CLEGG — It would have been better to have told me than to let Morrison find out. You'll have to leave Mr. Harper, now! . . .

HENRY CLEGG — I suppose so.

MRS. CLEGG — Oh, what a good job it was your uncle Tom died when 'e did, Jane. It was jus' like the 'and of Profidence. You'll be able to make some use of that money, now, 'stead of 'oardin' it up.

JANE CLEGG — Yes, that's true. Only it wasn't the kind of use I wanted to make of it.

MRS. CLEGG — What better use could you make of it than to save your 'usband's good name?

JANE CLEGG — (*beginning to clear away the remnants of the meal*). Yes, I suppose that's a great privilege.

After Mrs. Clegg has retired Henry, still worried as to Jane's real feeling toward him, stands with his back to the fire watching her as she clears the dishes from the table. The dubious look in her eyes worries him

HENRY CLEGG — What are you thinking about, Jane?

JANE CLEGG — Oh, I wish I could be sure of you, Henry!

HENRY CLEGG — Well, you are, aren't you?

JANE CLEGG — I don't know. Oh, yes, I suppose so. Come on, let's go to bed. (*She gathers up her sewing and moves towards the door*) Turn out the lamp, will you?

HENRY CLEGG — Yes, dear. (*He turns out the light.* JANE *stands in the doorway*) Don't be hard on me, Jane. I'm not really a bad chap. I'm only weak. That's all.

JANE CLEGG — I can't help thinking of that woman, Henry.

HENRY CLEGG — (*putting his arms about her*). You needn't dear. I swear to God I've not done anything against you. I promised you! . . .

JANE CLEGG — Yes, you promised! . . . (*She goes towards the stairs, and he follows, closing the door after him.*)

ACT III

When, the following evening, Mr. Morrison comes to collect the money his welcome is polite without being over warming. It has been agreed that the Cleggs shall go to Canada, and that nothing more shall be said of Henry's unfortunate mistake. Morrison has told Mr. Harper, however; felt that he had to to save himself future embarrassment. "The guv'nor was almost sure to find it out," he explains, in justifying himself; "and if he'd found I'd kept it from him, he might have thought I was in it, too. I've always kept *my* hands clean!"

MRS. CLEGG — You better touch wood, Mr. Morrison. You don't know 'ow soon it'll be before you get into trouble.

MR. MORRISON — I'm not that sort. I don't get into trouble. Trouble doesn't come to you: you go to it. That's my belief.

JANE CLEGG — You're a fortunate man, Mr. Morrison. I hope you will always be able to believe that. . . . I'll go and fetch the money. It's in notes, Mr. Morrison. I thought that would be more convenient.

MR. MORRISON — Yes, that was the best thing to do, Mrs. Clegg. (JANE *goes out and is seen to mount the stairs.*)

MRS. CLEGG — I do think Mr. 'Arper ought to 'ave come 'ere 'imself for the money.

MR. MORRISON — Oh!

MRS. CLEGG —'Ow do we know it'll be all right! . . .

MR. MORRISON — Do you mean to suggest that I might steal the money? . . .

MRS. CLEGG — I don't mean to suggest anythink, but I believe in bein' on the safe side.

MR. MORRISON — (*hotly*). Everyone isn't like your son, you know.

HENRY CLEGG — (*angrily*). You needn't put on the virtuous air, Morrison! . . .

MR. MORRISON — I'm not putting on any virtuous airs. I've tried to make things as pleasant for you as possible, and I get nothing but insults from your mother. You'd think to hear her that I'd stolen the money, not you . . . I've always kept *my* hands clean. There's nothing in my life I'd be ashamed to let anyone know about.

Mrs. Clegg — Well, you ain't yooman, then! I tell you this, Mr. Morrison, I don't believe you. Now!

Henry Clegg — Mother, mother!

Mrs. Clegg — No, 'Enry, I won't sit 'ere an' 'ear you made little of. 'Ow do we know 'e's any better'n you. We on'y got 'is word for it.

Mr. Morrison — I must say! . . .

Mrs. Clegg — There's things in everyone's life they don't want to talk about. If it isn't one thing, it's another. That's wot I've learned from bein' alive. It's on'y yooman. Wot 'ud be the use of 'avin' a Merciful Father if 'E 'adn't got nothink to be merciful about! That's 'ow I look at it! An' I dessay, Mr. Morrison. for all you're so good an' 'oly, you got somethink you don't want to go braggin' about. There's some people does things they're not ashamed of an' ought to be.

Jane returns with the money, but Mrs. Clegg refuses to yield the floor. She is still bitter against those who have brought disgrace upon her son — after the way he was treated. They had no right to give Henry a "dear round and then make 'im pay the bad debts." Henry, seeing more trouble ahead. tries vainly to keep her still, and to get Morrison out of the house before further revelations are forthcoming. But Morrison has heard enough to arouse his suspicions and he refuses to stir before he has set himself and the guv'nor straight.

Mr. Morrison — Look here, Mrs. Clegg, I've had enough of this, see! I don't know what tale he's been telling you! . . .

Henry Clegg — It doesn't matter, old chap, it

doesn't matter. Let's get this business settled! Jane! . . .

MR. MORRISON — I'm not going to be shut up. (To MRS. CLEGG) He's had the best and easiest round of the lot, and he hasn't had a single bad debt for a year past, and those he used to have, the guv'nor bore two-thirds. See! I'm not going to stay here and listen to you abusing the guv'nor for nothing!

JANE CLEGG — He hasn't had a single bad debt! . . .

HENRY CLEGG — It's all right, dear. I'll explain it all presently. Let's settle this affair first. Morrison doesn't want to hear our quarrels.

JANE CLEGG — I don't understand. You said you had to pay the bad debts, and that you took the money to make them up.

MR. MORRISON — All lies, that's what it is!

MRS. CLEGG — Don't you dare to insult my son, you!

JANE CLEGG — Please keep quiet, mother. Henry, is this true?

MR. MORRISON — Of course it's true!

JANE CLEGG — I'm speaking to my husband, Mr. Morrison. Henry, will you explain? . . .

HENRY CLEGG — It's all right, dear. It's quite simple. I can make it clear in a minute or two, but I prefer to do it when we're alone. I object to discussing private matters before strangers.

.   .   .   .

JANE CLEGG — That'll do, Henry. Mr. Morrison will stay until you've explained the position.

HENRY CLEGG — Then he can stay till he's blue in the face. I won't explain. I'm not going to be bullied by him or by you. I'm a man, not a child.

JANE CLEGG — I shall not pay the money until I hear your explanation.

HENRY CLEGG — I don't care. Keep your damn money. They can do what they like.

JANE CLEGG — Very well. I'm sorry, Mr. Morrison. Goodnight!

MR. MORRISON — This is pretty serious, you know.

JANE CLEGG — I know. Goodnight!

HENRY CLEGG — (*still blustering*). I don't care a damn!

MR. MORRISON — I shall go straight to Mr. Harper. and tell him what's happened. I shouldn't be surprised if he applies for a warrant at once

HENRY CLEGG — (*anxiously*). What, tonight!

MR. MORRISON — Yes.

JANE CLEGG — I can't help that.

MRS. CLEGG — Oh, Jane, an' 'im your own 'usband!

MR. MORRISON — (*hesitating*). I don't understand you, Mrs. Clegg. After all. he is your husband! . . .

JANE CLEGG — I wonder. I thought I was marrying a man I could trust. Henry's a liar. I can't trust him.

HENRY CLEGG — Go on. Make me out all that's bad.

JANE CLEGG — Henry, why are you talking as if you were being unjustly treated? You know that you have lied to me from first to last. Even now I don't know how you managed to get into debt as you did.

HENRY CLEGG — I've told you. Gambling.

MR. MORRISON — Good heaven! A gambler. a liar. and a thief!

MRS. CLEGG — It's none of your business.

MR. MORRISON — No, thank God.

JANE CLEGG — You just gambled the money away, Henry? Is that so?

HENRY CLEGG — Yes. I said that about the bad debts to make the thing look a bit better than it was. (*He comes up to her*) Jane, I'm sorry. I'm really sorry. I ought to have told you the truth. I know that. But I was ashamed, I was really. Get me out of this scrape, Jane, and I swear I won't give you cause to complain again. Morrison, you won't tell old Harper tonight, will you? Good God, man, I might be arrested this evening. Jane, you'll get me out of it, won't you. I couldn't stand it. Look here, I swear I'll be a good husband to you, I will. I'll swear it on the Bible, if you like. I didn't mean what I said just now. It was all talk.

JANE CLEGG — I wonder if you're worth saving, Henry! (MRS. CLEGG *bursts into tears.*)

HENRY CLEGG — I'll make myself worth saving, Jane. I will, I swear I will. (*He tries to kiss her, but she turns away from him*) Morrison, you say something. Mother.

JANE CLEGG — It isn't necessary, Henry. I'll pay the money.

Mr. Morrison is no sooner paid and out of the house before there is a loud, persistent knocking at the outer door, which threatens to throw the now thoroughly frightened Henry into a state of hysterics. He thinks it is the police, but it is only Mr. Munce, demanding entrance. A very wrathy Mr. Munce he is, seeing that he thought he was about to be cheated out of his twenty-five pounds. Payment on the spot is what he demands. Henry's promise to settle with him in the morning has no effect in quieting him. 'E's treated 'Enry Clegg fair and 'e expects to be treated fair. Jane Clegg is free to admit his rights in the matter — but she will not pay his twenty-five pounds.

JANE CLEGG — I have just paid the gentleman you saw here a few moments ago, one hundred and forty pounds to replace the money my husband stole from his employer less than a week ago.

HENRY CLEGG — You needn't advertise the fact.

JANE CLEGG — (*ignoring him*). My husband told me that he stole the money to pay gambling debts due to you.

MUNCE —'E never! . . .

JANE CLEGG — One moment, please. It now appears that he has not paid you anything.

MUNCE — Not a 'a'penny, 'e 'asn't.

JANE CLEGG — Well, then, the inference is that he still has the money he stole. You can't dispose of a hundred and forty pounds in a day or two can you?

MUNCE — (*to* HENRY CLEGG). Look 'ere, Clegg, 'ave you got the money or 'ave you not?

HENRY CLEGG — I tell you I haven't.

JANE CLEGG — Then what did you do with it?

HENRY CLEGG — I haven't got it. Look here, I'm not going to be cross-examined as if I were a criminal! . . .

JANE CLEGG — You are a criminal. You've robbed your employer.

HENRY CLEGG — (*throwing out his hands*). There, Munce, that's the sort of thing I have to endure. How'd you like it!

JANE CLEGG — Tell us what you did with the money. Mr. Munce and I have a right to know.

HENRY CLEGG — Well, you shan't know, see. Damn you, I've had enough of your questions. I'm sick of you!

JANE CLEGG — Yes, Henry, I think we've both about reached the end of things; but that won't help Mr. Munce, will it?

HENRY CLEGG — I don't care about Munce!

MUNCE — (*jumping up*). Oh, don't you. Don't you then. We'll soon see about that. I bin treatin' you jolly well, I 'ave. I 'eld my tongue all this time when I might 'ave said things, on'y I didden want to round on a pal. (*To* JANE CLEGG) 'Ere, ast 'im about 'is fancy woman! . . .

HENRY CLEGG — You swine!

MUNCE — Go on, ast 'im about 'er. Ast 'im what's the matter with 'er. Go on, ast 'im that.

HENRY CLEGG — You dirty dog! (*He rushes at* MUNCE, *and they close and struggle together*) I'll choke the life out of you.

JANE CLEGG — You'll be hanged if you do that, Henry!

HENRY CLEGG — (*snorting with disgust*). You're not worth killing!

.   .   .   .

JANE CLEGG — Listen, Mr. Munce, I'll pay you the twenty-five pounds on one condition.

MUNCE — What is it?

JANE CLEGG — That you tell me about my husband's fancy woman!

MUNCE — Gimme the money first?

HENRY CLEGG — Blackguard!

MUNCE — Gentleman!

JANE CLEGG — I haven't got the money in the house, Mr. Munce, but I'll give it to you tomorrow.

MUNCE — That's all very fine! . . .

JANE CLEGG — You'll have to trust me, Mr. Munce. After all, you've told most of the story to me already. haven't you? I know that there is a fancy woman . . . Henry didn't deny it . . . and I understand there will be a . . . fancy child! You see, the remainder of the story hardly matters, only I'm curious . . . I'm just curious to know all of it.

MUNCE — I don't know much meself about it, on'y one dy las' week I saw 'im an' 'er talkin' in the street! . . .

HENRY CLEGG — Look here, I can't stand this. I'll own up. It's true.

MUNCE — I said to 'im when I come 'ere that last time, "That was a fine bit o' skirt you 'ad to-dy!"

and then 'e tole me abaht it.   She'd on'y jus' been to
the doctor! . . .

JANE CLEGG — I see!

HENRY CLEGG — I tell you I own up.   Isn't that
enough?

MUNCE —'E said if 'e 'ad the money 'e'd clear out of
Englan' with the woman! . . .

HENRY CLEGG — You're a pal.   So help me God,
you are!

JANE CLEGG — If he had the money? . . .

MUNCE — Yes.   Go to Canada or somewhere!

JANE CLEGG — Canada!   Canada!   Oh!   (*Her
nerve fails for a moment; but she recovers herself*)
I suppose that was why he took the money.   He
wanted me to give him money!

HENRY CLEGG — I can't help it.   You've never understood me, never tried to.   You've always sort of
preached at me, and I'm not the sort that can stand
being preached at.   You're different from me.   You're
hard and you don't make allowances.   Kitty's more
my match than you are.   I've been happy with her,
happier than I've ever been with you, and that's
straight.

JANE CLEGG — (*to* MUNCE).   Will you come in the
morning, Mr. Munce, for the money, and we can go
to the solicitor together, and arrange the matter.

Mr. Munce goes — but not before he has turned
in the doorway to hurl a parting shot at Henry Clegg.
"Serve you right if she'd led you go to quod, an' your
fancy woman to the work'ouse!" he says.   "Tooloo
— absolute rotter!"

JANE CLEGG — (*sitting down before the fire*).
That's true, isn't it, Henry.

HENRY CLEGG — What?

JANE CLEGG — You *are* an absolute rotter.

HENRY CLEGG — I don't know. I'm not a bad chap, really. I'm just weak. I'd be all right if I had a lot of money and a wife that wasn't better than I am. . . . Oh, I know, Jane! You *are* better than I am. Any fool can see that! It doesn't do a chap much good to be living with a woman who's his superior, at least not the sort of chap I am. I ought to have married a woman like myself, or a bit worse. That's what Kitty is. She's worse than I am, and that sort of makes me love her. It's different with you. I always feel mean here. Yes, I am mean. I know that; but it makes me meaner than I really am to be living with you. (*He sits down at the table and begins to fill his pipe*) Do you understand, Jane? Somehow, the mean things I do that don't amount to much, I can't tell 'em to you, or carry 'em off as if they weren't mean, and I do meaner things to cover them up. That's the way of it. I don't act like that with Kitty.

JANE CLEGG — It's funny, isn't it, Henry.

HENRY CLEGG — (*lighting his pipe*). Yes, I suppose it is. Damned funny!

JANE CLEGG — It's so funny that we married at all. I used to think you were so fine before I married you. You were so jolly and free and light-hearted . . . Somehow, I feel as if I'd lost you in the church that day! Do you know? It's as if I went there to find you, and found someone else.

HENRY CLEGG — And you're not like what I thought you were!

JANE CLEGG — No. (*She picks up her sewing and makes a few stitches. HENRY CLEGG gets up from the table and draws a chair up to the fire. He sits for a second or two smoking*) Henry, have you spent all that money?

HENRY CLEGG — I haven't spent any of it. I've got . . . well, I *have* spent some of it.

JANE CLEGG — Why didn't you pay Mr. Munce, then?

HENRY CLEGG — What! Not likely. I need all of it!

JANE CLEGG — Yes, I suppose you do. When are you going to Canada?

HENRY CLEGG — Eh?

JANE CLEGG — You're going with her, aren't you?

HENRY CLEGG — (*after a short pause*). Yes.

JANE CLEGG — I suppose the money you spent was on the tickets?

HENRY CLEGG — Yes.

JANE CLEGG — When are you going?

HENRY CLEGG — (*with a great effort*). Tomorrow!

.   .   .   .

JANE CLEGG — What's Kitty like, Henry?

HENRY CLEGG — She's prettier than you.

JANE CLEGG — Yes.

HENRY CLEGG — Well, it's hard to say. You're a finer woman than she is, but she's my sort, and you're not. (*He pauses in his pacing, and then comes to the fireplace and stands before her*) You're a rum sort of woman, Jane. There aren't many women would talk about this the way you do.

JANE CLEGG — No?

HENRY CLEGG — It's just as if we were strangers talking about something that didn't matter.

JANE CLEGG — It is like that, isn't it, only I have two children, and you're their father.

HENRY CLEGG — (*sitting down*). Well, I don't know! It's a funny sort of a world; mixed-up like!

.   .   .   .

JANE CLEGG — I suppose so. (*Rising and extending her hand to him*) Goodbye, Henry!

HENRY CLEGG — How do you mean?

JANE CLEGG — Goodbye, of course. You'll go to

Kitty tonight. It . . . it'll be more convenient to-morrow.

HENRY CLEGG — (*standing up and gaping at her*). My God!

JANE CLEGG — You didn't think I'd let you stay here tonight with me! Oh, Henry. it wouldn't be decent! . . .

HENRY CLEGG — You mean I'm to go now.

JANE CLEGG — Yes.

HENRY CLEGG — But . . .

JANE CLEGG — There can be no argument about it. You must go now. It would be like committing a sin to let you stay with me tonight!

HENRY CLEGG — I don't understand you. Damn it. you're condoning the offence.

JANE CLEGG — (*again holding out her hand*). Goodnight, Henry, and goodbye. I'm very tired.

.   .   .   .

HENRY CLEGG — Oh, well! . . . I suppose I can go up and look at the kids?

JANE CLEGG — You might wake them, and they'd wonder! . . .

HENRY CLEGG — I could have a peep at them!

JANE CLEGG — It would be better not.

HENRY CLEGG — All right! (*He goes into the hall and puts on his hat and coat. He returns to the room*) How'll you explain?

JANE CLEGG — I'll tell your mother! . . .

HENRY CLEGG — You'll look after her, won't you? She's not a bad old soul though she does get on my nerves.

JANE CLEGG — Yes. I'll look after her. (*There is silence for a few moments.*)

HENRY CLEGG — Well! (*He looks at her as if he does not know what to do.*)

JANE CLEGG — Goodbye!

HENRY CLEGG — (*taking her hand*). Goodbye,

Jane. I've not been a good husband . . . You're well rid of me. (*He tries to put his arms round her, but she struggles out of his reach*) You might give me a kiss before I go.

JANE CLEGG — (*covering her face with her hand and speaking like one who is horrified*). I couldn't, I couldn't. It would be a sin!

HENRY CLEGG — (*with an affectation of jauntiness*). Well, of course, if that's how you look at it. Good-bye, once more!

JANE CLEGG — (*she turns her back to him*). Good-bye.

HENRY CLEGG — Well, I'm damned! (*He goes into the hall, and puts his hand on the door. He waits for a moment.*) I'm now·off. (*She does not reply. He opens the door, and then waits a little while. She does not move. He goes out and closes the door after him. She stands for a few moments gazing into the fire. Then she turns down the light and goes upstairs to bed.*)

(*Curtain*)

"THE JEST"

A Tragi-Comedy in Four Acts

By Sem Benelli

(American Adaptation by Edward Sheldon)

"THE JEST" was first presented at the Plymouth Theatre, New York, the evening of Wednesday, April 19, 1919. It ran until June 14, 1919, was withdrawn for the summer, and the run resumed September 19, 1919. It then continued through the better part of the current season, or until February 28, 1920. It is the work of one of the best known of the modern Italian dramatists and has been frequently played on the Continent. There are two characters of first importance to the dramatic action, Giannetto Malespini, a young painter of Florence at the time of Lorenza, the Magnificent, and Neri Chiaramentesi, a captain of mercenaries. Giannetto, because of his frail frame and effeminate ways, has inspired the ridicule of the brutal Neri and his brother, Gabriello. For years the poet, helpless to defend himself, has been the butt of the Chiaramentesi's jokes, the most brutal of which has been perpetrated the night before the opening of the play, when Neri and Gabriello, catching young Giannetto near the Ponte Vecchio, first etched certain grotesque designs upon his tender skin with the points of their daggers and then, when he had swooned from pain, threw him into the river.

Out of this terrifying experience is born in the mind of Giannetto not a new determination to be re-

venged upon his persecutors, for that thought has been
with him constantly, but a plan by which for the first
time he sees a chance of carrying his revenge to a
successful issue.   Tornaquinci. a friend of the Magnificent's, is to give a dinner in honor of Giannetto.   The
poet, instructed to select his own guests, invites Neri
and Gabriello.   It is at the feast he plans to set in
motion the " jest " that shall prove the trap into which
he hopes the lumbering Neri will unwittingly step.
The table is spread in the great hall of Tornaquinci's
house, and presently Giannetto, preceding his guests
in order to acquaint his host with something of his
plans, arrives.   He stands, " against a background of
the night sky and the stars — his small, wistful figure
almost covered with a great white mantle.   Close beside
him is Fazio, his aged dwarf, carrying a lantern."

To the astonished Tornaquinci Giannetto relates in
detail the latest humiliation he has suffered at the
hands of the Charamentesi and of Lorenzo's suggestion
that he meet his enemies at Tornaquinci's dinner.   But
Tornaquinci is still at a loss to understand.   " How
comes it," he demands, " that Lorenzo the Magnificent,
the Lord of Florence. the man of letters, patron of
the arts —"

GIANNETTO — (*interrupting*).   Should   bid   me
grovel at the feet of two base Pisan mercenaries?   Ah,
do not blame him, sir.   Never was the Magnificent
more worthy of his name!   Such tact!   Such taste!
(*He kisses his hand*)   Wait, sir, and you will see!
(*He sings a little tune and pirouettes a few steps.*)

TORNAQUINCI — Were   not   the   sack,   the   dagger
points, the jeering crowds enough to make you serious
for once.

GIANNETTO — (*changing his tone*).   No, honored
sir.   And if for a moment I am serious now, it is for
your sake and the last time.   You have reproached me

for my light heart. That proves there is no blemish in my smiling mask. Yet all I feel, asleep or waking, is a dull ferocity —

TORNAQUINCI — (*interrupting*). Not that! If that were true, after so many —

GIANNETTO — (*swept on*). Yes, yes, I know! The sack, the dagger points, the jeering crowds. And yet, ferocious, savage though I be, I am a coward. That's why the Chiaramentesi chose me for their victim. I'm seventeen. Five years ago I was twelve. Then's when I met them first. In May it was and I was going to school. They had just come to Florence and were wrestling before the barracks in the Via Fossi. I stopped to watch them. They were strong as lions. And as I stood there, wondering in my childish way if Ajax and Achilles had been half so glorious, they spied me out and as they looked at me my heart stood still. "Hi, Tickle-my-chin," the tallest one cried, "what are you, cock or hen?" I was so frightened I began to weep and then they spat on me and made me catch twelve big blue flies and eat them, one by one. (*Pause*) What could I do? I was so weak and small. And from that day to this we never met but they fell upon me with their fangs and claws.
Ah God, when I think of these last five years! To wake up trembling every morning. Night after night to cry myself to sleep — yes, I, Lorenzo's friend, young Messer Malespini! To know in my own soul I have no courage, and that I never will have — never — never —

TORNAQUINCI — (*soothing him*). My poor child.

GIANNETTO — (*after a pause*). Then came the miracle. Into the gutter of my life there dropped a rose. She was the daughter of the fishmonger near the Roman Gate, Ginevra. We loved each other. She was good and beautiful. I painted her as the Madonna in my "Annunciation." We were to marry. And

then, the night before the banns were published, they
— they came.

TORNAQUINCI — They?

GIANNETTO — The Chiaramentesi. They had found
us out. They paid her father fifty ducats and carried
her away. Neri as elder claimed her for himself. He
put her in a great, rich house and keeps her for his
pleasure. She is his slave, his toy, his animal. At
first I thought I should go mad. Each night she
drifted to me on my dreams, all white and piteous,
whispering my name — at last, sir, I gave way. I
wrote to her. I begged to see her just to say goodbye. She answered, telling me to come at sundown
to her garden gate beyond the city walls. I went.
That, sir, was yesterday. The rest you know.

TORNAQUINCI — She betrayed you?

GIANNETTO — My poor white rose.

TORNAQUINCI — Forget about her. Lose yourself
in work, my boy.

GIANNETTO — (sadly). In work? Yes. I should
have been a peaceful, happy painter of Madonnas.
Like young del Sarto, sir, and Raphael, too. But now
that dream has faded. . . . My heart is not the only
thing that died beneath their torments. My soul died,
too. (With a change of tone) But oh, sir! I have
one thing left — my wits! turned by my suffering into
gleaming steel! And these wits of mine, set free at
last, have shown me how to lure my enemies with flowers and feasting and with silver lutes to their eternal
ruin. Strong, wild and lustful though their bodies be,
my brain will blast them like a belt from hell. And
when last night that vision came to me, came as they
bled me like a vile buffoon, it was not agony that made
me shriek, but laughter! I laughed! And I laugh
still!

TORNAQUINCI — God save us. And I thought you
were resigned and meek!

GIANNETTO — I used to be. I was so good until these two brothers changed me to a devil. (*Feverishly*) Sir, shall I tell you something terrible? For three years, for three whole years I have not said a single prayer! Each time I pray — oh, I try so often! — my tongue grows thick. The words refuse to come — . . . I think it will be that way till vengeance falls. Revenge will give me back the power to pray.

TORNAQUINCI — (*goes over to* GIANNETTO *and sits*). Then, God be willing, you shall pray tonight. Come! Shall we stab them as they sit at meat? Mix poison with their wine?

GIANNETTO — No, no! The Magnificent and I wish peace. Yet peace from which revenge grows, like a scarlet blossoms.

TORNAQUINCI — But how?

GIANNETTO — (*smiling*). Patience, and you will . see. Beneath my smiles the red bud breaks into a flower. I, too, may play a little joke, who knows? The Charamentesi have made jokes the fashion. Look, sir, what am I holding between thumb and finger?

TORNAQUINCI — Nothing.

GIANNETTO — I hold a thread so fine, which I shall tie into a knot so hard that it would bind great Hercules himself. (*To the dwarf*) Come, Fazio! Come, old friend! Tell Messer Tornaquinci I have not gone mad. Tell him how cunningly the trap is laid. (*To* TORNAQUINCI) He knows my plan, sir. I confide in him. We are two weak small creatures, so we help each other — (*Suddenly*) Hark! (*There is the sound of a man's singing and distant laughter*) Neri! (GIANNETTO *and the dwarf cling to each other.*)

The doors are opened. "Without, red in the torches' smoky glare, stand Neri, Gabriello, and between them, Ginevra . . . They are all arm in arm and smiling and very splendid."

NERI — Hail, noble host! Three hungry gadabouts salute you! (*To the others*) Come, chicks, your nanners! One! Two! Three! (*They all bow very low, then burst into a roar of laugher.*)

TORNAQUINCI — Welcome, Messer Neri. For you, I think *are* Neri?

NERI — Yes, Neri, in whose beard doves nest. And this, sweet sir, is Gabriello, by the grace of God my brother. To him the lambkins born last May are playmates.

TORNAQUINCI — (*turning to* GINEVRA). And yonder radiance that deigns to honor me?

NERI — Ginevra. Late the daughter of a vile fishmonger. Now an Orient pearl, hung lightly in my ear.

GINEVRA — (*laughing and curtseying low to* TORNAQUINCI). Sir. do not heed him. He talks in cap and bells.

NERI — (*seeing* GIANNETTO *for the first time*). Ha! Body of God! Behold our little friend! What! Still alive? A miracle! Look, brother, he's put pomatum on his hair!

GABRIELLO — No, water. River water.

NERI — Bah! Soul of a cat! He sweats with fear! (*Taking* GIANNETTO *by the arm*) Come, wren, be happy. We've brought the jewel of your twittering heart, your little birdship's dream of wedding-bells. Come lick-pot. Present her with a kiss! On the hand. No lady gives her lips to mice.

GINEVRA — (*bursting into a peal of laughter*). I cannot help it, love. He looks so foolish —

NERI — Body of Bacchus! She's right! (*With a wink at* GABRIELLO) He bathes too much . . . that's how he lost his color! (*To* GINEVRA) Come, give the little fish your hand! (*To* GIANNETTO) So, minnow . . . touch it gently now. There, that's enough!

Off! (*Throwing him to the ground*) Scum! Would you beslime my food?

TORNAQUINCI — (*interrupting*). Come, softer names and gentler manners, sir! The Magnificent himself has had you meet here for the sake of peace.

NERI — A word that I am ill acquainted with. By the Eleven Thousand Virgins of Cologna, sir, war's my trade! I topple over dukes and princes, I give and take away crowns of kings. I'd pull the nose of any man in Christendom for two hairs from a blind dog's tail! Why, many's the joke I've cracked with your Magnificent . . .

TORNAQUINCI — (*interrupting*). Take care!

NERI — All Florence knows it! I'm a famous jester. I begin with puns, quips, barbs of fantasy. Then if my humor does not stick, I use my hands. And if my hands can tickle forth no laughter, I call for sacks and put a point on this! (*He shows his dagger*)

GIANNETTO — (*good humoredly*). You made me laugh last night, sir, I confess it. Since I am so helpless I ask for peace.

NERI — Now by the white breasts of St. Jezebel.

GINEVRA — (*interrupting*). Say yes, my soul.

NERI — What? I, who pick my teeth with a two-handed sword? I, to make peace with this white food for fleas?

GINEVRA — (*coaxing*). Say yes, love, for my sake!

NERI — (*sighing*). So be it. Peace it is.

GIANNETTO — Your hand, good Neri.

NERI — What? Shivering still? Poor jelly, calm yourself. Neri forgives you. Come, bantam, to a soldier's arms!

Giannetto eludes the embrace. He prefers, he says, to make his peace with Gabriello, with whom he feels

he is " united by a bond of pain." Does not Gabriello
also love Ginevra, his brother's beauteous mistress —
yet dare not breathe the words because he, too, fears
Neri? Gabriello whitens under the accusation, and
Neri is furious again. Yet he is made calm and forced
to laugh away the incident when both Ginevra and
Gabriello make light of the charge. Gabriello, however, is unhappy, and soon makes an excuse to withdraw. " May God forsake me, love, if I could so
much as name the color of his eyes," declares Ginevra,
when he is gone. " You know how faithful and how
true I am!"

GIANNETTO — Perhaps she pierced his heart, good
Neri, when she aimed at yours. Women are such bad
marksmen — eh, Madonna?
GINEVRA — True, sir, but more's the pity. Alas,
poor Gabriello. (*She puts her head on Neri's shoulder.*)
NERI — Well, honey pot, I'll believe you for tonight. (*Taking her in his arms, half savagely, half
tenderly*) What does it matter if those lips tell lies,
they are so warm and soft . . . (*He kisses her*) Ah.
mouth like the pomegranate flower! Red enemy of
men that never sleeps! Kiss me again . . .

The dinner proceeds and there is much drinking.
Neri grows mellow and quarrelsome by turns, until,
when Giannetto determines the time ripe to bait the
trap he subtly leads the argument to a doubting of
Neri's boasted courage. His voice grows shrill and
taunting as he shouts: " I say that if I were not
what I am, the vilest worm that ever crawled the earth,
you would not dare to treat me as you do! Last
night would you have cut another's back as you cut
mine? Never since Christ was king!"

NERI — (*leaping to his feet*). You lie! You lie in your rat's teeth! There's not a man in all this city, I'm afraid of! No, not the Magnificent himself! I shout it from the house-tops! The lord of Florence is a wooden spoon . . .

GIANNETTO — Tut! Just to put your bravery to the test! I'll wager twenty golden ducats you dare not go tonight, this very moment, now, to Ceccherino's wine-shop in the Vacchereccia!

NERI — (*rolling an eye*). What's that?

GIANNETTO — (*rapidly*). You know. The favorite lounging-place of half of Florence. Where all the young rips meet to gossip and shake dice. In short, the very animals you'd like to fry. You need not touch them, though. A joke's a joke! But, clad in steel, a weapon in your hand, stride through the crowd to where old Ceccherino sits, tweak his red nose, walk out . . . and the wager's won!

NERI — (*outraged*). What, lamb? What, lady-bird? Is that a fit test for a hero's heart?

GIANNETTO — (*sighing*). Ah, perhaps not . . . that would frighten anyone.

NERI — (*Interrupting*). What? Frighten *me?* Snakes of Purgatory! Here, put your wager in his hand! Quick, or I'll split you in two.

GIANNETTO — (*pretending to be terrified — emptying his purse into* TORNAQUINCI'S *hands*) Take it, sir.

NERI — There's armor here?

TORNAQUINCI — Enough to cover a brigade.

NERI — (*prodding* GINEVRA *with his foot*). Off, cat, you're in the way! These are men's matters. Trot home and go to sleep. I may be drunk when I come in tonight.

GINEVRA — (*rising*). How sweetly, love, you murmur your farewells!

NERI — (*rubbing his hands*). Death of my life!
They'll run like pullets when they see a sparrow-
hawk! (*To* GINEVRA) Go on! What are you
dawdling for . . . ?

TORNAQUINCI — (*smoothly*). Dear friend, I pray
you! . . . not so harsh!

NERI — (*grumblingly*). Hell's teeth! Am I a
troubador? (*To her*) To your kennel, wench!

GINEVRA — (*putting on her mantle*). I go, I go.
Would God I'd never come!

NERI — (*pointing to* GIANNETTO). You came to
watch that mongrel lick his lips at you. Well, he has
done it. Are you satisfied? To bed. (*Fuming*) To
bed, you fool!

GINEVRA — Good night, my lord. Good night, old
friend. (*To* NERI — *shaking her finger*) Good night
. . . you silly boy! (*She goes out the great doors at
the back.*)

NERI — (*Bawling after her*). Lock all the doors!
I have my key! (*To the others*) Now I am ready.
Where's the armor, sir?

They truss the bibulous Neri in the suit of armor
and put a great sword in his hand. Then Giannetto
proposes a stirrup-cup to speed him on his way. With
bawling gusto Neri drinks —" To the spavin-shanks
of Lorenzo's barnyard . . . To all his cowards and
mountebanks and clowns . . ."

NERI — (*cutting the air with the sword*). Now, by
Sir Lucifer, I could kill all Italy! . . . Fling wide
the gates of gold! (*They obey. Without is seen the
night sky blazing with stars*) Do you hear the blare
of trumpets and the crash of drums? The armies of
the world salute their conqueror! (*Brandishing his
sword*) Give way! Give way! The floods and thunder and the earthquake come! I shake the moun-

tains! I defy you, stars! I am Death! I am Truth!
I am God! (*He staggers out, roaring. The doors
close behind him.*)

GIANNETTO — Fool! You have walked into the
spider's web. (GIANNETTO *who has been hurriedly
searching for something in Neri's doublet now finds it
with a cry of joy.*)

TORNAQUINCI — What key is that?

GIANNETTO — The key to Paradise! (*Picking up
NERI'S doublet and mantle and giving them to the
dwarf*) Here, Fazio, take this cloak of his. Carry
t home and put it on my bed. Then run to the fencing-
master's in the Via Nuova. There'll be a crowd there.
Push your way in. Tell them your news — that
Messer Neri suddenly has gone mad! That he came
here howling like a dog, and when the servants shut
the door on him, he started for the Vacchereccia,
swearing he'd turn it to a slaughter-house! I'll go myself and warn them there. (*Throwing on his white
mantle and opening the doors*) Run! Shriek it in the
streets! Fly, Fazio, fly! (*The dwarf hurries away.
GIANNETTO turns to* TORNAQUINCI) You, sir, to the
Magnificent. Tell him my vengeance has begun —
atrocious, horrible, as he commands! (*With savage
exaltation*) Tell him that there are banners floating
in my heart tonight — And that tomorrow — tomorrow
— I can pray — (*He turns and goes blindly into the
night as*

(*The curtain falls*)

ACT II

In Ginevra's house next morning, just before dawn,
the servants are aroused by those who come to report
that Messer Neri is quite mad. The night before, in
Ceccerino's wine shop, after he had wrecked the place,
Lorenzo's guards had fallen upon him, " gagged him

with an old shirt, trussed his arms, and locked him up," confident that the devil was in him. Cintia, Ginevra's maid, hastens to acquaint her mistress with the news. But Ginevra, emerging sleepily from her bedroom, is far from startled.

GINEVRA — Good Cintia, it is *you* who has gone mad.

CINTIA — What? Me, madonna? When I am telling you the truth?

GINEVRA — (*contemptuously*).   A pack of lies!

CINTHA — But why?

GINEVRA — Because he's there.

CINTIA — Who?

GINEVRA — Neri.

CINTIA — In your bed?

GINEVRA — Where else, poor fool?

CINTIA — (*horrified*).   Madonna, you spent last night, then, with a madman!

GINEVRA — (*smiling*).   Ah, but a gentle madman! Poor Neri!   He must have drunk deep and slept sound to have lain so still.   I did not even know that he was there until you called me!

CINTIA — He may be crouching at the keyhole now, ready to leap at us and tear us limb from limb!

GINEVRA — Peace, woman!   He is sleeping like a frightened child, the bedclothes all drawn up above his head.   And when just now I stumbled over that red cloak of his and cried "God save us!" he never even waked to curse at me!

CINTIA — Perhaps he was feigning sleep to put you off your guard!

GINEVRA — You think so?   (*Rising*)   Come now, let's us go and see!   (*She takes Cintia firmly around the waist and leads her toward the bedroom door*).

CINTIA — (*resisting*).   No, no!   Have mercy on me!   Do not bring me near him!   I cannot bear it! I would rather die — (*With a loud shriek*)   Ah,

Mother of God! The door is opening! Fly! Fly —
(*It is Giannetto who stands at the bedroom door. He
is in his shirt-sleeves, adjusting his belt. Over his
arm he carries Neri's doublet and great scarlet mantle.*)

GINEVRA — (*gazing at him stupified*). You!

CINTIA — Why, who is that, Madonna?

GINEVRA — You! Giannetto! In God's name, how
were you — you — (*Unable to speak, she points
towards the bedroom.*)

GIANNETTO — By a trick, madonna.

· · · · · · · · ·

GINEVRA — (*haughtily, as she seats herself*).
Now, sir, I listen to your tale.

GIANNETTO — It is not long, madonna. Three little
words! (*Softly*) I love you.

GINEVRA — (*calmly*). Ah, *that* I understood last
night. Go on.

GIANNETTO — Go on? What else is there to tell?

GINEVRA —Why, how you came here, sir! What
demon gave you courage? You, who turned sick with
terror at my Neri's name!

GIANNETTO — Your Neri? So I did. How
strange to stand here in the poor man's house, knowing I shall never fear him any more!

GINEVRA — (*nervously*). Why?

GIANNETTO — Your Neri has gone mad.

GINEVRA — (*with a cry*). No! No!

GIANNETTO — (*politely*). What else, madonna,
since he is not here? (*Coming nearer*) This is the
hour when fruit hangs ripe and heavy on the bough.
Where is the owner? Has he ceased to care? Or
has he forgotten the old garden rule — that fruit, like
kisses, should be plucked at dawn?

GINEVRA — (*smiling*). Wine makes the memory
short sometimes. (*Severely*) But even so, the fruit
belongs to him. You stand, sir, in *his* orchard, not
your own!

GIANNETTO — According to the laws of **Florence**, one can inherit land from madmen as well as from the dead.

GINEVRA — So then! You are his heir perhaps?

GIANNETTO — (*humbly*). Madonna,   no.   What have I dared permit myself? Of what can **you** reproach me?

GINEVRA — (*smiling a little*). Not of greed, sir, truly.

GIANNETTO — Do you know why? Because I love the fruit so much I could not tear it like a robber from the bough. That is another's way, not mine. No, I must kneel beneath the tree and watch and pray until it drops down of its own sweet will and falls into my hands

GINEVRA — Indeed? And when, sir, will that moment come?

GIANNETTO — (*lightly*). Who   knows? Today? Tomorrow? Not at all?

. . . .

GIANNETTO — It was so still when I crept up the stairs. So deathly still! (*Pointing to the doorway at left*) Saints, how my heart beat coming through those curtains. This room was dark. (*Pointing to the bedroom*) But there, through the half-open door, a light was shining.

GINEVRA — (*softly*). The night-light by my bed.

GIANNETTO — For hours, it seemed to me, I dared not move. I waited, listening. But nothing stirred. Then, inch by inch, I tiptoed nearer — nearer — until I stood there on your threshold, and looked in, and saw —

GINEVRA — Well?

GIANNETTO — A pool of gold upon the pillow. One bare arm — oh God, how can I say the words?

My brain caught fire, I shook, I could not breathe —

GINEVRA — (*with irony*). And then, sir, you went in.

GIANNETTO — Yes. I went in. I blew out the light.

GINEVRA — But why?

GIANNETTO — To bathe in that warm, tempting darkness! To glide down black walls of velvet to a sacred orchard, whose guardian giant was bound with chains of steel! To lie there smiling through the slow, sweet hours, while you beside me slept and dreamed as the earth dreams of the coming of the spring!

GINEVRA — Why did you not wake me, Giannetto?

GIANNETTO — What?

GINEVRA — Perhaps — the fruit might have forgiven, might have even loved the hand that plucked it.

GIANNETTO — (*with a sudden sob of passion*). But now I wait no longer! Look! I reach, I seize —

GINEVRA — (*interrupting him*). Too late, my friend. Robbers turns beggars at the break of day!

GIANNETTO — So be it then. I beg. And not for love alone, madonna. No! For vengeance, too!

GINEVRA — (*puzzled*). For vengeance?

GIANNETTO —(*Pointing to the bedroom*). Yes, now you know what kept you safe last night. Fruit that is stolen cannot satisfy my hate. It hungers for a ten times richer feast, spiced with the poison of your soft consent.

GINEVRA — (*nervously*). Take care! If Neri should appear —

GIANNETTO — That madman? Tied up in a horse's stall? (*Urging her towards the bedroom*). Why do you think of him, madonna? Come!

GINEVRA — I am afraid —

GIANNETTO — Of what? My dwarf is stationed in

the street outside. He'll run to warn us at the first
alarm. (*Looking at her oddly*) They say fear whets
the razor-edge of love. I wonder! Come!

GINEVRA — (*half frightened*). I do not know you
when you talk this way —

GIANNETTO — I know myself! I long for you! I
want you!

GINEVRA — (*beginning to yield*). Let me go —

GIANNETTO — Our bridal night — at last, madonna!

GINEVRA — Thief!

GIANNETTO — My saint, my church, my altar-
candle —

GINEVRA —Thief!

GIANNETTO — My ruin, my hell, my black damna-
tion —

GINEVRA — Thief!

GIANNETTO — (*in   a   transport*). Revenge! My
beautiful revenge!

GINEVRA — (*half   fainting*). Dear   thief — (*A
pause, they listen*) Did you hear?

GIANNETTO — A door closed — (*A cry from below*).

GINEVRA — What is that? (*He does not answer*)
You are trembling!

GIANNETTO — (*forcing himself to be calm*). No!
(*He goes to the curtains and listens*). Someone is
running up the stairs.

GINEVRA — (*suddenly*). Oh,   I'm   afraid! I'm
afraid!

GIANNETTO — Madonna, trust me. (*He draws his
dagger and faces the curtains as the dwarf rushes
through them and into the room*) Fazio!

FAZIO — (*throwing his arms about Giannetto's
legs and clinging to him*). Dear master, save yourself! He has escaped!

GINEVRA — Holy God!

GIANNETTO — But how?

FAZIO — A squad of guards were taking him to the Palazzo Medici. Just as they came abreast of the Cathedral he broke loose, tore the sword from the captain's hands, killed two and fled like a mad dog as the crowd gave way.

GIANNETTO — In what direction?

FAZIO — Towards the Ponte Vecchio, they say.

GIANNETTO — I knew it! He is coming here!

GINEVRA — (*crossing herself*). The saints protect me!

FAZIO — Fly, master, fly! Escape while there is time!

GIANNETTO — I cannot leave her.

GINEVRA — Would you be my death? God knows he'll kill me if he sees you! Go! (*She pushes him towards doorway at left.*)

FAZIO — But not that way. You'll meet the madman, sir!

GIANNETTO — The guards! Oh God, have they forgotten him?

GINEVRA — Go this way. (*She opens the secret door at right*) . . . I'll lock myself in here. (*She pushes* GIANNETTO *through the secret door and locks herself in her bedroom.*)

With the crash of the outer door Neri bursts into the room. "He is dishevelled, wounded and streaked with blood. His armor is battered and his clothing torn. He still holds the great, two-handled sword. But its blade is broken off short. He is altogether a spectacle of horror." Like a mad man he rages of his wrongs and the revenge he will take. Frightening the last of Cintia's wits from her addled head he rushes to the door of Ginevra's room.

NERI — (*knocking*). Sweet   chuck,   awake! Awake! Your Neri calls! (*He knocks again*) Hey there! I'm tired! I want to go to bed! (*He listens, his ear to the crack*) I heard you, love! Cock-robin heard his little hen! You are standing with the door between us, eh? (*He pauses. Then, rattling and banging*) Come, stop your joking, trollop! Let me in!

GINEVRA'S VOICE — (*soothingly, from behind the door*) — God help you, dear. I know they do you wrong. You are not half as bad as they pretend! And so you are going to creep away without a word, this instant, now — to show you love me. Are you not, my soul?

NERI — (*grinding his teeth*). Lord God of Moonshine! You believe it, too. (*Roaring at her*) Bawd! Let me in! You'll see how mad I am!

GINEVRA'S VOICE — Be gentle, dear!

NERI — (*mimicking her*). "Be gentle, dear"! (*Ferociously*) Oh, I'll be gentle, when I lay my hands on you! I'll crack your little bones, dear, one by one!

GINEVRA'S VOICE — (*with a nervous laugh*). Ha, ha! You are so droll, love! Run away!

NERI — What, trull? You mock at me? I shall count three — If, when I cease, the door is still between us — then. hell-hag, God have mercy on your soul!

He knocks and curses without avail, until, as he is about to crash his way through the door the soldiers of the Medici swarm into the room. He turns upon them savagely, but they are too many for him and he is bound and held again. And while he lies thus Giannetto slips in through the secret door and with a gentle, pitying irony goads him to a greater and greater rage. Then he calls the frightened Ginevra to look upon her fallen lover.

GINEVRA — Poor Neri! Ugh! How hideous he is!

NERI — Harlot, be still!

GIANNETTO — (*to Neri*). Come, come! This is the last time you will ever look upon her face. Yes, from today she is alone. And yet not quite alone, for I am here.

NERI — O God — O God —

GIANNETTO — (*earnestly*). I swear to you by all the Saints, poor friend, I'll do my best to cheer and comfort her!

NERI — Oh, for a moment — only one, dear God! — to hold their white throats in my naked hands!

GIANNETTO — I fear we lash him into fury, sir. For his own sake, lead him to the place I spoke of.

NERI — No, no!

GIANNETTO — The best of care! A priest and doctor, sir!

NERI — (*frantically as they drag him away*). Your hands — take them off her — she belongs to me —

GIANNETTO — Fear not, dear Neri, I am in your place! I shall console her! Watch me! I begin! (*He kisses Ginevra. She drops her head with the old lascivious instinct into the same position she took with Neri in Act I.*)

NERI — (*shrieking*). Ah —!

GIANNETTO — (*triumphantly*). Mouth like the pomegranate flower! Red enemy of men that never sleeps! Kiss me again — (*She does so as he leads her slowly into the bedroom.*)

NERI — (*hysterically as he is torn through the other door*). No, no — Ginevra — Giannetto — no — for Christ's sake, no —

(*The Curtain Falls*)

Act III

" When the curtain rises the stage is perfectly black.
There is a moment of silence, broken only by the
steady drip-drip of water. Finally, at the right is
heard the faint jangle of keys and the turning of a
lock; the gate of rusty hinges and then, at last, a streak
of yellow light . . . Framed in the blackness, against
a narrow, winding staircase, Giannetto and the Executioner are seen, followed by the Doctor . . . They are
in a small, low, round cell. The vaulted ceiling rises
from a thick stone pillar in the center. Attached to
this pillar is a heavy iron ring, with chains and man-
acles hanging from it . . . The whole place drips with
moisture. It is evidently deep in the earth."

In the cellar below this vault Neri is confined, in
the keeping of the Executioner. Giannetto and the
doctor have come to see what can be done for the
" madman," the doctor holding confidently to the
newest treatment for madness now applied by men of
science in Florence. To Giannetto he explains the
treatment — the " ordeal of confrontation."

THE DOCTOR — That madness is the possession of
the human body by an imp or demon. Thanks to this
law — the fairest blossom on my tree of scholarship —
the cure of madness lies in confrontation. Sweet
remedy! I shall explain it, sir! Suppose that someone dear to you is killed, or that your wife is stolen
by the brigands. You pine with grief, you fret, you
lose your reason — or, as the vulgar put it, sir, go
mad. Good! Now suddenly the murderer or the
bandit, as the case may be, appears before your wild,
distempered eye. You foam, you cry out. Yet is it
truly you? No, no, dear sir. It is the fiend within
you, the demon whose dwelling-place you are! And it
is from this demon that we deliver the insane —

(*Breaking off suddenly*) Are you listening, sir?

GIANNETTO — (*examining the instruments*). To every word. Your mouth drips milk and honey, doctor. I respect you deeply. Indeed I spoke of you to the Magnificent when, full of pity for poor Messer Neri, he bade me call the wisest man in Florence. So you think, sir, you can cure our friend?

THE DOCTOR — I'll cure or kill him — with the help of God. (*Rubbing his hands*) We shall confront him here, sir, hanging from that ring. If he show no sign of black possession —

GIANNETTO — Pray Heaven he may not!

THE DOCTOR — Then we shall set him free like any fool. How many of them wander through the streets of Florence! I often stop to watch them burrow in some rubbish-heap and run off tittering with a crust of bread.

GIANNETTO — (*sentimentally*). Yes, God is good to simpletons.

The executioner and his men go to drag Neri from his damp cell, as Fazio, the dwarf, comes to warn his master of the threatened approach of Gabriello, the brother. But far from being alarmed at this news Giannetto rejoices. Gabriello, too, shall figure in his planned revenge, if he can arouse Neri's jealousy of him. He ponders the possibilities of this as the new plan takes shape in his mind. "Which flame burns hottest in his (*Gabriello's*) soul I wonder — love or hate?" he asks Fazio.

FAZIO — Love! Love, good master!

GIANNETTO — (*deep in his own thoughts*). And yet he loves his brother.

FAZIO — When you have lived as long as I, you will know one thing well.

GIANNETTO — What, Fazio?

FAZIO — That love of women transcends all other
loves. It is the breath of life, the voice, the cry, the
silver song that lifts the soul to God. It is the poisonous weed whose perfume kills the white flowers in the
garden of the heart. It is the cup of blood and burning wine that goads the father on to kill his child, the
brother to commit the crime of Cain — the mo —

GIANNETTO — (*his eyes gleaming*). The crime of
Cain! (*He pauses. Then turning to Fazio*) You
think, then, that Gabriello's passion for Ginevra is
stronger than his loyalty to Neri?

FAZIO — I do not think. I know.

GIANNETTO — (*with a terrible cry of joy*). At last
I am stronger than my enemies!

The executioner and his assistants drag Neri up the
steps from the cell below. "His head appears over
the trap; his face is white and bloody; his hair is
wet. . . . With a howl he suddenly tears himself from
the men who are holding him and rushes up the remaining steps, his mouth foaming, his bound hands up-
raised . . . Giannetto, cowering, clings to the executioner "— until Neri is beaten again into submission
and chained to the pillar.

GIANNETTO — At last! (*with exquisite tenderness*).
Poor Neri, are you very tired? Too tired to lift that
handsome head of yours? (*Neri stiffens and glares
at him silently*) How pale you are! Dear friend, I
fear that you have suffered much! But do not mope,
for all will yet be well. Come, come! Remember that
we only seek to cure you. We do what we must do
for your own good. . . . Poor thing, I wonder if he
understands? Perhaps. For he is smiling. How I
love that radiant, happy, sunny smile of his!

NERI — Wait till my brother hears of this in Pisa!
He'll tear the windpipe from that silky throat of yours.

GIANNETTO — (*easily*). Tush! How you fret!

Yet I can guess the secret of your petulence. It is
Ginevra!

NERI — (*interrupting*). No!

GIANNETTO — You chafe because the dear child may
be weeping for you — eh? How like a lover! Well,
I bring good news! Dawn found our young friend
raised upon one elbow, teasing my nostril with a lock
of hair.

NERI — You lie, you lie.

GIANNETTO — (*continuing*). I dreamed it was a
rose. She scents her hair with roses, you remember. . . . And then I woke and drew the baggage to
me. That velvet bosom, those slim ivory flanks —

NERI — (*gasping*). Enough! Be   still! (*Turns
away.*)

GIANNETTO — And as we lay and laughed in one
another's arms, she put her rosey mouth close to my
ear — like this — and whispered — (*Giannetto is leaning against Neri and whispering in his ear.*)

NERI — (*with a sudden howl*). The bawd! The
harlot!

GIANNETTO — Wait! There is more!

NERI — No — no — (*Looking up*) Oh God, where
are you?

GIANNETTO — (*in a burst of infernal joy*). God
cannot help you, Neri. You must call on me. On
me — for years the butt of all your bestial jokes! On
me, who bear upon my unhealed back the shameful
wounds of your vile cruelty!

FAZIO — Master!

GIANNETTO — (*resuming his former manner*).
And yet I do not wish to seem severe. I will have
mercy, friend, though you had none. I will loose your
bonds, restore you to the light and set you free if —
If you will beg forgiveness for the past and kiss my
hand in token of defeat.

NERI — Defeat.

GIANNETTO — You will not?

NERI — (*violently*). No! No, by the liver of Mahound!

GIANNETTO — (*singing to himself*).

> *Youth is fair*
> *But youth is fleet!*
> *Like the bee suck all its sweet —*

(*As he sings, he quietly and rather carelessly picks up the scourge, left by the executioner. NERI is terrified. GIANNETTO sings as he tries the scourge on the air. NERI is more and more terrified.*)

GIANNETTO — Will you submit?

NERI — No! (*GIANNETTO raises the scourge for the first blow.*) Yes! I can bear no more —

GIANNETTO — Repeat these words — Obediently and with many tears of shame —

NERI —" Obediently and with many tears of shame —"

GIANNETTO — I beg forgiveness for my past transgressions —

NERI —"I beg forgiveness for my past transgressions —"

GIANNETTO — And humbly beg the leave to kiss your hand.

NERI — "And humbly beg the leave to kiss your hand."

GIANNETTO — (*very graciously, throwing aside the scourge and putting his hand to NERI's mouth. NERI slowly leans forward his head. Then, with sudden ferocity, he seizes GIANNETTO's fingers with his teeth. There is silence as GIANNETTO, with a great effort wrenches his hand away.*)

NERI — (*bursting out — laughs madly.*) GIANNETTO *with the face of a demon, has picked up the scourge and is stealthily approaching him when suddenly, from up the stairway, comes the sound of women's laughter.* GIANNETTO *stops. The sound grows louder, snatches of song, etc.*)

For the ordeal of confrontation Giannetto has selected three women whom Neri had known and cast aside. " From the gutter where dear Neri flung them I have picked up three — three mildewed rags that once were clean as snow." They shall confront the madman and stir the devil that possesses him. " Then, with God's help," declares the doctor, " we shall drive him forth through a hole in the side, made with these iron pincers, blessed by two bishops and heated white hot with the brazier there." . . . " Thank God for science," solemnly adds Giannetto.

One of the three is Fiammetta, once beautiful but now disfigured by a great scar. She is stone blind and feels her way about with a stick. One is Lucrezia, " pale and thin, with great sunken eyes and yellow hair." And one is Lisabetta, " almost a child; sad and lovely. Her clothes are humble but very neat."

With these three Giannetto leaves Neri. " And now, farewelll, dear friend," he calls. "And may they give you back a million times the frenzy you gave them."

Lucrezia is first to face the shackled giant, a dagger gleaming in her hand.

LUCREZIA — Do you not know me, sir! Three years ago you found me exquisite. I am Lucrezia, the jeweller's wife who sold her soul for you. I had a home, and children too — Then you came. And now I lie in wait for soldiers on the street. (*Pause*) Do you remember? (*Wildly*) If, like a beast, you cannot speak to me, then you must suffer like a beast. (*She draws out a dagger — pause*) Holy Madonna, how my hand is shaking! Why do you stare at me?

(*Pause*) Stop! Stop, I say! What are you doing? (*In a strange voice*) I could have sworn I hated you, but now — (*She stops. Then, in a burst of emotion*) May God forgive me, I love you still! (*And she sinks down, kissing his feet, in a flood of passionate tears.*)

FIAMMETTA — (*disgusted*). Have done, you snivelling drab! What! Would you drown the camel in your tears? (*Reaching out with her stick*) Where is the frog? Let me commune with him! I'll make him croak or know the reason why! (*Her stick touches him*) Is that your carcass, pretty one? (*Kicking aside Lucrezia, dropping her stick and running her hands over his body*) How cold you are, my plunderer of virgins! Like some great sausage on the cellar wall. And thin! I can count each rib! Ha, does that tickle, and here's your face. So! Gaze in my sockets. (*Leaning on him and lowering her voice*) Do you recall a certain orchard nook, with a sly moon peeping through the apple blossoms — and how we kissed the jolly nights away? Ah, what brave times! But there was a child. You did not know that, did you? It lived two days. A girl. I'm glad she died. My father was a pious man — the fool! He tried to kill me with a water jug. I wish he had! It broke and blinded me. So now I am a worthless jug myself and sit a-begging by Giotto's Tower. (*Holding out her hand*) "A penny, signor, or the devil take you!" That is my life. I owe it all to you. (*Ominously*) But I am honest. Yes. I pay my debts. (*Drawing a silver hairpin from her hand*) You gave this to me once. Observe it well. It is the last thing you will ever see! And why? Because — (*feeling about his face*) — because those lecherous jellies that you call your eyes —

Before Fiammetta can strike Lucrezia and Lisabetta

drag her away from Neri and finally, by a subterfuge, get her from the room. Lisabetta alone is left.   And from her confession it transpires that she is not one of Neri's victims, but one who long has loved him.

LISABETTA — I wonder if you heard me lie to them. We never knew each other, did we, sir? You never even saw me till tonight. (*Sighing*) Poor soul, you cannot understand! (*She comes nearer him*) This is the moment I have prayed and longed for! How shall I use it, my beloved? Shall I pretend you are not mad, but love me? Yet granny says that love's a sort of madness. (*Passionately*) Then I am mad, for oh! I love you so! You never guessed? But, oh, your eyes! One glance, one careless glance as you rode by me on that horse of yours — and all day long I heard the harps of God! And though you never saw me as you passed, my soul shone in the light you left behind!

And now Lisabetta, convinced that Neri is not mad, plans to effect his release. "If they are cunning, you must be cunning, too," she says. "Why not pretend that you are really mad, as if this joke of theirs they are so proud of had in good truth addled your poor brains?"

NERI — They would but laugh the louder.
LISABETTA — That   may   be.   But   soon   they'll wonder what to do with you.
NERI — They   would   not   dare   to   give   me   to   my brother.
LISABETTA — To   your   brother,   no.   But   I   think they might to me. Now, listen! I will swear that I still love you, and that I want to take you far away and nurse you as I would a little child. And as I plead for you, you'll seem, by word, by look, by gesture, every-

thing, to be the simpleton that I claim you are. No
raving madman, howling threats of doom, but a poor
dunce — one of those mooncalves whom the street-
boys mock. If you but act this part — and act it well!
— they will not fail to put you in my charge —

NERI — (*in a burst of joy*). O star-eyed child!
Where did you learn such wisdom?

LISABETTA — (*shyly*). I think my schoolmaster
was Love.

Lisabetta's ruse is successful. When Giannetto and
the guards return to the cell Neri babbles witlessly and
is adjudged harmless. Even Giannetto is puzzled for
a time — until, catching his enemy off his guard, he
sees again the light of murder in his eyes and knows
he is shamming. Yet by now Giannetto has no liking
for the revenge he thought would be so sweet. He is
willing to cry quits.

GIANNETTO — I offered once to free you, Neri, but
I asked a base humiliation in return. That was unworthy. I confess it now. (*His voice deepening*)
Once more I offer you your liberty — this time if you
will only pledge your word never to hurt or frighten
me again. (*With broken gesture*) There! I have
said it, Neri. I have stripped my soul. You see me
as I really am — in all my weakness and my vanity.
Your joke had lasted for so many years and I had
suffered so — ah, was it strange that when the moment
came I struck at you? If I went too far, remember
that I am not used to triumph. But now — please
God! — the dreadful game is ended. Give me your
word and I shall set you free. (*He pauses, looking
anxiously at his enemy*) Your word, dear Neri! I
am waiting! (*Again he pauses. Turning wildly to*
LISABETTA) You, who say you love him, oh, for your
love's sake! tell him to consent —

NERI — (*grinning*). If ever a dog begins to say

his prayers — why, clap a muzzle on the filthy brute!

GIANNETTO — (*Fiercely, clasping his hands*). Oh, Neri! Neri! Will you not cry quits?

NERI — I see a spider, and the rogue has fur like cherry-colored velvet, soft and warm —

GIANNETTO — Neri, this joke of ours is like a whirlpool. To what vile depths have we already sunk! And who knows what the future has in store?

NERI — I am a cork. Around, around I spin.

GIANNETTO — (*at the height of his despair*). Peace! Peace! Upon my knees I beg for it!

NERI — (*Looking down at him*). Sir, are you hungry? Can you eat a cloud? They say that he who eats one will be king!

GIANNETTO — (*wiping the sweat from his own forehead*). Think, Neri, think! There is a moment left, but once the die is cast, your doom is sealed. Now let me warn you! I shall no longer keep you here in chains! I shall release you! Do not smile! Because the first thing that you do when you are free will be to walk again into my web and this time — this time you will be destroyed! (*More and more terrified*) Oh, Neri, keep me from that mortal sin! I am so young! I want so to be good — all good and clean, the way I used to be! Oh, I would never pray again than ask forgiveness for such wickedness! Now help me, Neri — no, you must — you shall —

NERI — Ah, what a swarm of cowardly little stars!

GIANNETTO — I humbly beg of you in our Saviour's name —

NERI —They fill the air! But this is how I catch them —

GIANNETTO — For the last time —

NERI — (*snapping savagely with his teeth*). Just like flies!

GIANNETTO — (*after a pause, crossing himself*). God's will be done. (*He goes to the door, opens it and calls*).   Come!   Set free this idiot.   I am convinced that he is harmless as the babe unborn.

But as Lisabetta leads Neri away Giannetto contrives to whisper in his ear: "And now a parting word.   You have not deceived me.   When they unbound you, not a moment since, I saw the murder blazing in your eyes —"

NERI — (*very gently*).   Dear little brother, will you come with me?   The path is strewn with roses, so they say!

GIANNETTO — (*continuing*).   But this is what I want to tell you, Neri.   Tonight, at my accustomed hour, I go to a certain house that you know well.   Yes, to Ginevra's!   For I love her so, to save my life I could not stay away!   Come there, my friend, and kill me if you can!   Oh, have no fear!   I shall be alone!   Yet say a prayer before you cross that threshold!   Sharpen your wits!   Keep all your senses keen!   For in some corner of that house of shame, in some dim passage or behind some door, there is a red shape waiting for its prey —

NERI — (*waving him off*).   Back, Satan, back! You cannot tempt me now!   Oh God, lean down from Heaven and pity us!   Yet courage, brothers!   Forward on our way!   (*He goes towards the stairs, preceded by the doctor, the executioners, and Lisabetta, who holds him by the hand*)   Over the moutains and across the sea, past snares and pitfalls of the Evil One, we come!   We pilgrims come!   Have mercy, Lord! We are Thy children!   We belong to Thee —

GIANNETTO — (*closing the door*).   No, no, you fiend from Hell!   You belong to me!   Oh, Fazio, now how my plans, my pretty plans, how they wriggle and squirm to get away. . . . Fazio, tonight, tonight, I must damn my own soul to hell!   O, Lucifer, stretch

out your blazing arms and catch me as I plunge into
the abyss. (*Fazio cries and falls on floor*) Pray
for me, Fazio, for I shall never, pray again — (*Breaks
in sobs.*)

(*Curtain*)

Act IV

In Ginevra's house, that evening, " the room is dim
and empty. Only the silver lamp above the toilet table
and the tapers at the shrine are burning. Through the
window a flood of moonlight pours softly on the floor.
Outside a nightingale is singing " The garrulous
Cintia is preparing Ginevra for the night. Their talk
is of Ginevra's lovers, of those she has cause to fear
and those she would welcome. " Moonlight! Spring-
time! And a poet's song! Madonna, teach me how
to love again! " is Ginevra's prayer.

Suddenly there is a noise outside the window, and
soon " Neri pulls himself up and perches on the
sill. . . His whole appearance is horrible and fantastic. He pauses for a moment, glaring at the two
paralyzed women, then drops into the room and comes
toward them slowly."

Cintia he casts from the room. Ginevra he commands with thunderous voice to stand before him.
" She comes slowly to where he points and stands
there. He takes her by the arms; she closes her eyes.
When he speaks his voice is soft and malignant."

NERI — If I am mad, why do you tremble so? The
mad are gentle as a little child. Only the self-
possessed are dangerous. And so to prove I am of
sober mind, I fear I must be very cruel to you.

GINEVRA — (*muttering*). Neri, I am not to blame.
I was — deceived —

NERI — (*very quiet*). I know you were. And yet

these arms have twined themselves about my enemy.
This breast — this snowy breast that he has soiled!
What was it but the altar of my love? So now love's
altar must be purified, and blood alone can wash the
stain away!

GINEVRA — Be merciful —

NERI — If not your blood, then his. I leave the
choice to you.

GINEVRA — Not that!

NERI — Well, do you throw him overboard?

GINEVRA — Oh God, have pity on me!

NERI — Yes or no?

GINEVRA — (*bursting into hysterical tears*). Yes!
Kill him if you must! But let me live — (*With a
cry, as he flings her to the floor*) I cannot help it! I
cannot die! (*She lies weeping at his feet.*)

NERI — (*contemptuously*). You love him, then, as
much as you loved me! What a rag you are!
(*Touching her with his foot*) Lift up your head.
(*She obeys*) What is Giannetto's usual hour?

GINEVRA — Last night — (*Breaking down*) Ah,
Holy Virgin!

NERI — (*again prodding her with his foot*).
Answer me!

GINEVRA — (*hoarsely*). He came at ten.

NERI — And the house was dark? (*Pointing to the
window*) You put the little alabaster lamp there in
the window-niche as in my time!

GINEVRA — (*as before*). Yes, Neri.

NERI — Take off that robe. (*She does so*)
There! Now you're ready for him! (*Half-fero-
cious, half-passionate*) How pink and white you
are — (*Feeling her body under the nightgown*)
How soft and small! Saints! Do you know I almost envy him? The lucky dog! To die on such a
breast!

GINEVRA — *(in a revulsion of feeling)*. Oh God,
this is too much! I cannot bear it! What you are
doing is monstrous, horrible —

NERI — Go to your bed!

.   .   .   .

NERI — Take care now! Not a sob or tear! You
cannot save this spider from his fate, so calm yourself
and meet him with a smile! Remember, I am very
close, concealed behind the curtains of your bed. If
you so much as breathe into his ear one word of warning, both of you shall die. He'll come — the little
coward — surrounded by at least a score of men.
He'll bring them up here, as he did before. But when
he cannot find a trace of me, and sees your light there,
meaning all is well, he will dismiss his body-guard and
creep, like a hound, through your chamber-door.
Then, as he slips between the silken sheers, I glide out
from my hiding-place and —

The speech is broken by the sound of the convent
bell striking the hour. It is ten o'clock. With a parting threat Neri bids Ginevra place the signal lamp
and go to her room. Outside a serenader is singing
the " Madrigal of May."

In a coffer Neri finds "a long, thin dagger with a
jewelled hilt. Sitting on the edge of a chest he tries
its point and polishes its blade with a fold of his
mantle. . . . He goes softly into the bedroom. . . .
The stage is empty. Only the music comes up from
below. Then, through the doorway at left, appears a
figure completely wrapped in Giannetto's white
mantle . . . crosses the stage. enters Ginevra's bedroom and gently closes the door . . . The poet's song
outside the window continues."

" The song ends. The music dies away. . . . There
is the stamp of feet, the fall of a heavy body, then the

door bursts open and Ginevra flies out shrieking, beside herself with terror. Her neck and nightgown are stained with scarlet. . . ."

NERI'S VOICE — (*in the bedroom*). At last, oh saints! At last! (*He stands at the threshold, looking back into the room and jeering. He holds the bloody dagger in his dripping hand*) Well, Giannetto? And did death taste sweet? Sweet as the taste of love — or sweeter still! (*In a burst of triumphant hate. He turns away, with a savage laugh, and strides rapidly towards the doorway — left, as if to leave the house. As he reaches the steps that lead to this doorway, he looks up, and stops short with a gasp of horror. Above him, between the curtains, in the full light of the moon, stands* GIANNETTO, *smiling down at him.* FAZIO *crouches at his master's feet. Both are very pale.* NERI'S *dagger falls to the floor. Choking, his hand at his throat, he looks from* GIANNETTO *to the bedroom, which he has just left, and then back to* GIANNETTO. *There is a silence. Then, in a dreadful whisper*) Not — you —?

GIANNETTO — (*clinging to the tapestry, and thrusting his head forward like a poisonous snake*) Yes, Neri. I! (*He pauses, looking at his victim with glittering eyes*) Your hands are wet with blood. Whom have you slain? My friend, I fear you have revenged yourself too hastily! We two are not Ginevra's only lovers. One of her minions came to me tonight with murder in his heart. To save my life, I bargained with the wretch. I said to him, " I tricked her once and you can do the same. Take this white mantle that she knows is mine. Go to her chamberdoor. Walk boldly in. The rest is easy! " That is what he did. But oh! You killed the dog! And so, when all is said, you acted wisely. We are both revenged!

NERI — (*hoarsely*). Who was he?

GIANNETTO — Guess, my friend!

NERI — I cannot! Speak —

GIANNETTO — (*in wild exultation*). It was your brother! Gabriello!

NERI — (*reeling*). No!

GIANNETTO — You killed your brother, Neri!

NERI — (*piteously*). No! No! No!

GIANNETTO — (*springing forward*). Fool! Do you doubt me? Take this lamp and see! Go lift him up! You'll find him where he fell! And when those dead eyes look into your face, remember it was you who murdered him! (NERI, *staggering like a drunkard, goes into the bedroom, lamp in hand.*)

FAZIO — (*as Neri disappears*). Quick! There is not a moment to be lost! (*There is a wail from the inner room*) Hark! Do you hear that? Fly, dear master, fly!

GIANNETTO — I cannot. Something is holding me. (*A burst of strange laughter from within.*)

FAZIO — (*frantically*). Enough! Enough! Are you not satisfied?

GIANNETTO — No, I must see the look upon his face. He is coming — (NERI *appears on the threshold of the bedroom. He holds the lamp in one hand; in the other* GIANNETTO'S *white mantle, all spotted with blood.* GIANNETTTO *steps forward, in an ecstasy of horror.* FAZIO *has fled*). Oh, my enemy! I give and take no quarter! Kill me, too! (*But* NERI *does not answer. He looks at* GIANNETTO *with glassy, unseeing eyes, then wanders rather uncertainly across the room dragging the mantle after him.*)

NERI — (*faintly*). Where are you, love? I have been hunting for you!

GIANNETTO — He is mad! Stark mad!

NERI — Come back! Come back! I am so lonely, dear —

GIANNETTO — (*turning to the shrine*). Ah, Holy

Virgin! Look into my heart and hear me as I pray
for both of us — (*He kneels and crosses himself*)
  (*From the garden below again comes the* SONG.)
NERI — Give me your hand! I cannot see the
way —
  GIANNETTO — *Ave Maria, gratia plena* —
            (*Curtain*)

"WEDDING BELLS"

An American Comedy in Three Acts

By Salisbury Field

"WEDDING BELLS" was produced at the Harris Theatre November 12, 1919, and continued there successfully until the middle of April. It proved a typical American comedy of the lighter type, dipping occasionallly into situations that are frankly farcical, and being dependent for its popularity rather more upon its cleverness of characterization than upon its smartness of dialogue.

Reginald Carter is about to be married to Marcia Hunter. In his New York apartment he is cleaning out such accumulated "incriminating evidence" as still remains in his desk. In the process he is sentimentally reminded of a romance that had threatened, a year and a half before, to "wreck his life." Though neither his friends nor his fiancee were aware of the fact, Reginald had been married. Now confession is being forced upon him. He relates the circumstances to Spencer Wells, "a gay, irrepressible young man, decidedly English in appearance and manner," who has long been his best friend and is to be his best man. "It happened on my way to Japan," he explains. "We met in Santa Barbara. We were at the same hotel. Her name was Rosalie."

Spencer—Rosalie. Pretty name, that.

Reggie — It was very romantic. I put my shoes outside my door to be cleaned. Her dog chewed one of them up.   And — and two days later we were married.

SPENCER — By Jove! You didn't lose very much time.

REGGIE — (*turns to Spencer*). You see, she was going to Japan, too, and she had her ticket on the same boat.

SPENCER — Oh, that's why you married her ?

REGGIE — (*hotly*). Nothing of the sort! It was a love match. You've no idea how wonderful she was, Spencer

SPENCER — Yes, I have. They're always wonderful. But what happened ?

REGGIE — (*sighing*). You know how I've always admired red hair.

SPENCER — Yes,— but what's that got to do with it ?

REGGIE — Everything! One day at luncheon, I admired a woman in the dining room who had red hair — and the next day Rosalie dyed her hair red. Oh! I was furious, and I told her she looked like a — a —

SPENCER — Yes, I know.

REGGIE — And she said it was plain I preferred that kind of woman, for the woman I'd admired looked like a — like a —

SPENCER — Exactly!

REGGIE — And then she left us.

SPENCER — Us?

REGGIE — Me and the dog.

SPENCER — And you didn't follow her?

REGGIE — I couldn't, old chap, I came down with the measles.

SPENCER — MEASLES?

REGGIE — Yes, measles. Caught 'em from some kids at the hotel. I was ill quite a long time.

SPENCER — Well, why didn't you send Jackson after her?

REGGIE — I didn't have Jackson then.

SPENCER — Yes, but after you got well. Didn't you try to find her after you got well?

REGGIE — Of course I tried. But by that time she'd disappeared completely. I couldn't find a trace of her — not a trace.

SPENCER — Yes, but somebody must have known where she was. Didn't her people know? Who were her people?

REGGIE — I don't know.

SPENCER — Don't know?

REGGIE — You see, the few days we were together I was so busy talking about myself — that I didn't have time —

SPENCER — Naturally — naturally. But go on. Tell me what happened.

REGGIE — Well, I was feeling awfully down at the time — blue, you know. And I knew she wouldn't have left me like that if she'd really cared — and I couldn't find her — and I had my ticket — and there was a boat sailing from San Francisco —

SPENCER — And so you went to Japan?

REGGIE — Yes. And a month later — at Kobe — or maybe it was Nagasaki — I received word from her lawyer that she'd divorced me.

SPENCER — Oh! She divorced you!

REGGIE — Of course. I couldn't be marrying Marcia tomorrow if she hadn't, could I?

SPENCER — Did you ever hear from her again?

REGGIE — Not a word. I don't mind telling you, Spencer, it nearly wrecked my whole life. I don't suppose I would ever have looked at another woman as long as I lived — if I hadn't met Marcia.

Reggie would have told Marcia, he explains. but "hang it all — a chap can't tell about the woman he loved yesterday to the girl he loves today. It isn't decent." But Marcia has discovered the truth. When

she went with Reggie to apply for the marriage license
the story of the first Mrs. Carter had to be told —
and she was furious. Also curious. Therefore she
has followed her intended to learn the details. " I
think it was outrageous for you to be married and
divorced like that without telling me a word about
it," she insists.

REGGIE — Well, you know about it now, don't you?

MARCIA — Yes, no thanks to you!

REGGIE — That's just it. I knew you wouldn't thank
me for telling you so — so I didn't tell you.

MARCIA — But you haven't told me anything.
(*Pause*) Why did you get *married* if you didn't intend to stay married?

REGGIE — I did intend to stay married.

MARCIA — Then why didn't you? Had you known
her long?

REGGIE — N-not very.

MARCIA — Who introduced you?

REGGIE — Nobody.

MARCIA — What?

REGGIE — I mean somebody who wasn't exactly
anybody. (*Lightly*) You see she had a little dog,
and — and I met her through the little dog.

MARCIA — (*turns away*). Oh! She was that
kind of a woman!

REGGIE — She wasn't that kind of a woman. Look
here, Marcia, I know you're disappointed in me and
— well, if you want to chuck me. it isn't too late, you
know.

MARCIA — (*horrified*). What! And not get married tomorrow?

REGGIE — Well, you don't seem to care for me very
much.

MARCIA — Why, Reggie! How can you say that?

REGGIE — Because if you really cared for me you wouldn't make me so unhappy.

MARCIA — Unhappy?

REGGIE — Yes, Marcia, unhappy. I want to forget about the past and you won't let me.

MARCIA — But Reggie!

REGGIE — When I asked you to be my wife, I thought the past was buried. But today has brought it all back. I want to forget it, I tell you! I want to forget it!

MARCIA — Did you — did you love her?

REGGIE — Yes.

MARCIA — (*to him*). Do you — love her now?

REGGIE — I tell you I'd forgotten until today. And I'll forget tomorrow. Only please don't think about it any more! Please!

So Marcia agrees to forgive — and forget as much as she can, though forgetting will be difficult. And that's settled. Then it transpires that Marcia also has loved another — and given him up. Douglas Ordway, a youthful poet, subject to attacks of verse and passion in the spring, has confessed his great love for her, and she has admitted her liking for him — but Reggie is the better match and Marcia has made her choice. Still she hopes Douglas will go on loving her. " It's very comforting to a girl to know that someone is going to love her after she's married." And she bids him a fond goodbye — forever.

That night Reginald is to give his farewell bachelor dinner. The arrangements are all completed, and his friends leave him that he may rest a bit before the great send-off. He has just stretched himself out on the lounge when Jackson announces a caller, a " Mme. Brousseau." Reggie doesn't know, and doesn't care to know, any Mme. Brousseau. He wants to rest. But Jackson is rather stubborn about it. Mme. Brousseau having given him $10 to arrange the interview he feels it must be arranged some way. So finally he prevails upon his master to see the lady, and —" Rosalie " enters. Her hair is no longer red, but she is so chic and charming that neither the Diety nor the audience can blame Reggie for what happens later. Jackson goes out, closing the door softly behind him."

Rosalie — Reggie! (*They stare at each other.*)

Reggie — Rosalie!

Rosalie — I — I suppose you're surprised to see me.

Reggie — Surprised! I should say I was!

Rosalie — I — I hope it's a pleasant surprise.

Reggie — Pleasant? Why, I was thinking about you only a minute ago. It's the nicest thing that ever happened to me, your dropping in to see me like this.

Rosalie — (*Who has been agitated and not at all sure of her welcome, gains confidence as she goes on*) Yes, that's it. I — I just dropped in. You see, I only arrived this morning, and I found your address in the telephone book, so — I — thought I'd call and get my dog.

Reggie — Your dog?

Rosalie — Yes, Pinky — the dog I left with you in Santa Barbara. (*As Reggie is silent*) Don't tell me anything has happened to him!

Reggie — I'm awfully sorry, Rosalie.

Rosalie — Then something has happened!

Reggie — Yes.

Rosalie — He — he's not dead?

Reggie — I hope he's not dead. He was stolen.

Rosalie — Stolen?

Reggie — Yes.

Rosalie — Poor Pinky! I think you might have taken better care of him.

Reggie — I couldn't take care of him, Rosalia. The day after you left me, 1 came down with — an illness — a severe illness. I was sick quite a long time.

Rosalie — You poor boy! What was it?

Reggie — It was — er — measles. (*As* Rosalie *laughs*) I can assure you, for a man of my age, measles is no laughing matter.

Rosalie — So you turned red — like my hair.

Reggie — Yes. And I looked like the devil — and so did you.

Rosalie — I know 1 did, Reggie. That's one reason I ran away.

Reggie — It was?

Rosalie — But J thought of course you'd follow me.

Reggie — Well, you see I was angry with you for leaving me like that. And when I got over being angry, I had measles. And you can't follow anybody anywhere when you've got measles. And then, when I did try to find you, I couldn't — and I knew you didn't love me any more — and I'd lost your dog —

Rosalie — Then you did try to find me?

Reggie — 1 should say I did! I hired detectives and everything!

Rosalie — Did you honestly.

Reggie — Yes, I did. And before I got through I had a photograph or description of every red-headed woman in California. (*Sadly*) But none of them was you.

Rosalie — Yet you went to Japan.

Reggie — Well, I had to go somewhere, didn't I?

Rosalie — Yes, but we were going there together. If you'd really cared, you wouldn't have gone there alone.

REGGIE — I would too, because I did. And I wouldn't do a thing I did if I wouldn't do it (*Pause*) Besides, you had no right to leave me like that and hide so I couldn't find you. (*Pause*) And then to divorce me on the grounds of desertion I didn't desert you. You deserted me.

ROSALIE — (*smiling*). I know. But the courts in California are so obliging. Did you like Japan, Reggie?

REGGIE — No.

ROSALIE — Did you go to China, too?

REGGIE — Yes.

ROSALIE — Did you like China?

REGGIE — No. And I went to India and I didn't like India. And I came back to California and I didn't like California and I returned to New York and I didn't like New York.

ROSALIE — Why didn't you like them, Reggie?

REGGIE — You know very well why — I missed you. Everywhere I went I missed you. And then to have you come and see me like this. (*Taking her card from pocket and studying it*) Somehow I'd hoped you wouldn't marry again.

ROSALIE — Marry again? What do you mean? (*As she sees card in his hand.*)

REGGIE — (*reading from card*). Madame Brousseau.

ROSALIE — Oh, that — (*Goes up to piano stands pensive over the keys, one of which she faintly strikes.*)

REGGIE — Oh, Rosalie, how could you?

ROSALIE — Then you don't believe in marrying again?

REGGIE — (*emphatically*). No! (*Startled by what he has said and hastily changing the subject*) I mean one doesn't — one shouldn't — (*Desperately*) Did — did Mr.— Monsieur Brousseau come to town, too?

ROSALIE — No, Reggie. Why?

REGGIE — (*throws card on table*). Oh, nothing! . . .

Reginald and Rosalie are very happy in that reunion — except when Reggie thinks of his wedding next day. Even then Rosalie, pretending to know nothing about it, is not exactly depressed. Two or three times Rosalie suggests that she really must be going. She is off for Santa Barbara next day, and there is packing to do. And Reggie is "going south, too." So it seems they must say "Goodbye, after all." But Reggie can't think of that. Surely they can have one more dinner before they separate — forever! Suddenly Reggie has an inspiration. They will dine together — in his apartment. He was giving a party — to some men. But he will put them off some way, if she'll only say she will come.

ROSALIE — No, Reggie, I won't let you.

REGGIE — But I want to, Rosalie, I never wanted anything so much in my life. Besides, it's only a stag party — just a lot of men.

ROSALIE — Oh, if it's only men! You're sure you'd rather have just me?

REGGIE — You know I would. You'll come?

ROSALIE — Why, yes, Reggie. I'll come with pleasure.

REGGIE — Rosalie! It's so sweet of you to come. I'm so glad you're coming. I don't know what to do.

ROSALIE — Well, you might tell me what time dinner is.

REGGIE — Any time you say.

ROSALIE — Eight o'clock . . .

.   .   .   .   .   .

REGGIE — You're sure this isn't all a dream, Rosalie? You're sure you're really coming back?

Rosalie — (*at door*). Yes, Reggie

Reggie — Cross your heart, and hope to die if you don't.

Rosalie — (*smiling and crossing her heart*). Cross my heart and hope to die if I don't. Au revoir, Reggie.

And so it is arranged that Reggie will send word to Spencer Wells that he is to take over the bachelor dinner at the club because he (Reggie) has suddenly been taken ill. " And remember," he warns Jackson, " Mme. Brousseau and I are not to be disturbed, no matter what happens. Are you quite sure you understand? " " I understand perfectly, sir," replies the knowing Jackson; " perfectly."

Act II

It is nine o'clock of the same evening. Reggie and Rosalie are still at dinner, and the echo of their laughter can be heard through the doors of the dining room Presently they appear. Rosalie never looked more charming, nor was Reggie ever in higher spirits. They have had such a good time remembering Santa Barbara and the glorious days that preceded their foolish quarrel over Rosalie's red hair. At the piano Rosalie plays the little song that used to make Pinkie howl so amusingly, and Reggie, to complete the picture, agrees to howl just as Pinkie did. They quarrel again, over the color of the rose on the piano, but it is a foolish love quarrel — and quickly made up.

Reggie — Oh, Rosalie, why didn't we end that other quarrel like this.

Rosalie — How could we when you didn't say you were sorry.

Reggie — Well, I was sorry — afterwards.

ROSALIE — Yes. But afterwards was too late.

REGGIE — It shouldn't have been too late. If you'd really cared it wouldn't have been too late. But you didn't care — And now you're married to someone else.

ROSALIE — I thought we agreed not to talk about that.

REGGIE — Yes. We're going to be happy while we can. (*Pouring out two liquers*) Have some?

ROSALIE — What is it?

REGGIE — What do you think?

ROSALIE — Not Cointreau? (*As* REGGIE *nods* "*yes*") Why, I haven't had any since I was in Santa Barbara.

REGGIE — (*coming down*). Well, I should hope not! Cointreau's our drink. (*Handing her glass*) The old toast, Rosalie.

ROSALIE — (*puzzled*). The old toast? (*Remembering*). Oh, you mean the one about — the one you taught me when —

REGGIE — (*eagerly*). Yes, that one.

ROSALIE — (*extending her glass*). Forever —

REGGIE — And ever — (*They touch glasses and drink.*)

ROSALIE — (*dreamily*). Today is forever. To-morrow comes never.

REGGIE — (*shivering at the thought of tomorrow, takes glass from her*). Let's not talk about tomorrow.

They go back again to their happy yesterdays. Reggie produces the very shoe that Pinkie had chewed the morning they met. "I didn't have a ribbon. I didn't have a photograph of you — or even a letter. I didn't have anything but this. . . I've always kept it, because if it hadn't been for Pinkie's chewing it, I'd never have met you. . . . I tell you, Rosalie, Pinkie was some dog. (*Proudly displaying scar on wrist*) See that scar? That's where he bit me."

ROSALIE — He didn't mean to bite you.

REGGIE — Of course not. Why that dog fairly wor-shipped me. Only bit me twice. I felt terribly when he was stolen, Rosalia. You see he was all I had left. (*Puts shoe in box.*)

ROSALIE — Let's not talk about Pinky any more.

REGGIE — (*lays box beside him*). Well, there's an-other thing. Your lawyer didn't — I mean he should have — I mean — Hang it all, Rosalie, I'm rich, and I ought to pay you alimony.

ROSALIE — Why, Reggie! Of course not.

REGGIE — But I'd love to. (*Eagerly*) You needn't tell anybody about it. Just send your lawyer to my lawyer and they'll fix it up between them. And then I'll know you'll never want for anything.

ROSALIE — But I have everything I need. I have really.

REGGIE — Yes, but the time might come when you didn't. Please let me settle something on you. Rosalie.

ROSALIE — I couldn't, Reggie. But you're a dear to think of it.

REGGIE — I'm not. I'm a swine. Rosalie, tomor-row I'm —

ROSALIE — (*rises, interrupting him*). I thought we agreed not to talk about tomorrow.

REGGIE — We did. But there's something I've got to tell you sooner or later.

ROSALIE — Let's make it later, then.

REGGIE — I ought to have told you this afternoon. Only if I had you wouldn't have come to dinner. And if I told you now, you'd go home.

ROSALIE — Then I forbid you to tell me. I don't want to go home yet. I'm having a wonderful time.

Is it — Is it because of Monsieur Brousseau that
you —?

REGGIE — No! Yes! Let's not talk about him,
either.

ROSALIE — Are you jealous of him, Reggie?

REGGIE — I hate him. Rosalie, if he ever — (*He
stops abruptly.*)

ROSALIE — What were you going to say, Reggie?

REGGIE — Nothing.

ROSALIE — That isn't true.

REGGIE — I know it. I *was* going to say something. Only it seems so disloyal to talk about someone who — (*He stops.*)

ROSALIE — Reggie, I'd no idea you were such a
Puritan.

REGGIE — I'm not a Puritan. If I were, I wouldn't
be making love to another man's wife.

ROSALIE — But you *haven't* been making love to
me.

REGGIE — I have, too. If you knew anything about
me, you'd know that every time I've looked at you
I've told you I loved you.

ROSALIE — But you don't love me.

REGGIE — I do love you. I've always loved you.
(*As* ROSALIE *puts her handkerchief to her eyes and
sits L of table*) Why Rosalie, dearest! What is
it?

ROSALIE — I — I suppose it's because I — I'm
happy, Reggie. You see, when I came here this
afternoon, I — I — didn't know what had happened
to you. I — I hadn't seen you for so long, and — and
I thought perhaps — perhaps there might be someone
else. (*She glances at him to see how he takes this.
REGGIE starts guiltily and looks front*) But when you
told me — and oh, it was sweet to hear you say it —
that you thought — you thought it was wrong to marry
again, I — I felt so guilty.

REGGIE — So did I — (*She looks at him*) I mean one does get lonely.   And one marries again just because —

ROSALIE — No! No! One doesn't marry again if one cares. (*As he looks at her wonderingly*) You — you really love me?

REGGIE — (*turns away*). Yes, God help me.

ROSALIE — (*rise, very alluring*). I've heard that God helps those who help themselves.

REGGIE — (*turning to embrace her, then stopping gloomily*). Not if they help themselves to something they've no right to.

At which moment the arrival of Spencer Wells interrupts the charming tete-a-tete. Spencer just ran over to see how dear old Reggie was getting on, knowing he was ill and all that. The boys, having dinner at the club, were worried, too. He is a little surprised at finding Reggie quite himself, and more surprised at sight of Rosalie. Reggie tries diplomatically to avoid introducing them, but Rosalie is not at all willing to help him. She, in fact, is quite insistent on meeting Spencer, who finally introduces himself. " My name is Spencer Wells. I'm Reggie's best friend."

REGGIE — You are not!

ROSALIE — And I once had the honor of being Reggie's wife for a few minutes.

SPENCER — Oh! I'm awfully glad to meet you. It's a great pleasure to meet any wife of Reggie's.

ROSALIE — Has he so many wives?

SPENCER — Oh, no! But he's going to —

REGGIE — (*sharply*). Spencer!

ROSALIE — He's going to what, Mr. Wells?

SPENCER — He — he's going to — to Florida.

ROSALIE — So he told me. But perhaps — I only say perhaps, Mr. Wells — he'll change his mind.

SPENCER — Oh, I say! You can't back out at the last minute like that.

REGGIE — Don't worry, I have no idea of backing out.

ROSALIE — (*smiling*). Wait and see, Mr. Wells, wait and see.

There is no end to the interruptions after that. Reggie has given orders to both his servants that he is not to be disturbed — but that does little good. None at all in the case of a newspaper woman who insists she will stay until she sees Mr. Carter, no matter how long it takes. Reggie simply has to see her — which gives Rosalie a chance to try to find out a few things from Spencer Wells. But she finds Spencer fairly alert, in his blundering way, and rather resentful of her continued interest in Reggie.

SPENCER — But must we talk about Reggie? Can't you be interested in me a little?

ROSALIE — My dear man! Do you think I would have asked you all these questions if I hadn't been interested in you. You see I wanted to find out what kind of a butterfly you were.

SPENCER — Well, did you find out?

ROSALIE — I found out one thing. You certainly can keep a secret.

SPENCER — I say! What's that got to do with it?

ROSALIE — Nothing, because I know what it is Reggie told you not to tell me.

SPENCER — (*amused*). Oh, you do?

ROSALIE — Yes, I do — You don't believe me?

SPENCER — Well, of course I believe you believe you know.

ROSALIE — But I do know. Reggie told you —

SPENCER — Yes.

ROSALIE — Not to tell me —

SPENCER — Yes.

ROSALIE — Frankly, Mr. Wells, I don't approve of it at all.

SPENCER — Don't approve of what?

ROSALIE — Of Reggie's marrying that Hunter girl tomorrow.

SPENCER — Well, I'm dashed! Then you did know!

ROSALIE — (*laughs*). Of course, I did.

SPENCER — Well, Reggie doesn't know you know.

ROSALIE — I know he doesn't. He's been trying to tell me all evening only I wouldn't let him. What I didn't count on was his marrying so soon.

SPENCER — Oh, Reggie always marries in a hurry.

ROSALIE — But his engagement was only announced two weeks ago.

SPENCER — Oh, you knew about it two weeks ago?

ROSALIE — Yes. I read it in the *Paris Herald.*

SPENCER — And you hopped on a boat and came right over. What?

ROSALIE — Well you don't think I was going to let Reggie wreck his life, do you? What is she like, Mr. Wells?

SPENCER — Who? Marcia? Oh, she's like a kitten — purrs and scratches and plays about.

ROSALIE — Has she — has she red hair?

SPENCER — No. Marcia's hair isn't red.

ROSALIE — (*with sigh of relief*). I'm glad she hasn't red hair. That's the one thing I was afraid of. You want Reggie to be happy, don't you?

SPENCER — Of course I do.

ROSALIE — Then we must keep him from marrying that Hunter girl. He'll never be happy with her.

SPENCER — How do you know he won't?

ROSALIE — Because he doesn't love her.

SPENCER — How do you know he doesn't?

ROSALIE — Because he — he likes me better.

SPENCER — How do you know he does?

ROSALIE — He just the same as told me.

SPENCER — Did you make him tell you?

ROSALIE — Yes. But if it wasn't true he wouldn't have told me.

SPENCER — Why not? I would.

ROSALIE — Yes, but you're a butterfly. Reggie's not like that.

Spencer, however, feels that he should remain loyal to Marcia. As he sees it, Rosalie had her chance and missed it. Now it's Marcia's turn. Reggie can't jilt her at the foot of the altar. That wouldn't be at all nice. A line of reasoning that does not impress Rosalie at all. Then Marcia and her mother are heard in the hall, and it transpires that Rosalie had told her maid to phone them just as it was Rosalie who had sent for the newspaper woman. She was so curious to see what Reggie's fiancée was like. Marcia, like Spencer Wells, suffers too distinct shocks: First, on learning that Reggie is not at all ill, and, second, that he has deliberately put off his bachelor dinner in order to entertain his divorced wife. Naturally she is furious. "Why should Reggie treat me like this?" she demands. "Why, he wasn't sick at all. He just said he was sick so he could invite women to dinner." She crosses the room to face Rosalie. "You can have your old last year's husband!" she almost shouts. "I don't want him!"

ROSALIE — I hope you don't think I want him.

MARCIA — Well, if you don't want him, why are you here?

ROSALIE — I've already told you Reggie invited me to dinner. What I didn't tell you, not wishing to hurt your feelings, was that Reggie not only didn't tell me he was going to be married — he didn't even tell me he was engaged.

MARCIA — But that only makes it worse.

ROSALIE — I'm very cross with Reggie. He should have told me about you the very first thing this afternoon.

MARCIA — Do you hear that mother? She was here this afternoon too.

MRS. HUNTER — But Marcia —

MARCIA — (*to Mother*). Well you don't think I'm going to marry a man who invites his divorced wife to tea and dinner the day before my wedding, do you? I tell you, I won't stand it. I suppose he thinks he's the only man in the world. Well, he isn't. There are plenty of others. Men much nicer than Reggie. Why, there's one breaking his heart for me this minute. (*Looks at* SPENCER.)

MRS. HUNTER — Marcia!

MARCIA — Well, there is. Spencer.

SPENCER — (*jumps from table*). Now look here, Marcia. There's no use.

MARCIA — Don't worry. I don't mean you. It's Douglas.

SPENCER — Douglas?

MARCIA — Yes. He's waiting in the motor. Tell him I want him.

SPENCER — Exactly. I'll fetch him. Oh! Douglas, tender and true.

MRS. HUNTER — Marcia, why are you sending for that Ordway boy?

MARCIA — (*indicating* ROSALIE). To show some one I mean it when I say there are others.

MRS. HUNTER — Yes, but —

MARCIA — I'm going to marry Douglas —

MRS. HUNTER — You're not. I won't have it. What will people say?

MARCIA — I don't care what they say. I'm going
to marry Douglas.

MRS. HUNTER — But I tell you —

MARCIA — Now don't argue, mother. It won't do
any good.

MRS. HUNTER — (*to* ROSALIE). You're to blame
for this.

ROSALIE — Yes, I'm afraid I am. But I shouldn't
worry about it if I were you. She may change her
mind.

MRS. HUNTER — Oh, I hope you're right. Not that
I believe in divorce, but I can't seem to like that
Ordway boy. It's very uncharitable of me, I know.
But I've read some of his poems, and they seemed
to me quite immoral — not at all the kind of poems
one would want the father of one's grandchildren
to write.

Marcia finds she has been leaning on a frail reed in
Douglas. He is still deeply, passionately, utterly, hopelessly in love with her, and nothing would give him
greater pleasure than to marry her — but — unfortunately — he is already married! It wasn't altogether
his fault, but — Marcia is not interested in the details. With Douglas gone, Marcia changes her tactics.
She will not lose Reginald, too. Rather than see a
designing divorcee get him she will magnanimously
overlook the past and forgive him. Forgive him —
and hold him to his promise to wed her next day. Reggie tries to convince her that she should not forgive
him, that he doesn't deserve forgiveness, but she is
satisfied. She will be waiting for him at the church.
Reggie shows her to her motor and returns, hopelessly
crestfallen.

REGGIE — Rosalie, I don't suppose you'll ever forgive me.

ROSALIE — Why should I forgive you? Has it occurred to you I might not have accepted your invitation to dinner if I had known you had a fiancée who would come stalking in like a policeman.

REGGIE — But I didn't know she'd come stalking in. I thought I'd provided against that.

ROSALIE — Oh, you didn't intend I should know you were going to be married?

REGGIE — I did intend you to know it. I was going to tell you before you went home.

ROSALIE — Oh! You were saving it for the end — as a nice surprise?

REGGIE — Well, i couldn't have told you before.

ROSALIE — Certainly you could have told me before.

REGGIE — No, I couldn't. Because if I'd told you this afternoon, you wouldn't have come to dinner. And I had to see you again — I just had to.

ROSALIE — And why did you have to see me again?

REGGIE — You know very well why. From the moment you came into this room this afternoon, the only thing I could think about was seeing you again.

ROSALIE — Well, now that you've seen me again, are you satisfied?

REGGIE — No.

ROSALIE — But you're going to marry Miss Hunter tomorrow, aren't you?

REGGIE — Yes.

ROSALIE — Why are you going to marry her, Reggie?

REGGIE — Why? I've got to. She expects me to marry her. Her mother expects me to marry her. Everybody expects me to marry her.

ROSALIE — What of that? My mother expected me to be a boy and I was a girl. But I didn't mind.

REGGIE — That's just it. You don't mind. If you'd minded, you wouldn't have come to see me this afternoon, and upset my life like this.

ROSALIE — I didn't come to see you. I came to get my dog.

REGGIE — You always did care more for that damned dog than you did for me.

ROSALIE — Well, at least Pinkie was loyal to me.

REGGIE — How do you know he was? He probably forgot all about you the day after you left him. And even if he didn't, you don't think I'm going thru life being loyal to another man's wife do you?

ROSALIE — Why not? Lots of men do.

REGGIE — Well, I'm not like that. I'm going to play the game.

ROSALIE — You mean you're going to be loyal to Miss Marcia Hunter?

REGGIE — Yes.

ROSALIE — That's good. Miss Hunter is charming, Reggie. I like her — quite as much as she likes me. I'm sure you'll be very happy with her.

REGGIE — I won't!! How can I be happy with her, when I love you?

ROSALIE — Do you call that being loyal to Miss Hunter?

REGGIE — I didn't say I *was* loyal to Miss Hunter — I said I was going to be.

ROSALIE — Oh —! Tomorrow?

REGGIE — Yes.

ROSALIE — Well, I hope you have a nice day for it. . . . (*Extending her hand*) Goodbye. (*They shake hands. She goes to the doors and throws them open.*)

REGGIE — Will you — will you kiss me goodbye, Rosalie?

ROSALIE — Do you think I should?

REGGIE — No, you shouldn't, but I wish you would. Will you?

ROSALIE — No, Reggie.

REGGIE — All right. I'm sorry I asked you. But

don't think I'm going to let you hang like a black cloud over my life. I'm not. ' Tomorrow I'll have a wife — one who appreciates me — one who is kind and thoughtful — one who forgives me when I do the wrong thing. There was a time, tonight, when I felt I'd made a mistake — when the few hours of happiness we've had together seemed worth more than all the future. But I know different now. My future is Marcia's. I'll be absolutely loyal to her. And I won't wait until tomorrow to begin. I'll begin now — tonight.

ROSALIE — Is this final, Reggie?

REGGIE — Absolutely!

ROSALIE — Even if I've changed my mind. Even if I'll say goodbye to you the way you want me to.

REGGIE — (*radiantly*). Rosalie! Will you?

ROSALIE — (*backs up*). No, Reggie. I only wanted to find out how loyal you really were. Goodnight.

She goes out, smiling sweetly over her shoulder at Reggie, who is doing what he can to " express rage " — and succeeding admirably.

ACT III

At 11:30 o'clock next morning all is in readiness for the wedding of Reginald Carter and Marcia Hunter at St. Martin's, the bishop himself having consented to perform the ceremony. Spencer Wells, feeling extraordinarily nippy after a good night's rest, is also ready, having had his white gloves sand-papered so there will be little danger of his dropping the ring. Reggie, however, is still a trifle low in his mind, and nothing seems to cheer him. Even Spencer's suggestion that he try a stimulant is frowned upon.

REGGIE — I don't want a cocktail.   Spencer, do you believe in God?

SPENCER — Good God, yes.   Why?

REGGIE — Nothing.   Only it's a damned solemn thing to get married — especially the second time. And you get to thinking about things, and wondering.   (*He kneels down by sofa.*)

SPENCER — (*in an awed voice*).   Are you going to pray?

REGGIE — No, you idiot!   I'm looking for something.   (*He reaches under sofa and secures Pinkie's chewed shoe.*)

SPENCER — (*Eyeing shoe*).   What are you going to do — throw old shoes at yourself when you get married?

REGGIE — This isn't a shoe, Spencer, it's a symbol. If it hadn't been for this shoe I mightn't have met Rosalie.   I said I was going to keep it as long as I lived.   But I'm beginning a new life today, and I'm going to begin it right.   I've got to.   After the way Marcia acted last night it's the only thing to do.   She has a noble nature, Spencer.   (*Picks up wastebasket and throws shoe into it*)   So that's the end of that.

SPENCER — Goodbye Rosalie, what?

REGGIE — Yes.   I've put Rosalie out of my life. I'm never going to even think of her again.

At which point the door opens and Rosalie enters, cheerily.   She has come, presumably, to see her maid, who happens to be the wife of Reggie's man.   But Reggie is suspicious.   He believes she is there merely to devil him.

ROSALIE — (*to* REGGIE).   I wish I could have found time to go to your wedding, Reggie, but you see how it is —

fering tortures you would only laugh at me.   If I was
dying you wouldn't raise a finger to save me.

ROSALIE — (*smiling*).   You're   wrong,   Reggie.   I
would raise a finger.   (*She raises one finger.*)

REGGIE — (*further   enraged*).   I   don't   know   what
I ever saw in you.   You're not even a human being.
You're a devil, that's what you are.   But I'm through.
If you don't believe me, look in the wastebasket.

As Reggie rushes away to church, not at all in the
humor of a happy bridegroom, Rosalie smilingly picks
the shoe out of the wastebasket, rings for Reggie's
valet and has him bring in one of Reggie's traveling
bags.   In the bag she carefully packs the shoe.   Then
she sends for Douglas Ordway, Douglas being the
youth who wanted so much to marry Marcia Hunter,
but could not because he had inadvertently, as it were,
already married another.   Rosalie has discovered acci-
dently, as frequently happens in farce, that she knows
the woman; that she was an English girl Douglas had
met on a Surrey farm, and that she had no right to
marry Douglas, because she, too, had been married
before to a man in her own class.   Later she had
gone into service and was even now Rosalie's maid.
This leaves Douglas free to marry Marcia — if she is
not already married to Reggie.   Which Rosalie has
reason to suspect she is not.   Her suspicions are confirmed when the wedding party comes trooping back
to the house.   The bishop, having learned from a note
he received just before the hour set for the wedding
that Reggie is a divorced man, had refused to perform
the ceremony.   Reggie has gone in search of a " regular " clergyman who will not be so strict, and everybody is terribly excited.

MRS.   HUNTER — Think   what   it   meant!   Everybody there — St. Martin's crowded — the bridesmaids

ready — the altar decorated — and Reginald divorced. (*She breaks down and wipes her eyes.*)

DOUGLAS — (*hopefully*). Mrs. Hunter, I've never been divorced.

MARCIA — Do you hear that, Mother? Douglas has never been divorced. He's never been married either. He only thought he was.

SPENCER — What?

MARCIA — Yes, Spencer. An unscrupulous adventuress took advantage of his youth and inexperience. She already had a husband.

SPENCER — By Jove! Did she though?

MARCIA — Yes. (*To* MRS. HUNTER) So you see, mother. I can be married in St. Martin's after all — if I marry Douglas.

DOUGLAS — (*takes her hand*). My angel!

MARCIA — (*she withdraws hand shrewishly*). Be quiet!

MRS. HUNTER — (*harshly*). But Marcia, you can't do a thing like that. People will think you're crazy.

MARCIA — I don't care if they do. Besides, they think I'm crazy, anyway, trying to marry a divorced man like that in St. Martin's.

MRS. HUNTER — But Marcia!

MARCIA — (*smiles at* DOUGLAS). Now don't argue, mother. I've made up my mind.

Making up her mind was easy enough — but who is to tell Reggie? And what will he think? Perhaps he will hold her to her promise, after all. Then Reggie enters, all enthusiasm at having found his clergyman.

REGGIE — It's all right. I've got him. He's a Presbyterian. He's a regular human being, too. Didn't seem to care that — (*he snaps his fingers*) when I told him I'd been divorced. (*Others have listened indifferently. Seeing* DOUGLAS) Oh, hullo, Douglas! Did you hear about the way they treated us at St. Martin's? A nice thing to do to us, wasn't it? Why I've been a stockholder — I mean pewholder — in that Church for years.

MARCIA — But Reggie, *they* couldn't help it.

REGGIE — Certainly they could. Who gave them the land they built their old church on? My father. Who left them a hundred thousand dollars in his will? My father. And that Bishop? Who got him his job?

SPENCER — Your father.

REGGIE — Exactly! And they wouldn't even suspend one of their bylaws for me! Talk about gratitude — they don't know what it means! (*Suddenly conscious that they are all regarding him gravely*) What's the matter? Anything wrong?

MARCIA — Tell him, mother.

MRS. HUNTER — (*up and down L*). I will not.

MARCIA — (*appealingly to* SPENCER). Spencer!

SPENCER — Not on your life!

MARCIA — Douglas?

DOUGLAS — (*stepping forward bravely*). Yes, it's my place to tell him. Reggie, I'm about to impart — we think you should know — it has become necessary that you should be informed — (*He pauses and clears his throat*) Reggie — (*Stopping and glancing desparingly at* MARCIA) I can't tell him.

REGGIE — (*irritably*). Tell me what? What's the matter with everybody?

MARCIA — It's about the minister you telephoned to, Reggie.

REGGIE — Didn't you tell me to telephone for a minister?

MARCIA — Yes, but — Reggie, you know how mother has set her heart on my being married in St. Martin's.

REGGIE — Yes, Marcia. But it can't be done. There isn't any way.

MARCIA — I know a way, Reggie.

REGGIE — You do? What is it?

MARCIA — Well, you see, the only reason *we* can't be married in St. Martin's is because you've been divorced. So I thought, in order not to disappoint mother —

REGGIE — Yes. *Go* on.

MARCIA — In order not to disappoint mother — (*She begins to weep, and flies to her mother, burying her face in her shoulder, in a muffled voice*) Mother, you tell him.

MRS. HUNTER — Yes, darling. (*To* REGGIE) Reginald, if I had a son I couldn't be any fonder of him than I am of you. If my little Stephen had lived he would be almost your age. First my poor dear husband passed away. Then my little Stephen — (*Overcome at the tender recollection, she weeps on* MARCIA.)

REGGIE — (*to* SPENCER *in a hushed voice*). For God's sake, Spencer! What's the matter?

SPENCER — (*in a hushed voice*). Little Stephen. He passed away, you know.

REGGIE — Oh! (*After a pause*) But what's that got to do with it?

SPENCER — (*in a low voice*). Nothing.

REGGIE — (*bewildered*). But hang it all. (*To* MARCIA) Look here, Marcia. You're hiding something from me.

MARCIA — (*uncovering a tearful face*). Yes.

Finally the truth is told and Reggie knows that Marcia has definitely decided to marry Douglas. It will be much simpler that way, she explains, seeing that mother would be so disappointed without a wedding in St. Martin's. " Oh, I'm so ashamed to tell you,

Reggie. I don't suppose you'll ever forgive me. But I don't think I ever loved you as much as a girl should love the man she's going to marry. And even if I did, I don't now, because I love Douglas more, and —

REGGIE — Do you mean to tell me you want to marry Douglas instead of me?

MARCIA — (*humbly*). Yes, please.

REGGIE — (*looks around*). Well, I think you might have mentioned it before. This is a pretty time to tell me about it.

MARCIA — Then you won't give me up?

REGGIE — Certainly I'll give you up. I'm delighted to give you up. Nothing would please me more.

MARCIA — You darling!

So Reggie finds himself with a Presbyterian minister, a wedding ring and a developing grouch on his hands. Nobody loves him and he is quite depressed. Even Rosalie's increasing good humor fails to cheer him.

ROSALIE — Reggie — can I be of any help?

REGGIE — I don't need any help — I'm going away.

ROSALIE — Where are you going?

REGGIE — I don't know where I'm going — if I knew I wouldn't go there.

ROSALIE — Oh, if that's where you're going. Here's your bag. (*Picks up bag — brings it down.*)

REGGIE — (*grabs other handle of bag*). Leave that bag alone.

ROSALIE — But I want to help.

REGGIE — I don't want any help — I want my bag. (*Pulls bag open. Seeing shoe*) Who put that shoe in my bag?

ROSALIE — (*snatching shoe and returning it to bag*). I did. (*They drop bag on floor.*)

REGGIE — (*taking it out and throwing it on table*).
Well, I don't want it.

ROSALIE — Why, Reggie! You said you were going to keep that shoe as long as you lived.

REGGIE — Yes. And you said you were going to
love, honor and obey me as long as you lived. And
what did *you* do? You left me three days after you
said it.

ROSALIE — And why did I leave you? What did
you tell me I looked like?

REGGIE — Well, you did look like one with that
damned red hair.

ROSALIE — I had a perfect right to dye my hair.
Not many women would have made the sacrifice I
did.

REGGIE — Sacrifice?

ROSALIE — Certainly it was a sacrifice. You don't
suppose I wanted red hair, do you. But my husband
liked red hair. So I — poor deluded creature — tried
to give him what he wanted.

REGGIE — I never wanted you to have red hair. I
hate red hair. But of course I'm to blame. Oh, yes!
I'm to blame for everything! It's my fault you ran
away — it's my fault you dyed your hair — it's my
fault your dog was stolen.

But it transpires that " Pinky " was not stolen.
Rosalie had had him all the time. "It seemed too
much to lose a husband and a perfectly good dog,"
she explains to Reggie, " so I wired the porter at your
hotel, and he sent me ' Pinky ' by express."

"Well, I'm damned!" shouts Reggie. "And I
paid that porter five dollars a day just to keep looking
for that dog."

ROSALIE — (*to* PINKY). Do you hear that, Pinky?
He thought it was wonderful. And he had your boo-

ful shoe all ready for you. (*To* REGGIE)   Give Pinky his shoe, Reggie.

REGGIE — (*happily*).   Yes. (*He picks up shoe*) No! (*He throws it down*)   I'm damned if I'm going to give my shoe to another man's dog.

ROSALIE — But he isn't, Reggie.   He's our dog — yours and mine.

REGGIE — Yes.   That's what you tell all your husbands.

ROSALIE — But I haven't any husband

REGGIE — My God!   Did you divorce that Frenchman, too?

ROSALIE — There wasn't any Frenchman.

REGGIE — What?

ROSALIE — No, Reggie.   When I called on you yesterday afternoon, I was afraid you wouldn't see me so I sent in my dress-maker's card.

REGGIE — Then you didn't marry anybody?

ROSALIE — No, Reggie.

REGGIE — Oh, Rosalie! (*There is broad smile of joy flitting over* REGINALD's *face as he embraces* ROSALIE, *followed by an expression of determination suggesting that she will certainly have a time of it if she ever tries to get away from him again.*)

"MAMMA'S AFFAIR"

An American Comedy in Three Acts

By Rachel Barton Butler

WHEN Oliver Morosco, the New York producer, heard that John Craig, of the Castle Square Stock Company in Boston, had withdrawn his annual offer of a $500 prize for the best play written by a student of Prof. George Baker's " English 47 " class of Harvard and Radcliffe, he immediately substituted a prize of his own for a like amount, to be awarded under the same terms.

As a result of this offer some forty plays were submitted to the Morosco office during the fall and early winter, and of the forty " Mamma's Affair," a satirical comedy written by Rachel Barton Butler, an alumnus of the Baker class, was awarded the prize. It was produced at the remodeled Little Theatre in New York, Monday evening Jan. 29, was well received, both by its reviewers and a public attracted to it, possibly by reason of its exploitation as " the Harvard prize play." After five weeks in this theatre the play was transferred to the Fulton Theatre, (Feb. 9,) where it added an additional eight weeks to its run.

" Mamma's Affair " is the story of a sentimental hypochondriac. " It pleases her to think that she is ill and thereby absorb all the energy and attention of every human being in contact with her." For two years Eve Orrin and her mamma have been traveling in search of Mrs. Orrin's health. They have been accompanied on this pilgrimage by Mrs. Orrin's dearest girlhood friend, Mrs. Marchant, and the latter's son, Henry. It is the desire of both mothers that Henry shall marry Eve, in the expectation that the great love they bear each other will thus be perpetuated. Henry is quite agreeable to the arrangement and Eve has accepted him, though more "on mamma's account" than her own. They have now arrived at "The Willows," a hotel in the Massachusetts hills where Mrs. Orrin and Mrs. Marchant had gone to school, and it is here the wedding of the young people is to take place within the month.

In the hotel Mrs. Orrin's room has been selected with great care, with Mrs. Marchant superintending the arrangements, Henry executing them and Eve bustling about nervously to see that they are perfect.

MRS. MARCHANT — Henry dear — Did you speak to the proprietor about the extra pillows for Grace?

HENRY — I did, Mother.

MRS. M.— And did you explain dear Grace might have to have all her meals in her rooms?

HENRY — Yes.

MRS. M.— Is this the quiet side of the house?

HENRY — It is—

MRS. M.— And could you arrange for our suite near, so I can be close to dear Grace?

HENRY — It is directly across the hall.

MRS. M.—(*letting out a breath of relief*). *Henry* dear, you're perfect.

HENRY —(*modestly*). Thank you.

MRS. M.— I have the strangest feeling! It's as if something *terrible* were going to happen.

HENRY —(*impatiently*). My dear mother —

MRS. M.— My son! My feelings are an infallible guide! Poor Grace —

HENRY — There's nothing going to happen to Mrs. Orrin, mother.

MRS. M.— I can't help it. I have a terrible premonition that Grace is going to be ill.

HENRY — Mrs. Orrin will be delighted to be ill if you'll just speak to her about it, mother.

Henry, " a tall, hay colored young man, with soulful eyes and a sonorous voice," is much more concerned about his approaching marriage and Eve's attitude toward him than he is about Mrs. Orrin, a state of mind he reveals in their first scene together.

HENRY — Only a month — just for a short month — and there will be no separation — no moment we must share with others — no time when we shall be apart !

EVE —(*steadily but without warmth*). No, Henry.

HENRY — To call you — my wife ! I cannot believe such happiness awaits for me. " Forsaking all others, cleave only unto him so long as ye both shall live."

EVE —(*absently and slowly*). It's a very long promise — isn't it?

HENRY — Long! (*He takes her hand in his*) Don't you wish it were longer? Don't you wish we could promise for eternity?

EVE — Henry — if you'll open the shutters —

HENRY — O !

EVE — Dear ! Mamma tires so — when she has to wait —

HENRY — Everything tires your mother except having you hang over her, kissing and petting her. If it comes to fatigue, *I'm* tired of never having you to myself for an instant without a howl from your mother.

EVE — Henry ! You know how delicate Mamma is !

HENRY — She isn't delicate ! She only thinks she is.

EVE — Henry ! You're cruel ! Every doctor we've ever had has said —

HENRY — Every doctor you've ever had has been a fashionable toadier — who's found out what your mother wanted to have and has let her have it — from brain fever to floating kidney!

EVE — Henry!

HENRY — The one doctor in Kalamazoo who was poor enough to tell her the truth — you dismissed at his first call.

EVE — And perfectly properly! He was not a competent physician. To dare to speak so to mamma! Please, please, Henry, try to *understand* her!

HENRY —(*grimly, exasperated*). I understand your mother — you yourself look a great deal sicker than she does.

EVE — Will you get mamma, Henry? I'll open the shutters. (*They bring* MRS. ORRIN *in. She is a frail, slender little lady, very pale-eyed, with a sweet, indefinite voice and lifeless hair. Whatever the prevailing mode she always somehow conveys the idea of trailing. She is a determined sentimentalist and her voice drips as honey from the comb. Her smile matches the voice."*)

MRS. ORRIN — Ah! what a charming room! (*Smiling the wan but determined smile of an accomplished invalid*) Too bad of me, Eve, little daughter, to spoil our perfect trip with one of my headaches!

EVE —(*tenderly*). You haven't spoiled it, Mamma darling.

MRS. ORRIN — How patient all of you are with me. I had hoped not to intrude even one of my headaches on yours and Henry's happiness. I wanted no cloud to darken the sunshine of these lovely, tender days before your marriage. (*Smiling sweetly to* HENRY) You are very good to me, Henry.

HENRY — (*sourly*). Not at all, Mrs. Orrin.

MRS. O.— You are your mother's son, Henry. Who could dream of anything but gentleness and kindness from dear Judith's boy Do you see my salts bottle anywhere, Henry?

EVE —(*anxiously*). On the table Henry. (*Henry goes to get it.*)

MRS. O.—It's so distressing to be so dependent on others. Was there a little tea in the thermos, Eve, Dear?

EVE — I'm not sure — (*She goes to thermos and opens it*).

MRS. ORRIN —(*to* HENRY *who presents salts*). Thank you, Henry, how sweet you are!

HENRY — Not at all, Mrs. Orrin.

EVE —(*referring to tea*). There is only a little — let me make you some fresh!

MRS. ORRIN — No, no! That will do — just a swallow — my poor head. Does it seem cool in here to you, Henry?

HENRY —(*wrathfully*). No, Mrs. Orrin, I can't say that it does.

MRS. ORRIN — Then it must be I — my circulation's so poor.

EVE — Dear, are you chilled? Henry dear, there's a knitted shawl — on the bed — I think (*Henry goes into the inner room.*)

MRS. O.—(*to* EVE *who has put the tea in a cup*). Thank you love. Now kiss me — (EVE *does so.* HENRY *returns in time to witness it*). (*To* HENRY *who carries the shawl as if it were a dangerous breakable*) Just around my shoulders, Henry dear — How patient you are, Henry —

HENRY — Not at all, Mrs. Orrin.

MRS. O.— What a son you will be to me.

EVE — Dear, you'd better not try to talk for a little.

MRS. O.—(*leaning back in her chair and closing her eyes*). Perhaps you are right, my pet! Ah! (*Her face contracts as if with pain. Murmuring*) The light!

Eve — Too much for your poor head? I opened the shutters because I thought it would be more cheerful — but we'll shut them again.

Mrs. O.— The coming back here — to the scene of my early girlhood. The sight of the place — so familiar and yet so strange.

Eve — O, mamma! Perhaps we shouldn't have come.

Mrs. O.— No, no, my pet! It has been Judith's and my dream — ever since Henry and you have been bethrothed — to come back for your wedding to this scene of our old school days! This headache — this nervous collapse — it is only the result of too great happiness. Happiness overwhelms me — like a wave! I suffer — but I suffer an ecstasy! Kiss me! (*During this Henry enters and slams door on the "Kiss me."*)

With Mrs. Orrin comfortably settled the next most important thing is to get a physician to attend her. " Mamma never travels without a list of physicians in every large town and city where we are going to be." In this instance a certain Dr. Jansen has been recommended. He is a " tall, smooth-shaven, somewhat ruddy young man in the pink of condition. . . . He pleasantly but never aggressively radiates health and fine spirits. He is bubbling over with the very latest scientific ideas and bounteous enthusiasm, but his professional repose would do credit to a man of 50." Dr. Jansen is quick to note the unnatural paleness of Eve, and assumes that she is his patient. But Mrs. Orrin promptly corrects him.

Mrs. O.— The child is so intense. Sometimes, I think our love for each other is an agony.

Doctor (*grimly*). I am quite prepared to believe that, Mrs. Orrin —(*as the door closes on Eve, briskly*)

Now, my dear lady, what can I do for you? (*Sits chair left of chaise lounge.*)

Mrs. Orrin — Ah, Dr. Jansen, how many physicians have asked me that question. And how recurringly difficult I find it to answer them! (*She applies her handkerchief to her eyes.*)

Dr. Jansen —(*prosaically taking her wrist to feel her pulse*). You've been motoring all day, do I understand?

Mrs. Orrin — All the way from town — since early this morning.

Doctor — That would readily account for fatigue. Pulse is good.

Mrs. Orrin —(*opening her eyes anxiously*). Doesn't it miss a beat?

Doctor — Quite regular.

Mrs. Orrin —(*removes her hand and feels her own pulse*). How strange! Dr. Schell always finds it misses a beat, when one of these collapses is on me.

Doctor — You have Dr. Schell in town?

Mrs. Orrin —(*with enthusiasm*). Yes. Ah, there is a man who has given his life to the understanding of just such women as I.

Doctor —(*drily*). He has indeed, Mrs. Orrin, done just that.

Mrs. Orrin — He is the only one who has ever really understood my case. How many times has he said to me: "Dear Mrs. Orrin, you live too intensely!" And I have replied: "Can you deaden a heart too aware of the joys and sufferings of others? Can you cure me — of life?"

Doctor —(*prosaically*). How is the appetite?

Mrs. Orrin — Fitful — always fitful! When my emotions are stirred, my appetite goes.

Doctor — You have been under a nervous strain for some length of time?

Mrs. Orrin — For the past three months, I have

suffered — exquisite pain — my daughter — my little
Eve —   (*She breaks off.*)
    DOCTOR —(*waking up*).   Your daughter — yes?
    MR.. ORRIN — She is soon to be married.
    DOCTOR —(*patiently*).   Yes.   (*Short pause*)   You
do not approve of her choice of a husband?
    MRS. ORRIN — Ah, how little a man can read a
mother's heart.   She has chosen the one man of all
the world who would have been my choice.   But can
you not guess what it means to me to give her to
another?   To share the sweet intimacy of her daily,
hourly presence!   Dr. Jansen, I have lived in her
since her first breath.   I have been a widow since she
was a year old.   All that was denied me in my early
wifehood, I have poured into living in my motherhood!
She is more than my daughter — she is the heart of
me.   Every beat of her pulse I can feel is mine.
When she goes from me to another, one part of me
will die.   I — (*As she opens her mouth on the pro-
noun the doctor deftly inserts the thermometer which
he has taken out of his pocket*).
    DOCTOR —(*very politely*).   Please pardon me —
just a moment.   (MRS. ORRIN *is reduced to reproach-
ful silence sucking the thermometer*)   Now, Mrs. Orrin, we must set about mending these nerves of yours.
And first of all, I am going to prescribe the simplest
remedy I know — rest.   (MRS. ORRIN *tries to protest
around the thermometer*)   Just a moment, please.
Absolute rest — and quiet.   No one in your room —
particularly not your daughter —   (MRS. ORRIN *again
tries to speak around the thermometer*)   Just a moment now —   (*He looks at his watch*)   No conversation that will tend to excite her — I mean you —
just a moment — above all — rest —   (*He takes the
thermometer*)   Thank you —   (*He rises, crosses to
center, looking at thermometer, shows his disgust at
her having no temperature.*)

MRS. ORRIN —(*disappointed*). Nothing to take?

DOCTOR —(*as to a child*). O yes, indeed. You shall have something to take. There will be a nerve tablet every half hour — unless you are sleeping. Light nourishment at six — a powder at eight and I'll have my druggist send up a new prescription I've found very successful in er — just such cases as yours.

MRS. ORRIN —(*in great relief*). Thank you. I thought there must be something to take.

DOCTOR — Now may I suggest you retire — at once, (MRS. ORRIN *rises as if hypnotized and moves toward the door into the chamber*) while I'm still here — and will you send your daughter to me for — er — instructions?

MR.. ORRIN —(*turns at door R*). O — you didn't tell me! Have I a temperature?

DOCTOR —(*cheerfully*). Not a fraction of a degree.

MRS. ORRIN.— How very odd! Dr. Schell always finds I have a temperature when I've had one of these emotional collapses.

Dr. Jansen tries to reassure Eve that her mother is in no great danger. She needs rest and quiet — and a good supper —"two soft boiled eggs, a good dish of milk toast, a substantial salad and some cooked fruit."

EVE —(*guilelessly*). Is that — a light supper?

DOCTOR —(*at his most professional*). Nothing there that will not agree in this case. In fact — I think you'll find she can take it — all.

EVE —(*looking up for more instructions*). Yes?

DOCTOR — That's all.

EVE — All?

DOCTOR —(*with finality*). All.

EVE — You're *sure* it's not serious?

DOCTOR — I stake my professional reputation on it — it is not. (EVE *gives a sigh of relief*.)

DOCTOR —(*casually. At window*). Have you noticed — we are paying our devotions to you with a glorious sunset?

EVE —(*absently*). Yes. (*Starts up.*)

DOCTOR — Come — look.

EVE —(*going up to the window.*) It's very lovely, isn't it? But I don't believe I care much for nature. Sometimes sunsets make me tired.

DOCTOR —(*encouraging her to talk*). Really! Now I imagined you enjoyed that sort of thing.

EVE — I have looked at some sunsets that only made me want to go into a dirty kitchen and fry eggs.

DOCTOR —(*laughing*). That's a stiff reaction — unless you're particularly fond of eggs.

EVE — Not particularly — but I'd like to try frying some.

DOCTOR —(*turns to look out of window*). Well, you'll not deny our godly chapel spire does the proper thing. Lifts its head to Heaven against the evening glow, et cetera.

EVE — That's the chapel where I'm to be married next month.

DOCTOR — What!

EVE — That's the chapel where I'm to be married next month.

DOCTOR — Pardon me — I didn't understand it was so soon — nor here.

EVE —(*in a monotonous voice, hardly noticing him*). That's why we've come here. Mother and Mrs. Marchant learnt their prayer book in that chapel. So now that — that — Henry and I are to be married, we came up here to crown their joy — they say — by being married here. (*Sits on chaise longue.*)

DOCTOR —(*quietly*). You will forgive me, I am sure, a professional question. How old are you, Miss Orrin?

Eve — Eighteen.

Doctor — Good God!

Eve —(*in the same monotonous voice*). It has been the dream of their lives that Henry and I should marry. And now we're going to — next month. Do you know — in the service — you have to say —" Forsaking all others, cleave only unto him?" (*Short pause.*)

Doctor —(*to himself*). Eighteen! (*Aloud*) Miss Orrin, you can't have been out of school long.

Eve — I never went to school, really. Never to go away. Mother couldn't have me far from her — so I went to a little day school. And then there were governesses and lessons at home.

Doctor — And when were you through with those?

Eve — Last year. Then we travelled — out through Northern Canada and down through California.

Doctor — The Marchants were with you, I suppose?

Eve — O — of course. The scenery was lovely.

Doctor —(*smiling*). And did you want to fry eggs?

Eve — O — a good many times.

Doctor —(*gravely*). Did you go to Santa Barbara?

Eve — Yes. Henry and I got engaged there.

Doctor — I've heard it's a heady place. (*Pause*) (*Abruptly*) Miss Orrin, you must forgive me if I seem officious — but won't you let me give you something for yourself. You look fagged out.

Eve —(*as if bringing herself back from far off*). O thank you, no. I am quite well. Only tired.

Doctor — I suppose you've not had much appetite the past few days?

Eve — How did you know? (*Turning to him.*)

Doctor — I — guessed. Not sleeping much?

Eve — Not much. (*Rises*) But mamma mustn't know that. Don't tell her. I keep perfectly still all night — and she doesn't guess.

Doctor — You mean — you have been sleeping in the same room with her?

Eve — (*simply*). O yes! Of course. I have never slept away from my mother.

Doctor — (*grimly*). Pardon me, that is a very bad practice. Then you won't let me prescribe for you?

Eve — (*very politely but wearily*). O, thank you! You are very kind to bother — but — I'll manage — somehow! (*The doctor grips his jaw over some very evident violence. Short pause.*)

Doctor — Well, then, since I can be of no professional service to you I'll not keep you. Goodnight. (*He puts out his hand.*)

Eve — (*putting hers into it*). Goodnight — and thank you. (*The doctor starts. At the door he turns as if to make one last effort.*)

Doctor — I —

Eve — (*noticing that he has stopped*). Can you find your way?

Doctor — Thank you. I think I know my **way** — in fact it's quite clear.

After the doctor has gone Eve continues to stare at the sunset. So intent is she upon the scene, and so wrapped in thought, she does not hear her mother enter the room. At the touch of her hand she starts, and moves excitedly away from her. Nor are her sentimental mother's efforts to soothe her effective.

Mrs. Orrin — Look! The evening star! How many times have I said: Star light, star bright — and made a wish for you, my darling. I have wished for you the only real crown of a woman's life — love, love, love! (*Half playfully*) It's love that makes the world go 'round. (EVE *makes a curious sound as if she took in her breath sharply*) (MRS. ORRIN *crossing quickly to her*) Love, you are crying — I know how perfect joy can end in tears —

EVE —(*rushing past her in terror*).—Don't touch me — don't come near me — (*She crosses to center and throws herself on the floor, pounding and crying, hysterical, until the curtain*) Go away, I can't stand it — I can't stand it — I hate sunsets — I hate the moon — I hate the stars — Oh, why was I ever born — why — why?

MRS. ORRIN —(*thoroughly frightened she goes to door left, calling*). Someone come — help — the bell — where is the bell — (*She sees* HENRY *coming*) Oh! Henry, Henry, come quick —

HENRY —(*entering quickly*). (*He sees* EVE *huddled on the floor*) What is it — for God's sake, Mrs. Orrin, what is it?

MRS. ORRIN —(*hurrying him off*). Go, go for the doctor at once, hurry go — (HENRY *exits*) Eve, Eve — my baby — my baby —

(Curtain)

ACT II

A month later Eve is living in a private suite on the top floor of the hotel. Dr. Jansen, following her collapse, ordered that she should be kept there, in charge of his own housekeeper, Mrs. Bundy —"a small, round, brown-eyed, rosy-cheeked, snowy-haired, motherly, cozy little lady"— and should neither be permitted to see nor to communicate with any member of her party. All the letters that her mother and Henry have attempted to smuggle in to her have been pigeonholed. Under this " rest cure " treatment Eve has fairly blossomed. " Her cheeks are faintly pink and her eyes bright, but not from excitement." She has acquired an electric stove and revels in the preparation of her own breakfast. Still she is a little worried about her mother. " You're sure Mamma is perfectly well, Mrs. Bundy ?"

MRS. BUNDY — Perfectly. my dear.

EVE — What does she do all day?

MRS. BUNDY — These warm days she and Mrs. Marchant sit for hours on a corrugated iron bench at the end of the yard — and talk —

EVE — What about?

MRS. BUNDY — Well, Mrs. Marchant talks about Henry and your mother talks about you.

EVE — What does Henry do?

MRS. BUNDY —(*with a touch of severity*). Henry prowls. He haunts the stairway — and the corridor — I've almost fallen over him in the dark once or twice.

. . . .

EVE — I've been happy, Mrs. Bundy, these past few weeks. Perfectly, *gloriously* happy! After those first ten days in bed of course —   But now I can do things — cook — and go out each morning with the doctor on his rounds! I just sit in the sun and *am*! (*Pause*) He's a very remarkable physician, isn't he, Mrs. Bundy!

MRS. BUNDY — Yes, my dear, he's a very remark-able — physician.

. . . .

EVE — It's strange. isn't it. Mrs. Bundy. that the doctor never married.

MRS. BUNDY — Never! Good gracious child! Give him time!

EVE — O, but he's never going to marry!

MRS. BUNDY —(*drily*). So he tells me every time he meets an attractive woman.

EVE — But the doctor's never going to marry as a matter of principle.

MRS. BUNDY — Indeed. He's full of notions. What's the principle for never marrying, pray?

EVE — He says there's a strong prejudice against *un*-married physicians. So he's going to remain unmarried and succeed, too, just to put the damned public in its place.

MRS. BUNDY — Miss Eve!

EVE — O, that's not my " damn," Bunny. It's the doctor's.

MRS. BUNDY — So I'm aware. I've broken him of many of his bad habits but I haven't succeeded in breaking him of swearing — (*shutting her mouth tight*) yet.

Suddenly there appears a slight flaw in the amber of Eve's new-found happiness. She discovers that having paid no attention to the flight of time she has approached her wedding day without realizing it. To-morrow, according to the calendar, she should become the wife of Henry Marchant — and the idea is plainly disturbing. But Dr. Jansen has foreseen that interruption to the continued progress of his patient and counseled the postponement of the wedding. Which rather interests the observing Mrs. Bundy.

MRS. BUNDY — You're very much interested in this case, aren't you?

DOCTOR — Very.

MRS. BUNDY — (*significantly*). I noticed.

DOCTOR — (laughing). Wrong scent, Bunny; I'm interested — purely scientifically — in Miss Orrin. She's criminally and needlessly neuresthenic.

MRS. BUNDY — (*with knowing look*). O — I see.

DOCTOR — Now, Bunny, use your reason. Didn't I withstand the new organist even when you said she played " Abide With Me " right at my head?

MRS. BUNDY — She was fifty and had a squint.

(*Slight pause*)   Has it by chance occurred to you that
Miss Eve might fall in love with you?

DOCTOR — What! ! !

MRS. BUNDY — I thought you hadn't considered the
possibility.

DOCTOR —(*crisply*).   Rot!   (*Short pause*)   Rot!
You're incurably romantic!   (*Another short pause
—somewhat uncomfortable . . . on the part of the
doctor*)   Utter nonsense! ·

MRS. BUNDY —(*with   placid   maliciousness*).   O.
I'm not implying, it's because of your hopeless at-
tractiveness.   But she's young and inexperienced.
Your cure of her has had certain romantic aspects.
Being up here by herself the past month has left her
little to think about, *but* you.   It could easily happen.

DOCTOR —(*after a moment's growing conviction, his
scientific mind taking it in*).   Hell!   I beg your pardon, Mrs. Bundy, but — hell!   That's psychologically
sound.

MRS. BUNDY — It's humanly sound.

DOCTOR —(*in growing alarm*).   I'm old enough to
be her father —(MRS. BUNDY *smiles*) but what difference does that make?   To her I'm not an individual
— I'm a reaction — a natural, logical reaction from
Henry!   It would have been just the same if I had
been the ashman!   I don't want her to fall in love with
me!   It's got to be stopped at once.   Do you hear me?

MRS. BUNDY — O yes; it would be difficult not to
hear you, Dr. Brent.

DOCTOR — Why the devil should I take an infant to
rear!   She's about as interesting, emotionally, as a
frilled baby pillow with a blue satin bow stuck somewhere about it.   Why in hell —

MRS. BUNDY — Doctor Jansen!

DOCTOR — I *will* swear, Bunny.   So if you don't
want to hear me — leave the room!   If there is any
woman on God's earth who will let a man enjoy an

innocent, impersonal relationship with any girl and not want to label it with the sticky label of romance.   My God —

Mrs. Bundy — Dr. Jansen —

Doctor —(*defiantly*).   *My God!* You've spoilt every moment I shall ever have with that child!   I feel as if I'd been dipped in warm molasses and rolled in confectioner's sugar!   (*He stamps out savagely.*)

Mrs. Bundy — Dear, dear!   How hard you do take things.

Doctor — Hard?   I take a sheer delight in that little girl because I made her well —   She's my novel, my poem, my symphony, my sculptured masterpiece!

Mrs. Bundy —(*as if to herself*).   Wasn't there a sculptor named Pygmalion?

Doctor —(*stamping*).   Be still, woman!   While I make you understand I *don't want* to be in love with my masterpiece.   Pygmalion *did,* and see what a damned mess he *made* of it.

Dr. Jansen is really quite irritated at the thought of Mrs. Bundy's suspicions.   He doesn't want to marry anyone; he is not a marrying man.   And furthermore, seeing that Miss Orrin's wedding day has only been postponed, he has no intention of interfering further with the affair.   He will withdraw from the case as soon as he reasonably and gracefully can do so.   He is still rather irritable when Eve arrives to take her morning ride, making his rounds with him.   Nor does Eve lessen his irritability by forcing him to analyze further his personal feelings toward her.

Eve — When I was taken sick — why did you put me up here all by myself — and shut Henry and Mamma away from me?

Doctor — I've been expecting that question for the past ten days.   I wonder if I can make you fully understand? (*Smiling*) You know you are — so *exceedingly* young.

EVE —(*quaintly*). I'm not so young as all that.

DOCTOR — Do you remember the afternoon of your arrival, when I was called to attend your mother? I insisted, rather forcefully on prescribing for you.

EVE — Yes.

DOCTOR — Well, I decided then, you must control conditions. In order to do that it was necessary to remove you from all your old environments. You are nearly well, and you *must* control conditions. It's a big burden to put on young shoulders, but it's really up to you. Live your own life, somehow; in the end that will be really helping your mother. (*After an uncomfortable pause, and watching her closely*) And — your marriage will make a difference.

EVE — Yes — I suppose so — it's tomorrow, you know.

DOCTOR —(*still watching his effect*). Perhaps not.

EVE —(*very startled*). You mean — (*Her breath catches in a sob*) What do you mean?

DOCTOR — Three days ago I told your mother I thought it ill-advised to carry forward the plans for the original date.

EVE — And Mamma —

DOCTOR — She put the matter entirely in my hands. And I decided at once that there must be a postponement — how long a one depending on your recovery. I am quite sure you're not to be married, tomorrow. Will you pardon me, Miss Eve, if I seem intrusive — but — you are quite happy in the thought of your marriage to Mr. Marchant?

EVE —(*simply*). I am engaged to Henry.

DOCTOR —(*whimsically*). So I understand.

EVE — An engagement is as binding as a marriage.

DOCTOR — Will you pardon my saying it — there are

those nowadays who believe a marriage itself is in no-wise binding —

Eve — I could never believe that. It would kill Mamma.

Doctor — Oh! Damn Mamma — I mean to say I thought I made it clear to you, you must think independently of your mother.

Eve — But — I think the same about this.

Doctor —(*looking at his watch*). I guess I'd best be getting on. Will you come?

Eve — Please don't think I appreciate your interest. You have been very good to me. Very good!

Doctor —(*lightly*). What am I for if not to look after my patients? Are you coming for your ride?

Eve — Yes — (*She goes to the door of her room and pauses there*) Do you take the *same* care of *all* your patients? (*With something akin to chill.*)

Doctor —(*pause*). I try to.

Eve —(*disappointedly*). Oh!

It is while the doctor is attending other patients in the hotel, and Eve is getting her things preparatory to her drive with him, that Mrs. Orrin decides to take again a hand in Eve's affairs, doctor or no doctor. Quietly she slips into the sun-parlor of the suite on the top floor. Eve is naturally overjoyed at sight of her, but still her sense of fairness to the doctor forbids her taking pleasure in defying his orders. " Mamma, we promised the doctor not to see each other," she says.

Mrs. Orrin — What is your promise to a man you've not known a month to my humiliation — my heart-break.

Eve — Mamma! Darling! I'm only trying to do all the things he tells me so as to get well quickly — for your sake, darling, darling! Don't you see?

Mrs. Orrin —(*darkly*). I see, I see, plainly enough! A stranger has alienated my daughter from me — my only child — whose happiness has been my sole thought since the day she was born. Now — *my* unhappiness, *my* heart-break — means nothing to her! My cup is full of bitterness indeed! (*She weeps.*)

Eve —(*struggling hard to control herself*). Darling — don't cry! Please! All I want is to be well so I may be with you always.

Mrs. Orrin — But you *are* well, Eve. you are! I never saw you look so well and happy.

Eve — Yes, darling, I am. I am really well and happy.

Mrs. Orrin — All this without me. You have never been happy in your life before without *me*. Another has taken my place. I am only a lonely woman whose heart-blood has been drained from her and the sapping of that crimson flood has left her a lifeless wreck!

Eve —(*crossing to her*). Oh! Mamma, try to understand.

Mrs. Orrin — Oh, I understand! And the understanding is breaking my heart. Well, let it break. I have not much longer to live! The symptoms of my decline are growing every day.

Eve — Mamma! What is it?

Mrs. Orrin — I fear I haven't much longer, dear little Eve —

Eve —(*going to her with a sharp cry, kneeling*). Mamma! No, no!

Mr.. Orrin —(*clasping her arms tightly about Eve and lifting a pitiful face*). My darling, you'll come back with me, now, won't you? Let me have my last days with you, as we have always been?

Eve — Yes, yes, yes! I'll never forgive myself. Let me take you to your room. Come dear! Come with me.

Mrs. Orrin — Ah! This is as it should be. This will prolong my last days! Kiss me, darling.

They are on their way out when Dr. Jansen suddenly returns. His demand to know their intentions reveals Mrs. Orrin's renewed hold upon Eve, and he promptly orders that young woman to her room. Eve is still a little afraid of the doctor and reluctantly obeys. Mamma's new "illness" is then discovered to have been brought on largely by her worry about Henry Marchant's keen disappointment when he learns that his wedding day has been postponed. She has not had the heart to tell him. Henry expects to marry Eve the next day, and it is Mrs. Orrin's idea that the ceremony — just the ceremony — could be gone through with without fuss or excitement. But Dr. Jansen is firm.

Doctor — Mrs. Orrin, you are, of course, at liberty to do as you like in this matter. I have no way of forcing my will upon you . . . unfortunately. But I must tell you now, that if you consider such a course, I shall at once withdraw from the case. I cannot take the responsibility of Miss Orrin's condition, if you consider putting her through her own wedding tomorrow.

Mrs. Orrin — But she goes out every day with you. I have never seen her look so well! She is radiant!

Doctor — That is because she has been untroubled. (Quietly) Mrs. Orrin, help me to help her. Let her live a few weeks more of healthy, happy, normal existence.

Mrs. Orrin — How can I tell Judith . . . and Henry . . . poor Henry!

Doctor — Surely it will not be difficult to make it clear to him.

Mrs. Orrin — Oh, but Henry's soul is like a sensitive plant. . . . He will never understand. (*The* DOCTOR'S *set jaw bears silent witness to what he thinks of Henry.*)

DOCTOR — Mrs. Orrin, do you love . . . Henry's soul . . . more than you love your daughter?

MRS. ORRIN — Oh, no, no!

.   .   .   .

DOCTOR — Then will you inform the Marchants of the postponement of the wedding?

MRS. ORRIN — Yes!

DOCTOR — You'll do so this morning.

MRS. ORRIN — Yes — even if it breaks my heart.

But the Marchants still have something to say. While the Doctor and Eve are away they, too, invade the forbidden rest cure. Mrs. Marchant slips in first — and finds Mrs. Orrin there. Her suspicions naturally are somewhat stirred by the encounter.

MR.. MARCHANT — Grace, you are my life-long friend. But before all I am a mother. Eve is Henry's promised wife. What befalls her befalls him. He is a marvel of patience and forbearance. All the more reason why I must insist for him. What ever has happened to Eve I must know. Am I or am I not to see her?

MRS. ORRIN — Judy, dear, I want to tell you . . . I want to explain . . . (*There is a knock at the hall door*) There's . . . there's someone at the door. (*Mrs. Marchant opens it. Henry enters. That he is in a state of mind, is evident at once.*)

MRS. MARCHANT — Henry!

MRS. ORRIN — Henry, dear!

HENRY — (*striding in and up to* MRS. ORRIN *who is center*). Excuse me, Mother! (*In suppressed rage*) May I ask, Mrs. Orrin, if you're aware of Eve's whereabouts at the present moment?

Mrs. Orrin —(*fluttering*). Well, Henry . . . not her exact whereabouts . . . of course . . . but her general whereabouts, oh, yes!

Henry — Oh, yes! Her general whereabouts are in Dr. Jansen's noisy tin runabout.

Mrs. Marchant — No?

Mrs. Orrin — Oh, Henry, dear . . .

Mrs. Marchant —(*aghast*). Grace, Eve is out with that medical person . . . again? I — I —felt it — and my feelings are . . .

Mrs. Orrin —(*weakly*). The doctor says what she needs now is fresh air and sunshine.

Henry — And his society . . .

Henry is excessively pained at the way he has been made game of by a country physician and he does not purpose standing any more of it. When they weakly tell him of the proposed postponement he is quite furious, and when Eve unexpectedly returns, having forgotten her gloves, he promptly assures her that he has decided their wedding shall take place, as scheduled, the next day. At the announcement of this decision Dr. Jansen appears in the doorway, looking for Eve. He is a little surprised and quite angry at finding the Marchants and Mrs. Orrin there, and annoyed at their new tone of defiance. Henry repeats that Eve is to marry him next day. The doctor turns to her for confirmation. She shrugs her shoulders helplessly. " Sooner or later — what difference does it make? "

Doctor —(*coldly*). As you please, of course, I have no authority over you . . . (*To* Mrs. Orrin) Mrs. Orrin, it is evidently quite impossible for me to secure any results in your daughter's case. Therefore, kindly permit me to withdraw. (*He crosses to door left, opens it.*)

Eve —(*startled*). No, no!

Mrs. Marchant — An excellent idea.

Henry — Since it spares us the task of discharging you!

Doctor —(*furious*). Good morning.

Eve —(*starting after him*). Please . . . I ask you . . .

Doctor — Under the circumstances you can hardly expect me to remain . . . Goodbye.

The doctor starts out the door, and as Eve realizes that he is deserting her she begins to laugh, covering her face with her hands. She evidently is in for another attack of hysterics. The more they try to quiet her, the harder she laughs — until they are forced again to appeal to the doctor, who is still at the door.

Doctor — Mrs. Orrin, if I take over this case again temporarily, I shall brook no interference from anyone! I shall only undertake it on this condition.

Mrs. Orrin —(*herself beyond control*). Do what you like, only help her . . help her . .

Doctor — Very well. Leave the room, every one of you.

Mrs. Marchant — I do not think Henry should be asked to leave.

Doctor — Then let Henry quiet her!

Henry —(*he goes to her*). Eve!

Eve —(*thru her wild laughter*). No, no, no . . . (*She goes off again.*)

Henry — O, my nerves won't stand this. Come, Mother! (*To* Eve) When you're quiet, I'll return.

Mrs. Orrin — Henry! Please come! O, Eve, Eve! (*The* Doctor *drives them all out without ceremony.* Mrs. Orrin *clings to* Mrs. Marchant, *whose fighting blood is almost boiling over. When they are gone the* Doctor *comes quickly back to* Eve.)

DOCTOR — (*emphatically*). St-op! Stop this at once, do you hear me?

EVE — (*her hands still over her face, whispering*). Are they all gone?

DOCTOR — What!!! (*He is completely surprised.*)

EVE — (*still seated*). Gracious. I couldn't have kept that up much longer.

DOCTOR — Do you mean to say you were *tricking?* (EVE *nods*) Well, on my soul . . . (*In a manner amused.*)

EVE — I know it was mean . . . low . . . to lie and frighten you all! But I won't let them drive you away! That's what they would have done! The night I really had hysterics, everything was made so easy for me . . . so that was the only way I could think of to make them let you stay! (*She rises.*)

DOCTOR — (*matter of fact*). Well, you've found a way to manage your family! Plenty of women have used the method for years. Keep on using it! But my services are hardly required. (*He starts for the door.*)

EVE — Oh! Please don't leave me! If you go, there'll be no one to stand back of me, no one who understands! I know I can never stand against them all alone. Until I knew you I never seemed to have breathed fresh air, I never seemed to have known how warm and bright the sun could be! I've lived in a room where the shades were always drawn, I've always breathed air that was warm and stale, and perfumed. I've been taken South in the winter, to be kept from the cold. I want to *be* cold — so cold I ache with it. I want clear bright sunshine, so pitiless it stabs my eyes, I want to be hurt — I want to live — live — (*During this she has worked very close to him, and on the end of the speech she has her arms extended. He lifts her from her feet in his arms, kisses her hard and fiercely on the lips. Then as suddenly*

releases her)   I beg your pardon . . . I am . . . pro-
foundly   . ashamed!   I don't know . . . what possessed me . . . I shall not expect you to see me again.
Goodbye! Goodbye! (*In a very honest shame and
confusion, he goes to the door and out.*)

Henry, bursting into the room, finds Eve standing
as the doctor's sudden embrace had left her, staring
fixedly at the door through which he had just disappeared.   She is in no mood to listen to Henry then.
He attempts to embrace her, but she repulses him with
both hands, and also with ardor.   She even throws the
sofa pillows at him as she cries out: "Go away! Go
away! Go away!"

Act III

It is early evening of the same day.   Dr. Jansen has
just returned to his office "five calls behind his afternoon schedule" and still trying to think of some reasonable excuse for his having kissed Eve Orrin that
morning.   The sudden appearance of Mrs. Marchant
acquaints him with the fact that Eve has disappeared
from the hotel and has not been seen for hours.

Mrs. Marchant — After you left this morning, she
behaved in a most unnatural manner.   She treated my
son to an hysterical scene — the *details* of which it is
unnecessary to repeat.   Then she locked her door and
remained in her room!   Her mother — my son — I —
all spent a futile day begging her to see us!   At last
my son telegraphed to Dr. Schell.   About five this
afternoon he arrived.   When we went with him to
Eve's room again she was gone!   Her mother is pros-
trated.   Dr. Schell is — making an effort to revive her
— her heart is at its worst.

Doctor — With Orme Schell to feel her pulse — I

don't doubt it.   If Doctor Schell is here, why do you come to me?

Mrs. Marchant — I have not come to you *professionally,* be sure of that!   Dr. Jansen, your orders in Miss Orrin's case have been most peculiar —   You have persistently denied to all of us access to her. She has reccvered rapidly — and yet you have continued to forbid her seeing her mother or her affianced husband.   Miss Orrin will some day inherit great wealth.   You are a country physician —   It's not hard to believe —

Doctor — (*interrupting*).   Mrs. Marchant!   Are you presuming to suggest — that I —

Mrs. Marchant — Just that!   That you have influenced an inexperienced girl for your purposes.   Do you deny that you desire her to break her engagement to my son?

Doctor — I don't deny that I *hoped* she'd break it.

Mrs. Marchant — Ah!

Doctor — Because I have been quite sure she didn't love your son.

Mrs. Marchant is not to be easily convinced the doctor is not a kidnapper and openly accuses him of having Eve hidden somewhere in his house at the moment. He offers to let her make a search of the premises if she will, and then changes his mind.   He will not give her that satisfaction.   Just as well that he did not, for Eve had that minute entered Mrs. Bundy's kitchen and been taken in by the kindly housekeeper.   As soon as Mrs. Marchant is gone she appears.   The doctor is not at all pleased.

Doctor — A nice position you've placed me in — the two of you!   What am I to do?   What am I to say?   I have just told Mrs. Marchant that you were not in the house.   I feared when I heard the bell — but I didn't know!   (*Breaking out again*)   I should have expected better judgment from you, Mrs. Bundy! At least, more discretion!

MRS. BUNDY — (*still weeping but with a return of spirit*). Discretion! Judgment! I don't know why I thought you were flesh and blood! Upon my soul! I don't! This — child — (*indicating* EVE) — has come here worn out battling with herself and her family problems!

EVE — Mrs. Bundy, please —

MRS. BUNDY — No, I'll say my say She has no place to go — no soul to turn to! And you had been — kind to her — (*with significance*) — at least! And she has turned — as any human being not made of sawdust would — to the only soul who has ever entirely understood her — and you — you — Oh! You're not a man — you're an emotional vivisectionist. (*She goes out into the kitchen and closes the door. There is a short pause EVE breaks it, speaking in a voice that is evidently holding back tears, but determinedly steady.*)

EVE — I'm — I'm very sorry! I didn't mean to come here when I left the hotel this afternoon! I only wanted to think — But all day long they kept coming to my door — (*With a little break*) They wouldn't give me time to think. You — you have been very kind to me — always. This morning — when you — kissed me — I thought — you cared for me — that way. Now I see — I was mistaken. Please forgive me for — bothering you — and I'll go. (*She starts for door in hall.*)

DOCTOR — Listen to me, my dear. Perhaps you were not — mistaken. (EVE *turns to him with a little cry*) No — no — Wait! Think just a moment of my — point of view — How much respect do you think I should have for myself — if I asked you to marry me. You are eighteen — I am twice your age. You are straight from the school room. You are even more immature emotionally than most girls of your age. They handed you over to Henry and you've played at a hideous mockery of something beautiful and sacred — to gratify an abnormal sentimentality in your mother and Mrs. Marchant — and soothe and feed Henry's vanity. I have been — you say — kind to you. You were in sad need of kindness and understanding. How could I ever face you, if I took you now? You don't love me! (Eve *looks at* Doctor) Love wears a different face, my dear! Go live — and learn — and wait — and the man will come to whom you really belong!

Eve — (*looking directly front, sadly*). It is lonely — waiting!

Doctor — It would be lonelier — with the wrong man! You're going to live — and find how beautiful the world can really be. Some day you're going to love — (*he hesitates*) — and marry. Only wait — wait till you know! Wait! Wait!

Eve — (*she turns to him*). O, but I know now —

Doctor — (*across the table to her*). Listen, my dear. Quite aside from what you know or feel. Are you going to ask me to do something that will cost me my self-respect?

Eve — (*crying out*). Ah, no!

Doctor — That is what this would mean to me.

The doctor plans to send Eve back to the hotel in a cab. While he has gone to fetch one, Henry Marchant makes his way into the Jansen house and discovers Eve. It was quite as Henry suspected, but he is still considerably flabbergasted, both at finding her there and at her assurance in telling him that she has about decided she cannot marry him. Before he can fully recover from the shock Mrs. Orrin arrives. She, too, is surprised, not to say shocked, at finding Eve there and in so rebellious a state of mind. Still, it serves to confirm what Mrs. Marchant and Henry have told her.

MRS. ORRIN — (*not making an effort to rise*). Eve, my daughter, come to me!

EVE — (*going to her*). What is it, Mamma?

MRS. ORRIN — Kneel here beside me.

EVE — (*kneeling*). Mamma, please —

MRS. ORRIN — Can it be! Do you love — *this* man? (*She indicates the* DOCTOR.)

EVE — (*protestingly*). Mamma! Don't!

MRS. ORRIN — Ah, then! You do — you do! That's why you no longer love dear Henry. You've come to care for — *him!*

EVE — (*looking squarely at the doctor*). Yes.

MRS. ORRIN — (*to the* DOCTOR). The dream of my life is shattered. I am a broken-hearted woman at last. (*To the* DOCTOR) But I'll not stand before my daughter's happiness. Take her — I will resign all my dreams — as I always have — for her! Marry her — marry her! And let me die somewhere alone! I cannot survive this! (*She drops back and closes her eyes.*)

EVE — (*rises; firmly*). Mamma! Listen to me! Listen! (MRS. ORRIN *opens her eyes.* EVE *catches her mother's eye and holds it*) I — I asked — practically asked — Dr. Jansen — to marry me — and he will not have me! Now will you come?

MRS. ORRIN — Eve! What are you saying? (*Rises and crosses to* EVE) Has he led you on, only to break your heart. Forgive me. I did not understand. My poor, poor darling — come to me. Your mother's arms are always aching for you. Fold your crushed wings in my breast. Broken-hearted women, we shall wander the world alone — just we two — always — always. (*She trails dramatically towards the door.*)

DOCTOR — I'll be damned if I let you go to that!

Listen to me, Mrs. Orrin. If I marry your daughter I wish you to understand exactly with what promises I do so. What she says is true. I declined to marry her earlier this evening. For reasons I have fully explained to her. But what none of her most eloquent pleadings could accomplish, you've managed to get away with in just two minutes. Mrs. Orrin, I'm going to marry her.

.   .   .   .

DOCTOR — (*coming down to* EVE). Now, Miss Eve, I'm going to talk plainly to you. Do you understand?

EVE. I'm quite used to that from you, Dr. Jansen.

DOCTOR — I wish I could tell you that I'd marry you and let you live here in my house as my niece or my youngest grandchild. But I'm not big enough to do that. I'll marry you. But — if you ever want to leave me — if I ever suspect you want your freedom — I'll set you free. Goodnight!

EVE — (*quietly*). Goodbye, Dr. Jansen.

DOCTOR — Good —?

EVE — Goodbye. I hardly can hope to see you again.

DOCTOR — What do you mean?

EVE — We shall be leaving tomorrow.

DOCTOR — But — but —

EVE — Yes?

DOCTOR — What are you going to do?

EVE — Why, I think I shall marry Henry — tomorrow.

DOCTOR — Marry —!!

EVE — *Henry — tomorrow.*

DOCTOR — Are you out of your head?

EVE — I don't think so. But I'm very tired. (*Starts to door.*)

DOCTOR — But Henry —

EVE — He's a very poor bargain, you mean. I suppose so. But I don't know anyone else to marry —

DOCTOR — I've just told you — I'd marry you —

EVE — (*flaming*). You've just told me — you'll take me on as a ward — and endure me as a wife. That's what you've just told me.   You don't love me — (*she comes down to him*) — but you'll take me in. Because you see no other way to prevent my becoming a chronic neuresthenic — you'll make your house a soft of permanent preventive institution! You don't want me — but you'll take me in as you might a kitten — out of the cold! That's what you've just proposed to me, isn't it?

DOCTOR — (*utterly taken aback*). I'm — I'm — sure I —

EVE — (*interrupting*). "You're sure!" Yes, you are — very sure — always! And now you're sure I'll accept such a proposal — until an hour ago I admitted your sureness — I adored it! But now I'm tired of it — along with being tired of a good many other things. I'm tired of Mamma's tantrums. And I'm tired of Mrs. Marchant's tragicness and always expecting the worst! And now I find I'm even tired of being told what to do by you! — I'm even tired of that! But — you've helped me make up my mind. I'll marry Henry. I'll keep him on till I grow up — and then — if he doesn't divorce me — I'll divorce *him* — but what I'll set him free! (*She flings herself to the door and opens it.*)

DOCTOR — Eve!

EVE — (*to without*). Mamma!

DOCTOR — Eve!

EVE — Mamma! I've something to tell you!

DOCTOR — You shan't marry Henry Marchant.

EVE — O, yes, I shall.

DOCTOR — (*softly*). Eve!

EVE — (*quietly*). Yes?

DOCTOR — Eve! Please don't marry Henry.

EVE — Why not?

DOCTOR — Because —   (*He pauses.*)

EVE — Well?

DOCTOR — Because — I love you!

EVE — (*with a little happy sigh*).   Ah!

DOCTOR — (*assumed severity*).   You bold faced — shameless — little — darling.   (*He suddenly seizes her in his arms, lifting her clear of the ground as in the preceding act, he kisses her again and again roughly and repeatedly.*)

(*Curtain*)

"ADAM AND EVA"

An American Comedy in Three Acts by Guy Bolton and George Middleton.

EARLY in September, the thirteenth to be exact, Guy Bolton and George Middleton, the collaborateurs whose "Polly with a Past" had scored a success the previous season, came forward with a characteristic comedy of American home life bearing the musical comedy title of "Adam and Eva." It was much to the liking of its first audiences, the reviewers were kind when they were not enthusiastic, and there was every indication the new play would continue until spring, which it did.

The hero and heroine of this romance are Adam Smith and Eva King. Adam is the general manager of the King Rubber Company, and Eva is the daughter of James King, head of that concern. Father King is very much disgusted with his family of "idle wasters"—the family including his two daughters. Eva and Julie; Julie's husband, Clinton, a foppish, ambitionless youth; Aunt Abby Rooker, the late Mrs King's sister, and Uncle Horace Pilgrim, a humorous old gentleman who came to spend a week-end with Cousin James and stayed fifteen years.

It is the first of the month and the bills are in, which intensifies James King's disgust. Something drastic must be done, he realizes, if any member of his household is ever to amount to anything, and after serious thought he has decided to close up the city house and reopen the old King farm in New Jersey for the summer. They can at least raise chickens, and although he has little hope that much good will result, he thinks perhaps they "can learn something by seeing how hard they have to scratch for a living."

The family is properly horrified. The idea of suggesting anything resembling work to *them*, when not one of them has ever been taught to do a useful thing! They immediately decide that father must be crazy, and begin to search for some way of diverting his thoughts from so wild a scheme. Perhaps if they can induce Dr. Delamater, the family medical adviser, to suggest to Mr. King that he needs a rest, and a change — a long rest and a complete change — they can get him to go out of town, and by the time he comes back he will have forgotten all about New Jersey and the silly chicken business. Dr. Delamater is easily won over to the conspiracy. Being quite in love with Eva he realizes that if she moves to New Jersey he will see but little of her, while if she stays on in New York, and father is away, she may grow more dependent upon him. So he agrees to advise Mr. King to make a tour of inspection of his rubber plantations up the Amazon, a trip that will keep him away from home for three months.

The family conspiracy is an entire success until it is exploded by Uncle Horace, who has heard the plotting and deliberately exposes the plotters. Then James King waxes exceeding wroth. So that's the scheme, is it? Well, wait until they hear from him —

Before he has a chance to turn on his family, however, Adam Smith, his general manager, arrives. He is a good-looking, exceedingly personable young man. Innocently he stumbles right into the middle of his employer's grouch as he greets him.

ADAM — You're not looking *well* this morning, Mr. King.

KING — No?

ADAM — You know, what you need is a holiday?

KING — You think I ought to take a trip. too — eh?

ADAM — I suppose you'll say you can't bring yourself to leave this place — and really I don't blame you.

KING — You like it here, eh?

ADAM — *Like* it? It's perfect. It's a *home.*

KING — Yes, it's a *home* all right!

ADAM — It takes a homeless lonely fellow like me to appreciate the way you're blessed, Mr. King! As I came up the drive and saw this lovely, big house hedged about with honeysuckle and roses, and looking so sweet and peaceful, I just realized all I was missing in life — (*looks at window*) And then when I turned the corner and saw your family sitting out on the porch — Oh, but it must be wonderful to have a family!

KING — They were all on the porch?

ADAM — Yes, sir — And they looked so happy. They were all laughing.

KING — (*getting up*). *Laughing?* They were all laughing?

ADAM — Yes. They seemed as merry and carefree as a lot of kids when the day school closes —

KING — (*thru his teeth*). Just wait — just wait!

ADAM — (*startled*). I beg pardon, Sir?

KING — (*recovering himself*). Nothing — Nothing. I mean if you just wait you'll have a family yourself some day.

ADAM — I hope you're right, sir, but I hate to think of all the time I'm losing. You're simply not living when you've only got yourself. Can you imagine what it would be like to come home and not find your loved ones waiting for you with outstretched arms?

KING — Outstretched *arms?* Outstretched hands,

you mean. You know a hell of a lot about families, don't you?

ADAM — Why, Mr. King!

KING — They made a pretty picture out there on the porch, didn't they? The smiling faces — I know why they were smiling all right — and the sunshine filtering thru the honeysuckle and the soft-colored summer dresses. (*Snatches up a bill, hands it to* ADAM) See that?

ADAM — What is it? (*Takes bill.*)

KING — The *bill* for those soft-colored summer dresses! How'd you like to pay that? Have you seen their hats? No, neither have I, but I've seen *this*. (*Hands another bill*) And here's the things they wear underneath. (*Hands lingerie bill*) Sometimes on Monday afternoon I go out and sit in the clothes yard to try and get my money's worth on the lingerie bill.

ADAM — If you'll pardon me, Mr. King, why do you encourage them to be so extravagant? You ought to speak to them.

KING — *Speak* to them!

ADAM — I s'pose you're afraid of hurting their feelings — but if you were *very careful* of the way you expressed it — All you need to do is just drop a hint — love is a wonderful interpreter.

KING — Say, where have you been all your life?

ADAM — For the most part I've been up at Manouse looking after your rubber plantations.

KING — Then I'm partly responsible for your innocence, am I? And I was just planning to send you back there, to-morrow.

ADAM — Yes, sir. That's what I want to talk to you about. Can't you send somebody else, Mr. King?

KING — Why don't you want to go?

ADAM — It's so lonely. I don't believe I could

stand it again.   You can't realize what it's like never
to see a woman.

KING — Aren't there any women there?

ADAM — There were just three Anglo-Saxon women
there when I first went there and one of them left and
one's dead.

KING — What's the matter with the other one?

ADAM — She was almost killed by our kindness too.
The whole club used to paddle six miles up the river
on Sunday afternoon just to sit and look at her.   She
was the only relative any of the boys had.

KING — You had to paddle six miles up river to see
a relative?   You're not describing Manouse — you're
describing Heaven.

ADAM — Heaven?

KING — (raptly).   I have always longed for a place
like that — longed for adventure — to get off in the
wilds — I love to picture myself sitting by the camp
fire, listening to a cougar howling in the forest, or
watching the crocodiles heave about in the river like
drifting logs, while a pink cloud of flamingoes floats
across the window of blue sky that opens between the
palm trees.

ADAM — (quite unmoved).   Sounds very wonderful, but take my word for it, it doesn't compare with
a wicker chair out on your porch.   Oh, gee — Life's
a funny thing, isn't it?   Here I am envying you everything you've got and you're envying me everything I
have had, and you talk about the place I call hell as
Heaven.

KING — Adam — why can't we change places?

ADAM — (startled).   Change places — how do you
mean?

KING — I mean that I will go to Manouse — if you'll
take over my family.

ADAM — You're joking.

King — Oh, no, I am not. You're longing for a family and I'm longing for a rest.

Adam — You mean that you'd actually leave me in charge of your family?

King — I mean I'll install you here as Father. They don't think much of me as father — so I should like to let them try a new one.

Adam — If you will pardon me, Mr. King, I think that is one of the wildest ideas I ever heard.

King — Not at all. It would be a liberal education for you — and believe me you *need* it. It's really awful to think of a poor innocent fellow going about with the idea that if you want to stop women from being extravagant, all you need to do is *drop a hint!* You long for the touch of a woman's hand, do you? You'll get it, boy, you'll get it, if you're not darn careful! You've done a lot for me, Adam. Your honesty and faithfulness have helped me to make a large fortune — so I'd like to do something for you. I want to open your eyes before you've landed yourself with a wife, a mother-in-law and a couple of kids.

Adam — But what would your family say to the scheme?

King — We don't need to care *what* they say. I've still got *one* hold over my family. They all sit up on their hind legs and woof when I hold this little book. (*Holds up check-book as if it were a piece of sugar for a poodle.*)

Adam — (*shocked*). You rule them with a check-book! That isn't right, Mr. King.

King — If you can discover any other way to rule them, I shall be most grateful.

Thus it is arranged that young Mr. Smith shall for the time being become the " father " of the King family. His word is to be law. The girls are to be given their regular allowances, and there will be a certain sum set aside for the maintenance of the home. But all charge accounts are to be cut off, and, as their father explains to them: " If Smith doesn't approve your purchases all your C O D's will be S O S's." Even Adam is a little frightened at the prospect, as he notes the hostility of the family when he is introduced to them. " Really, Mr. King," he protests, " if they don't want me — and it is only natural that they shouldn't —"

KING — Of course they don't want you. They'd like a chance to do all the silly, extravagant, idiotic things that they can't do while I'm here.

JULIE — But, Dad, Mr. Smith is a stranger. He doesn't know us.

KING — No, and it's a damn good thing he doesn't. Mr. Smith has a very limited idea of family life. Hence he's longing for it. He has a charming picture in his mind that I hope you will all help him to realize. It is evening, the lamps are lit, the curtains down. Father is sitting by the log fire with his family all about him. Aunt Abby is knitting, Julie and Clinton are playing parchesi, Uncle Horace is reading out loud some interesting excerpts from the *Literary Digest,* while Eva is seated at the piano playing very softly and sweetly that dear old melody, " Home, Sweet Home." (*Says this very sweetly thru his teeth with an exaggerated smile.*)

ADAM — That's very charming, indeed, but really I shall feel like an intruder within the sacred circle — After all the atmosphere of the home is hallowed, an alien presence might shatter its mystic charm.

KING — You see! He can't talk about a home without getting poetical. (*To* ADAM) Oh, my boy, my boy,— what an awakening you're going to get!

Eva is the only one who is the least sympathetic, and it is Eva to whom any impressionable young man would most naturally turn. "Dad deserves a vacation," says she; "we have led him an awful life. . . . I'm sure Mr. Smith will make a splendid father."

ADAM — Thank you. Really, Miss King, if you feel that way about it I feel inclined to accept. Of course, I appreciate it's rather a wild idea, but after all you will want *someone* to lean on.

KING — *Lean* on? They won't want to *lean* on you, they'll *sit* on you. . . .

.   .   .   .

JULIE — But after all, father, do you think you'd better go on such a *long* trip?

ABBY — Yes, if you want a little rest, why not let us *all* go down to White Sulphur Springs.

CLINTON — Pious idea —

KING — I'm going to South America and I'm going *alone*.

EVA — He wants romance. Poor dear, he's never had it.

ADAM — He'll be sick of it soon enough. You don't realize it, Mr. King, but you're going to be terribly lonely.

KING — Don't realize it, don't I? Why that's the whole reason I'm going. All my life I've been longing for it. Lonely! I'm going to try to be so blame lonely that maybe I'll be able to understand why a man is darn fool enough to raise a family!

.   .   .   .

ABBY — (*after Mr.* KING *has gone*). I'm sure Mr. Smith must feel as uncomfortable as we do.

ADAM — (*thoroughly abashed in the presence of the ladies — he hesitates — starts to speak — cannot — smiles — tries again*) Don't call me Mr. Smith — call me — Adam.

Eva — Oh, no. I'm going to call you " Father."

Adam sinks weakly into a chair as the curtain falls,
overcome either by the prospect of his new " job " or
the enticingly mischievous smile with which Eva observes him.

Act II

Ten days later James King is well on his way to
South America and Adam Smith is comfortably installed in the King home as substitute father — as
comfortably installed, at least, as circumstances have
permitted. He has been rather obviously tolerated by
the members of his " family " and has felt considerably out of place. But he has done his best, taking
tips from Clinton as to the way he should dress for
dinner, and overcoming his proletarian liking for sleeve
guards and tie-clips. Eva continues the most friendly
of the group, but even she has not been as friendly
as he could wish, one reason for which he learns when
she comes to consult him about her particular problem.
Shall she marry Lord Andrew Gordon, an affable
Scotchman whom everyone suspects of being a fortune
hunter, or Dr. Delamater?

ADAM — Good evening, Miss King.
Eva — Miss King? That's rather a formal way of
addressing your daughter.
ADAM — Don't you think we've had about enough of
that father and daughter joke?
Eva — Don't you want me to think of you as a
father?
ADAM — No.
Eva — Why not?
ADAM — Why not? Because — (*He pauses and
his courage fails him*) If you think of me as a fa-

ther you'll begin to think of me as old — not old in years perhaps, but stoggy and serious.

Eva — No — you're just the thing I've been asking for.

Adam — (*eagerly*)   Am I really?

Eva — Yes — a young father — one who's not too old to understand my problem.

Adam — Oh —   (*Laughs embarrassedly*)   I suppose, Miss King, you want to ask my advice about something?

Eva — Yes, my own father took a dislike to Andy on principles, so it was no use to try to talk it over with *him*.

Adam — Andy — you want my opinion of Lord Andrew?

Eva — I've been trying to make up my mind which would make the better husband, Dr. Delamater or Lord Andrew.

Adam — Good Heavens.   Do you *have* to marry one of them?

Eva — Well, I suppose I've got to marry — someone.

Adam — I suppose — I've never met Dr. Delamater.

Eva — He's coming here tonight — they both are.

Adam — For an answer?

Eva — Not exactly.   You see, Lord Andrew hasn't proposed as yet.

Adam — But you *know* they both love you?

Eva — Of course.   Why a girl can always tell when a man is in love with her.

Adam — *Always?*

Eva — (*nodding*).   *Always.*

Adam — That opens up a new line of thought —

.   .   .   .

Eva — . . . I don't think it can be very nice to marry anyone whose tastes and habits are on a different plane from your own.

ADAM — Oh, you wouldn't marry a man who (*pause*) — I understand — However, both the men you're considering have got the right tastes and habits, so *that* doesn't enter into your problem, does it?

EVA — No.

ADAM — Which one do you love?

EVA — I'm not sure that I love either — neither the doctor nor Andy quite fills the bill.   You see, I like one for one thing — and the other for something else.

ADAM — I see — if you could marry them both, they would add up about a hundred percent.

EVA — Yes.   One to take me to a Polo Match, and one to take me to the Opera.   Oh, you understand?

ADAM — Oh, yes, I understand.   I've met lots of ideal women — ideal fifty percent of the time.   But if I can't have my hundred percent girl, I don't want any.

EVA — Oh, have you found a hundred percent girl?

ADAM — I've carried the picture of one around with me a long time.   She rode into my dreams when I was up the great river — she was just a dim phantom then.   It's only lately that she's grown real to me. I don't want one woman to go to a Polo Match with me, and another to sit by my side when I hear beautiful music.   I want *her* all the time — everywhere I go.   And most of all I want her to come home to — for after all it's the thought that the woman you love is waiting for you there that makes " home " the most beautiful word in all the languages of the world.

EVA — Why, Father, I had no idea you were so romantic.   (*She says it with a whimsical smile, not really meaning to tease him.*)

ADAM — Romantic? — Yes — I suppose I am.   You see, being alone a lot forces a chap to live on dreams.

Adam soon faces the first family crisis.   A new dinner gown arrives for Julie, C O D, and the amount due is $435. "C O D," Eva explains to the puzzled Lord Andrew, is an Americanism meaning "Call on Dad." Adam, going over the books, knows that they have all overdrawn their accounts and are blithely running into debt, just as they were accustomed to do with their real father. He realizes the time has come for him to take a stand and he frankly tells both Eva and Julie that he does not feel that he can pay for the gown.

EVA — Julie, the Secretary of the Treasury declares our domestic government is facing a deficit.

JULIE — Really, Mr. Smith, you mean —

ADAM — (uncomfortably). I'm in a very awkward position, Mrs. DeWitt. That package was sent C O D.

JULIE — Well, what is the difficulty, Mr. Smith? Father supplied you with funds to pay our C O D's, didn't he —

ADAM — Yes, up to a certain amount. But he's been gone only ten days and we've already exceeded our month's allowance.

JULIE — Then we'll have to start drawing on next month's — Father grew quite used to that. (Takes out dress and holds it up.)

LORD ANDREW — Oh, I say — that's a rip-snorter, if you like!

JULIE — A Poiret model — nobody else can combine colors like that. (Drapes it on herself) Isn't it a poem?

EVA — More like a song, I should say —

JULIE — A song? —

EVA — Sweet and low. (To ANDY) You see, Julie beleives in candor. No secrets among friends, even where moles and freckles are concerned.

ADAM — You say that when you exceeded one

month's allowance your father would let you begin to draw on the next?

JULIE — Yes.

ADAM — Well — that was all right for him — but I don't see how I can do it. You see, he limited me and I — I'm very sorry —

JULIE — Then you propose that I should send this dress back?

ADAM — I should think that would be the best solution — yes.

JULIE — And what do you suggest I should wear at dinner tonight?

ADAM — Really I — that frock you have on looks very nice to me.

JULIE — A tea gown at dinner?

ADAM — I beg pardon. I'm afraid I'm not very well up on these things.

EVA — Don't be a chump, Julie. You know you've got a closet full of dinner gowns.

JULIE — That's no reason why I should be treated like a school girl and humiliated by having my purchases sent back.

ADAM — If you feel that way about it, Mrs. DeWitt. I'll pay it out of my own account.

JULIE — Oh, please don't be so preposterous. (*Swings dress to* CORINTHIA, *who puts it in the box*) Send the dress back. Tomorrow I'll take my pearls up to town and pawn them. I think I can raise enough money to pay my bills until father returns —

ADAM — (*going to her*). Oh, no — you mustn't do that, Mrs. DeWitt. If we can just get together and see where we can save.

JULIE — *Save!* You talk as if the King Rubber Company were on the verge of ruin —

LORD ANDREW — (*alarmed*). It isn't, is it?

Nor does the matter of Julie's dinner gown end the

troubles of the worried father for the day. Distasteful as the task is, he suddenly discovers that he also is forced to discipline Eva. " I'm afraid," says she, by way of opening the conversation, " that dinner gown will rankle for sometime."

ADAM — I'm awfully sorry to hurt her feelings.

EVA — Before you put that check book back, I may as well make my application.

ADAM — Certainly, how much do you need, please?

EVA — I think a hundred and fifty will do. We're going to teach Andy to play Red Dog after dinner.

LORD ANDREW — I'm always very quick at picking up games.

ADAM — Red Dog? — is that gambling?

EVA — Yes. Why? Do you object to my gambling?

ADAM — I have no reason to object to your gambling, as long as your father doesn't mind.

EVA — Oh, I can't say father doesn't mind. He kicks up an awful fuss whenever he hears about my losses. Now isn't that just like a man who gambles with millions in the rubber market to object to his children playing cards for money?

ADAM — The King Company is forced to gamble in order to protect its supply of raw material, but if you knew what a risky business it is you wouldn't wonder that your father dislikes gambling.

EVA — Well this is an occasion where his feelings are spared. (*Holds out hand*) One hundred and fifty, please.

ADAM — (*miserably*). I'm dreadfully sorry.

EVA — Sorry?

ADAM — Your father left me in charge and I promised him I'd try and look after his home and family just as he would himself!

EVA — So because I tell you he objects to my gambling you won't give me any money?

ADAM — I'll give it to you if you'll promise you won't use it for that purpose.

EVA — Well, if Julie felt like a school girl I feel like an infant.

ADAM — (*trying to smile*). You insist on calling me 'father.' Please don't be annoyed the first time I act like one.

EVA — No, I can appreciate a joke — even though it's on myself — but when you ask me for promises of good behavior it is too idiotic to be even funny. However, praises be — I also have a pearl necklace. So your lesson in Red Dog is postponed merely until tomorrow, Andy.

LORD ANDREW — Right, Oh!

ADAM — Oh, please don't take it that way, Miss King. I feel perfectly rotten.

EVA — Don't trouble to apologize. Come out on the terrace, Andy. (ANDY *rises*) And you shall tell me what that thing is that is weighing on your mind.

LORD ANDREW — I don't know — I don't think it would be quite judish to tell it while you're in a bad mood.

EVA — (*sharply*) Nonsense, I am in the right mood, if you only had sense to see it.

ADAM — (*stopping her at door*). Miss King, please don't go like that — I've been awfully clumsy.

EVA — Why, no. You acted very conscientiously and creditably. It's only that I think I've had about enough of parental authority. It's about time I became my own mistress.

Adam now realizes that he has reached the point in his parental experiment when either he must control the situation or acknowledge himself beaten. Both girls have threatened to pawn their jewels. It would be perfectly simple for them to raise sufficient funds in that way to keep them in money until their father returned. Therefore, Adam determines there shall be a burglary while the family is at dinner — and that will dispose of the pearls. About which time he is struck with another idea. Word is telephoned from the offices of the King Rubber Company that there has been a flurry on the stock exchange that has hit the King Company pretty hard. What would happen if it were made to appear that not only a part, but all of the King money had been lost? Adam is revolving this thought in his mind when Dr. Delamater, returning from a private conference respecting his chances of winning Eva away from Lord Andrew, suggests practically the same thing. " I'm not going to ask you to forbid the match," he explains. " I've thought of a way you can get rid of this adventurer. It's pretty drastic, I admit, but then the case is becoming desperate and calls for a desperate remedy.

ADAM — All right, Doctor — prescribe —

DR. DELAMATER — To begin with you are Mr. King's business manager — (ADAM *nods*) So anything you say about the business is going to be pretty conclusive — and then remember none of the family knows any more about business than a child.

ADAM — I don't catch your drift, Doctor.

DR. DELAMATER — Well, I see by the paper that there's been quite a flurry in the rubber market to-day —

ADAM — Flurry hardly describes it.

DR. DELEMATER — Mr. King was known to be a large speculator.

ADAM — Yes —

DR. DELEMATER — Why not announce privately to the family that Mr. King is ruined?

ADAM — Eh?

DR. DELAMATER — Eva will of course tell the Scotchman that she is penniless and as he is penniless too, he'll be forced to show his real colors and back out as gracefully as he can. (DR. DELAMATER *stops and looks at* ADAM *to see how he likes the idea.*)

ADAM — (*slowly*). You know, Doctor — it's a darn funny thing that you should propose this.

DR. DELAMATER — (*surprised*). Yes — why?

ADAM — (*after a second's pause*). Because **Mr.** King really *is* ruined.

DR. DELAMATER — Eh — *WHAT?*

ADAM — That little flurry you spoke about has wiped him out clean.

DR. DELAMATER — But, good God, man, do you mean to say that with a business like Mr. King's — it's — *impossible.*

ADAM — Seems so to me, too — I just can't realize it.

DR. DELAMATER — Why, I'd always understood King was worth millions. And you stand there and tell me he's lost *everything?*

ADAM — I'm afraid it's going to be an awful shock to the family.

DR. DELAMATER — SHOCK? I should say it is a shock! (*A soft chime is heard off, the* DOCTOR *starts*) What's that?

ADAM — Oh, that's the dinner gong. I thought I wouldn't tell them till after dinner. It would be a shame to spoil their appetites.

DR. DELAMATER — Yes, of course — I'd better slip out before they come down — I couldn't talk to them now as if nothing had happened. (*Looks around*) All this gone — just think of it! What will they *do?*

ADAM — Well, Doctor, I suppose Miss King will marry a man who can look after her.

Dr. Delamater — Yes — yes — she's an awfully attractive girl.   Of course some fellow is bound to come along.

Adam — (*turning his head rather quickly*).   To *come* along?

Dr. Delamater — (*a trifle embarrassed*).   Oh — er — when you tell them please say that if there's anything on earth I can do to send for me.

Adam — Thank you, Doctor!

Dr. Delamater — And that check for my bill — I shall tear it up.

Adam — How good of you.

Dr. Delamater — I only wish I could do more but — (*Confidentially*)   My income is much smaller than people suppose —

Adam — Well — there's just one bright side to this thing.

Dr. Delamater — Yes, what's that?

Adam — Miss Eva will be quite safe from fortune hunters.   (*He looks at the* Doctor *meaningfully, as the latter makes an embarrassed exit.*)

It was while the family was still at dinner that the wall safes in both Eva's and Julie's rooms were pried open and their jewels extracted, but the girls did not discover their loss for some time.

.   .   .   .

An hour later, after dinner, the family is entertaining itself in the drawing-room.   Eva has just announced her engagement to Lord Andrew and Julie has gone upstairs to start a list of those socially eligible for invitations to an announcement party, when the substitute father walks in upon his home circle.   He is plainly disturbed and anxious, and this leads them to inquire the cause.   It is quite evident that he has an unpleasant announcement to make.

ADAM — I've been trying to muster up courage to
tell you — I even put these clothes on so as to give
myself another reason for delay — but it's no use
stalling any longer.   You've *got* to know.

EVA — (*really alarmed*).   Why, Mr. Smith, you
don't —

UNCLE HORACE — (*breaking in*).   Your father's
boat has gone down, just what I dreamed this afternoon.

ADAM — No. Mr. King is all right.   That is to say
— he's safe and well.

UNCLE HORACE — Go on, then.   Explode your
bomb and bury our fragments.

ADAM — My dear people — Mr. King is ruined.

ALL — (EVA *rises*).   Ruined?

ABBY — (*speaking on same cue*).   Did he say
ruined?

CLINTON — (*speaking above the omnes*).   Not
really *ruined?*   (*There is a moment's hushed silence
— ADAM nods his head slowly.*)

ABBY — It's incredible!   Fantastic!

LORD ANDREW — I say, does " ruined " mean the
same thing here that it does in England?

ADAM — Yes, I mean financially ruined.

EVA — But how — *how* could it happen?   Surely,
he can't suddenly —   Why he's been gone only ten
days.

ADAM — The Brazilian Government placed an embargo on rubber shipments — that means a nation-wide
shortage on raw material.   This afternoon prices
soared to the skies.   The King Company is carrying
a tremendous short account and that account has got
to be covered if it takes *every* dollar.   (EVA *goes
above chair* L.)

LORD ANDREW — Every dollar?

CLINTON — But look here, Brazil has no right to do
this to us.

LORD ANDREW — No, I say, can't we get the good old U. S. A. to send some battleships? That's what we always do in England.

EVA — Have you sent for father?

ADAM — No, he's probably way up the river by this time, and he won't hear of it till he reaches Manouse.

ABBY — Does it mean that *everything* is gone? (ADAM *nods his head*) His *private* fortune?

ADAM — I'm afraid there is no private fortune; it is all in the business. Perhaps we can save the home. I'm going to try. But it can't be kept up. We've got to rent it.

UNCLE HORACE — Rent it?

CLINTON — Good God!

UNCLE HORACE — Then where the devil are we going to live?

ADAM — That's the problem we've got to face.

ABBY — Well, there's only one thing to do — we'll just have to wait till Mr. King comes back.

.   .   .   .   .   .

ADAM — You actually propose to sit down and fold your hands until Mr. King gets back to earn your living for you?

CLINTON — Well, if we don't know how to earn one ourselves?

ADAM — You'll have to do like other people, Mr. DeWitt, and find out how. Mr. King is over fifty years old. All his life he has worked for his family — for you. He has supported you — made a beautiful home for you — a home that none of you appreciate because you've never had to do without it. He's given you education, food, clothes,— everything you asked for within reason — and a great deal that was out of reason. And now, after years of office drudgery, of fighting and struggling for you, are you going to ask him to start in all over again — at his age — with a family hanging around his neck?

Eva — Of course we're not, Mr. Smith! Though I don't blame you for thinking us quite capable of it.

Adam — I beg your pardon. I had no right to talk to you that way. After all, I'm only an outsider.

Eva — We'll be glad if you won't consider yourself an outsider — You see, we're a dreadfully helpless crowd, and we shall need someone with business experience to advise us.

Adam — (*goes to* Eva). That's what I want to do. I'm tremendously fond of your father. I've been with him ever since I was a kid and he's been so *damned white* to me —

There is little time to consider what's to be done before Julie arrives with the news of the jewel robbery — and that is the last straw. They might have lived some time on what the jewels would have brought, as Clinton sadly suggests, but — Well, there seems to be nothing to do but for them all to go to work. It is a terrible thought, but they must make the best of it. It is Clinton's suggestion that they look over the " Help Wanted " and " Business Opportunity " ads in the newspapers, which they do, with the result that Uncle Horace decides to become an insurance agent and Clinton purposes to take a new line of " snappy clothes " into the small towns. When it comes Eva's turn to choose Adam becomes somewhat excited. " The only job that I can find that doesn't need previous experience," she admits, " is a shop assistant. I shall make a try for that."

Adam — Oh, great Scott — no! I can't let you do that — I mean you mustn't do that.

Eva — Why not?

Adam — Because you musn't. You don't realize what it would be like — to stand behind a counter all day.

EVA — Well, if other girls can do it, I can.

ADAM — No, no, wait a minute. Tell me, doesn't your father own an old place over in New Jersey?

EVA — Yes — he's kept it out of sentiment. It's the place where he spent his boyhood.

ADAM — Why couldn't we turn it into a chicken farm?

EVA — I believe there are chickens there now.

ADAM — I mean on a large scale. For instance — special brands of eggs for invalids — packed in fancy boxes and delivered by express. And honey the same way. Have little jars shaped like a bee hive. You and Mrs. DeWitt could run it. It would be better than taking some ill-paid job as a secretary or companion.

EVA — What a splendid idea!

JULIE — Yes, isn't it. And I know all about bees since I read that book of Maeterlinck's. Oh, Clinnie. Have you read Maeterlinck's " Life of the Bee "? *So* fascinating — And the part about the Queen Bee and her young lover is deliciously risque. Poor dear, just like Cleopatra, she always murders him after the honeymoon.

ADAM — Really with your acquaintance to help get the thing started we could make a go of it.

It is thus decided that Eva and Julie will go to the farm and that Adam will board with them, build chicken coops on Sundays and sort of look after the business details. Aunt Abby decides to take a position as housekeeper and companion, until the bee and chicken enterprise is well under way. Which makes a place for everybody but Lord Andrew. Naturally, everyone expected with the King money gone his lordship would fade away, but as it transpires he is not that sort of a fortune hunter at all. " I say, look here," says he to Eva, " I'm going to make a confesh.

I came over here to America with the idea of marrying money. That's true — absolutely. But I've found
out tonight that the money hasn't a dashed thing to do
with the way I feel about you."

EVA — Why, Andy, that's very nice of you, but —

LORD ANDREW — So if good old Smith will help me
I'm going to be naturalized and settle down in America an — an — an — and get a job.

ADAM and EVA — A job?

LORD ANDREW — (*a trifle anxiously*). Yes, you
won't think any the less of me for working, will you?
And of course, I'll have to drop the title —

EVA — Andy, you're a dear!

ADAM — (*holding out his hand*). Put it there, old
man. I'll never say a word against the Scotch as
long as I live.

LORD ANDREW — Thank you.

.   .   .   .   .   .

EVA — But — one minute, Andy — your family —
surely they are counting on you?

LORD ANDREW — To bring home an heiress? Yes,
I suppose they are. But then I've been a sore disappointment to my family from the very first. Will you
believe it, they had it all planned out to christen me
Victoria and marry me to a Duke.

When Adam finds himself alone he decides to make
way with the "loot." He can't go around with several
thousand dollars' worth of pearls in his pocket, so he
thinks he will hide them in some good place — perhaps
back of the books. He takes an envelope from the
desk and is just dropping the pearls into it when Eva
re-enters the room and sees him. She is surprised —
not to say shocked, but all she can say is: "I don't
understand."

ADAM — (head down). It is quite simple, Miss

King. I am the man who took those jewels. (*Holds them in his hand*).

Eva — Yes, but why —

Adam — Those jewels mean you don't have to work — none of you. You can live on the money they fetch until your father gets back, and starts in again. (*He hands the jewels to her, she takes them mechanically.*)

Eva — Those jewels would be a big help to Dad; you want us to keep them and give them to him. That's it, isn't it?

Adam — It will be great if you can.

Eva — Can. Of course we can. (*Offers them to him — he does not take them*) Take them back, I won't say a word to the others.

Adam — You mean that?

Eva — I suppose we may have rather a hard time at first. It would be a temptation if they know we still had these.

Adam — You're splendid.

Eva — Oh, no, but we'll see if the Kings can't go thru like Andy did. (Adam *takes the jewels*) Goodnight — Father.

Adam — I am glad I am something to you.

Eva — I didn't say it that time to tease you, I just want to tell you how grateful I am for all you've done for me — for us —

Adam —" Me " was right.

Eva — You've been — what was your expression? —" damned white."

She turns and leaves the room as the curtain falls.

Act III

Thanksgiving day, three months later. The King family, represented by its present and prospective members, is reassembling at the King farm in New

Jersey for a celebration dinner. The "Queen Bee" honey and chicken business is booming; Clinton has made a success as a salesman of nifty clothes for nifty lads; Uncle Horace is the most persistently successful of insurance agents; Aunt Abby has married an aged widower with gout and a fortune, for whom she had been keeping house, and Lord Andrew has become the most popular riding master in New York. Adam is quite well satisfied with the way everything has worked out. He is even becoming reconciled to the thought of Eva's marrying Lord Andrew, though he finds that the hardest feature of the situation to accept. This Thanksgiving morning he is painting the coop that is to be sent to the poultry show with the prize Dorkings. Eva, carrying a glass bowl of corn-meal for the chickens, and a big red apple for Eva, spies him as she comes from the house.

EVA — Don't tell me it's all done?

ADAM — Yes, I got up and finished it early this morning. *I* was the man with the hammer that you were cursing for waking you.

EVA — I didn't hear you.

ADAM — No! Well of course I tried to hammer softly.

EVA — Nonsense. I'll bet I was up before you. I took a little holiday and went riding with Andy.

ADAM — (*trying to be airy about it*). Must have been a perfect morning for horse-back riding.

EVA — It was lovely. The air like crystal and that nice woody smell that comes in late fall. Do you know I really love this place, Adam. And our funny little gray house makes me understand what you used to mean when *you* talked with so much feeling about a home.

ADAM — Yes, it'll be nice to look back at this time we've all spent here together.

Eva — Look back?

Adam — Andy is doing pretty well now, isn't he?

Eva — (*running her fingers thru the chicken food*) He's getting on.

Adam — Well, when is it going to be? (*His attempt of carelessness is over done.*)

Eva — When is what going to be — Oh, the wedding, you mean?

Adam — Uh — huh! (*Whistles and regards his painting thru half closed eyes.*)

Eva — Oh, not for a long time yet.

Adam — But isn't he getting pretty anxious? I know if I loved a girl 1 simply couldn't wait for the day when — I could really call her mine.

Eva — *If* you loved? I thought you told me once that you had found the woman you'd always dreamed of? Your hundred-percent girl you called her.

Adam — Did I say that?

Eva — Yes, but maybe she turned out not to be a hundred-percent after all.

Adam — No. She turned out even better than 1 expected. Too good.

Eva — Too good?

Adam — Too good for me.

Eva — (*shaking her head*). I *don't* believe that.

Adam — Yes, I think even you'd have to admit it if you knew her as I know her — and saw just how splendid she is.

Eva — (*piqued — she heedlessly spills the chicken food as she runs her fingers thru it*). And does this female paragon realize that you think so highly of her?

Adam — (*painting away*). No, sir — I should say not — Oh, no — and what's more, she never will. (Eva *gives him a look but he doesn't see it.*)

Eva — Too bad. Have a bite of my apple, Adam?

And the unwary Adam takes quite as generous a bite as his ancient ancestor gobbled up in Eden, just as Lord Andrew himself appears on the scene manfully shouldering a bag of meal he has brought in from the village for the " jolly old poultry." Lord Andrew is growing a little impatient, too, at being constantly put off by Eva whenever he suggests an early marriage. He can't altogether understand it — until an observing member of the family helps to open his eyes. Can't he see that Adam is head over heels in love with Eva, and Eva in love with him? No, he can't, dash it all. He can't. And before he has much of a chance to try James King appears suddenly on the scene and everything else is forgotten. His return from South America is what he intended it should be, a complete surprise. But —" what on earth are my family doing out here in this God-forsaken spot?" he promptly demands.

ADAM — Raising chickens.

KING — Raising *what?*

ADAM — Chickens. Oh, they love it here — the peace and quiet are wonderful.

KING — Peace and quiet — don't you ever say those words to me again.

ADAM — Why, what's the matter?

KING — I've had enough peace and quiet to last me a life time. I want my family.

ADAM — I told you so.

KING — Oh, shut up — I'm trying to grasp this thing — I came back expecting to find my whole family on Long Island raising hell and I find them in New Jersey raising chickens.

Adams leaves Mr. King while he goes in search of the family, that they may welcome their father home. When they assemble and the greetings are over, they try to make him understand the situation. He may not know it but he is a ruined man. Adam will tell him the details when he comes and he will understand that when the blow fell there was nothing else for them to do.

CLINTON — (*swaggering a bit*). Well, of course we could have sat down and cabled for you to come back and work for us, but that never even suggested itself to us.

UNCLE HORACE — (*stoutly*). I should say not.

EVA — Wait till you hear what we've all done. You'll be proud of us. Why these past three months we've actually saved three times as much as we spent.

KING — (*looks from* EVA *to* JULIE *dumbfounded*). Poor old Rip Van Winkle! I know just how he felt.

JULIE — So you see if you need any help, Dad. *We've* got some money to give you for a change.

KING — Good Heavens! You're all talking as if I'd gone broke.

JULIE — Well so you have, dear.

EVA — That's the reason that we —

KING — Broke. *I'm broke?* Say, is this whole thing a joke?

CLINTON — (*to* HORACE). Poor old Father. He doesn't realize what has happened to him.

HORACE — Of course, tropical heat. (*Taps forehead.*)

JULIE — Father, dear, have you forgotten what happened ten days after you left us?

EVA — The Brazilian embargo on rubber shipments!

JULIE — And the way the rubber shares jumped.

CLINTON — You had sold short and of course you had to cover.

UNCLE HORACE — Even though it took the last dollar.

KING — My last dollar? Nonsense! I only lost about seventy thousand in that little rubber panic.

JULIE — (*surprised*).   Seventy *thousand?*

CLINTON — (*whisper hoarsely to Horace*).   I dare say that's what Adam let him think.

KING — You mean that something has happened to the business that I haven't been told about?

EVA — Adam almost cried when he broke the news to us.

JULIE — And he spoke so beautifully of you and of how you had always worked for us.

KING — I see what has happened.   They made a mess of things down at the office — Adam and that fellow Russell.   I was a fool to go away and trust a tricky business to a couple of underlings.

So, that's it.   The business ruined and knowledge of it kept from him by his general manager!   Where is Adam?   The last anyone had seen of him he was riding toward the station.   And there is a train for New York at a quarter to one!   But Eva will not listen to such silly suspicions.   They may all think what they like, but she will stake her life on Adam.   None of the others are ready to share her trust, however.   The elder King doesn't believe Adam is dishonest, but he does believe he has made a mess of the rubber business and is trying to cover his tracks.   Which reminds Lord Andrew that when he was investigating the jewel burglary he had found one of Adam's sleeve garters in Julie's room.   And when he told Adam about it he blushed.   It's true, admits Eva.   Adam did take the jewelry.   She had known that all the time.   But he had a " splendid motive " for it.

EVA — I don't understand about the failure or whose fault it was that Dad's business was smashed, but after it had happened Adam knew that we would never go to work if we had those pearls to sell, so he stole them.

KING — And you knew about it?

EVA — Yes I knew.

JULIE — How did you manage to keep a secret like that?

EVA — And do you realize Adam took all that trouble just for us. Look at us! What were we when father went away? A lot of worthless idle wasters. And look at us now! He has given us self respect. He has shown us there is more fun in working and earning money than there is in spending it. He's fine, and no matter how things look — whatever you may say, nothing can break my faith in him.

And then Adam comes in. He had been to town to get more paint. He laughs at their surprise at seeing him. " Oh, I see, you thought now your real father had come back it was time for me to abdicate. What do you think of my chicken coop, Mr. King? "

KING — Smith, my family have just been telling me that the King Company has gone to the devil.

ADAM — Oh yes, bad business isn't it?

KING — Very bad.

ADAM — But on the other hand the Bee and Chicken Industry is thriving.

KING — Tell me straight out, how did it happen? You must have been gambling with futures.

ADAM — Yes, sir, I was.

UNCLE HORACE — Oh, perhaps I had better take down his confession in shorthand.

ADAM — Only it wasn't rubber futures I was gambling with — but human futures — the futures of all these people here.

KING — Yes, if you have ruined me — you have ruined them.

ADAM — Ruined them? Good Heavens, look at them! Are they ruined? Look at Uncle Horace — why he has even learned shorthand, isn't that marvelous — and look at my daughters — your daughters — our daughters — aren't you proud of them? As a business man and a captain of industry you're a marvel, but as a father you're simply not in it with me.

KING — (*realizing the truth*). Do you mean to say —

ADAM — Yes, the story of the ruin was a fake. You are still rich and can support them all as a crowd of spongers (*they all resent this*) if they will let you, but I miss my guess if they do.

CLINTON — To think this man faked up the whole story of the ruin just to make us work. Good God!

ADAM — That's it.

JULIE — Wasn't that a cute idea?

KING — I can see why you did it, but I'm darned if I can see how you did it.

ADAM — Well, I had to take the office into my confidence.

It is all over now, but the understanding between Adam and Eva. Lord Andrew makes that possible, by confessing that he has discovered they do really love each other. "I've just been watching you both, and I've noticed a few things."

EVA — You noticed? Oh, no. Andy, you dear old silly — you couldn't notice anything *of that* sort. Not any more than Adam could.

ADAM — Eh? How's that?

ANDY — It — It's true enough — isn't it? (EVA *nods her head "yes"*) Then that's settled — it's been deuced well worth while knowing you and being one of the family.

EVA — You'll always be that Andy, dear.

ANDY — Congrats, Adam, old boy an'— an' all that sort of thing. (*Starts into house, turns again in doorway*) 1 say that turkey smells devilish good. (*Goes in whistling with an attempt at jauntiness.*)

EVA — (*pause — looking after him*). Isn't he a dear?

ADAM — Eva —(*he breaks off*).

EVA — Yes — Adam?

ADAM — I don't know what to say — it — it doesn't seem possible.

EVA — Maybe you don't love me. Do you? Or don't you?

ADAM — Oh, Eva — there aren't any words to tell you. (*He now finds the courage to hold her in his arms and is about to kiss her.*)

EVA —Father?

ADAM — (*thinking she means* MR. KING, *jumps back*). Where?

EVA — No, dear — not daddy. (*Takes his hands —" helping him out "*) It's you that I'm calling that — don't you like the name?

ADAM — Oh, gee, I forgot.

EVA — Then I'll tell you something — I think *maybe* — after we're married we'll be like good old-fashioned country folk — and I'll always call you " father." (*She says it slowly, he holds her closer and kisses her — one long kiss*).

UNCLE HORACE — (at the window with a turkey bone *in his hand*). Say, if you don't hurry, there'll be nothing left for you but the neck — 1 say the neck. (*He sees the situation*). OH-H!!

(*Curtain*)

" CLARENCE "

An American Comedy in Four Acts.
By Booth Tarkington.

" CLARENCE " was produced at the Hudson Theater, New York, Saturday evening, September 20, and
achieved an immediate popular success.   It is written
in a spirit of what, for lack of a better classification,
may be termed " high farce."   It relates the experience
of a young entomologist who, having served as a
drafted man in the American army, seeks employment
in New York after his discharge.   After several days
of patient waiting he succeeds in making his way into
the inner offices of Henry Wheeler, the " president of
an impressive financial institution with offices on the top
floor of the institution's building in Nassau Street,
New York."

The opening of the play finds the Wheeler family
rather seriously upset, and Mr. Wheeler much concerned with the straightening out of its domestic tan-
gles.   Mrs. Wheeler, his second wife, much younger
than he and entirely superficial, is nursing a growing
jealousy of Violet Pinney, a youthful and attractive
governess employed to look after Cora Wheeler.   Cora,
a sweet, but self-willed child " about 16," fancies herself deeply in love with Hubert Stem, a middle-aged
grass widower.   " Bobby " Wheeler, a budding Tarkington adolescent of the Willie Baxter type, is just
home after having been " fired " from his third school,
and, having forcibly kissed Della, the housemaid, finds
himself seriously entangled in an " affair."

The opening scene is played in the ante-room of the
Wheeler offices beginning with the entrance of Wheeler,

Sr.   He consults his secretary, Mrs. Martyn, concerning his engagements for the day.

WHEELER — Have I appointments with any of those people waiting?

MRS. MARTYN — No; I haven't made any appointments at all for you this morning.   At one o'clock you go to Mr. Milly's lunch for the Secretary of the Interior; you have a directors' meeting at three . . . the Unity . . . and the Pitch Pine consultation at three-thirty.   Mr. Lindsay and Mr. Vance will do for all the people in the ante-rooms.   Except one, perhaps.

WHEELER — Who's that?

MRS. MARTYN —It's a soldier who . . .

WHEELER — In a private's uniform . . . rather a sickly-looking fellow?

MRS. MARTYN — Yes.

WHEELER — I noticed him waiting out there yesterday too.

MRS. MARTYN — They sent him to Mr. Vance, but he wouldn't tell what he wanted; said he had to see you.   Of course Mr. Vance told him that was impossible; he didn't even have a letter of introduction.

WHEELER — Oh, well, he's a soldier; see what he wants.

MRS. MARTYN — Very well.

WHEELER — It's possible my daughter and her governess, Miss Pinney, will come to town this morning to see me   Miss Pinney spoke to me just as I was leaving the house, and I understood her to say — I'm not just sure I caught her meaning — (*His manner is the least bit confused*) — She spoke in a low voice, for some reason . . .

MRS. MARTYN — Your daughter did?

WHEELER — No.   My daughter's governess — uh — Miss Pinney.   I understood her to say that she wanted to see me in private   I think she meant she wanted to talk with me about my daughter.

MRS. MARTYN — I understand.

WHEELER — I think she implied that she and my daughter might come in town and turn up here at the office . . .

MRS. MARTYN — I'll look out for them.

Mr. Wheeler's surmise that he will be followed by certain members of his family is entirely correct. He has no sooner retired to his private office than Mrs. Wheeler herself appears. She has heard something of Miss Pinney's intention of coming to the office, and though she is prideful of the fact that she never, never interferes with her husband's business, she believes it just as well to keep a watch on his movements when he isn't concentrating.

Mrs. Wheeler is followed by "Bobby." "He is hovering on the elder side of 16," explains Mr. Tarkington. "His hair is to the mode of New York, according to the interpretation of his years, and so is his costume, which includes an overcoat. *He also wears* a pair of pale spats, too large for his shoes — he is strongly conscious of them at times, and also of a large hook-handled cane, too long for him. He removes his hat at sight of Mrs. Martyn. At all times he is deathly serious; and speaks quickly; when he doesn't stammer. THIS IS BOBBY."

"Bobby" is anxious to avoid a meeting with his father, but eager to effect a meeting with Violet Pinney, who happens to be his latest passion. "Have they been here yet?" he demands of Mrs. Martyn, and in reply to her query as to whom he means he continues:

BOBBY — Why, my sister Cora and — (*Suddenly gulps*) . . . look! I mean my sister Cora and . . . (*Gulps again*) . . . and Violent. I don't mean Violent . . . (*Hurrying on in helpless confusion, but with abysmal gravity*) Listen; I mean her and Cora.

Look; I mean Cora and Miss Pinney. Miss Pinney.
Cora's governess, Miss Pinney.

MRS. MARTYN — No. They haven't been here.

BOBBY — Well, they'll be here pretty *soon* then. I
don't want my father to know I'm here if it's convenient. We haven't got along too well lately and
besides I took his spats. Look, do you suppose he'll
care? He's never had 'em on; I don't think he likes to
wear 'em. It's right, isn't it? I mean you don't haf
to be very old to wear spats, do you?

MRS. MARTYN — Oh, I don't think so.

BOBBY — Look; they haven't gone *out* in New York,
have they? I been away at school for practik'ly a lifetime; and I haven't had a good chance yet to see what
they're wearing.

MRS. MARTYN — I didn't know you were interested
in "what they're wearing." The last time I saw
you . . .

BOBBY — Well, I said that was about a lifetime ago!
Look; I used to go around like a scarecrow, but you
can't do that all the time because, look; why how do
you look if you do? Do you think it's right to carry
a stick over your arm like this? With shammy gloves?
Or do you think you ought to kind of lean on it?

MRS. MARTYN — (*gravely*). Oh, I'd lean on it.

BOBBY — (*nervously*). Look; I think a single eye-
glass may be all *right,* but look, I think it's kind of silly
to *wear* one, don't you?

MRS. MARTYN — I suppose it all depends.

BOBBY — Look; I guess it wouldn't be any harm to
own one, would it? Another thing I was goin' to ask
somebody, well f'r instance s'pose, I found a lense that
dropped out of a pair of somebody's spectacles, listen;
Do you think it wouldl damage your eyes if you had
a hole put in it for a string and kind of practised with
it in your own room? What I mean; look, if you don't
wear it all the *time* it wouldn't damage your eyes any.

would it? I guess it wouldn't look too well to have it
on when — well, look. what I mean . . .

The arrival of Cora and her governess precipitates
the first of the scenes indicating the domestic inhar-
mony prevailing at the Wheelers'. At sight of Miss
Pinney Bobby is visibly flustered. Sister Cora, however, is only amused.

CORA — What do you mean calling Miss Pinney
" Violet "? You've only known her these four days
since you got fired from this *last* school, and certainly . . .

BOBBY — You show a little delicacy, please! (*With
emotion to* VIOLET) Vio-Violent . . . Violet . . . I
only ask you to show me at least this much consideration that you would certainly observe to a mere — dog!

VIOLET — I'm not going to speak to your father
about *you* at all, Mr. Wheeler.

CORA —" Mister " Wheeler! Miss Pinney, *do* call
the child " Bobby "!

BOBBY — Haven't you got any sense at all?

MRS. MARTYN — He will see you and Cora now.
Miss Pinney.

VIOLET — I wanted to see him alone first.

MRS. MARTYN — That's all right. I'm sure.

VIOLET — Thank you.

(CORA *goes across to the door* L. *and listens.*)

BOBBY — (*bitterly*). That's a woman's honor. *that*
is! Eavesdropping!

CORA — Door's too thick to hear, anyhow. That's
papa's stick. The idea of a child of your age — oh!
(*Shouting*) Look! (*Pointing*) Those are papa's
spats too! Well, aren't you ashamed of yourself!

BOBBY — You 'tend to your own petty affairs.

CORA — Golly! I wish they *were* petty! She's
come to tell papa on me!

BOBBY — What about?

CORA — You 'tend to your own petty affairs.

BOBBY — Whyn't she discipline you herself?

CORA — She thinks I'm getting so dissolute something in the father line has to be done.   She'll get into a scrape all right.

BOBBY — *How* will she?

CORA — Mama'll have a fit if she finds out about her coming here to papa's office.

BOBBY — Why will she?

CORA — School boys needn't ask too many questions.

BOBBY — I'm not a school boy!

CORA — No; that's so!   Bobby, what *did* they fire you for?   Papa wouldn't tell me.

BOBBY — I want to know why will Miss Pinney get in a scrape.

CORA — Oh — Mama thinks Miss Pinney's too young and pretty to be a governess, anyhow!

BOBBY — What you talkin' about?

CORA — Of course *I'm* not goin' to tell Mama we made this secret excursion to tell on me and discuss how my character's to be saved . . . but when she finds *out* .   whoopee!

The entrance of Clarence is effective.   Mrs. Martyn, thinking to avoid the confusion of the outer room, asks him to step into the inner office.   " The soldier shambles in slowly, his hat in his hand," according to the author's instructions.   " He is very sallow; his hair is in some disorder; he stoops, not only at the shoulders, but from the waist, sagging forward, and, for a time to the left side; then, for a time, to the right; his legs ' give ' slightly at the knees, and he limps, somewhat vaguely.   He wears the faded, old, shabby khaki uniform of a private of the Quartermaster's Department. and this uniform was a bad misfit for him when it was new.   A large pair of spectacles shield his blinking eyes; his hands are brown; and altogether he is an unimposing figure.   Cora watches him closely as he comes down C. and stands, turning the rim of his army hat in his hands with an air of patience. He seems unaware of anybody, and continues so throughout the next speeches. This is CLARENCE."

MRS. MARTYN — I am Mr. Wheeler's secretary . . .

CORA — She's papa's *confidential* secretary. It's just the same as talking to papa.

MRS. MARTYN — We didn't want to keep you waiting any longer, when there's no opportunity . . .

CORA — (*interrupting her impulsively, but not unsympathetically*). What makes you sag so much to one side?

CLARENCE — (*Turning his head to look at her solemnly*). It's my liver!

CORA — (*blankly*). Oh!

MRS. MARTYN — You see Mr. Wheeler himself *can't* see *everybody;* and as you haven't even a letter to him, wouldn't it be the simplest thing for you to state your business to me?

CLARENCE — Wuw . . . Well . . . I haven't **any** business . . . exactly.

MRS. MARTYN — Well, your desires, then.

CLARENCE — Well — I thought I'd better see *him.*

MRS. MARTYN — Have you ever *met* Mr. Wheeler?

CLARENCE — Not — not yet.

MRS. MARTYN — Of course we want to show consideration to any *soldier* . . . (*As she speaks she takes a note-book and a fountain pen from a drawer of the desk*) What is your name, please?

CLARENCE — Clarence Smum. (*He does not actually say "smum." This word represents* MRS. MARTYN'S *impression of what she hears. His voice disappears casually, as it were, during the pronunciation of his surname, though he pronounces "Clarence" distinctly enough.*)

CORA — I do think . . . Clarence is a poetic name!
Some people don't, but I think it is.

MRS. MARTYN — Clarence what, please? (CORA
after blurring CLARENCE'S *reply by speaking at the
same time as* CLARENCE, *she continues the thought of
the preceding speech.*)

CORA — There used to be Dukes of Clarence in history, you know — very wealthy people that the king
drowned in a barrel of cider or something. There
could hardly be a nicer name than Clarence no matter
what people say. Were you in the war?

CLARENCE — I was in the — army.

BOBBY — (*sternly in a low voice*). You don't know
him.

CORA — It's right to speak to soldiers. Isn't it?

CLARENCE — If you . . . don't mind . . . what they
say . . . back.

CORA — (*to* BOBBY). *I told* you.

MRS. MARTYN. Now, if you please, Mister . . .

CLARENCE — Well, I thought I'd better see *him*.

MRS. MARTYN — If you're looking for a position,
I'm sorry, we've taken on more returned soldiers,
really, than we have places for. It would only waste
your own time . . .

CLARENCE — Well — I thought I'd better —

MRS. MARTYN — I know Mr. Wheeler would never
decline to see you, but — your first opportunity, even
for a few minutes wouldn't come until about Wednesday of next week.

CORA — Oh, yes, it could! When Miss Pinney gets
through telling about *me* in there, I'll *cheerfully* give
this soldier *my* time with papa!

MRS. MARTYN — My dear, that wouldn't . . .

CORA — Why, yes, it would. It'd be the best thing
that could happen for everybody! (*Determinedly*) I
atchally insist on it, Mrs. Martyn. (*To* CLAR-

ENCE) It's all right. Why don't you sit down?
CLARENCE — (*solemnly*). I will.

The children are greatly interested in Clarence as a soldier, their curiosity intensified by their habit of looking upon all men in uniform as heroes of one kind or another. " How did it feel when you first enlisted? " queries Cora, " her expression concentrated and serious," while Bobby kneels on the settle near him.

CLARENCE — It felt all right. There was nothing the *matter* with it then.
CORA — I don't mean your liver. I mean how did you feel when you first enlisted?
CLARENCE — I was drafted.
CORA — Were you just a private all the time?
CLARENCE — Yes, all the time after I was drafted, I was.
BOBBY — I hope there'll be another war in about a couple o' years or so.
CLARENCE — You want another war?
BOBBY — You bet!
CLARENCE — So you could be in it?
BOBBY — Yes, *sir!*
CLARENCE — I wish you'd been in this one. What would you do?
BOBBY — *Flying Corps.* That's the life!
CORA — What did *you* do in the war?
CLARENCE — (*with a faint note of pathos*). I drove a mule.
CORA — What in the world did you do that for?
CLARENCE — Somebody *had* to.
CORA — But what *for?*
CLARENCE — They won't go where you want 'em to unless you drive.

.   .   .   .

Bobby — You don't haf to ask so many *personal* questions, do you?

Cora — It's *right* to be personal to soldiers, isn't it — so as to look after their welfare?

Clarence — It's very public-spirited.

Cora — I think our American uniform is *so* becoming, don't you?

Clarence — Do you mean you think I'd look worse in other clothes?

Cora — No, but I *would* like to know why you drove a mule.

Clarence — I didn't *select* that branch of the service myself.

Cora — You mean somebody told you to?

Clarence — Yes. I thought it was better to do what they said.

Cora — Did you have to learn to swear at the mules to make them obey?

Clarence — (*thoughtfully*). No. No, I didn't.

Cora — Were you ever wounded?

Clarence — Yes, I was.

Cora — Oh, he was wounded! Where was it?

Clarence — At target practice!

Cora is summoned into the conference with her father and Miss Pinney. "Oh, murder," says she; "here is where I get wounded!" During her absence Bobby takes Clarence more completely into his confidence. "Listen," says he; "you been in the army. I'd like to ask your advice about some'p'm."

Clarence — I hope you've come to the right man.

Bobby — Listen; I'd like to ask you because, look, you been in the army and I can tell by your conversation you been around a good deal. Listen, do you think when a man's taken advantage of a woman's inexperience and kissed her he's bound to go ahead and marry her even if he's in love with another woman?

CLARENCE — (*gravely*).   Did you kiss somebody?

BOBBY — Yes.   I wouldn't again ; not her, I mean.

CLARENCE — Was it against her will?

BOBBY — She claims so.

CLARENCE — Does she claim you ought to marry her?

BOBBY — She says if I don't, she'll tell the whole family because, look, the person that was engaged to her saw this thing happen, and he got mad at her and she says I either got to pay her damages or run off and marry her.   Well, I haven't got any money for damages.   I wouldn't tell this to everybody.

CLARENCE — No ; I wouldn't either.   Who *did* you tell?

BOBBY — Well, I told Cora's governess, Miss Pinney — that just came in here for her.

CLARENCE — What did you tell Miss Pinney for?

BOBBY — Well, I told her because, listen, this *other* affair, it was just a passing fancy, but, look, I think when something higher and more spiritual comes into your life, why look, you're just hardly responsible for what you do, don't you?

CLARENCE — You mean when the higher love comes, then you get really wild?

BOBBY — That's it!   You see when this first thing happened I'd hardly even noticed what Miss *Pinney looked* like.

CLARENCE — Miss Pinney is the spiritual —?   And this other person that has a claim on you —?

BOBBY — It's horrible!   Look, you been in the army and everything.   What would you do about it?

CLARENCE — I'd go away to school again.

BOBBY — Yes, but look, when you've been fired from three prominent schools you get kind of a reputation, and, listen, it's kind of hard to get you in.   Father's already had quite a rebuff from *one* principal and he says himself I'm about as big a responsibility for him as anyone in the family.

CLARENCE — He does?

BOBBY — Oh, yes, and besides, well look, I don't want to go 'way just when this *other* thing's happened to me. It's the biggest thing in my *life*.

CLARENCE — You want to stay near Miss Pinney. (*Assenting.*)

BOBBY — Sure. Wouldn't you?

CLARENCE — Yes, I think I should.

The efforts of her governess and her father to discipline Cora disgust that young woman utterly. " They can go to thunder," she announces on her return from the inquisition. " If two people ever made me tired it's papa and Miss Pinney! Puritans! "

" I believe you been up to somep'm again with that ole grass widower! " ventures Bobby.

" Hush up! " returns his excited sister : " he's one of the most perfect characters that ever came into my life. I leave it to you (Clarence) if grass widowers aren't just as perfect as the other kind of widowers? "

" Yes," agrees Clarence, " just about."

CORA — I *did* go out motoring with him and I did dine at his country club with him, and danced there till twelve o'clock — and then Miss Pinney came and got me, but I leave it to you; is there any harm in that?

BOBBY — Well, of all the vile confessions —

CORA — You hush up! Of course I *said* I was going to spend the evening with a girl friend, but Miss Pinney found out — and *what* I want to know . . . if *you* were my father . . . (*To* CLARENCE) Would you go into thirty-five fits over a thing like that?

CLARENCE — No. Not that many.

CORA — Why, you ought to *see* those two in there;

you'd think they were judges of the Ex-treme Court of the United States in Washington! What I'm afraid of, they'll never let me see him again! (*Sits, sobs suddenly.*)

BOBBY — They ought to drown you; I never heard such a disgusting story in all my . . .

CORA — Hush up! She dee-lib'rutly comes to father with this just because mama's only our step-mother and hasn't got any idea of discipline — and you just ought to *hear* her in there, the way she goes on about being responsible for the shaping of my character because she's my governess! She'll get papa so prejudiced against me . . .

BOBBY — At that, I bet she hasn't told him half she knows about you! (*To* CLARENCE) Don't some women make you sick sometimes?

CLARENCE — No; to me she seems attractive. You see, she isn't *my* sister.

CORA — Listen; you've been in the army and all that. What would you do if *you* were a girl and in a fix like that?

CLARENCE — I don't know what I'd do if I were a girl in a fix like that; I don't even know what I'd do if I were a girl.

.   .   .   .

CORA — I kept trying to talk to papa about *you* all the time. I told him again and again there was a soldier waiting to see him, but they wouldn't let me change the *subject!* I tried to tell 'em about the cannibals, and how you'd been wounded, and about your liver, and I *did* tell 'em how you could drive mules without swearing —

CLARENCE — That wasn't what I said. I said I didn't have to learn how to swear at 'em. But did your father believe you when you *said* I could do it without?

CORA — He didn't say; he switched the subject right back to me. Never mind! (*Vindictively*) They'll be in a fix, all right, if *mama* hears about it!

BOBBY — *How* will they?

CORA — Why, they can't *tell* her they ignored her in the matter because she's merely an incompetent *step-mother,* can they? Besides that, there's somep'm else about mama and Miss Pinney and papa.

BOBBY — What?

CORA — I told you once and you were too dumb to understand. I'm not goin' to tell you again.

BOBBY — Aw, blub!

Wheeler Sr. attempts to dismiss Clarence, much to the disgust of both Cora and Bobby. Having told the soldier " everything " they feel that he may prove a friend in need. The climax is precipitated by the return of Mrs. Wheeler. Without intending to, Clarence is forced to overhear her side of the controversy as well as that of the children. Her suspicious of Miss Pinney have reached a height that makes her partly hysterical. " Has Cora been in there with them all the time? " she demands of Bobby.

BOBBY — No, not all.

MRS. WHEELER — I fancy not!

BOBBY — They let her out once, but they had to take her back.

MRS. WHEELER — What a farce!

BOBBY — It certainly was! What's the matter with you, mama; you're kind of excited.

MRS. WHEELER — Oh no; I'm not.

BOBBY — I s'pose Cora makes you perty mad —

MRS. WHEELER — No, she doesn't. I love Cora. I love both of you, Bobby. It's only that being a step-mother's an unfortunate position. One has to leave " discipline " to fathers and — governesses — which means that fathers and governesses have to consult, very frequently!

BOBBY — Cora was sayin' somep'm about that herself. She said: How could they ever tell you it was no use puttin' it up to you about her, but she thought herself it was goin' to make you perty mad.

MRS. WHEELER — So, even Cora thought I had a right to be angry, did she? Oh, Bobby —

BOBBY — Say, what's the matter?

MRS. WHEELER — (*just barely keeping the sobs from becoming vociferous*). Oh, Bobby, don't any of you see what I have to suffer? Don't you understand what I have to bear every day from your father and — these "consultations for discipline"! He and Miss Pinney — (CLARENCE *interrupts this emotional confidence with a loud, diplomatic cough*) Is some one — (CLARENCE *rises.*)

BOBBY — Papa told him to wait there. I would like you to meet my friend, Clarence.

CLARENCE — How do you do?

MRS. WHEELER — Have you been in here most of the morning?

BOBBY — Oh, he knows everything that's been goin' on.

MRS. WHEELER — I should think he would! Well, you've been in the army; I don't suppose there's any real reason to mind your having seen that we're a rather measly family.

Clarence is attempting to withdraw as gracefully as possible, when Wheeler discovers him. "Oh, murder — I forgot you!" confesses Wheeler. "I don't wonder at all," meekly responds the soldier.

Rather than have Clarence leave bearing with him so much of the family gossip, Wheeler decides to employ the soldier. As he is about to leave, Mrs. Martyn, after a conference with Wheeler, calls him back.

Mrs. Martyn — Where are you going, Mr.— Mr.—

Clarence — I thought he — forgotten me again. He seemed to have several other things on his mind — so I —

Mrs. Martyn — He wants you to sit down, please.

Clarence — Thanks.

Mrs. Martyn — He thinks he can find a position for you. But first — he wants me to ask you if it's really true you can drive mules without swearing.

Clarence — Does that mean he expects to give me a position — at his house?

ACT II

Three weeks later Clarence is comfortably installed in the Wheeler home. He has made himself a sort of high-class " handy man about the house." When the hot water system has given trouble, Clarence has repaired it. When the piano needed tuning, he has borrowed the chauffeur's tools and sought to improve the tone of that instrument. He has also served Mr. Wheeler as a sort of private secretary. Yet he is still a good deal of a mystery.

" Clarence," demands Della, the housemaid, " what line was you in *before* you went in the army? "

" I was working in a laboratory."

" Oh? In a hotel, I s'pose! "

Dinwiddie, the butler, is also puzzled. " You been here about three weeks now," he explains to Clarence; " and the domestic side of the household ain't able to settle what you are."

" What *I* are? "

" I mean, are you one of us, or do we treat you as one o' the family? "

" It doesn't matter," replies Clarence.

The Wheelers have all grown to depend on Clarence. Cora is sure he is the only one who understands her great love for the grass widower. Bobby is looking to him to settle his " affair " with Della, the housemaid, and even Violet. in whom he is most interested, permits him to help her be rid of an unwelcome suitor, one Hubert Stem. Hubert was really Cora's grass widower, but it transpires that he had been using her infatuation only to cover his attempts to be near the governess.

" Don't you think it is pretty odious of a man, when he knows a girl dislikes him, to pursue her by pretending to pursue a younger girl who's in her charge?" Violet asks Clarence.

CLARENCE — Are you consulting me on this point because I've been in the army, or more on the ground that I'm a person?

VIOLET — (*smiling faintly*). More on *that* ground.

CLARENCE — That surprised me. However, speaking to your point that a pursuer belonging to the more cumbersome sex becomes odious to a fugitive of the more dexterous sex, when the former affects the posture of devotion to a ward of the latter . .

VIOLET — Were you a college professor before the war?

CLARENCE — No. Not a *professor.*

VIOLET — Surely, not just a student?

CLARENCE — No. Not a *student.*

VIOLET — Well, then what . . .

CLARENCE — What I was leading to, was, that I personally, am indifferent to your reason for finding this young man, or any other young man, odious.

VIOLET — Thank you. I didn't put it on *personal grounds,* I believe.

CLARENCE — The *reason,* I say, is indifferent to me. I merely experience the pleasure of the *fact.*

VIOLET — What fact?

CLARENCE — That you don't like him.

VIOLET — I believe you are the queerest person I ever met.

CLARENCE — That's what my grandmother always said of my grandfather, and they *had* been married sixty-one years.

VIOLET — Your grandfather was as queer as that?

CLARENCE — No. Only to grandmother.

VIOLET — Are you *very* much like him?

CLARENCE — I'm just as much like my grandmother; you see, I'm descended just as much from her as I am from him.

VIOLET — I never thought of that!

CLARENCE — Well, after this, won't you think of me just as much like her as like him?

VIOLET — (*rather stiffly*). Isn't *that* a little " *personal* "?

CLARENCE — Personal? Good gracious! *You*'ve just been discussing *my* most intimate family affairs: my grandfather, my grandmother . . .

VIOLET — Never *mind!* I *will* think of you as just as much like your grandmother as your grandfather!

CLARENCE — It's very kind of you to think of me.

VIOLET — I didn't say . . .

CLARENCE — It's kind because you've got so many to think of : I want you to think of me; Mr. Stim . . . Stem! . . . wants you to think of him; Bobby wants you to think of him; Mr. Wheeler wants you to think . . .

VIOLET — That will do, please!

CLARENCE — Well, but doesn't

VIOLET — You *know* my position in this house; do you think it's manly to refer to it?

CLARENCE — I don't know about " manly "; maybe this is where I'm more like my grand*mother*. My idea was merely that since so many want you to think about them, if you'd just concentrate your thoughts on somebody that had been in the army, it might avoid . . . complications.

VIOLET — (*bitterly*). Do you suppose I'd stay in this house another hour, if I hadn't given my word to Mr. Wheeler I'd stand by Cora until she comes through this nonsense? He asked me to just stick it out until the child comes to herself again, and I gave him my word I'd do it. It seems *you* take Mrs. Wheeler's view of me!

CLARENCE — But, Mr. Stem . . . he's . . .

VIOLET — If I told Cora the truth about him, she'd only hate me. If I left her, she'd do the first crazy thing she could think of. She's *really* in *love;* it's a violence, but it may last a long while.

CLARENCE — She tells *me* it's " forever "! I'm her only friend and she made me her only confidant . . . except her stepmother, and Della, and Dinwiddie, and both of the chauffeurs. She told us that when she first saw him, she knew it was forever. (*Amiably*) Do you think it's advisable, Miss Pinney, for . . . anybody . . . to fall in love . . . permanently?

VIOLET — (*turning away coldly, then facing him*). I don't think I feel like holding a discussion with you about such things . . . or anything else.

CLARENCE — That must be all then.

VIOLET — When you first came here, I thought you were another friendly person, like me; pretty well adrift in the world. so that you had to make yourself useful in whatever you could find, just as I did. I did make that mistake; I thought I'd found a friend!

CLARENCE — Couldn't I keep on . . . being found?

VIOLET — Thank you, no! Not after what you said a moment ago! I'm glad you said it, though, because I like to know who my enemies are!

CLARENCE — (*blankly*). Oh?

Clarence could not continue long in such an anomalous position. "He's awful sympathetic and useful around the place," admits Cora; "and so mysterious and likeable; but I overheard Mama telling Papa last night she thinks he must be crazy for hiring him just because he could drive mules without swearing, and nobody knows a thing about him. Papa said it was mostly because Clarence was a stranded soldier and he didn't have any place for him except to dictate his letters to when he was home, but he guessed maybe he was crazy to do it."

The elder Wheeler's conviction was strengthened the same evening when he came home to find the entire family "at it again"; the children quarreling, Mrs. Wheeler with her tender feelings hurt over some new fancied slight; Violet insisting that she must be relieved of her promise to him that she would stay on. She is convinced now that she should go.

WHEELER — I can't let you do that.

VIOLET — What did you say —

WHEELER — I said I couldn't let you do that. See here; I suppose I've seemed to you just a commercial machine — head of a big business and head of an unhappy, rowing family, like so many of us machines. Well, I'm *not* — not altogether. I'm a pretty tired man. The naked truth is I'm pretty tired of the big business and pretty tired of the family. It's so. Sometimes I don't know whether I'm an old man or just a sort of worn out boy; I only know the game I play isn't worth the candle, and that I want to get away from the whole thing. I don't think I *could* stay with it, if *you* don't stay and help me.

VIOLET — (*touched*). Oh, poor Mr. Wheeler!

WHEELER — If you give *me* up, I'll give everything up.

The fact that Mrs. Wheeler overhears this statement

does not in the least help matters, but just as the final domestic crash seems imminent, a curious wailing noise is heard off-stage. Wheeler is convinced that it is Cora indulging in another tantrum, but "it ain't," as Della, dancing into the room in a state of high excitement, explains. " It's him; it's Mister Clair'nce all dressed up and wastin' his money on musical instruments."

" The sound has now resolved itself into the loud cry of a saxophone rendering a march," explains Mr. Tarkington. " Clarence marches on in the sun-room; he is the musician. Behind him Cora prances, clashing the silver covers of two dishes together for cymbals and loudly singing the air. Behind her Dinwiddie pompously dances, beating a tray with a large spoon, and whistling. This procession evidently intends to move along the sun-room from off R. to off L. but is arrested by Wheeler's vehemence."

WHEELER — What in the name of — (*They stop: so does the music.* MRS. WHEELER *has stopped crying and has risen.*)

DINWIDDIE — Oh!

WHEELER — What in the —

CLARENCE — (*removing the saxophone from his mouth*). We didn't know there was anybody here.

CORA — (*enthusiastically*). Look at him, Papa! (CLARENCE *has made a remarkable change in his appearance; he wears a beautifully fitting new suit of exquisite gray or fawn material, and he has been at pains to brush his hair becomingly; has a scarf-pin in his tie; buttonhole; and altogether is a most dashing figure.* CORA *goes on, without pausing*) Isn't he *wonderful*, Mama?

MRS. WHEELER — (*seriously and emphatically*). Why, *yes!* He *is!*

CORA — He went and bought *those* (his clothes) and the most *glorious* evening things all out of what he made in the war, and he borrowed the Swede's saxophone and never ever told us he could play it! Just look at him! Turn around! (*Obeying her gesture, made as she speaks, he solemnly turns round, so that they may see his back.* CORA *is carried away by helpless admiration. She almost means this; then as he faces front again*) Oh, Clarence!

MRS. WHEELER — It's beautiful! It's the most beautiful music I ever heard in my life. *I'll* play your accompaniment, Clarence; I'd adore to!

The saxophone solo is entirely successful as a harmony restorative, but all the joy is taken out of it for the performer when Violet abruptly leaves the room.

ACT III

Following the incident of the saxophone, the power and influence of the peacemaker grow apace. Soon Mrs. Wheeler is beaming upon Miss Pinney; Cora, transferring her affections completely from the forgotten Hubert Stem to Clarence, is ideally happy, and Bobby, seeing that even Della is fascinated by the new idol, is greatly relieved. There is no letup in the family effort to clear up the mystery of Clarence's past, however.

" Will you answer me one question, Clarence? " pleads Cora.

CLARENCE — What is the question?

CORA — It's simply, Clarence, what *was* the matter with your liver?

CLARENCE — If I answer you this time, will you promise never to ask me again?

CORA — Yes. What *was* the matter with your liver, Clarence?

CLARENCE — I was *shot* in it!

MRS. WHEELER — (*with eager loudness*). At Chateau Thierry?

CLARENCE — (*explosively*). No! At *target* practice!

CORA — What else did you do that was heroic, Clarence?

CLARENCE — I beg your pardon?

CORA — What was the next thing you did in the war?

CLARENCE — That was the *last* thing I did. I didn't do any more after that.

When they seek to discover how he became so proficient a performer on the saxophone, he is again evasive. " It's only an accident that I ever knew how to play at all."

" How was that? " demands Wheeler. " How could you learn to play the saxophone by accident? "

CLARENCE — Why, we used it to see whether certain species of beetles found in Montana are deaf, or if they respond to peculiar musical vibrations.

CORA — Beetles! How wonderful! How could you tell if the bettles responded to the vibrations?

CLARENCE — We placed them in a dish filled with food, that they were passionately fond of, and then I played to them. If they climbed out of the dish and left this food and went away we knew they'd heard the music.

BOBBY — Are the *hotels* good out in Montana?

CLARENCE — I don't know. I was living in a tent.

WHEELER — Hunting these beetles?

CLARENCE — Yes. They live outdoors.

BOBBY — And you were playing the saxophone to
'em?

CLARENCE — Yes.   Hours and hours at a time — to
the deaf ones.   It got very tedious.

CORA — I wish I'd been one.

BOBBY — You wouldn't haf to *change* much!

The family is more deeply mystified by the recital,
but Violet is moved frankly to laughter.   This troubles
Clarence and he seeks an explanation.

VIOLET — You want to know why I laughed?

CLARENCE — I'm not *sure!*   I'm not at all sure I
do; people aren't usually made much cheerfuller by
finding out why other people laugh at them!

VIOLET — You told *them* you had a *question* to ask
me.   You oughtn't to keep them waiting.

CLARENCE — A question?   Yes.   You said this afternoon we couldn't be friends any more.   My question
is: if that wasn't just an afternoon rule that we could
consider not operating in the evening?

VIOLET — Hardly!

CLARENCE — Couldn't?

VIOLET — It was on account of what you said this
afternoon that I laughed at you this evening.   You
have so many to think of, you know!

CLARENCE — I?   To "think" of!

VIOLET — Doesn't it seem rather funny, even to you:
your giving me that little lecture this afternoon about
the people that you said wanted me to "think" of
them?

CLARENCE — Oh, you mean when I said I wanted
you to think of *me!*

VIOLET — (*scornfully*).   Oh!

CLARENCE — You mean you got to thinking about
that this evening, and that's what made you laugh

You thought it was so funny my wanting you to think
of me.

VIOLET — No; I thought it was so funny your giving me that lecture; you see, *you* seem to have so many
to think of that I *don't* want you to think of *me!*

CLARENCE — I'd like to do what you want: I don't
know. I don't know whether it could be stopped or
not. A person goes around thinking — it wouldn't
make any *noise,* just thinking. It needn't disturb you
at all.

VIOLET — I think you'll be able to stop it.

CLARENCE — But it's the only pleasant thing I do!

Della does not help in the clearing up of the Clarence
mystery by repeating to Bobby that the soldier told her
he formerly was employed in a "hotel lavatory,"
though Violet firmly refused to credit this statement
when Bobby brings it to her. "Well, anyway," admits Bobby, "it is only another of his stories about
himself. Look, whenever he says anything about himself, it's somep'm a body can hardly believe, or else dis-
graceful like that. I and father been havin' a talk
about him and we both think it'll be better if you don't
have any more to do with him, Violet."

VIOLET — Why?

BOBBY — Look: the way *I* look at it is simply; look
at the way Cora and Mama and Della *are!* Look, you
don't want to get like that; you got an awful high
nature. It brings out all the most spirichul things I
got *in* me, and *we* think this is gettin' to be a serious
matter.

VIOLET — (*puzzled*). Clarence is?

BOBBY — Look; don't even let him talk to you.
'Course we don't feel it makes so much difference about
Cora and Mama — but with your spirichul nature, Vio-
let, and all this and that, and he telling about these
Montana beetles, and them listening to a saxaphone,

and being brought up by cannibals, and this mule story about bad language, and then workin' in a hotel lavatory — and all thus and so, why *we* think it's time somep'm'll haf to be *done* about it!

Something, the elder Wheeler agrees, will have to be done " with this fellow Smun." But his mere mention of the name starts another explosion. Clarence's surname is not " Smun," insists Violet. It's " Moon." Mr. Wheeler knows it must be " Smun " because that is the name his secretary wrote down the day Clarence was employed. But, insists Violet, no one was ever named " Smun."

Young Bobby has a different version. As he understood it, Clarence said " Smart." Into the midst of the discussion Hubert Stem projects himself with a clipping from a newspaper. He, taking an instinctive dislike to Clarence as a piano tuner, has made certain investigations on his own account and is positive that Clarence is none other than one " Charles Short, wagoner in the Quartermaster's Department; deserted three weeks ago; sought both by war department and divorced wife seeking alimony. Also wanted in Delaware."

This bomb is something of a " dud." Violet laughs at it. But the Wheelers admit it is worth investigating. Outside Clarence is playing an obligato on the saxophone while Mrs. Wheeler and Cora are striving to pitch their voices to the same mournfuul tune. Clarence is summoned that Mr. Stem may interrogate him.

STEM — (*fiercely*). My question is simply and plainly this : Did you ever hear the name of Charles Short?

CLARENCE — (*quickly*). Charles Short? Yes.

STEM — Do you know anybody by the name of Charles Short?

CLARENCE — Of course I do.

STEM — Do you know anybody by the name of Charles Short *well?*

CLARENCE — Charles Shortwell? I do not.

STEM — But you *do* know a person named Charles Short?

CLARENCE — Yes. Don't you? What do you mean? *Everybody* knows somebody named Charlie Short!

STEM.— I'm talking about the one *you* know!

CLARENCE — I know three!

STEM — I mean the one we're talking about!

CLARENCE — Well, good heavens, my dear sir, which one of them *are* we talking about? *I'm* not talking about any one of 'em. If you want to ask me a simple, direct question about somebody named Charlie Short, surely you ought to be able to say something more about him than that he's the one we're talking about.

STEM — More quibbles! Quibbles!

CLARENCE —" Quibbles "? I'm trying if possible to reach your mind! It seems you think we have a mutual acquaintance named Charlie Short, and you want to find out something about him from *me,* and you immediately proceed to lose your temper because your own powers of description are too limited for you to tell me which of the three *I* know is the one *you* know!

.   .   .   .

STEM — I want to know —

CLARENCE — Well, I'll answer you: *No!* I'm not this Charles Short! I'm not this one here in the paper, understand! About my being either of the other two, or both of 'em, I won't commit myself, but I'm not *this* one!

STEM — Isn't that quibbling, Mr. Wheeler?

CLARENCE — Does Mr. Wheeler think . . . Have

you been sharing Mr. Stem's suspicious as to his friend, this Mr. Charles Short?

WHEELER — (*emphatically*). I have not. It might have been possible, so I let him ask you. I'm glad it came up because we certainly need to know more about you than we do. We need to know just *who you are!*

CLARENCE — You need to know who *I am!* Why, I supposed you *did* know from the time I gave my name to Mrs. Martyn in your office!

WHEELER — Well, I didn't! We don't know anything about you!

CLARENCE — Why, good heavens, all you had to do was to look me up in the last edition of "Who's Who" —I don't mean that I'm a great man, but I certainly *am* one of the authorities on the coleoptera!

WHEELER — On the *what?*

CLARENCE — (*shouting*). On the COLEOP-TERA!

The mystery might have been cleared up right there — but just at that moment the butler rushes in to warn Clarence that the hot water pipes have " busted again " and the " authority on the coleoptera " dashes madly to the rescue.

" Well, what d'ye think about it, father? " demands Bobby. " Don'cha think he's probably crazy? "

" I don't know," shouts Wheeler in reply. " Go get me a dictionary! And a copy of ' Who's Who? '."

ACT IV

The discussion relative to Clarence's name and the recently added mystery of the strange science upon which he was an accepted authority occupied the evening and was resumed the next morning. Cora, her nose buried in mighty tomes, was sure Clarence had said " coal-something-or-other," but though her search had been diligent she was still unenlightened. " But," as she explained to her equally puzzled father, " the encyclopedia's absolootly more than useless whenever you need it the most. You can't get any help out of it at *all* unless you know just what you want to look up. *I'd* have *willingly* gone and asked Clarence last night while he was working in the cellar only you wouldn't let me."

MRS WHEELER — I don't just see you you couldn't have asked him yourself, Henry.

WHEELER — Don't you? I suppose you think I'm so ridiculous already I needn't have minded making myself more so!

MRS WHEELER — But I don't see the ridiculousness —

WHEELER — You don't see the ridiculousness of going down in the cellar to ask a man you've been badgering and who's repairing a heating plant for you — to ask him what a word was that he'd already *told* you *twice!*

There is neither a " Smun " nor a " Moon " in " Who's Who?" which adds to the distress of the investigating Wheelers. One point Clarence does make clear, however. He had not, he explains, told Della that he had previously been employed in a " lavatory." What he said was " laboratory."

He makes further admissions of interest when he discovers that Violet, convinced that her usefulness at the Wheelers' is ended, has decided to leave. As he is also about to make a change he sees no good reason why they should not go away together.

CLARENCE — I suppose the important thing is that we're both going away — and don't know where. You've never told me. Haven't you got any father or mother or anything?

VIOLET — No. I've got a second cousin in Belfast — I've never met him.

CLARENCE — I've got an aunt — in Honolulu. She used to write to me for money sometimes. I don't believe she'd be much help.

.   .   .   .

CLARENCE — There's something I want to tell you. It's about myself. I don't believe I've mentioned it. I *have* mentioned a lot of things about myself —

VIOLET — Well, not a " lot "— but — some.

CLARENCE — Nothing's so stupid as a man going about telling every one all about his private affairs — I'm afraid I talk about myself too much altogether. Of course, it was disgustingly conceited on my part to think Mr. Wheeler had looked me up — but wasn't it natural to think he'd do that when Mrs. Martyn had my *name?* I suppose I often forget I'm a specialist and that business men of *course* don't know about such people as entomologists.

VIOLET — I — suppose — they — don't.

CLARENCE — On the other hand, doesn't it seem strange they don't? My subject is of the most august proportions in the world. The coleoptera are the largest division of the animal kingdom. They outnumber mere human beings by billions of billions. Not held in check they would sweep the whole of mankind from the earth like a breath!

VIOLET — They would?

CLARENCE — I say I am an expert on them; that only means I know most of the little we know about them; our ignorance is still of the dark ages! Mr. Wheeler is an expert on dollars. Anybody can know *all about* dollars. Put all the wealth of the nations together and you get a sum that can be spoken in hundreds of billions, whereas the coleoptera consist of _eighty thousand species_ and the population of a _single one_ of those eighty thousand species alone outnumbers the dollars of all the nations of the earth as stupendously as the dollars of those nations outnumber the dollars in Mr. Wheeler's pocket! No, no; there's no reason for _him_ to feel superior. No, no, indeed! _Nobody_ need set up to be snobbish about _beetles!_

VIOLET — Beetles! Are the co-cole-optera — are they just _beetles?_

CLARENCE — Why! Didn't you _know?_

VIOLET — I — I don't believe many people — do.

CLARENCE — No. I suppose they don't. Each man to his trade — I've heard a politician get as excited about politics — or a minister about his congregation — as I do about the coleoptera! You wouldn't believe it, but —

VIOLET — Yes, I believe it. I believe everything you say — but you said you wanted to tell me something about your private affairs. You didn't mean the co-leoptera, did you?

CLARENCE — Yes; in a way their affairs are mine. What I wanted to tell you is that it's possible we shan't need to worry about money.

VIOLET — Possible that "_we_" shan't?

CLARENCE — We might not, after this morning mail. You see, before the war I was on potato bugs —

VIOLET — You were?

CLARENCE — Oh, yes; I was a _long_ time on potato bugs.

.   .   .   .

Now, the potato bug — the potato bug has several acknowledged authorities, and I was one of 'em.

VIOLET — Of course.

CLARENCE — My assistant was even more so; _I'm_ a more general authority; he's all potato bug; he's spent *sixteen years* on potato bugs; and he's the oldest bug man in the world to-day! He is! He's a good general bug man, too, a fine all round bug man, but when it comes to potato bugs, he can eat any other bug man alive!

VIOLET — He can?

CLARENCE — Yes, when I went into the army, this assistant of mine was appointed to the position I'd held; and it was what he deserved. When I got out of the army I knew if I went back there the trustees would put me in again, and he'd be dropped, so I decided it was only decent not to disturb him, but I had spent a lot of money on outside experiments, and I had to do something. However, I discovered that during a period of economic reconstruction after a world war there are extremely limited openings for a specialist on the coleoptera.

.   .   .   .

CLARENCE — It will all depend on the letter. You see, several days ago the papers said my assistant had been called to Washington by the Department of Agriculture and he'd accepted. So you see where that might put *us,* right away.

VIOLET —" Put us "? I don't see where it might put anything!

CLARENCE — But my dear —

VIOLET — What?

CLARENCE — My dear Miss *Pinney.*

VIOLET — Oh!

CLARENCE — Don't you see; that left me free to write the laboratory that I was out of the army — so I *did* write 'em yesterday, and if they think half as much of me as a coleopterist as I do of myself, they'll have my re-appointment in this morning's mail and we'll be all right.

VIOLET — But " we," " we "! You keep saying " we "!

CLARENCE — Well, by that I mean us. I couldn't ask for a better salary.

VIOLET — Oh, it's *you* that are going to lend money now — if your letter comes? Would you lend me — half of it?

CLARENCE — I thought probably — the best way would be — would be for you to take charge of all of it — as it comes in — and let me have what I need when I need it!

For a time it appeared that even the arrival of the mail would fail finally to clear up the mystery of Clarence. There was no letter, either for " Mr. Smun," " Mr. Moon," or " Mr. Smart."

CORA — No. That's all there is: there isn't a single solitary other letter except just this one that'll have to be sent to the Dead Letter Office because it's addressed to somebody that doesn't live here at all. It's addressed " *C. Smith, Esquire,*" care of Papa.

CLARENCE — But good heavens, that's *it!*

CORA — What?

CLARENCE —" C. Smith," Clarence Smith ; — of *course* it's it! You gave me a fright!

WHEELER — Smith? Clarence Smith!

VIOLET —" Smith "!

CORA — It's a 1916 " Who's Who in America "— before the war, that is. " S "—" S "—" Satterthwaite"—" Smalley "— *Smith! Clarence* Smith! He's the very first Smith there is in it! (*Reading*) " Clarence Smith, zoologist. Born June 13, 1890, at Zubesi Mission Station, Congo River, Africa — I should say he *did* have cannibals! — Son of Gabriel C. Medical Missionary and Martha S. Grad. Coll. Physical Science Newcastle-on-Tyne, England, Postgrad. Polytechnique, France. D. S. C.— D. S. C.?"

BOBBY — It means he's a Doctor of Science.   I had a prof. was one — ole Doc. Toser!

CORA —" Doctor of Science.   Chief en — en — tom-*ologist* "—

CLARENCE — En*tomolog*ist.   It   means   somebody that studies bugs.

CORA — Bugs?   How lovely!   " Chief ento-tomologist and curator of entomology.   Sturtevant Biological Laboratories.   Fellow N. Y. Acad. Science; mem. N. Y. Zoological Soc — society — Address Sturtevant Biological Laboratories, N. Y."   Did you ever hear anything like it?   And that just means Clarence!

VIOLET — Smith!   Clarence *Smith!*

CLARENCE — Why, *you* knew it was Smith, didn't you?

VIOLET — No.   No, 1 didn't.

CLARENCE — Is it — is it going to make a difference?

VIOLET — I couldn't — I couldn't —

CLARENCE — You mean you couldn't — because it's Smith?

VIOLET —" Smith's "— beautiful!

CLARENCE — Yes — it *will* be.

CORA — (*disturbed*).   What are they talking about?

MRS.   WHEELER — Sh!   They're   going   to   be married.

And so Clarence and Violet drove away in a taxi, waving their goodbys to a united family of Wheelers. Only Cora was unhappy.   Her latest " amour " had been shattered and her spirits plunged into the abysmal depths of unrequited love.   Clarence was gone — and she probably would never, never love again.

THE PLAYS AND THEIR AUTHORS

"Abraham Lincoln." Copyright, 1919, by John Drinkwater. Published by Houghton, Mifflin & Co., Boston. Mr. Drinkwater, born in England, June 1, 1882, devoted his early working days to the insurance business. He left this to become the manager of the Birmingham Repertory theater. He is the author of several short plays, including "The Storm," and "X-O," and is at work on three historical dramas patterned after "Lincoln," "Mary Stuart," "Oliver Cromwell," and "Gen. Robert E. Lee."

"Beyond the Horizon." Copyright, 1919, by Eugene G. O'Neill. Published by Boni & Liveright, Inc., New York. Mr. O'Neill is the son of James O'Neill, the veteran actor. He was born in Provincetown, Mass., in 18—. He is the author of several short plays, notably "The Moon of the Carribees," "Bound East from Cardiff," "Ile," "In the Zone," and "Where the Cross Is Made." His full length plays include "Chris," "The Straw," and "Gold."

"The Famous Mrs. Fair." Copyright, 1919, by James Forbes. All acting and recitation rights reserved. Mr. Forbes is a native of the province of Ontario, Canada, where he was born Sept. 2, 1871. He became interested in the theatrical business in 1897, and took up writing for the theater in 1904. His first play, and his most successful until he wrote "Mrs. Fair," was "The Chorus Lady," written first as a vaudeville sketch for Rose Stahl and played by her for many years in its expanded form. Other Forbes plays have been "The Traveling Salesman," "The Commuters," and "The Show Shop."

"Jane Clegg." Copyright, 1919, by St. John Ervine. Excerpts printed by arrangement with the publishers, Henry Holt & Co., New York. This is the second of St. John Ervine's plays to achieve unusual success in America, his "John Ferguson" having run for several months a year ago.

"Clarence." Copyright, 1919, by Booth Tarkington. Mr. Tarkington, born in Indianapolis, Ind., in 1869, gained wide fame as a novelist before he attempted writing for the stage. His first play was a dramatization of "The Gentleman from Indiana." In collaboration with Evelyn Greenleaf Sutherland he dramatized "Monsieur Beaucaire." With Harry Leon Wilson he wrote "The Man from Home," "Cameo Kirby," and "Up from Nowhere," and with Julian Street "The Country Cousin." Recently he has worked alone, producing "Your Humble Servant," "Mister Antonio," and "Clarence."

"Declasse." Copyright, 1919, by Zoe Akins. Miss Akins was born in the Ozark mountains of Missouri, in the town of Humansville, in 1886, but has spent most of her life in St. Louis. She is the author of "Papa," a three-act comedy, "The Magical City," a one-act drama, and "Footloose," a modern version of the old melodrama, "For-get-me-not." She has also done much writing for the magazines.

"The Jest." Copyright, 1919, by John Barrymore. The author of "The Jest," Sem Benelli, is one of the most popular of the younger Italian writers for the stage. In America he is known only for this drama and the libretto he prepared for the opera, "The Love of Three Kings," but on the continent his "Centaur's Nuptials," "The Mask of Brutus," and "Il Manbellaccio" have been generously acclaimed.

"Adam and Eva." Copyright, 1919, by George Middleton and Guy Bolton. All rights reserved. Working as collaborateurs, Mr. Middleton and Mr.

Bolton have written " Polly With a Past," " The
Light of the World," " The Cave Girl," and, with
George Cohan, " Hit-the-Trail-Holliday."   Mr. Mid-
dleton, born in Paterson, N. J., in 1880, has been
writing for the stage since 1902, when he helped Paul
Kester with a dramatization of " The Cavalier."   He
is also the author of " The House of a Thousand
Candles," " A Wife's Strategy," " The Prodigal
Judge," and numerous volumes of short plays.   Mr.
Bolton is author, or co-author, of " Oh, Boy," " Oh,
Lady, Lady," " Oh, Dear," " The Rose of China,"
" The Five Million," " The Rule of Three," and
" The Fallen Idol."

" Wedding Bells."   Copyright, 1919, by Salisbury
Field.   Mr. Field is a Californian and one of the
newer playwrights.   With Margaret Mayo he was
co-author of the farce, " Twin Beds."

" Mamma's Affair."   Copyright, 1919, by Rachel Barton Butler.   Miss Butler, born in Cincinnati, O.,
an alumnus of Prof. George Pierce Baker's " English 47 " class at Harvard, won, with " Mamma's Affair " a $500 prize offered by Producer Oliver Mo-
rosco.   She also sold the same manager another play,
called " Mom," and at the same time disposed of a
third, entitled " The Lap-dog."   Previous to this sudden success she had been writing plays for several
years without much encouragement.

NEW YORK

Including the plays of 1919–20 that will hold over,
and the new plays scheduled for a New York hearing
with the intention of remaining on or close to Broadway as long as their success warrants, a tour of the
eastern territory to follow:

John Barrymore in " Richard III."

Maude Adams in " Mary Rose."

Henry Miller and Blanche Bates in " The Famous Mrs. Fair."
David Warfield in " Peter Grimm."
Ina Claire in " The Gold Diggers."
George Arliss in " Podelkin."
Margaret Anglin in " The Woman of Bronze."
Ruth Chatterton in " Just Suppose."
Alice Brady in " Anna Ascends."
Billie Burke in " The School for Scandal."
Frances Starr in " One."
Lionel Barrymore in " Blood and Sand."
Florence Reed in " The Love Woman."
Walker Whiteside in " The Master of Ballantrae."
William Hodge in " The Guest of Honor."
Taylor Holmes in " Crooked Gamblers."
Nora Bayes in " Her Family Tree."
Emma Trentini in a new play.
Frank Tinney in " Tickle Me."
Frances White in " Jimmie."
Martha Hedman and Arthur Byron in " Transplanting Jean."
Raymond Hitchcock, Julia Sanderson and C. P. Huntley in " Hitchy-koo, 1920."
James K. Hackett in " The Great Adventurer."
Willard Mack in " His Grace, the Loafer."
Leon Errol in a revue.
William Rock in " Silks and Satins."
Eddie Cantor in a revue.
George White in " Scandals of 1920."
Richard Carle in " The Jolly Colonel."
Grace George in a new play.
Louis Mann in a new play.
Guy Bates Post in a new play.
Charles Purcell in " The Poor Little Ritz Girl."
Ruth Shipley in " Wild Cherries."
Lou Tellegen in " Blind Youth."
" Abraham Lincoln."
" Bab," with Helen Hayes.

" The Champion," with Grant Mitchell.
" Dear Me," with Grace LaRue and Hale Hamilton.
" Borderland," with Holbrook Blinn.
" Rollo's Wild Oat," with Roland Young.
" Man and Woman," with Mary Nash.
" The Jury of Fate," with Lowell Sherman.
" Arabian Nighties," with Hazel Dawn.
" Crucible," with Henry Hull.
" Paddy, the Next Best Thing," with Eileen Huban.
" Little Old New York," with Genevieve Tobin.
" Broadway Brevities," with Dorothy Jardon, Bert Williams and Geo. LaMaire.
" The Maid of the Mountains," with Fred Wright and an English company.
" Call the Doctor."
" Welcome, Stranger."
" The Straw."
" Golden Days."
" Scrambled Wives."
" Come Seven."
" The Man from the West."
" Cinderella on Broadway."
" Genius and the Crowd."
" The Innocent Violet."
" The Checkerboard."
" The Winged God."
" Pitter Patter."
" Opportunity."
A George Cohan revue.
" The Americans in France."
" Abie the Agent."
" The Bat."
" The Meanest Man in the World."
" Self Defence."
" Sweetheart Shop."
" Broadway to Piccadilly."
" Blue Bonnet."

" The Charm School."
" The Cave Girl."
" Dearie."
" Honeydew."
" Happy-go-lucky."
" Kissing Time."
" Ladies' Night."
" The Lady of the Lamp."
" Little Miss Charity."
" Mecca."
" Man of the People."
" The Nightwatch."
" Nothing Doing."
" The Rose Girl."
" Sonny."
" Spanish Love."
" Tattle Tales."
" The Dream Girl."
" Maid to Love."
" Peggy."
" Broken Wing."
" The Thrust."

EAST AND MIDDLE WEST

Including cities and important towns between the
Atlantic seaboard and Kansas City, Mo.:
  ** Ethel Barrymore in " Declassee."
  ** Henry Miller and Blanche Bates in " The Famous
      Mrs. Fair."
*** Richard Bennett in " Beyond the Horizon " and
      " For the Defense."
   * Fay Bainter in " East is West."
  ** William Gillette in " Dear Brutus."
   * Ina Claire in " The Gold Diggers."
   * Louis Mann in " Friendly Enemies."
  ** Barney Bernard in " His Honor Abe Potash."

Raymond Hitchcock in " Hitchy-koo, 1920."
* Lenore Ulric in " The Son-Daughter."
** Marjorie Rambeau in " The Sign on the Door."
* Jane Cowl in " Smilin' Through."
* Leo Ditrichstein in " The Purple Mask."
* Otis Skinner in " Pietro."
* William Collier in " The Hottentot."
* Ed Wynn's " Carnival."
* Charles Cherry in " Scandal."
* Grace George in " The Ruined Lady."
* Nance O'Neill in " The Passion Flower."
** Walter Hampden in " Hamlet," and " Romeo and Juliet."
* Robert B. Mantell in Shakespearean repertoire.
May Robson in " Nobody's Fool."
George White's " Scandals of 1919."
** " Wedding Bells," with Margaret Lawrence and Wallace Eddinger.
* " Mamma's Affair," with Effie Shannon and Robert Edeson.
* " The Storm," with Helen MacKellar.
McIntyre and Heath in " Hello, Alexander."
* " Civilian Clothes," with William Courtenay.
** " Buddies," with Peggy Wood and Donald Brian.
* " Shavings," with Harry Beresford.
* " The Wonderful Thing," with Jeanne Eagels.
* Al Jolson in " Sinbad."
*** " Abraham Lincoln."
** " Jane Clegg."
** " Irene."
** " Clarence."
** " Adam and Eva."
** Ziegfeld " Follies, 1920."
** " Apple Blossoms."
* " My Lady Friends."
" The Girl in the Limousine."
" The Little Blue Devil."

* " Nighty-Night."
* " The Little Whopper."
" Linger Longer Letty."
" The Magic Melody."
" The Rose of China."
* " Aphrodite."
* " The Acquittal."
*** " Monsieur Beaucaire."
" Angel Face."
" Always You."
" Frivolities of 1920."
* " The Nightboat."
* " As You Were."
" My Golden Girl."
" Breakfast in Bed."
* " The Ouija Board."
" Look Who's Here."
" Mrs. Jimmie Thompson."
* " Floradora."
** " Lassie."
* " Honey Girl."
" Betty Be Good."
" His Chinese Wife."
" Up in Mabel's Room."
* " Experience."
* " The Wanderer."
San Carlo Opera Co. (see note).
Dunbar Opera Co. (see note).
* " Chu Chin Chow."
" Greenwich Village Follies, 1919."
* " Passing Show, 1919."
* " What's in a Name? "
" Three Showers."
" The Hole in the Wall."
* " The Bird of Paradise."
* " Maytime."
" Man Who Came Back."

" The Blue Flame," with Theda Bara.
" Martinique," with Josephine Victor.
" Footloose," with Emily Stevens.
" Jack-o-Lantern," with Doyle and Dixon.
Bertha Kalich in " The Riddle : Woman."
Guy Bates Post in " The Masquerader."
Anna Pavlowa in a ballet repertoire (see note).
Thurston the Magician (see note).
" The Man of the People " (see note).
" The Royal Vagabond."
" Three Wise Fools."

NOTE.— These attractions have not been seen by the author. He is therefore unable to venture an opinion as to their 'quality as entertainment.

WEST AND NORTHWEST

From Kansas City, Mo., to the Pacific Coast, and including the larger towns and cities of the Southwest:

*** " Abraham Lincoln."
*** William Gillette in " Dear Brutus."
 ** Otis Skinner in " Pietro."
 ** Leo Ditrichstein in " The Purple Mask."
 ** Robert B. Mantell in Shakespearean repertoire.
 ** Jane Cowl in " Smilin' Through."
 ** Grace George in " The Ruined Lady."
  * Bertha Kalich in " The Riddle: Woman."
    McIntyre and Heath in " Hello, Alexander."
  * Anna Pavlowa in a ballet repertoire.
  * Nance O'Neill in " The Passion Flower."
 ** Milton Nobles in " Lightnin'."
 ** Guy Bates Post in " The Masquerader."
 ** " The Passing Show of 1919," with the Howard brothers.
 ** " The Blue Flame," with Theda Bara.
  * " Tiger Rose."

* " Buddies."
" Gaieties of 1919."
** " Clarence."
** " Chu Chin Chow."
* " Nighty-Night."
* " The Storm."
" Hitchy-koo, 1919."
" The Girl in the Limousine."
* " The Little Whopper."
" Linger Longer Letty."
** " The Sign on the Door."
" Angel Face."
" Frivolities of 1920."
* " As You Were."
" Breakast in Bed."
" My Golden Girl."
* " Mamma's Affair."
** " Floradora."
" Jack-o-Lantern. '
George White's " Scandals of 1919."
" Sweetheart Shop " (see note).
* " Experience."
* " The Wanderer."
" Keep Her Smiling."
" Good Morning, Judge."
" Up in Mabel's Room."
** " The Acquittal."
* " Listen Lester."
" Flo-Flo."
" Twin Beds."
" The Man Who Came Back."
* " The Bird of Paradise."
San Carlo Opera Co. (see note).
Dunbar Opera Co. (see note).
Kolb and Dill (see note).
Fanchon and Marco (see note).
NOTE.— These attractions have not been seen by the

author. He is therefore unable to venture an opinion as to their quality as entertainment.

SOUTH

*** William Gillette in " Dear Brutus."
*** Mrs. Fiske in " Miss Nelly of N'Orleans."
  ** " Wedding Bells," with Margaret Lawrence and Wallace Eddinger.
   * Robert B. Mantell in Shakespearean repertoire.
*** Milton Nobles in " Lightnin'."
  ** " The Acquittal."
  ** Walter Hampden in " Hamlet," and " Romeo and Juliet."
     " Robert E. Lee " (see note).
  ** " Clarence."
   * " Nighty-Night."
     " Hitchy-koo, 1919."
     " The Girl in the Limousine."
   * " The Little Whopper."
     " Passing Show of 1919," with the Howard brothers.
  ** " Buddies."
  ** " Irene."
     " Linger Longer Letty."
     " The Rose of China."
     " My Lady Friends."
     " As You Were."
   · " My Golden Girl."
     " Breakfast in Bed."
   * " Floradora."
     " The Man Who Came Back."
     " Twin Beds."
     " Listen Lester."
     " Flo-Flo."
   * " Experience."

* " The Wanderer."
  " Keep Her Smiling."
  " Good Morning, Judge."
  " Up in Mabel's Room."
* " Tiger Rose."
  " Three Showers."
** " Lassie."
** Bertha Kalich in " The Riddle: Woman."
  McIntyre and Heath in " Hello, Alexander."
  San Carlo Opera Co.
  Fields' Minstrels (see note).
  Neil O'Brien Minstrels (see note).
** " Three Wise Fools."

NOTE.— These attractions have not been seen by the author. He is therefore unable to venture an opinion as to their quality as entertainment.

THE SEASON IN LONDON

By Sidney Dark

(Editor *John O'London's Weekly*)

IT was inevitable that during the war the English theatre should have practically ceased to have any artistic existence and that the playhouses should have been monopolised by ephemeral and generally banal entertainments. Most of the younger actors and dramatists were in the army. All the older men shared the insistent anxieties that for over four years made any sort of imaginative work almost impossible. Moreover, the theatres catered entirely for the boys home on leave from the front and they certainly did not want plays that made them think. All they wanted was to laugh and to forget. The armistice was signed nineteen months ago. The army is demobolised. New conditions (it would be false to say "normal" conditions) have come into existence. The London theatres are still in most cases content to be merely houses of entertainment, but there are signs (at present little more than clouds the size of a man's hand) that our theatre is again ambitious and that the art of drama may once more flourish in the country of Shakespeare. There is one fact, however, that must be accepted, in considering (so far, at least, as England is concerned), both post-war literature and post-war drama. That is that a literary era definitely came to an end on August 4th, 1914. With a few notable exceptions, the most considerable writers before the war ceased to count when the war began. We must look to new

men and new women for the real work of the present
and the future.

It should be said at the outset that this review of
the London theatre is confined to the last six months
of 1919 and the first five months of 1920. During
this period there have been, as I have said, many in-
dications both of the desire of the English actor and of
a minority of English managers to produce plays of
genuine dramatic value and of the English public to
pay to see artistic plays when they have the chance.

The older generation of actor managers, who cared
for something more than box-office returns, has practically disappeared. Sir Herbert Tree and Sir George
Alexander died during the war. H. B. Irving has
died since the peace. But a notable addition to the
actor manager ranks occurred towards the end of last
year when Henry Ainley became a partner with the
American Gilbert Miller in the management of the St.
James'. Mr. Ainley is without question the most
gifted of contemporary English players. He possesses
good looks, imagination, intelligence and unusual ver-
satility. He began his stage career with Sir Frank
Benson, who has trained most of the considerable
players on our stage, and he learned a great deal from
Mr. Granville Barker, the best producer England has
seen for many a year and who, unhappily for us, now
spends most of his life in America. Mr. Ainley began
his management with the production of Tolstoi's
" Reparation " and followed this gloomy drama with
a revival of " Julius Cæsar." When one remembers
how much the English theatre owed to the enthusiasm
of the late Charles Frohman, it is interesting to repeat that Ainley is aided and abetted in his artistic
ambition by another American.

Even more interesting is the new management of
the Lyric Theatre, Hammersmith, a small playhouse
in a distant western suburb. This house is controlled

by a syndicate of which Mr. Arnold Bennett is the
head and which includes two of London's newspaper
millionaires. Its first production was John Drinkwater's "Abraham Lincoln," perhaps the most considerable play seen since the war. America has thoroughly endorsed London's verdict on "Abraham Lincoln." Its financial success here was as surprising as
it was significant. It was followed by "John Ferguson" by St. John Ervine, the young dramatist who
lost a leg during the war. "John Ferguson," which
was a success in America before it was seen here, only
had a short run, despite its distinction and despite
the fact that it was magnificently acted by a company
largely recruited from the notable players associated
with the Abbey Theatre, Dublin. "John Ferguson"
was followed by a revival of "As You Like It" and
this will give way shortly to a production of Gay's
famous "Beggar's Opera."

Incidentally it should be recorded as further proof
of what I have stated that during the winter, two large
theatres in the crowded mean streets of south London
have been packed every evening by performances of
Shakespeare and grand opera at popular prices.

John Galsworthy's "The Skin Game" is far and
away the most interesting new play produced in the
West End. Plays with actual war incidents have a
small chance of success in London. We are so weary
of it all. But though Mr. Galsworthy does not refer
to the war, he has evidently written under the influence
of the events that have followed the peace. His play
deals with the quarrel of an old aristocratic family
settled for generations in a sleepy village and a pushing "new" millionaire. But the play is really an
allegory and there is a world of sad significance in the
words of the aristocrat after he has won the fight.
"We went into this fight with clean hands, are they
clean now?" The acting of "The Skin Game" is

altogether worthy of the play and it gives a definitely
high place in the English theatre to Mr. Edmund
Gwenn who plays the " new " man with splendid sincerity and intensity.

Sir James Barrie's " Mary Rose " at the Haymarket
is, of course, one of the successes of the season. Barrie is a sure card both in England and America. But
this play emphasizes my assertion that the pre-war
writers really finished their course in 1914. " Mary
Rose " may be described as " freakish sentimentality "
and to me anyhow sentimentality cloys after the ultra-
realism through which we have so recently lived.
Once more, the excellence of the acting may fairly be
noted. For nearly a generation English critics have
been obliged to admit that, while we possessed a number of actors who could be safely compared with the
best in America and almost with the best in France
and Germany, we were woefully poor in really capable
actresses. Our Ellen Terrys and Mrs. Kendalls had
no successors. Now we have actresses of far more
than first rate promise and conspicuous among them is
Miss Fay Compton who plays the Barrie heroine.
Miss Compton is a sister of Compton Mackenzie, the
novelist.

Mr. Alfred Sutro's " The Choice " has had a long
run at Wyndham's Theatre, owing to some extent,
perhaps, to the fact that Gerald Du Maurier is Su-
burbia's favourite actor. Mr. Sutro can never forget
his insistent admiration for " the strong silent man "
who never exists in real life and has become a bore
on the stage. Mr. Arnold Bennett's " Sacred and
Profane Love," produced at the Aldwych in the late
autumn, was a deft dramatization of an old novel.

Mr. James B. Fagan, a dramatist of some distinction, has been among the season's new managers. He
produced at the Court Lennox Robinson's " The Lost
Leader," the play written round the life of Parnell

which has since been seen in America. This well written drama was another success and again one had a proof of the old truth that good plays make good actors or rather that good plays give good actors the opportunity to show how good they are. The "lost leader" was admirably acted by Mr. Norman McKinnel, the fighting head of the Actors' Association. Mr. Fagan followed this play with a production of "The Merchant of Venice" in which the famous Jewish actor, Maurice Moscovitch, gave a powerful performance of Shylock, interesting particularly to English audiences because he disregarded almost all the conventions established by Henry Irving and copied by all subsequent English Shylocks.

Among the other outstanding new plays of the season one may mention "Mr. Pim Passes By," a deft light comedy written by A. A. Milne, one of the "Punch" group of humourists, in which Miss Irene Vanbrugh and her husband, Dion Boucicault, play with their usual charming light touch, and "The Young Person In Pink," by Gertrude Jennings. The latter may be described as an entertainment with brains. With amusing incident and bright dialogue it contains one character that Dickens might have created had he lived today. Mrs. Badger is, indeed, the most irresistible cockney type seen on our stage for many a day — unscrupulous but good natured, humourous and unfailingly resourceful. The part is played with abounding humour by Miss Sydney Fairbrother. "The Young Person in Pink" is the first essay in management of Mr. Donald Clayton Calthrop, whose father, John Clayton, was a distinguished Victorian actor manager and produced the famous Pinero farces at the Court Theatre. Mr. Calthrop's mother was one of the many talented Boucicaults. He is a capital actor, in the early thirties, who looks about eighteen both on the stage and off.

Miss Marie Löhr, who is established as the actress manageress of the Globe, produced a dramatic version by Mr. Macdonald Hastings of Joseph Conrad's great novel, " Victory," and followed it with Robert Hichens's " The Voice from the Minaret." Mr. Hichens is well known in America and all that need be said of this play is that it has most of the highly coloured qualities of its author's novels. Mr. Norman McKinnel was conspicuous in the part of an evil minded husband. Miss Löhr has revived the late Sydney Grundy's costume comedy, " A Marriage of Convenience," and has appeared in the rôle created by Sarah Bernhardt in Rostand's " L'Aiglon."

Colonel Robert Lorraine, actor and super-flying man, also chose Rostand for his first production since the war. His revival of " Cyrano de Bergerac " was altogether delightful and his performance of Cyrano was a joy even to those of us who can remember Coquelin in what was one of his greatest parts. Colonel Lorraine afterwards revived Bernard Shaw's " Arms and the Man." The Shaw plays do not, however, appear to have much attraction for the present race of English playgoers. " Arms and the Man " had a comparatively short run, as had a revival of " Pygmalion " with Mrs. Patrick Campbell in her original part.

John Masefield's " Pompey the Great," a thing for the study rather than for the stage, was played by Sir Frank Benson for a few nights at the St. Martin's. The production of a dramatization of the well press-agented " The Young Visiters " should be regarded as a theatrical curiosity and not a dramatic event. Miss Constance Collier returned home from America to produce the dramatic version of Du Maurier's novel " Peter Ibbetson," which has, I believe, been seen on your side. Du Maurier regarded this gloomy story as by far his best literary work and the play written by the late John Raphael, an English journalist who lived most of his life in Paris, has real dramatic quality. Mr. Cyril Maude, who is also home again after a long stay in America, has been playing for months with Miss Connie Ediss at the Criterion in a näive farce called "Lord Richard in the Pantry."

Captain Harwood's "The Grain of Mustard Seed," recently produced at the Ambassadors', is the cleverest political comedy we have had for many seasons. This is another instance of brains in the theatre with most satisfactory financial results. Incidentally, this play has added to Mr. McKinnel's acting successes.

I have mentioned several Shakespearian revivals. To them must be added Sir Frank Benson's "Hamlet" and Mr. Matheson Lang's "Othello," both interesting, but neither epoch-making. Mr. Matheson Lang has produced a version of the Italian play called "Sir-rocco," a colourful drama slightly bowdlerised for English consumption and rechristened "Carnival."

American plays have had a large place in theatre programmes during the past months. They have been, for the most part, bright, well constructed entertainments, exactly suited to the spirit of the times. "The Bird of Paradise," which is just finishing a long run at the Lyric, attracted by the pretty novelty of its Hawaiian atmosphere. "Business Before Pleasure" and "Nothing but the Truth" made us laugh when we badly wanted to laugh. Among the other American productions may be noted "Three Wise Fools," "Daddies," "In the Night" (written by an Englishman but produced in America with a different title in 1916), "The Lilac Domino," "The Man Who Came Back" and "Mr. Todd's Experiment." America may be assured that the unfortunate incident that occurred on the first night of Mr. Hartley Manner's "One Night in Rome" was certainly not caused by any hostile feeling to American players. Miss Laurette

Taylor was already an established London favourite, one of the many clever American women, of whom Miss Edith Day is the latest, who have been warmly welcomed in London. The London theatre is, indeed, traditionally cosmopolitan, and because the American player speaks our language (though in his own characteristic way) his place here is always assured. During this last season Mr. Walter Catlin, a comedian with admirable restraint and attractive personality, made a great personal success in " Baby Bunting," a musical comedy composed by the American Mr. Nat D. Ayer, whose success in London has made him a permanent resident here. This is one incident among many.

Little need be said of the new musical comedies and revues. These productions are written to pattern. They are generally devised to exploit the talent of some one expensive performer. They are rarely hampered by wit or originality. They always have long runs and make much money — and then they are forgotten. Mr. George Robey is the greatest London revue " star," with the American Miss Ethel Levey, the American Miss Lee White and the English Miss Violet Lorraine running him close. Mlle. Delysia has become a considerable draw here and the exotic " Afgar," in which she has been appearing has been one of the season's striking successes. Mlle. Delysia will be seen in America in the autumn.

Among the interesting artistic happenings of the season have been the visit of the remarkable Guitry family from Paris, Pavlova's dancing at Drury Lane and a series of revivals of Greek tragedy in which Miss Sybil Thorndike has played the leading parts.

I have summarised the facts that give hope for the future of the theatre in England. I have suggested the facts on the other side. Unhappily one must include with them the ever increasing commercialism of the theatre and the growing power of the mammoth managers.   Profiteering has forced up theatre rents in London to such figures that experiment, which is the life blood of every art, is only possible to a multi-millionaire.   And more than half the London play-houses are controlled by half a dozen men (with mysterious backers who include a Greek and an Armenian) who laugh at all talk about art and profess to care for nothing but profits.   The art of the theatre would be far, far safer in the hands of the actor managers whom, a dozen years ago, we all used so constantly to attack.

STATISTICAL SUMMARY

(June 1919–June 1920.)

Plays	Performances	Plays	Performances
Abraham Lincoln	193	Crimson Alibi, The	51
Adam and Eva	312	Cæsar's Wife	81
All Soul's Eve	21	Civilian Clothes	150
Always You	66	Clarence	300
An Exchange of		Curiosity	28
Wives	19	Declassee	257
An Innocent Idea	7	Dancer, The	61
Angel Face	57	Ed. Wynn's Carnival	64
Aphrodite	148	Elsie Janis and Gang	55
Betty Be Good	31	Faithful, The	49
Beyond the Horizon	111	Famous Mrs. Fair,	
Apple Blossoms	256	The	183
Acquittal, The	138	First Is Last	62
A Regular Feller	31	Five o'Clock	41
As You Were	143	Five Million, The	91
At 9:45	139	Fifty-Fifty, Ltd.	40
A Young Man's Fan-		Florodora	64
cy	13	Forbidden	18
A Voice in the Dark	134	For the Defense	77
Big Game	21	Footloose	32
Blue Flame, The	48	Frivolities of 1920	61
Bonehead, The	24	George Washington	16
Boys Will Be Boys	45	Girl from Home, The	24
Breakfast in Bed	75	Girl in the Limousine,	
Buddies	259	The	137
Carnival	13	Gold Diggers, The	282
Cat-bird, The	33	Greenwich Village	
Challenge, The	72	Follies, The	232

"AT 9:45"

A melodrama in three acts by Owen Davis, produced by William A. Brady, Ltd., at the Playhouse. New York, June 28, 1919.

Cast of characters —

Judge Robert Clayton	George Backus
Howard	Noel Tearle
Jim Everett	Leo Mielziner, Jr.
Jack Grover	Harry Green
Captain Dixon	Clifford Dempsey
Doane	Frank Hatch
Doyle	Frank Hilton
Mack	Peter Lang
Dr. Norton	Robert Thorne
Gillaini	Gustave Rolland
Mrs. Clayton	Edith Shayne

Molly .... Nedda Harrigan
Ruth Jordan......................... Marie Goff
Mary Doane........................ Madeleine King
Margaret Clancy .. .. -- - ....Idalene Cotton
Tom Daly......................... John Harrington

Act I.— Scene 1 — Judge Clayton's Library. Scene 2 — Waiting Room at the Ritz-Carlton. Act II.— Judge Clayton's Library. Act III.— Scene 1 — The Library. Scene 2 — Another Room at Judge Clayton's. Place — New York City. Staged Under the Direction of John Cromwell.

The son of Judge Robert Clayton is mysteriously shot and killed at 9:45 on an evening when the family is away from home dancing at the Ritz. Upon the discovery of the body the work of untangling the mystery is turned over to Capt. Dixon of the police, who follows a variety of clews implicating practically every member of the cast. Not until the end of the play does the confession of the member of the household least suspected relieve the situation.

"THE FIVE MILLION"

An American comedy in three acts by Guy Bolton and Frank Mandel, produced by F. Ray Comstock and Morris Gest, at the Lyric Theater, July 8, 1919.

Cast of characters —

Ruth Hunter .... Sue MacManamy
Mary .... Marie Ahearn
Ada .... Lucile Webster
Rhy MacDonald .... Helen Barnes
Lill .... June Holbrook
Phil Bishop .... Ralph Stuart
Nini Bishop .... Marjorie Poir
" Mac " .... James Gleason
Albert Weaver ...., ...Purnell Pratt
" Midge " Monahan .... Beatrice Noyes
Douglas Adams .... Ralph Morgan
Grant Adams .... Percy Helton
Jefferson Adams.................... Charles Abbe
Otis Weaver .... Robert McWade
Colonel Van Alstyne .... Edward Poland
Dan Monahan .... Harry Harwood
Al Higgins .... Harry MacFayden
Queenie .... Amy Ongley

Act I.— School Room at Clinton Falls, N. Y.

Act II.— Law Offices of Weaver & Weaver. Act III.— Dining Room of Monahan's Boarding House. Staged by Robert Milton.

"GREENWICH VILLAGE FOLLIES"

A revue in two acts and twelve scenes by Philip Bartholomae and John Murray Anderson, produced by the Bohemians, Inc., at the Greenwich Village Theater, July 15, 1919.

Principals engaged —

- Susanne Morgan
- Charles Derickson
- William Foran
- Robert Edwards
- James Watts
- Jane Carroll
- Homer Rosine
- Gordon Drexel
- Warner Gault
- Edgar Thornton

Jere Delaney
Bessie McCoy Davis
Irene Olsen
Rita Zalmani
Irene Mathews
Rex Story
Ada Forman
Cynthia Perot
Edmond Makalif
Olga Ziceva

Staged by John Murray Anderson.

"THE CRIMSON ALIBI"

A melodrama in a prologue and four acts by George Broadhurst, produced by George Broadhurst, at the Broadhurst Theater, New York, July 17, 1919.

Cast of characters —

Chuck Brown ....Gardner James
David Carroll ....Harrison Hunter
Professor Bristol ....Wm. H. Thompson
James Leverage ....Robert Vaughn
Loomis ....Thomas Traynor
Andrew Quincy ....Robert Barrat
Collins ....Roy LaRue
Robert Dorrington ....George Graham
Larry Conover ....·.. .... .Robert Kelly
Red Parks ....William E. Lemuels
Mrs. Williams ....Mary Foy
Judith Darrel ....Edna James
Mrs. Dean ....Thais Lawton
Mrs. Burrage ... .Inda Palmer
Mary Garrison ....Bertha Mann
Mrs. Wrench ....Mary Foy
Julia ....Cathrine Cozzens

Prologue — A Room in the Home of Joshua Quincy.

Act. I.— Scene 1 — A Room in the Home of David
Carroll. Scene 2 — Office of Police Inspector Lever-
age. Act II.— Scene 1 — Veranda of the Quincy
Home. Scene 2 — Joshua Quincy's Study. Act III.
— Scene 1 — Office of Carter's Hotel. Scene 2 —
Room 118. Scene 3 — Office of Carter's Hotel. Act
IV.— Office of Police Inspector Leverage. Play
Staged by and Entire Production Under the Supervi-
sion of Mrs. Lillian Trimble Bradley.

Joshua Quincy is stabbed in the dark, and likewise
the heart, by a person, or persons, unknown. David
Carroll, a local Sherlock Holmes who devotes most of
his time to the composition of music, is prevailed upon
to take the case. His suspicions shift from character
to character, each with seemingly a plausible motive
for making way with the old man, until the entire
company, including Carroll's sweetheart, appears
guilty. Then the investigator succeeds in fastening
the crime upon the guilty party and forces confession
from him.

" SHUBERT GAIETIES 1919 "

A revue in two acts and twenty-five scenes, produced
by J. J. and Lee Shubert, at the Forty-fourth
Street Theater, New York, July 17, 1919.

Principals engaged —

Henry Lewis	Gladys Walton
Jack Bohm	Jimmie Fox
Arthur Hull	Gilda Gray
Stewart Baird	Llora Hoffman
Harry Fender	Clayton and White
Marguerite Farrell	The Glorias
Irving Fisher	Ina Williams
Marie Stafford	Billie Williams
Ted Lorraine	

Staged by J. C. Huffman.

"A VOICE IN THE DARK"

A melodrama in three acts and nine scenes by Ralph E. Dyar, produced by A. H. Woods, at the Republic Theater, New York, July 28, 1919.

Cast of characters —

IN THE PROLOGUE

Mrs. Maria Lydiard	Florine Arnold
Amelia Ellinham	Arleen Hackett
Miss Meredith	Harriet Ross .
Madge Conroy	Anne Sutherland
The Coroner	John Ravold
Tip Wilkins	William Phinney
Doctor Franklin	Rexford Kendrick
Harlan Day	William Boyd
Hugh Sainsbury	Richard Gordon

The Office of Dr. Franklin, Briarcliff, Tuesday, June 22, 4:30 P. M.

IN THE PLAY:

Miss Gridley	Doris Kelly
Sam Cloyd	Frank Monroe
Robert Farrel	W. L. Thorne
Harlan Day	William Boyd
Tom Hemmingway	Stewart E. Wilson
Adele Warren	Georgia Lee Hall
Blanche Warren	Olive Wyndham
Mrs. Maria Lydiard	Florine Arnold
Amelia Ellingham	Arleen Hackett
Miss Meredith	Harriet Ross
Hugh Sainsbury	Richard Gordon
Madge Conroy	Anne Sutherland
John Malone	John Sharkey
Joe Crampton	William B. Mack

Act I.— Scene 1 — The Law Office of Day and Farrel, Wednesday, June 23, 9 A. M. Scene 2 — The Wood Near Briarcliff, Tuesday, June 22, 3 P. M. Scene 3 — Same as Scene 1. Time, 10 A. M. Act II.— Scene 1 — Office of Day and Farrel June 23, 10:30 A. M. Scene 2 — The Wood, June 22, 3 P. M. Scene 3 — Same as Scene 1. Act III.— Scene 1 — Office of Day and Farrel, June 23, 11 A. M. Scene 2 — A Railway Station, June 22, 10 P. M. Scene 3 — Same as Scene 1.

Staged by W. H. Gilmore.

Hugh Sainsbury, a profligate youth, has been murdered. Mrs. Lydiard, a deaf old lady, has been witness to the crime, but has heard no word of the quarrel preceding it. She saw Blanche Warren bending over the body with a revolver in her hand. The scene is re-enacted in pantomime as she describes it. Miss Warren, declaring her innocence, relates her version of the same scene, and it is again acted, with the dialogue supplied. Finally a blind newsman, selling papers in the railroad station, overhears another young woman confess that she did the killing. As he gives his testimony the scene he describes is acted in the dark. His recognition of the guilty person's voice leads to a confession that clears the mystery.

" OH, WHAT A GIRL! "

A musical farce by Edgar Smith, Edward Clark; music by Charles Jules and Jacques Presburg, produced by Lee and J. J. Shubert, at the Shubert Theater, New York, July 28, 1919.

Cast of characters —

Downes	Larry Francis
Carr	Mat Murphy
Taylor	George Stifter
Smathers	William Zinnel
Holmes	Harold Hulen
Williams	William Barry
Ross	Dave Dreyer
Washington	Lew Cooper
Bill Corcoran	Frank Fay
Jack Rushton	Sam Ash
Margot Merrivale	Hazel Kirke
Lola Chappelle	Vera Groset
Luigi Fravola	Ignacio Martinetti
Deacon Amos Titmouse	Harry Kelly
Perkins	Sam Curtis
Susie Smith	Patsy De Forrest
Amanda Titmouse	Elizabeth Moffat
Cinderella	Clarice Snyder
Prince Charming	Ethel Mary Oakland
Fairy Godmother	Veronica Marquise
Head Waiter	Lester Scharff

Act I.— Jack Rushton's Apartment. Riverside Drive, New York. Act II.— Scene 1 — Lawn of Uncle's Home. Cemetery Corners, N. J. Scene 2 — A Country Lane. Scene 3 — Century Midnight Whirl. That Night.
Staged by Edward Clark.

A country deacon and his nephew are flirting with the same cabaret singer. The nephew wins the girl by exposing uncle's duplicity to his family.

"THE CHALLENGE"

A drama in three acts by Eugene Walter, produced by
The Selwyns at the Selwyn Theater,
New York, August 5, 1919.

Cast of characters —

Harry Winthrop	Holbrook Blinn
Mary Winthrop	Jessie Glendenning
A Nurse	Ruth Benson
Richard Putnam	Alllan Dinehart
Mrs. Bemis (A Maid)	Georgie Lawrence
Mrs. Mather	Louise Macintosh
William Mather	Wilson Reynolds
John Shanley	Ben Johnson
A Police Reporter	Charles A. Sellon
A Copy Reader	Fred Karr
Harry Day (A Reporter)	Leonard Doyle
Taylor Warren (City Editor)	Hallett Thompson
Reddy Smith	Frank Torpey
A Telegraph Editor	C. M. Van Clieve
First Accountant	Francis S. Merlin
Second Accountant	F. C. Bronson
Third Accountant	A. D. Glaser
A Stereoptican Operator	C. R. Brown
Andrew Bemis	Wm. T. Morgan
John Hayes	David Landau
Tony Bertalini	Vici Ioucelli
Mat Smith	Herbert Bostwick
1st member of committee	Frank Vogel

Prologue — A Garden adjacent to one of the French
Hospitals near the front. Acts I. and II.— Home
of Harry Winthrop. Act III.— Committee Room.
House of Representatives State Legislature. Epilogue
— Harry Winthrop's Home.

Richard Putnam, a parlor socialist home from the
war, becomes the head of a working men's committee
seeking to bring about a social revolution. As a leading propagandist, he is instrumental in electing a socialist governor and is ready to declare a general strike,
when his fellow workingmen turn against him. They
have learned that their socialist governor has been
bought by the capitalists and believe young Putnam has
had a hand in the deal. Beaten and disillusioned,
Putnam is finally made over into a good conservative
by Mary Winthrop, the daughter of the capitalist for
whom he worked.

" THE RED DAWN "

An American play in three acts by Thomas Dixon,
produced at the Thirty-ninth Street Theater,
New York, August 6, 1919.

Cast of characters —

Tess Maloney	Mattie Ferguson
Fabia	Miriam Battista
Maria	Flora MacDonald
Richard Stanton	DeWitt C. Jennings
Zorin	Edward Emery
Cargin	Austin Webb
Margaret	Frances Grayson
John Duncan	Averill Harris
Pierre	Marcel Rousseau
Rev. Luke Jones	John Saunders
Napoleon	Will Evans
Jane	Ethel Jennings
Simpson	George T. Meech
The Cub	Billy Wells
Bolo	K. Bianche
Miss Vera Devere	Doraldina
McCarthy	Cassius Quimby
Smith	Hank Bovie
First Dancing Girl	Betty Mack
Second Dancing Girl	Frances Burns
Third Dancing Girl	Bobbie Reed
First Musician	Walter Kolomoku
Second Musician	Frank Kema
Third Musician	Dave Ploloka
Corporal of the Guard	B. F. Carew

Act I.— Interior of the Red Leader's house.
Morning. Act II.— Before the Red Leader's house.
overlooking the Pacific Ocean. Evening. Act III.
— Same Act I. The following morning.

On an island off the coast of California an attempt
is made by a young visionary to establish a socialistic
colony to prove that the theories of socialism are prac-
tical. The " central Soviet of Russia " attempts to
gain control of the colony to help along the " universal
revolution." Five billions in counterfeit money are to
be used in financing the scheme, and the aid of a million ex-convicts, three million laborers, and ten million
dissatisfied negroes is to be invoked. The scheme is
frustrated after the dreamer realizes his mistake. The
timely arrival of an off-stage U. S. cruiser helps.

"THOSE WHO WALK IN DARKNESS"

A drama in three acts by Owen Davis, produced by Lee and J. J. Shubert, at the Forty-eighth Street Theater, New York, August 14, 1919.

Cast of Characters —

Nelson, a policeman	L. J. O'Connor
Dowd, a chauffeur	Percival Reniers
Bob, a waiter	Alfred Knight
"Doc" Hedges	Howard Kyle
Alec Breen	Arthur Shaw
Mrs. Moss	Helen Tracy
Mrs. Spencer	Millie Freeman
Rufus Underwood	Donald Gallaher
A Girl	Mabel Maurel
Sally	Kathryn Sheldon
Viola Swan	Laura Walker
Dr. Bradford	Everett Milburn
Jessie Schofield	Consuela Bailey
Mrs. Alma Jenvey	Amy Ricard
Judge Joel Kennedy	George W. Wilson
Andy Jenvey	Godfrey Matthews

Act I.— A night lunch wagon on a New York Street, and Mrs. Moss' lodging house on 39th Street. Act II.— Rufus Underwood's house. Act III.— Outside Underwood house.

Rufus Underwood of Chenango County, New York, goes to the city in search of employment. Taken ill in a 39th Street boarding-house, he is nursed back to health by Viola Swan, herself a small town girl who, coming to New York in search of a career, has failed and fallen. Falling in love with Viola, young Underwood marries her, even though she confesses her somewhat lurid past. They return to the boy's home, where the town gossips make it unpleasant for them. Viola is finally forced to confess her New York experiences in order to save another young woman from a similar fate. Then she tries to go away, but her young husband's faith in her is unbroken and they agree to stay in Chenango County and defy the gossips.

" HAPPY DAYS "

A musical spectacle in three acts by R. H. Burnside
and Raymond Hubbell, produced by Charles
Dillingham, at the Hippodrome, New
York, August 23, 1919.

Principals engaged —

Albert Froom	Vera Bailey ,
Henry Mallia	Clyde Cook
Charles Bart	Bert Nagle
William Williams	Thomas Colton
Joseph Frohoff	Arthur Hill
Bert Bowlen	Alice Nash
Chinco and Kaufeman	Edna Nash
The Agousts	" Happy " Jack Lambert
Salbini	Valodia Vestoff
Hartley	Belle Story
The Perezoffs	Hattie Towne
The Great Hanneford Family	The Four Amaranths
	Maud Mallia,
Dane Claudius	Lalla Selbini
Lillian Scarlet	Minnie Kaufman
Ventian Quartette	Henry Taylor

The usual succession of vaudeville and circus acts inter-
spersed with musical comedy and elaborate scenic effects.
Staged by R. H. Burnside.

"UP FROM NOWHERE"

A comedy in four acts by Booth Tarkington and Harry
Leon Wilson, produced by John D. Williams,
at the Comedy Theatre, New York,
September 8, 1919.

Cast of characters —

George Washington Silver..........Norman Trevor
George ⎤   Frederick Howard
Georgianna ⎟ His children....   Olive Murray
Martha ⎟   Leotta Miller
Etta ⎦   Margalo Gillmore
Linski, his secretary.............George Casselberry
Sato, his valet...................................Sato
Captain Hercules Penny................Cecil Yapp
Mrs. William Grenoble Somerset........Grace Reals
Frederic Valentine, her brother.....Clarence Bellair
Edith, his daughter..................Ann Andrews

The action, passing within twenty four hours takes
place at Silver's home in a suburb on the Hudson.

George Washington Silver, a "new American" boasting a Portuguese father and Irish mother, as well as traces of Swedish and Italian blood, acquires a fortune and a family. To discourage his snobbish son, bent on marrying Edith Valentine, whom the father believes to be a fortune hunting daughter of an old New York family, Silver invites Edith to his house. In his efforts to expose her mercenary motives Silver falls in love with the girl himself and finally marries her.

"LUSMORE"

A play in four acts by Rita Olcott and Grace Heyer, produced by Rita Olcott at Henry Miller's Theatre, September 9, 1919.

Cast of characters —

Eithne	Eva le Gallienne
Mother Weir	Beth Fox
Taman Weir	John McFarlane
Lusmore	Grace Heyer
Mal O'Flynn	John Hamilton
Big Dermac Malone	John Todd
Daragh Murray	William H. Malone
Widow Ni Leary	Elsa Sheridan
Una O'Brien	Mary Stephens
Ellen of the Grey Locks	Louise Poe
Brother Bertram	John Todd
Brother Michell	Richard Wallace
Princess Oirein	Regina Wallace
Lady Margreadh	Louise Poe
Lady Cathleen	Elsa Sheridan
Wounded Knight	Edwin Strawbridge
Hugh de Lacy	William H. Sams
Aide	Richard Walllace
Soldier	William H. Malone
Fairy Queen	Mary Stephens

Acts I. and IV. at the dwelling on Carrick Hill. Act II.— The woods of Conmaicne. Act III.—Camp of Hugh de Lacy.

A poet hunchback named Lusmore, suspected of being a changeling left by "the good little people" of Conmaicne wood, in Ireland, is not popular in the community. Being driven away he wanders in the wood until he meets some of his fairy ancestors. They take away his disfiguring hump, turn him into a handsome knight and send him back to fight for his king. Finally he wins the heart of the loyal Eithne, a blind girl, whose sight is also restored by the good fairies.

" NIGHTY-NIGHT "

A farcical comedy in three acts by Martha M. Stanley and Adelaide Matthews, produced by Adolph Klauber, at the Princess Theater, New York, September 9, 1919.

Cast of characters —

Porter	George W. Pierpont
Trixie Lorraine	Suzanne Willa
Billy Moffat	Francis Byrne
Waiter	Oscar Knapp
Dr. Bentley	Cyril Raymond
Ernestine Dare	Marie Chambers
Mollie Moffat	Dorothy Martimer
Philip Burton	Grant Mills
Norah	Ruby Craven
Jimmie Blythe	Malcolm Duncan

Prologue — Section of a Washington-New York Pullman; Acts I. and II.—Billy Moffatt's apartments. Act III.—The Moffat kitchen.

Trixie Lorraine, an ex-dancer, has married a second time without telling her new husband that she had been married before, or that she is the mother of a child by the first marriage. Running away from her jealous mate on the eve of his discovery of her past, she rents an apartment in New York, which happens to be owned by an old friend of the second husband who promptly follows her and becomes more jealous than ever. The usual farcical complications, followed by the usual explanations.

"SHE WOULD AND SHE DID"

A light comedy in three acts by Mark Reed, produced at the Vanderbilt Theatre, September 11, 1919.

Cast of characters —

Frances Nesmith...	Grace George
Mrs. Nesmith........................	Isabel West
Pearl...............................	Esther Howard
Elsie Goward.....................	Cora Witherspoon
Frank Goward.....................	John Cromwell
Charlie Vincent....................	Edward Arnold
Bess Trull..........................	May Collins
Wallie Byrnes......................	John Adair Jr.
Dr. Coburn.......................	Fletcher Harvey
Fisher Brigham..................	George MacQuarrie
Worthen Bennett...................	John Stokes
Harley Hunt.......................	Lemist Esler
Major Wilson........	Ned Burton
Herbert............................	Arthur Keith

Act I.—Drawing room at the Nesmiths. Act II.—Office of Brigham and Bennett. Act III.—Library of the Gowards. Staged by John Cromwell.

Frances Nesmith has been suspended from her golf club because she lost her temper and deliberately dug holes in the eighth green. In her efforts to have the suspension lifted she flatters, cajoles and tricks enough members of the greens committee to effect her triumphant reinstatement.

"CIVILIAN CLOTHES"

A comedy in three acts by Thompson Buchanan, produced by Oliver Morosco, at the Morosco Theatre, New York, September 12, 1919.

Cast of characters —

Billy Arkwright, late lieut. A. E. F.	Glen Anders
Nora, the maid....................	Millie Butterfield
General McInerny, U. S. A..........	Edward Mackay
Jack Rutherford, late lieut. N. A.	Arthur Albertson
Florence Lanham....................	Olive Tell
Mrs. Lanham, her mother..........	Isabel Irving
Elizabeth, her sister..............	Grace Kaber
Sam McGinnis, late Capt. A. E. F.	Thurston Hall

Mrs. Margaret Smythe.... ....Marion Vantine
Belle Henderson......................Bessie Eyton
Zack Hart........................William Holden
Mr. Lanham.......................Frank Sylvester
McGinnis, Sr.....................James K. Applebee
Bell Hop.........................Edward Colebrook
Maid at Hotel......................Mary Melrose
    Acts I. and II. in the Lanham home, Louisville,
Ky. Act III.— Hotel in New Orleans. Staged by
Frank Underwood.

Florence Lanham, a proud southern beauty from
Louisville, while Red Crossing in France, marries Captain Samuel McGinnis. After an exciting honeymoon
back of the lines she returns to Paris and later hears
Captain Sam has been killed. Some months later in
Louisville, where she has said nothing about her marriage, Captain Sam turns up and is so disappointing
a figure out of uniform that she hesitates to acknowledge him as her husband. Refusing to be put aside
so easily, Captain Sam determines to give his snobbish
wife a lesson and accepts a position in her home as
butler. His experiment results in Florence's falling in
love with him all over and her complete capitulation
follows.

" SCANDAL "

A comedy in three acts by Cosmo Hamilton, produced
by Walter Hast, at the 39th Street Theatre.
New York, September 12, 1919.

Cast of characters —

Pelham Franklin....................Charles Cherry
Malcolm Fraser.....................William David
Sutherland York...................Malcolm Fassett
Major Barnet Thatcher.............Robert Ayrton
Pewsey........................Mr. Leonard Wood
Sarah............................Margaret Collinge
Mrs. Henry Vanderdyke......... .....Alice Putnam
Miss Honoria Vanderdyke.........Isabel O'Madigan
Mrs. Brown............................Mary Cecil
Regina Waterhouse..................Marjorie Hast
Helene...............................Doris Duane
Beatrix Vanderdyke............Francine Larrimore
    Act I.— York's studio, New York. Act II.—
Beatrix's bedroom Vanderdyke country house. Act
III.—Franklin's home in Connecticut.

Beatrix Vanderdyke, to save herself from the consequences of an embarrassing situation, informs her family and friends that she has been secretly married to Pelham Franklin. Franklin, resenting the liberty taken, purposes to teach the young woman a lesson and insists upon following her to her room. Here, when she is properly frightened, he reads her a lecture on morals and a young woman's responsibility and then leaves her. This high handed treatment has the effect of awakening her love for him, and in the end she is thoroughly humbled and they are legally married.

"ADAM AND EVA"

A comedy in three acts by Guy Bolton and George Middleton, produced by F. Ray Comstock and Morris Gest at the Longacre Theatre, New York, September 13, 1919.

Cast of characters —

James King.. .... .Berton Churchill
Corinthia, his parlor maid.............Jean Shelby
Clinton DeWitt, his son-in-law.......Reginald Mason
Julie De Witt. his eldest daughter....Roberta Arnold
Eva King, his younger daughter........Ruth Shepley
Aunt Abby Rocker, his sister-in-law...Adelaide Prince
Dr. Jack Delamater, his neighbor...Richard Sterling
Uncle Horace Pilgrim, his cousin................
.......................Ferdinand Gottschalk
Adam Smith, his business manager......Otto Kruger
Lord Andrew Gordon. his would-be son-in-law......
......................Courtenay Foote

Acts I. and II.—The King home, Long sland.
Act III.— The King farm in New Jersey.

See page 248

"A REGULAR FELLER"

A comedy in four acts by Mark Swan, produced by Charles Emerson Cook, at the Cort Theatre, New York, September 15, 1919.

Cast of characters —

Dan Brackett..................Ernest Glendinning
Charlie Winter..................Everett Butterfield

```
"Butch" Hawkins................Dudley Clements
Cyrus Pond.......................James Bradbury
Everett Davis.......... ......  .... Albert Busher
Joseph Brackett, Dan's father..........Edwin Holt
Milton Cross......................Charles Abbott
Leslie Purvis........................Roy Gordon
Vinton, chauffeur..................George Cukor
Bessie Winter.....................Miriam Sears
Jocelyn Cross....................Margaret Greene
Emelia Vandergrift, her aunt....Charlotte Granville
Mandy, waitress..................Kitty O'Connor
    Acts I. and III.—Interior of Roadside Garage.
Act  II.—Outside  the  Garage.  Act  IV.— "The
Little House Across the Road."
```

Dan Brackett, after a quarrel with his rich father, determines to make good on his own. He promotes the sale of a punctureless automobile tire and in a race from a Long Island village to New York he arrives in time to prevent the villain's voting the wrong way at a directors' meeting. Thus he wins the admiration of his stern parent and the hand of Bessie Winter, the heroine. Most of the scenes are laid in the Long Island village and the contrasts are those of the smart town boy and the country rubes.

"FIRST IS LAST"

A comedy in three acts by Samuel Shipman and Percival Wilde, produced by William Harris, Jr., at Maxine Elliott's Theatre, New York, September 17, 1919.

Cast of characters —

```
Doug..............................Hassard Short
Harvey............................Robert Strange
Lowell............................Franklyn Ardell
Phil.................................Richard Dix
Steve............................Edward Robinson
Madge............................Phoebe Foster
Ethel............................Kathleen Comegys
Annabelle........................Mary Newcombe
Helen..............................Elise Bartlett
Selby (a butler)...................James Kearney
    Act I.— Columbia College.  Acts II. and III.—
Library in Lowell's home.
```

A group of co-eds graduating from Columbia University agree to pool their futures. Meeting three years later to divide their profits, they discover they are, with one exception, all failures. The one success, the class poet, has become a garbage king and made a fortune. Dividing the profits of this enterprise, some 5,000 cans of garbage, they start forth again. At their next meeting, two years later, they are still mostly failures. The poet, however, has given up his garbage contracts and gone in for mechanical toys, and is still a rich man. He marries the girl who had believed in him as a poet and the others go their various ways disillusioned. but still hopeful.

"THE JEST"

Adapted from the Italian of Sem Benelli's " La Cena delle Beffe," produced by Arthur Hopkins, at the Plymouth Theatre, New York, September 19, 1919.

Cast of characters —

Giannetto Malespini	John Barrymore
Neri Chiaramantesi	Lionel Barrymore
Gabriello Chiarmantesi	Charles Kennedy
Tornaquinci	Arthur Forrest
Fazio	E. J. Ballantine
Calandra	Paul Irving
Nencio	W. J. McClure
Camus	H. Charles Smith
Cintia	Maud Durand
Ginevra	Maude Hannaford
Lapo	Arthur Rankin
A Lieutenant	Jacob Kingsberry
The Doctor	Cecil Clovelly
The Executioner	L. R. Wolheim
Lisabetta	Margaret Fareleigh
Lucrezia	Martha McGraw
Fiametta	Gilda Varesi
A Singer	Thomas Williams

Act .—At Tornaquinci's house. Acts II. and IV. — At Ginevra's house. Act III.— The pillar.

See page 149.

" CLARENCE "

A comedy in four acts by Booth Tarkington, produced
by George C. Tyler, at the Hudson Theatre,
New York, September 20, 1919.

Cast of characters —

Mrs. Martyn	Susanne Westford
Mr. Wheeler	John Flood
Mrs. Wheeler	Mary Boland
Bobby Wheeler	Glenn Hunter
Cora Wheeler	Helen Hayes
Violet Pinney	Elsie Mackay
Clarence	Alfred Lunt
Dinwiddie	Barlowe Borland
Della	Rea Martin
Hubert Stem	Willard Barton

Act I.—Ante room to Mr. Wheeler's private
office, New York. Acts II., III. and IV.— Living
room at Mr. Wheeler's home, Englewood, N J.
Staged by Frederick Stanhope.

See page 280.

" THUNDER "

A comedy in four acts by Peg Franklin, produced by
John Golden, at the Criterion Theatre, New
York, September 22, 1919.

Cast of characters —

Ma McBirney	Marie Day
Pa McBirney	Guy Nichols
Mandy Coulter	Liela Bennett
Jeff Coulter	Chas. McDonald
Buck Babb	Horace James
Mr. Carson	George Wright
Mrs. Carson	Eva Dennison
Sam Disbrow	Chester Morris
Mr. Disbrow	Wilson Day
Dick Babb	Benjamin Kauser
Azalea	Sylvia Field
Preacher	Burr McIntosh
Pliny Doane	Sam Reed
Hi Kitchell	John Talbot
Mrs. Kitchell	Marion Kerby
Mrs. Doane	Blance Talbot
Fidler	Charles Althoff
Tom Gerson	Mart E. Heisey

Acts I. and IV.—Dooryard of the McBirney cabin.
Acts II. and III.—Cabin of Simeon Pace.
(" Thunder " was afterwards called " Howdy
Folks? ")

Azalea is an orphan and a circus performer travelling under the protection of a guardian. When the guardian dies he asks " Old Thunder," a circuit preacher, to take charge of her. The preacher abducts the child, carries her to the cabin of friends in the mountains and protects her when she is pursued and threatened by the proprietor of the circus. A neighboring miser without kith or kin dies leaving a small fortune. The preacher, confident God will forgive the lie, swears this money belongs to Azalea as the dead man's heir. Azalea is thus able to establish a local store and build a schoolhouse in which she and the juvenile hope eventually to acquire sufficient book " larnin' " to guarantee their success and happiness.

" SEE-SAW "

A musical comedy in two acts, book and lyrics by Earl
Derr Biggers, music by Louis A. Hirsch, produced by Henry W. Savage, at Cohan's
Theatre, New York, September, 23,
1919.

Cast of characters —

Helen	Elizabeth Hines
Billy Meyrick	Guy Robertson
Captain Starboard	Horace M. Gardner
Harkins	Frederick Graham
Lord Harrowby	Charlie Brown
Kinkaid	John H. McKenna
Cleo Ray	Helen Bolton
Spencer Meyrick	George Barbier
Aunt Mary	Jeanette Lowrie
Cynthia Meyrick	Dorothea McKaye
Jephson (of Lloyds)	Charles Esdale
Richard Minot	Frank Carter
Henry Trimmer	Charles Meakins
Bell Boy	Jimmie Parker
Bird Byron	Byron Halstead

Act I.— On board steam yacht " Lilith." Act II.
— Courtyard of Florida Hotel.

Cynthia Meyrick's mother wishes her to marry an
English lord. Cynthia's father prefers a hustling

young American. Lord Harrowby, the English candidate, has insured his chances of marrying Cynthia with Lloyds of London for $100,000. Richard Minot, as Lloyds' agent in America, is assigned to keep an eye on his lordship and to protect the interests of the company. Falling in love with Cynthia, he finds himself in an unhappy predicament. If he prevents her marrying Harrowby he is disloyal to his company and if he does not marry her he is disloyal to himself and likewise to her. A clause in the contract that was overlooked in the first act is instrumental in providing a satisfactory conclusion.

" KATY'S KISSES "

A farce in three acts by Neil Twomey, produced by Edward B. Perkins, at the Greenwich Village Theatre, New York, September 24, 1919.

Cast of characters —

Ned Summers	Carl Jackson
Nat Foster	Frank Dawson
Fred Jones	William I. Clark
Sam Levy	Alfred Winn
Mathew Davis	Neil Twomey
Katy Hartman	Mary Ann Dentler
Margaret Lang	Geraldin Beckwith
J. Q. Rockmirh	Harry Maitland
Johnnie	Clifford Robbins
Hez Huckins	Robert Craig
Ambrose Quirk	T. C. Hamilton
Bill Griggs	Reynold Williams
Delia Dunn	Agnes Kelly

Acts I., II. and III. at Summers' Law Office.

Matthew Davis, an " apostle of bluff," believing that the world accepts every man at his own estimate of himself, drifts into a small New England town. He is broke. So is the lawyer to whom he attaches himself. But he (Davis) lies and bluffs his way to success, finally marrying his partner to the village wash-lady's daughter and himself to a rich widow.

" ROLY-BOLY EYES "

A musical comedy in three acts, book and lyrics by
Edgar Allan Wolff, music by Eddy Brown and
Louis Gruenberg, produced by John Cort, at
the Knickerbocker Theatre, New York,
September 25, 1919.

Cast of characters —
```
Judge Robert Warren.................Hugh Chilvers
Mrs. Robert Warren.................Adora Andrews
Ida Loring.........................Queenie Smith
Myron S. Rentham.............Harry Anson Truax
Mrs. Penelope Giddings.................Maud Leone
Dorothy Giddings...................Kate Pullman
Buddie Montrose........................Earl Gates
Michael Fiachetti...... ..... ......Frank Martins
Peter.............................H. D. Blakemore
Dances by.........................Margaret Edwards
Billy Emerson.......................Eddie Leonard
Billy Rice..........................Eddie Mazier
Billy West..........................Bert McGarvey
Fred W. Wambold..................G. Clayton Frye
Kitty Rice............................May Boley
     Act I.—Garden of Judge Warren's country home.
Acts II. and III.—Sleeping porch of same.
```

Billy Emerson runs away from home when threatened with arrest for a crime the villain committed.
He joins a minstrel troupe and later returns to sing
serenades to his mother and his boyhood sweetheart.

" AN EXCHANGE OF WIVES "

A comedy in three acts, by Cosmo Hamilton, produced
by Walter Hast, at the New Bijou Theatre,
New York, September 26, 1919.

Cast of characters —
```
William Armitage..................Forrest Winant
Viola Hay.........................Chrystal Herne
Meakin.......................Stanley Harrison
Stanner............................Miriam Doyle
Archibald Hay........................Lee Baker
Margaret Armitage..................Margaret Dale
     Acts I. and II.—The Living Room.  Act III.—
Mrs. Armitage's sleeping porch.
```

The Armitages and the Hays. intimate friends, take a cottage for the summer on Long Island. Under these living conditions Mr. Armitage and Mrs. Hay decide that they are much more suited to each other than they are to their respective mates. Realizing what the situation may lead to Mr. Hay and Mrs. Armitage decide the only way to cure the misguided ones is to pretend to accept the situation, and suggest a literal exchange of wives. Thereupon they pretend to become violently interested in each other and carry the joke as far as the sleeping porch. By this time it has ceased to be a joke. and as a result all parties are more than willing to return to their proper mates at the play's conclusion.

" MOONLIGHT AND HONEYSUCKLE "

A comedy in three acts by George Scarborough, produced by Henry Miller, at Henry Miller's Theatre, New York, September 29, 1919. .

Cast of characters —

```
Pet Baldwin......................Flora Sheffield
Tod Musgrave......................James Rennie  '
  .Hallie Baldwin..................Katherine Emmett
Senator Baldwin...................Edward Fielding
Jefferson ......................Lawrence Eddinger
Congressman Hamill.................Sydney Booth  ₋
Courtney Blue..................Charles Trowbridge  ᵃ
Judith Baldwin....................Ruth Chatterton
Mrs. Langley......................Lucile Watson  ᵃ
    The Three Acts of the Play Take Place in the Liv-
ing Room of the Baldwin Home in Washington Dur-
ing an Evening in May. The Action is Continuous
— the Intermissions Marking no Lapses of Time.
```

Judith Baldwin seeks to test the love of three men who have asked her to marry them — a society fop, a congressman and an educated cowboy. She invents a story of a scandalous past. tells it in turn to each of them and intimates that it is the story of her own life.

The fop and the congressman shy away, but the cowboy is ready to shoot anyone who intimates that Judith
has ever been less than 99 per cent. pure.   Thus he
wins the ingenious heroine and happiness impends.

" THE DANCER "

A drama in three acts by Edward Locke, produced by
Lee and J. J. Shubert, at the Harris Theatre,
New York, September 29, 1919.

Cast of characters —

Paul Kerinski	Effingham Pinto
Olga	Mary Mitman
Mrs. Penfield-Clarke	Eva Lang
Elvira Jargo	Miriam Elliott
Bojdan Borivenko	Jose Ruben
Nina Kosoloff	Renee Adoree
Roy Lingart	George Burnett
Mascha Kosoloff	Helen Salinger
Lola Kerinski	Isabelle Lowe
Peter Quincy Hale	John Halliday
Richard Penfield-Clarke	William Morris
Stetson	Philip Dunning
Higgins	Richard Freeman

Acts I. and III.— Lola's studio, New York. Act
II.— Peter Quincy Hale's home in the Berkshires.

Lola Kerinski, a dancer, falls in love with Peter
Quincy Hale, a New Englander who reflects the un-
yielding attitude of his puritanical forebears.   She
marries him, is unhappy and returns to her life with
the joyous vagabonds of the theater.   Hale's relatives
attempt to place her in a compromising position that
they may force her to divorce her husband, but he
returns from the war in time to prevent the success of
the conspiracy.

" THE GOLD DIGGERS "

A comedy in three acts by Avery Hopwood, produced
by David Belasco, at the Lyceum Theatre,
New York, September 30, 1919.

Cast of characters —

Stephen Lee..........................Bruce McRae
James Blake... ....H. Reeves-Smith
Barney Barnett.................Frederick Truesdell
Wally Saunders.....................Horace Braham
Freddie Turner.....................Austen Harrison
Fenton Jessup......................Harold Christy
Tom Newton.............. ....D Lewis Clinton
Marty Woods.........................Frank Lewis
Jerry Lamar...................... ....Ina Claire
Mabel Munroe.....................Jobyna Howland
Violet Dayne........................Beverly West
Mrs. Lamar,......................Louise Galloway
Topsy St. John........................Ruth Terry
Cissie Gray...... - ....Pauline Hall
Trixie Andrews...................Lilyan Tashman
Eleanor Montgomery..................Luella Gear
Gypsy Montrose...................Gladys Feldman
Dolly Baxter.....................Katherine Walsh
Sadie................................Louise Burton
    Acts I., II. and III.—Jerry Lamar's apartment,
New York City.

" Jerry " Lamar is one of a band of pretty little
salamanders known to Broadway as " gold diggers,"
because they " dig " for the gold of their gentlemen
friends and spend it being good to their mothers and
their pet dogs. In a pinch, which is to say in the second act, Jerry is willing to sacrifice her own reputation to prove to the guardian of a little chorus girl she
has taken under her wing that all the ladies of the
ensemble are not as bad as they are painted. The
guardian, becoming slightly alcoholic, accepts this as
the life and asks Jerry to marry him. In love with
him she honorably confesses the trick that she has
played upon him, but he is sufficiently noble to forgive
and marry her.

ZIEGFELD MIDNIGHT FROLIC

A revue in two parts, lyrics by Gene Buck, music by
Dave Stamper, produced by F. Ziegfeld, Jr., at
the New Amsterdam Theatre Roof, New
New York, October 2, 1919.

Principals engaged —

Frances White
Fannie Brice
Chic Sale
Ted Lewis
W. C. Fields
Savoy and Brennan
Arthur Rose

Martha Mansfield
Allyn King
Irene Barker
Keegan and Edwards
Arthur Uttry
Hal Hixon

Staged by Ned Weyburn.

"THE STORM"

A melodrama in four acts by Langdon McCormick,
produced by George Broadhurst, at the 48th
Street Theatre, New York, October
2, 1919.

Cast of characters —

Burr Winton.....................Edward Arnold
David Stewart.....................Robert Rendel
Maniteekwa.....................Charles Hend:rson
Jacques Fachard.....................Max Mitzel
Manette Fachard.............. .....Helen MacKellar

Act I.—Exterior Burr Winton's cabin. Act II.—
Living room in the cabin. Manette's bedroom. Act
III.—Same as Act I. Act IV.—Same as Act III.

Manette Fachard, a young French Canadian and an
orphan, is cut off from civilization in the depths of the
Canadian woods, her companions being Burr Winton,
a rough prospector of the northland, and David Stewart, a travelled and cultured Englishman. All winter
the three are imprisoned in a cabin. Both men are in
love with Manette and she refuses to choose between
them. In the spring the test of their loyalty is intensified. One of the men must make his way to Calgary
to bring provisions back to the others. The girl still
refuses to indicate which shall go, but by a trick Stew-

art makes it appear she has named Burr. Before Burr can leave they are surrounded by a forest fire. Their lives are saved by a series of happy accidents and out of this experience the girl's true love for Burr is revealed and Stewart retires with more or less grace.

"WHERE'S YOUR WIFE?"

A mystery farce in three acts by Thomas Grant Springer, Fleta Campbell Springer and Joseph Noel, produced by F. C. Thompson, at the Punch and Judy Theatre, New York, October 4, 1919.

Cast of characters —

Florence Hentley	Nila Mac
Jane	Ruth Parry
Mrs. Hope-Barrellton-Howe	Grace Goodall
Walter McLane	Charles White
Mr. Ewell	Harry Quealy
Joseph Hodgens	Jack Pollard
Howard Hentley	Jack Pendleton
Taxi Driver	Elmer Edwards
Officer Casey	James A. Boshell
Matthew Ward	Murray Phillips
James J. Barnes	Geo. Howell
Madam Zeller	Dorothy Newell
Charles Whiting	Roy MacNicol
Carpenter	Frank Atwell
Rowan Taylor	Maud Gilbert
Mr. Watson	Arthur Keith

Act I.— 5.45 P. M.   Act II.—Two Hours Later. Act III.—One Minute Later. Place — Living Room of the Hentley's Apartment in the Keystone Apartment House, New York City. Staged by George Howell.

A mystery farce in which an inquest in ordered to investigate the murder of a woman who has disappeared. The discovery of bloodstains and a rusty knife provide circumstantial evidence, which is humorously pursued until it transpires that there has been no killing at all. The woman had merely gone to the Grand Central station with her husband. The blood stains were those of a freshly killed duck and the rusty knife didn't mean anything.

"DECLASSEE"

A drama in three acts by Zoe Atkins, produced by Charles Frohman, Inc., at the Empire Theatre, New York, October 6, 1919.

Cast of characters —

Rudolph Solomon	Claude King
Edward Thayer	Vernon Steel
Harry Charteris	Charles Francis
Sir Emmett Wildering	Julian Royce
Sir Bruce Haden	Harry Plimmer
Count Paolo del Magiore	Ralf Belmont
Walters	Edward Le Hay
Lady Helen Haden	Ethel Barrymore
Lady Wildering	Clare Eames
Charlotte Ashley	Beatrice Beckley
Mrs. Leslie	Katherine Harris
Alice Vance	Madeline Delmar
Zellito	Gabrielle Ravine

Act I.—Sir Bruce Haden's house, London. Act II.—Lounge of a New York hotel. Act III.—Rudolph Solomon's house, New York City.

See page 95.

"HAMLET," "TAMING OF THE SHREW," "TWELFTH NIGHT"

Shakespearean repertoire presented by E. H. Sothern and Julia Marlowe on their return to the stage, October 6, 1919, and the two weeks succeeding, at the Shubert Theater, New York, under the direction of Lee Shubert.

HAMLET

Cast of characters —

Claudius, King of Denmark	E. L. Granville
Hamlet	E. H. Southern
Polonius	Frank Peters
Laertes	Henry Stanford
Horatio	Frederick Lewis
Rosencrantz	Vernon Kelso
Guildenstern	Boyd Clarke
A Priest	Malcolm Bradley
Marcellus	Colville Dunn
Bernardo	Arthur Ames
Francisco	Boyd Clarke
Reynaldo	Charles J. Sims
Osric	Vernon Kelso

```
First Player........................Colville Dunn
Second Player.....................Malcolm Bradley
First Gravedigger...............Rowland Buckstone
Second Gravedigger...............Leon Cunningham
Ghost of Hamlet's Father...........J. Sayre Crawley
Fortinbras.........................William Adams
Gertrude.....................  .......Alma Kruger
Ophelia............................Julia Marlowe
Player Queen.......................Norah Lamison
```

THE TAMING OF THE SHREW

Cast of characters —

```
Baptista.......................... ....Frank Peters
Vincentio..........................Malcolm Bradley
Lucentio........    .. .............Frederick Lewis
Petruchio...........................E. H. Sothern
Hortensio..........................E. L. Granville
Gremio.............................J. Sayre Crawley
Tranio.............................Henry Stanford
Blondello...........................Colville Dunn
A Pedant...........................Vernon Kelso
Tailor......... ..................Malcolm Bradley
Haberdasher......................Leon Cunningham
Grumio.........................Rowland Buckstone
Katharina...........................Julia Marlowe
Bianca.............................Norah Lamison
Widow.............................Alma Kruger
Curtis.............................Ursula Fawcett
```

TWELFTH NIGHT

Cast of characters —
TWELFTH NIGHT

```
Orsino.............................Frederick Lewis
Sebastian..........................Henry Stanford
Antonio.............................Frank Peters
A Sea Captain.......................E. L. Granville
Curio............................Leon Cunningham
Valentine.........................Andrew Souther
Sir Toby Belch........  ....... ....Rowland Buckstone
Sir Andrew Aguecheek.............J. Sayre Crawley
Malvolio............................E. H. Sothern
Fabian.............................Colvil Dunn
Feste, a Clown......................Vernon Kelso
A Priest............................Boyd Clarke
Olivia.............................Alma Kruger
Viola................................Julia Marlowe
Maria.............................Norah Lamison
```

"THE GIRL IN THE LIMOUSINE"

A farce in three acts by Wilson Collison and Avery Hopwood, produced by A. H. Woods, at the Eltinge Theatre, New York, October 6, 1919.

Cast of characters —

Kargan	Edward Butler
Benny	Dann Malloy
Betty Neville	Doris Kenyon
Dr. Jimmie Galen	Charles Ruggles
Tony Hamilton	John Cumberland
Riggs	Barnett Parker
Freddie Neville	Frank Thomas
Bernice Warren	Vivian Rushmore
Lucia Galen	Claiborne Foster
Aunt Cicely	Zelda Sears
Giles	Harry Charles

Acts I. and II.—Betty's Bedchamber. Act III.—Verandah.

Betty Neville is obliged to leave a house party and go to bed with the grip. Tony Hamilton, who had been in love with her before she married Freddie Neville, while on his way to the party is set upon by a pair of taxicab bandits, robbed of his valuables, including his clothes, pummelled into a state of insensibility, and dumped into Betty's room. Aunt Cicely, who has never met Betty's husband, finding Tony in her bedroom, jumps to the conclusion that he must be the husband and orders him into bed with Betty. Tony spends the rest of the evening in, out and under the bed, the situations being arranged to give as little offense as possible pending the usual explanations.

" HITCHY-KOO. 1919 "

A revue in two parts, book by George V. Hobart,
music and lyrics by Cole Porter, produced by
Raymond Hitchcock, at the Liberty
Theatre, New York, Octo-
ber 6, 1919.

Principals engaged —

Raymond Hitchcock
Sylvia Clark
Charles Howard
Waneta Means
Charles Witzell
Maurice Black
Mark Sullivan
James J. Doherty
Joseph Cook
Chief Eagle Horse
Dan Brennan

Lucille Ager
Eleanor Sinclair
Ursula O'Hare
Ruth Mitchell
Florence O'Denishawn
Billy Holbrook
Josephine MacNicoll
Elaine Palmer
Lilliam Kemble Cooper
Princess White Deer

" HELLO, ALEXANDER "

A musical extravaganza in two acts, book by Edgar
Smith and Emily Young, lyrics by Alfred Bryan,
music by Jean Schwartz, produced at the 44th
Street Theatre, New York, by Lee and
J. J. Shubert, October 7, 1919.

Cast of characters —

Col. Winslow	Dan Quinlan
Lieut. Jack Winslow	Jack Cagwin
Aunt Kittie	Esther Walker
Ethel Winslow	Jean Tyne
Capt. Chomendley	Earl Rickard
" Toots " McSwat	Sid Williams
Joe	Joe Hamilton
Simons and Slocum	Boyle and Brazil
Lieut. Clay	Fred Bliss
Lieut. Allen	Murry Salet
Lieut. Gordon	Harry Forsyeth
Lieut. Jackson	Martin Griffin
" Muggs " Casey	Charles Judson
Spike Murphy	Eddie Flynn
Jim Delilly	Larry Clifford
Bull Conners	Joe Hamilton
Leader of Crowd	Milton Pohs
Maude Bradbury	Rosie Quinn
Mrs. Carter	Gabriel Grey
Gloria Carter	Chick Barrymore
Gilda	Gilda Gray

Eczema Johnson.......................Mabel Elaine
Susie Folsom..........................Lottie Reick
Mary Lawton........................Peggy Dempsey
Mollie Bragg..........................Dot Mantell
Aunt Jeminma........................Vivian Holt
Mammy Cloe. .. . .Lillian Rosedale
Alexander ....James McIntyre
Henry Clay Jones................Thomas K. Heath
    Act I.— Scene 1 — Tampa Bay Hotel. Scene 2 —
Exterior of Aviation Camp. Scene 3 — Grand Min-
strel First Part. Jones' Ever-Ready Minstrels. Act
II.— Scene 1 — Levee, on the Mississippi. Scene 2
— At the Drug Store. Scene 3 — Villa of Col.
Winslow. Scene 4 — In New Orleans. Scene 5 —
Jazz Valley. Scene 6 — Ballroom, Col. Winslow's
Mansion. New Orleans.

A revamping of " The Ham Tree " story, with
Henry luring Alexander away from a perfectly good
hotel job that he may introduce him as a dusky poten-
tate at a costume ball.

"APPLE BLOSSOMS"

An operetta in a prologue and two acts, music by Fritz
Kreisler and Victor Jacobi, book and lyrics by
William Le Baron, produced by Charles Dill-
ingham, at the Globe Theatre, New
York, October 7, 1919.

Cast of characters —
Julie ....Rena Parker
Polly ....Juanita Fletcher
Molly ....Adele Astaire
Johnny ....Fred Astaire
Nancy ....Wilda Bennett
Lucy Fielding.......................Pauline Hall
Anabel Mason.......................Hildah Reeder
Richard (Dickie) Stewart...........Percival Knight
Mail Carrier.......................Frank Snyder
Chauffeur ....George Fordyce
George Winthrop Gordon.......Harrison Brockbank
Harvey ....Roy Atwell
Phillip Campbell...............John Charles Thomas
Mrs. Anne Merton................Florence Shirley
    Prologue — Garden of Castle Hall School. Act
I.— Phillip Campbell's house. Act II.— The Ball
Room.

Philip and Nancy marry to please their parents.
They agree, however, that immediately after the cere-

mony each will be permitted to live an unfettered, or
Greenwich Village, life Nancy is in love with the
comedian and Philip prefers the ingenue. Finding
that the free life is not as attractive as they had an-
ticipated it would be, and falling more hopelessly in
love with each other with each successive duet, they
end by acknowledging their mutual happiness in the
married state.

" TOO MANY HUSBANDS "

A comedy in three acts, by Somerset Maugham, produced by A. H. Woods, at The Booth Theatre.
New York, October 8, 1919.

Cast of characters —
```
Victoria .........................Estelle Winwood
Miss Dennis...........  .............Beatrice Miller
Taylor ...........................Carolyn Darling
Mrs. Shuttleworth..............Marguerite St. John
Leicester Paton..............4.........Fritz Williams
Major Frederick Lowndes, D.S.O..Lawrence Grossmith
Major William Cardew, D.S.O.... Kenneth Douglas
Nannie ...........................Marion Buckler
Mr. Raham.......................J. H. Brewer
Miss Montmorency................Florence Edney
Boy ..............................Richard Gray
     Acts I and II.— The Bedroom  Act. III.— The
Drawing Room.
```

Victoria, a clinging vine type of young English
woman, is married to Major William Cardew, D.S.O.
Hearing that William has been killed at Ypres, she
consoles herself by marrying his best friend, Major
Frederick Lowndes, D.S.O. A year later Bill returns unexpectedly from the war, having been imprisoned in Germany, and Victoria finds herself em-
barrassingly encumbered with two husbands, as well
as a mixed assortment of offspring. Which of the
men will she divorce? They, it happens, are equally
willing to give Victoria up, Bill insisting that she should
cling to Freddie and Freddie being equally determined
that she shall return to Bill. Victoria saves the situa-

tion by divorcing them both and marrying a flirtatious war profiteer.

"THE FAITHFUL"

A drama in three acts by John Masefield, produced by Augustin Duncan, at the Garrick Theatre, New York, October 13, 1919.

Cast of characters —

Asano	Rollo Peters
Kurano	Augustin Duncan
Hazama	Henry Travers
Kodera	Robert Donaldson
Hara	Erskine Sanford
An Old Samurai	Wm. J. Nelson
A Widow's Son	Noel Leslie
Shoda	Walter Geer
Kira	Henry Herbert
Sagisaka	Boris Korlin
Kamai	Walter Howe
Honzo	Erskine Sanford
The Envoy	Henry Stillman
One	Milton Pope
Captain of Kira's Guards	Albert Lester
Wild Cherry	Mary Blair
Lady Kurano	Helen Westley
Chikara	Richard Abbott
Starblossom	Julia Adler

Act I.— Scene 1 — open space near Asano's Palace. Scene 2 — Room in Kira's Palace. Act II.— Open space near Asano's Palace. Act III.— Scene 1 — The Retreat of the Ronin. Scene 2 — Room in Kira's Palace.

Kira, a crafty and cruel usurper, seeks to rule a province of old Japan. By trickery he succeeds in causing the death of Asano, a kindly leader of the people. As his lust for power grows, Kira lays waste the land and makes outcasts of Asano's followers. Under the leadership of Asano's friend, Kurano, the people bide their time and finally sacrifice their own lives to reek deserved vengeance upon their enemy.

" BOYS WILL BE BOYS "

A comedy in three acts dramatized by Charles O'Brien Kennedy from an Irvin S. Cobb story, produced at the Belmont Theater, New York, October 13, 1919.

Cast of characters —

Willie Bagby	Harold Bergh
Georgie Green	Edward Hayden
Tommie Martin	Donald MacPherson
Jeff Poindexter	Frank I. Frayne
Mrs. Gafford	Eugene Dubois
Peep O'Day	Harry Beresford
Dr. Wells	C. H. Reigel
Nick Bell	Claude Cooper
Breck Quarles	Erville Alderson
Horace Gafford	Charles Gibney
Lucy Allen	Winifred Wellington
Tom Miner	Robert Armstrong
Mrs. Hunter	Edna Archer Crawford
Judge Priest	William St. James
Mr. Sublette	Robert Harrison
Frankie Alton	Michael Hanlon
Harry Varney	Edwin Mouhot
Katie O'Day	Rose Mary King
Sergeant Bagby	George Park
Minnie Summers	Eldean Steuart
Mary Kelly	Noel Steuart
George Foster	Maury Steuart, Jr.
Tommy Bell	Philip Hayden
Dan Spencer	Gus Anderson

Act I.—Our Favorite Gathering Place. Act II.— Our Old Schoolhouse. In the Morning. Act III.— Same Place. Same Evening.

A dramatization of Irvin Cobb's story in which " Peep " O'Day, a sweet-tempered, simple, kindly old bit of " white trash " in a Kentucky village, inherits $40,000 and " busts out." Never having had any youth he accepts this as a chance to make up for lost time. So he buys the school house for the privilege of throwing stones through the windows and a field of melons so the boys can " hook 'em."

" THE LITTLE WHOPPER "

A musical comedy in two acts, book by Otto A. Harbach, music by Rudolf Friml, lyrics by Bide Dudley and Otto A. Harbach, produced by Abraham Levy, at the Casino Theater, New York, October 13, 1919.

Cast of characters —

Janet MacGregor	Mildred Richardson
Miss Granville	Nellie Graham-Dent
Kitty Wentworth	Vivienne Segal
George Emmett	Sydney Grant
John Harding	Harry C. Browne
Harry Hayward	Louis Coombs
James Martin	Sidney Hall
Oliver Butts	W. J. Ferguson
William } Robert {	Wilton Sisters
Judge MacGregor	David Torrence
Mrs. MacGregor	Lotta Linthicum
Frances	Lucille Williams
Teenty	Rose Wilton
Tonty	May Wilton
Jack Dodge	Edward Tierney
Fred Rood	Birnie Prevost

Act. I.—Scene 1 — Grounds of the Arlington Academy. Scene 2 — Corridor of Blenheim Hotel, Philadelphia. Scene 3 — Harding's Rooms at The Blenheim. Act II.— Scene 1 — The MacGregor Drawing Room, Baltimore. Scene 2 — The Same.

Kitty Wentworth, attending boarding school near Philadelphia, tells her preceptress she is going to the city to meet some friends of the family — which is a " little whopper." She is going to meet her fiancée with the intention of marrying him. In Philadelphia she gets into the wrong young man's room in a hotel, is followed by the schoolmistress and has considerable trouble fibbing her way out of her adventures. " The Little Whopper " was adapted from the screen comedy, " Miss Geo. Washington, Jr.," played by Marguerite Clark.

" FIVE O'CLOCK "

A comedy in three acts by Frank Bacon and Freeman Tilden, produced by Walter F. Wanger, at the Fulton Theatre, New York, October 13, 1919.

Cast of characters —

Davis	Paul Porter
Mrs. Burdette	Vivia Ogden
Daniels	Joseph Conyers
Higgins	David Higgins
Dr. Marsh	Tim Murphy
Dr. Gould	Paul Everton
Alice Gould	Alberta Burton
Orville Stackwood	Leslie Austen
Jimmy	Robert Schilling
Mrs. Murray	Mina Gleason
Holliday	Hayward Ginn
George Stackwood	Perce Benton
Emma Stackwood	Gertrude Maitland
Percival Brighton	Byron Rusell
Katherine Brighton	Sarah Edwards
Watkins	Charles T. Lewis
Dr. Doyle	G. Lester Paul
Miss Carroll	Elizabeth Burbridge

Act I.— Office of The Mansion House, Paulham, Mass. Act II.— Office of Dr. Gould in the Institution. Act III.— Orville's cottage in " Hope Village."

Orville Stackwood was a backward child; also an orphan. His guardians, who were his relatives, decided to send him to an institution for the feeble minded, partly to be rid of him and partly to have a freer hand in the disposition of the trust fund provided by his parents. For thirteen years they kept Orville in the home; then, having ceased to be backward and having become a thoroughly normal young person, he is helped to escape by Alice Gould, the superintendent's daughter, who loves him. After securing his legal release he devotes the later years of his life to the establishment of a home in which other backward children are treated kindly and given a chance to grow well and strong. " Five o'clock " is the hour at which all inmates, including the trusties, must return to the home.

"THE LUCK OF THE NAVY"

A naval play in three acts by Clifford Mills, produced
by F. Ray Comstock and Morris Gest, at the
Manhattan Opera House, New York,
October 14, 1919.

Cast of characters —

Lieut. Clive Stanton, V.C., R.N.....Percy Hutchison
Sub-Lieut. Louis Peel............... Aubrey Mather
Lieut.-Commander Perrin, R.N.......Geoffrey Webb
Midshipman Wing Eden............Patrick Ludlow
Admiral Maybridge......................A. P. Kaye
Francois ....Marcel Rousseau
Schaffer .... J. H. Croker-King
Briggs ....Tracey Barrow
Police Inspector....................Barry Whitcomb
An Airman.........................R. Huddlestone
Mrs. Gordon Peel.......................Kate Carew
Cynthia Eden...............Muriel Martin-Harvey
Dora Green........................Elsie Stranack
Anna ....Blanche Le Roy
Maidservant ....Eleanor Street
Newspaper Boy...................Edward Crompton
Prologue — 1 — Lieut. Stanton's Submarine, 5-A,
Below Surface. 2 — The 5-A Coming to the Surface.
3 — The British Fleet in Action at Night Against
a Zeppelin. Act I.— Stanton and Peel's Apartment at
Dunton, a Small Town on the East Coast of England.
Time — Afternoon. Act II.— The Lounge at " Hill-
side," Mrs. Peel's House at Brookridge, About
Two Miles from Dunton. Time — About a Quarter
to Seven in the Evening. Act III.— The Same.
Time — Shortly After Dinner. Period — The Clos-
ing Months of the Great War. Staged by Percy
Hutchison.

Lieut. Clive Stanton is engaged in a contest of wits
with a stageful of German spies, including the mother
of an English naval officer who was German by birth
and had been sent to England as a boy to grow up as
a spy in the service, and another German posing as a
wounded Belgian colonel. Stanton, after several narrow escapes, succeeds in outwitting the enemy and in
helping to win the war.

"HIS HONOR, ABE POTASH"

A comedy in three acts by Montague Glass and Jules
Eckert Goodman, produced by A. H. Woods.
at the Bijou Theatre, New York, October
14, 1919.

Cast of characters —

```
Rosie Potash.....................Mathilde Cottrelly
Irma Potash......................Lucille English
Abe Potash.......................Barney Bernard
Henry Gooding....................George Barnum
Harry Potash.....................Ted W. Gibson
Robert Stafford......- ........ ..Robert Cummings
George Block.....................James Spottswood
Crawford ........................Bertram Miller
Rothwell ........................Stanley Jessup
Evans ...........................Frank J. Kirke
Mr. Brady........................Harold Vosburgh
Riggs ...........................Kalman Matus
Detective Baker.......... .... ....William Vaughn
Henry Block......................Edwin Mordant
```
Act I.— Living Room of Potash Home. Acts II
and III.— Mayor's Office in City Hall, Damascus,
N. Y.

Abe Potash, a Jewish merchant in the village of
Damascus, New York, holds his honor, both as a Jew
and as a business man, as his creed. He accepts the
nomination for mayor tendered him by the political
boss of the town with the intention of using him as
a tool. After Abe is elected, however, though the
politicians try by all the familiar tricks of politics to
bend him to their wishes, he refuses to weaken and
in the end is still triumphantly honest.

"NOTHING BUT LOVE"

A musical comedy in three acts, book and lyrics by
Frank Stammers, score by Harold Orlob, produced by Maddock and Hart, at the Lyric
Theater, New York, October
14, 1919.

Cast of characters —

```
Billy Marbury....................Easton Yonge
Lucy Cotton......................Marion Sunshine
```

June Marbury... .. .   .Ruby Norton
Allyn Hicks........................Andrew Tombes
Dictor Tibbetts......................Donald Meek
" His Majesty "..................Millicent Gleeman
Drake ....Robert Woolsey
Bella ....Florence Enright
Mrs. Maud Winchester...........Arline Fredericks
Teddy Winchester.............Clarence Nordstrom
Brooks ....Philip Bishop
Stacey Adams.........................John Roche
Commodore Marbury........... .Stanley H. Forde
Fleming ....Jack McSorley
Mignon ....Mignon Reed
Muriel ....Muriel Reilly
Luvah ....Luvah Roberts
Grace ....Grace Weeks
Nell ....Nell Hall
Rose ....Rose De Vere .
Jere ....Jere Fitzgerald
Elizabeth ....Elizabeth Darling
Gracie ....Gracie La Rue
Josephine ....Muriel Wilson
Betty - ....Betty Warlow
Alice ....Alice Fessenden
Claire ....Claire Stevens
Dorothea ....Dorothea King
Beatrice ....Beatrice Darling
Florence ...., ...Florence Allen
Kathryn ....Kathryn Kelly
    Prologue — Living Room of the Marburys. (Note
— Curtain will fall 30 seconds to denote lapse of six
hours.) Act I.— Same as Prologue. Act II.— At
the Yacht Club. Act III.— Plaza Mrs. Winchester's
Home. Staged by Frank Stammers.

Allyn Hicks, a hero who does not know that he is a hero because he is afflicted with a dual personality, saves the heroine from drowning and then forgets all about it. He hates the water and he can't swim. He tries vainly to escape the consequences of his heroic act until a friendly doctor clears his subconscious complexes and he feels justified in claiming the girl as his by right of conquest.

" A YOUNG MAN'S FANCY "

A fantastic comedy in three acts by John T. McIntyre, produced by George C. Tyler, at The Playhouse, New York, October, 15, 1919.

Cast of characters —

Pickering ....Philip Merivale   ·
Martin ....Harry Barfoot

Handel ....Frank Allworth
Leftwich ....Alfred Kappeler
Costigan ....J. M. Kerrigan
Devine ....Walter C. Percival
Congo ....Krank Boyd
Miss Halsey.......................Mary Kennedy
Miss Carter.......................Jessie Busley
Laramy ....Howard Lindsay
Mary Darling...................Jeanne Eagels
The Blonde Girl...................Bessie Owens
The Pink Youth... ....Morgan Farley
The Hostess ....Eugenie Blair
The Brown Haired Young Man.......Sidney Elliott
The Dark Young Man..............John Davidson
The Tall Girl...................Symona Boniface
The Girl in Blue....................Viola Cain
Mary's Image......................Jeanne Eagels
The Man Servant...............John D. Seymour
   Act I.— Pickering's Home   Act II.— Inside the
Store.   Act III.— The Street.

Pickering, a poet and recluse, falls in love with a
dry goods store dummy. Her waxen features so
closely resemble those of a lost love that it is easy for
him to weave romances about the various groups of
which she is made the center by the window dresser —
romances in which he invariably figures as the hero.
Finally, he meets Mary Darling, the young woman who
posed for the model, and confesses his love for her.
She is really the assistant window dresser at the store,
but she may also have been the young woman whom
the poet had loved and lost before he became a recluse.

" ON THE HIRING LINE "

A satirical comedy in three acts by Harvey O'Higgins
and Harriet Ford, produced by George C. Tyler,
at the Criterion Theatre, New York, October
20, 1919.

Cast of characters —

Sherman Fessenden....................Cyril Scott
Dorothy Fessenden...................Vivian Tobin
Steve Mack.............. ....Donald Gallaherr
Mrs. Sherman Fessenden........Laura Hope Crews
Ronnie Oliver........................John Blair
Mrs. Billy Capron.................Minna Gombell

Ritchie ....Sidney Toler
Billy Capron........................Robert Hudson
    Acts I, II and III.— Living-Room of Fessenden
Country Home in New Jersey.

The Sherman Fessendens, living in New Jersey, have a great deal of trouble keeping servants — partly because Mrs. Fessenden, eager to move back to New York, does whatever she can to discourage them. Mr. Fessenden, in love with the country, finally meets the servant problem by engaging two detectives, one to serve as cook, the other as butler. To explain his need of them he tells them they have been hired to watch things. They do — and discover what they believe to be an affair between a visiting actor and Mrs. Fessenden. Mr. Fessenden is greatly excited until it is explained that the love letter the actor is supposed to have written to Mrs. Fessenden is really a copy of an old one he himself had written her before they were married.

" THE PASSING SHOW OF 1919 "

A revue in two acts and fourteen scenes, produced by Lee and J. J. Shubert, at the Winter Garden, New York, October 23, 1919.

Principals engaged —

Walter Wolf	Jack Donnelly
Harry Turpin	Frank Martin
Beth Elliott	Frankie Heath
Lon Hascall	James Barton
Hazel Cox	Tillie Barton
Charles Adams	Katherine Witchie
Eddie Miller	Grace Haley
Ralph Riggs	Bernice Haley
John Crone	Mabel Haley
Joe Opp	Grace Keeshon
Olga Cook	Blanche Ring
Roland Woodruff	Ray Oddo
James Grant	Charles Winninger
Reginald Denny	Mlle. Madge Derny

" PALMY DAYS "

A comedy-drama in three acts by Augustus Thomas,
produced by Arthur Hopkins, at The Playhouse, New York, October 27, 1919.

Cast of characters —

Sweeney	John Robb
Mrs. Curley	Lillian Dix
Big Lil	Eugenie Campbell
Jose	Alexis M. Polianov
Bud Farrell	Harry D. Southard
Leavenworth	Thomas Walsh
Texas	Emmet Shackleford
Kaintuck	Wilton Lackaye
Red Morgan	George Spaulding
Davy Woodford	George Le Guere
The Cricket	Genevieve Tobin
The Queen	Mattie Keene
Robinson	Edward J. Guhl
Fargo Bill	Olaf Skavlan
One-Eyed Conover	Edgar M. Wolley
Mrs. Woodford	Grace Reals

Acts I and II.— Mrs. Curley's Bar at Lone Tree.
Act III.— Hallway of the Hotel.

As a young man Kaintuck had been a dresser for
the actor Edwin Forrest. Marrying an actress member of the Forrest company, he later named Forrest
as correspondent in a sensational divorce case and left
for the West. Three months after Kaintuck's desertion of his wife she bore him a daughter, and eighteen
years later the daughter, having taken to the stage,
is the toast of the mining camp district in which her
father is a picturesque character. She is loved by
many men, but prefers Kaintuck's young partner Davy
Woodford, and Kaintuck, despite his divorced wife's
interference, makes the consummation of their romance
possible.

" BUDDIES "

A musical comedy in two acts and an epilogue by
George V. Hobart, lyrics and music by B. C.
Hilliam, produced at The Selwyn
Theatre, New York, Octo-
ber 27, 1919.

Cast of characters —

Biff	Robert Middlemas
Buddy	Bert Melville
Hank	George B. George
Abie	Adrian H. Rosley
Johnny	Horace A. Ruwe
Pete	Frank R. Woods
Rube	Richard Cramer
Babe	Roland Young
Sonny	Donald Brian
Madame Benoit	Camile Dalberg
Marie	Annette Monteil
Babette	Pauline Garon
Julie	Peggy Wood
Alphonse Pettibois	Edouard Durand
Louise Maitland	Maxine Brown

A squad of American doughboys is billeted with the
Widow Benoit in Brittany. The time is immediately
following the signing of the armistice. One of the
boys, called " Babe," brave in war but bashful in love,
is deeply enamored of the Widow Benoit's daughter,
Julie. Julie is also in love with him, and, thinking
to give him courage to propose to her, she tries to
arouse his jealousy by pretending to love his favorite
" buddie." The conspiracy, halted momentarily by
the discovery and exposure of a German spy in the
camp, is finally successful and Julie and her " Babe "
are united.

" FIFTY-FIFTY. LTD."

A musical comedy in three acts, book by **Margaret Michael** and **William Lennox**, lyrics and music by Leon DeCosta, produced by the Scibilia Theatrical Enterprises, at the Comedy Theatre, New York, October 27, 1919.

Cast of characters —

Phyllis Wyndham	Marguerite McNulty
Rosabelle Wyndham	Elsie Douglas
Katy	Margaret Michael
Monty	William Lennox
Judge Geoffrey Wyndham	Lynn Pratt
Kenneth Patterson	Barrett Greenwood
Fluffy La Grange	Gertrude Vanderbilt
Marian Carter	Norma Hark
Poultney Steele	Frank Bernard
Prof. Josephus Dabney	John Slavin
Cornwallis Crosby	Herbert Corthell
Phineas Tanner	Frank Walsh
Minerva Crosby	Jean Newcombe
Claire Crosby	Doris Arden
Dolly Manners and Angelica Manners	Gosman Twins
Toodles Gray	Alice Cavanaugh
Miss De Bath	Ann Lemeau
Giovannina Yon	Elsie Young
Tommy Gallagher	Wilma Bruce
Pauline Bell	Lillian Lee
Betty Roberts	Beatrice Moran
Claire Campbell	Kathryn Richards
Frederica Ashton	Rose King
Polly Leeds	Fanny Driscoll
Cissie Merideth	Marian Driscoll

Acts I and III.— Reception Room, Judge Wyndham's Home, New York City. Act II.— Second Floor, Judge Wyndham's Home.

A musicalized version of the old William Gillette farce, " All the Comforts of Home." So much of the plot as is retained repeats the adventure of the young man who rented his father's house furnished during the family's absence on a vacation. In this instance the tenants include a musical comedy chorus and the rented home becomes a sort of jazz boarding house.

"JUST A MINUTE"

A musical comedy in two acts by Harry L. Cort,
George E. Stoddard and Harold Orlob, produced
by John Cort, at the Cort Theatre, New
York, October 27, 1919.

Cast of characters —

The Song Girls..Niobe Warwick and Mae Terresfield
The Saleslady.................. .... .Merle Hartwell
The Demonstrators ....
　　　　Messrs. Green, Murphy, Fenn and Curren
The Girl............................Mabel Withee
The Other Girl.............../..........Mona Celete
The Porter............................Billy Clark
The Aunt..............................May Vokes
The Executor....................Wellington Cross
The Trouble....................George F. Moore
The Pilot.........................Percy Pollock
The Bathing Girl...................Virginia Clark
The Dancers........................Morin Sisters
　　Act I.— The Boardwalk, Atlantic City. Act II.—
Private Yacht " Sweet Stuff."

An heir to millions, under promise to keep his identity secret for a certain length of time, on penalty of
losing the money, falls in love with the heroine and
tells his real name too soon. The discovery that the
setting ahead of the clocks to conserve daylight saving has also saved the hero's money by " just a minute " permits a happy conclusion.

"THE LITTLE BLUE DEVIL"

A musical farce, book and lyrics by Harold Atteridge,
music by Harry Carroll, produced by Joe Weber,
at the Central Theatre, New York, November 3, 1919.

Cast of characters —

Tom ⎫ ....Jack Geier
Dick ⎬ ....Bookkeepers Edward Bisland
Harry ⎭ . ...James Buckley
Billie ....Eddie Cox
Freddie ....James Wheeler
Mary ....Eleanor Griffith
Stella ....Frances Dunlop

```
Pansy .............                ........Anne Sands
Augustus Rollett.................Bernard Granville
Paulette Divine (' The Little Blue Devil ").........
                                  Lillian Lorraine
Mrs. Lewellyn.....................Eleanor Gordon
Mr. Lewellyn.....................Wilfred Clarke
Phillip Scarsdale..................Jack McGowan
George Wallus...................Edward Martindel
Lizzie ............................Marion Mosby
Purkiss ...........................W. H. Powers
Moss ..............................Eddie Cox
Tiney, a dancer.................Katherine Hatfield
      Act I.— Office of New York Inter-County Rail-
road. Act II.—" The Little Blue Devil's " Apart-
ment. Act III.— The Home of Augustus Rollett.
```

Augustus Rollett, secretary to the president of a railroad, is eager for promotion. Knowing that his employer is fond of the ladies Augustus conceives the idea of engaging a chorus girl to pose as his wife and to flirt with his boss. The girl engaged is known as " The Little Blue Devil " and so successful is she in compromising the railway man that the secretary gets his promotion, is able to explain everything to his real wife and all is as it should be at the end. " The Little Blue Devil " is a musicalized version of Clyde Fitch's " The Blue Mouse."

" THE UNKNOWN WOMAN "

A melodrama in four acts by Marjorie Blaine and Willard Mack, produced by A. H. Woods, at Maxine Elliott's Theatre, New York, November 10, 1919.

Cast of characters —

```
Joel Emerson.......................Felix Krembs
Gerald Hastings...................Lumsden Hare
Margaret Emerson..............Marjorie Rambeau
Mr. Warrington...............Dodson L. Mitchell
Mr. Crosby........................Lincoln Plumer
Richard Normand...................Hugh Dillman
Mr. Mannering......· ................Roy Walling
Millicent Emerson....................Fan Bourke
Mrs. Lyons...................Annie Mack Berlein
Lizzie ...........................Florence Burdett
Claire Hastings....................Jean Robertson
Mrs. Burns......... ·· .......... ...Alice May
Quinlan .........................John Sharkey
Patrolman Kelly.....................Willis Reed
```

Act I.— Drawing Room of Emerson Home. Act
II.— Study in Gerald Hasting's Apartment. Act
III.— Same as Act I Act V.— The Governor's
Home, Albany.

Margaret Emerson, married to a philandering district attorney of New York, disgusted with her husband's repeated infidelities, turns for comfort and advice to Gerald Hastings, with whom she had at one
time been in love. The night of their meeting Hastings' wife, a drug fiend, escapes from a sanitarium
and kills herself. Hastings is accused of her murder,
and refuses to clear himself by proving that he was
with Mrs. Emerson because to do so would involve
that lady in a scandal. He is convicted on circumstantial evidence, and sentenced to be electrocuted. The
district attorney, now become governor, knowing the
situation. tortures his wife by promising to pardon
Hastings and then breaking his word at the last minute. Mrs. Emerson gets help from the outside, however, and Hastings is saved in time to promise he will
marry her as soon as she can divorce the governor.

" WEDDING BELLS "

An American comedy in three acts by Salisbury Field,
produced by the Selwyns, at the Harris Theatre,
New York, November 10, 1919.

Cast of characters —

Fuzisaki...........................George Burton
Reginald Carter...................Wallace Eddinger
Jackson ....John Harwood
Spencer Wells ....Percy Ames
Douglas Ordway...................Clarke Silvernail
Mrs. Hunter.................Mrs. Jacques Martin
Marcia Hunter...................Jessie Glendenning
Rosalie ....Margaret Lawrence
Hooper ....Maud Andrew
    Act I.— Five O'Clock of an Afternoon in February.
Act II.— Nine O'Clock in the Evening of the Same
Day. Act III.— Eleven Thirty in the Morning of
the Following Day. The Scene is a Room in Reginald
Carter's House in Madison Avenue, New York City.
Staged by Edgar Selwyn.

See page 185.

"THE LOST LEADER"

An Irish play in three acts by Lennox Robinson, produced by William Harris, Jr., at The Greenwich Village Theatre, New York, November 11, 1919.

Cast of characters —

Augustus Smith.... .. .. Hugh Huntley
Lucius Lenihan......................Frank Conroy
Mary Lenihan........................Mae Melvin
James Powell-Harper...............Robert T. Haines
Frank Ormsby......................Frank Compton
Peter Cooney, J.P..................J M. Kerrigan
Kate Buckley........................Ruth Boyd
James Clancy.....................Edward O'Connor
Major White, J.P....................Arthur Barry
Michael O'Connor.................Frederick Arthur
Thomas Houlihan..................Joseph Macaulay
Long John Flavin....................Eric Maxon
First Man.................. ....John Ahearn
Second Man..................Theodore A. Doucet
    Acts I and II.— The Smoking Room of the Hotel
at Poulmore. Act III.— The Standing Stones on
Knockpatrick.

Founded on the legend that Charles Stewart Parnell lived on obscurely in Ireland following his reported death. Lucius Lenihan, an aged, bent old man, is proprietor of a hotel at Poulmore, Ireland. Falling under the hypnotic influence of a visiting psychoanalyst, Lenihan declares that he is in reality Parnell, and he is prepared, if the call shall come, to lead Ireland out of her difficulties. Before those who had known Parnell can arrive to substantiate the old man's claims, he is struck down in the midst of a typical Irish political squabble — by the only man who had believed his story, a blind street singer.

"THE MAGIC MELODY"

A musical play in a prologue and two acts, book and lyrics by Frederic Arnold Kummer, music by Sigmund Romberg, produced by Max R. Wilner and Sigmund Romberg, at the Shubert Theatre, New York, November 11, 1919.

Cast of characters —

PROLOGUE

Anita	Jeannette Kahn
Delarose	Marie McConnell
Teresa	Adele Freeman
Salvatore	Walter Armin
Pietro	Gus Stevenson
Antonio	Louis Morrell
Beppo Corsini	Charles Purcell
Lisa	Bertee Beaumont
Gianina	Julia Dean
Beppino	Billie Roth
Postman	Jack Manning
Bianca	Jean Rebera
Maria	Nellie Crawford

THE PLAY

Carmencita	Fay Marbe
Prince Vladimir	Robert Bentley
Lady Chester	Aileen Poe
Captain Arthur Stanley	Charles Purcell
Isabel de Vernon	Renee Delting
Richard Palmer Adams	Earl Benham
Mrs. Fishbacker	Flavia Arcaro
Sophie (her daughter)	Carmel Myers
Sir Reggie Chester	Tom McNaughton
Lulu	Dorothy Wallace
Cluclu	Marie McConnell
Madame Jessonda	Julia Dean
Marquis de Vernon	Emile de Varny
Eifine	Bertee Beaumonte
Melody of Dance	Lois Leigh
Lola Winwood	Fay Marbe
Salvatore	Walter Armin
Madamoiselle Cherie	Legotie Hoover
Madamoiselle Nitouche	Marion Dixon
Madamoiselle Fleurie	Claire Hodgson
Madamoiselle Marguerite	Mary Cunningham
Madamoiselle Yvonne	Eleanor Leigh

Act I.— Reception Room at Prince Potemsky's House, Paris. Act II.— Garden of Madame Jessonda's Villa, Versailles.

Beppo Corsini, a composer, has his opera rejected

the same day he is led to suspect his wife's faithlessness. Under the pressure of the two disappointments he takes his young son and runs away. Corsini is lost at sea, but the boy is rescued, and is found twenty years after in London, his recognition by his mother being made possible by his remembering the principal aria of his father's opera. Mother was innocent all the time and the opera had really been stolen by the villain.

"IRENE"

A musical comedy in three acts by James Montgomery, music by Harry Tierney, lyrics by Joe Mc-
Carthy, produced at the Vanderbilt
Theatre, New York, No-
vember 18, 1919.

Cast of characters —

Donald Marshall	Walter Regan
Robert Harrison	Hobart Cavanaugh
J. P. Bowden	Arthur Burckly
Lawrence Hadley	John B. Litel
Clarkson	Walter Croft
Irene O'Dare	Edith Day
Helen Cheston	Eva Puck
Jane Gilmour	Gladys Miller
Mrs. Marshall	Florence Mills
Eleanor Worth	Bernice McCabe
Mrs. O'Dare	Dorothy Walters
Mrs. Cheston	Lillian Lee
Madame Lucy	Bobbie Watson

Act I.— Scene 1 — Marshall's home, Long Island. Scene 2 — O'Dare Home, New York City. Act II. — Scenes 1 and 3 — The Tenement. Scenes 2 and 4 — The Garden of Bowden's Home.

Irene O'Dare is a shop girl. One day, calling at the home of Donald Marshall, she is rescued from an unpleasant situation by the young man of the house. Being a philanthropic youth, with a good heart and a clean mind, Donald wishes to help Irene. He finds a position for her as a model for a ladies' tailor and after she has carried off all the honors at a great party on Long Island, where, as the model, she sings and dances and wears ravishingly beautiful gowns, he asks her to marry him. The opposition of Irene's mother, who suspects the rich, provides the suspense to this particular Cinderella story.

" THE SON-DAUGHTER "

A play of New China in three acts by George Scarborough and David Belasco, produced by David Belasco, at the Belasco Theatre, New York, November 19, 1919.

Cast of characters —
```
Lien Wha...........................Lenore  Ulric
Doctor  Lum  Low...................Marion  Abbott
Toy  Yah...........................Jane  Ferrell
Doctor Dong Tong..................Thomas  Findlay
Tom  Lee.......  ...........  ...  ...Edmond  Lowe
Sin  Kai..........................Albert  Bruning
His  Excellency,  Fang  Fou  Hy........Frederic  Burt
Fen-sha............................Harry  Mestayer  -
Wing .............................John  Willard
Kang  ...........................Richard  Malchien
Chao  Pingkium.......................Nick  Long
General  Yuan.....................Henry  Weaver
Wu  Git...........................John  Amory
Kai  Pai.........................W.  T.  Clark
Chow  Chang..................Charles  R.  Burrows
    Act  I.— Dong  Tong's  home  in  Pell  St.  New  York.
Act  II.— A  Few  Hours  Later.  Act  II.— At  Lien·
Wha's  Window;  The  " Sea  Crab "  at  Work;  Chamber
of  the  Smiling  Joss.
```

Lien Wha is the daughter of Dong Tong, an influential Chinese merchant in New York. Tong has been called upon to raise a large sum of money as his assessment for the revolutionary party operating in China. Not having the money, the leaders of the revolution suggest his selling Lien Wha to one of the wealthier Chinese merchants for the sum needed. Lien Wha, torn from the arms of her lover, who is none other than the son of the revolutionary leader in China, accepts the sacrifice she is obliged to make and forces the bidding of the merchants to a large sum. In the end she kills the wicked imperialist who buys her and there is a last-curtain rumor that she and her lover escaped from their enemies by way of Vancouver and a Chinese steamship line.

" LINGER LONGER LETTY "

A musical comedy in three acts, music by Alfred Goodman, lyrics by Bernard Grosman, produced by Oliver Morosco, at the Fulton Theater, New York, November 20, 1919.

Cast of characters —

Letty	Charlotte Greenwood
Nancy	Eleanor Henry
Mayme	Olga Roller
Juliet	Majorie McClintock
Mrs. Brewster	Louise Mink
Ethelmay	Bernice Hirsch
Roberta	Frances Victory
Marie	Virginia Travares
Jim	Olim Howland
Walter	Arthur Hartley
Colonel	Cyril Ring
Lazelle	France Bendsten
Father	Oscar Figman

Act I.— Kitchen of the Larkin Home. Act II. — Letty's Boudoir. Act III.— On the Lawn. Staged by Oliver Morosco.

Letty is the ugly duckling of an ambitionless family. When her sisters go strawberry festivaling, Letty is left at home to do the work. Finally she rebels and, after contributing several specialties to the entertainment, is paired with Jim, the comedian with whom she has been in love from the first of their duets.

" CÆSAR'S WIFE "

A drama in three acts by W. Somerset Maugham, produced by Florenz Ziegfeld, Jr., at the Liberty Theatre, New York, November 24, 1919.

Cast of characters —

Sir Arthur Little, K.C.B., C.C.M.G.	Norman Trevor
Roland Parry	Ernest Glendinning

```
Henry  Pritchard.......................Harry  Green
Richard  Appleby,  M.P..........T.  Wigney  Percival
Osman  Pasha.................Frederic  DeBelleville
Mrs.  Etheridge.......................Margaret  Dale
Mrs.  Pritchard........................Hilda  Spong
Mrs.  Appleby.................Mrs.  Tom  A.  Wise
Violet ...............................Billie  Burke
   Acts  I  and  II.— House  and  Garden  of  the  British
Consular  Agent,  Cairo.  Act  III.— Terrace  and
Garden  of  Same  House.
```

Violet Little, married to Sir Arthur Little, twenty years her senior and a British Consul General in Egypt, finds herself violently in love with her husband's young secretary, Roland Parry. She frankly confesses her passion to Sir Arthur and he as frankly informs her that, though he feels he has done her a great wrong in marrying her, it is her duty, as the wife of a British official, to conquer her weakness. The solution of her problem is made easier for Violet by the discovery that young Parry has met an American heiress in the third act in whom he has become seriously interested, and by curtain fall she is convinced that Sir Arthur is really worth a whole dancing floor full of jumping juveniles.

"THE RISE OF SILAS LAPHAM"

A comedy in four acts by Lillian Sabine, produced by The Theatre Guild, Inc., at the Garrick Theatre, New York, November 25, 1919.

Cast of characters —

```
Silas  Lapham.....................James  K.  Hackett
Batty  Hubbard.......................Milton  Pope
Persis  Lapham...................Grace  Henderson
Katie ............................Nell  Hamilton
Milton  Rogers.....................Henry  Stillman
Penelope  Lapham.................Majorie  Vonnegut
Irene  Lapham.......................Grace  Knell
Tom  Corey...........................Noel  Leslie
Anna  Bellingham  Corey............Helen  Westley
Bromfield  Corey.....................Walter  Howe
Nanny  Corey.........................Mary  Blair
Lily  Corey..........................Grace  Ade
Edith  Kingsbury....................Mildred  Keats
Mrs.  Henry  Bellingham... .........Nell  Hamilton
Charles  Bellingham.................Richard  Abbott
Mrs.  James  Bellingham..............Sara  Enright
```

```
James Bellingham................William Nelson
Mr. Sewell......................Erskine Sanford
Mrs. Sewell.........................Mary True
Mr. Seymour............ ...... ..Robert Donaldson
Robert Chase......................Walter Geer
Mr. Dunham.......................Henry Travers
```
Acts I and III.— Living Room in Lapham House,
Boston. Act II.— The Drawing Room at the Coreys'.
Act IV — The Lapham Cottage at Lumberville.

A dramatization of William Dean Howell's novel.
In the play version Silas, made rich by his discovery
of a mineral paint, seeks social position for himself,
his wife and his daughters in Boston. He finds so-·
ciety cold, disgraces the family by becoming slightly
alcoholic, later loses all his money, but saves his honor,
and finally drifts back to the sun-bathed cottage in
Lumberville from whence he started.

"THE ROSE OF CHINA"

A musical comedy by Guy Bolton, lyrics by P. G.
Wodehouse, music by Armand Vecsey, produced
by F. Ray Comstock and Morris Gest, at the
Lyric Theatre, New York, November
25, 1919.

Cast of characters —
```
Dum Tong............................Paul Irving
Ton Ka............................Louise Brownel
Ling Tao........................Jane Richardson
Ting-Fang-Lee ....................Stanley Ridges
Tsao Ling.........................Wm. H. Pringle
Tommy Tilford.......................Oscar Shaw
Wilson Peters.....................Frank McIntyre
Polly Baldwin....................Cecil Cunningham
Priest .............................Leo Dwyer
Chung ..........................Thos. E. Jackson
Grace Hobson......................Cynthia Perot
Mrs. Hobson......................Edna May Oliver
```
Act I.— The Garden of Tsao Ling. Act II.—
Tommy Tilford's Bungalow. Act III.— The Ter-
race Outside the Bungalow.

Tommy Tilford, a handsome young American adventuring in China, is forced to marry Ling Tao,
the daughter of a Chinese dignitary, because he is the

first male person to look upon her naked face. The situation is not serious, however, as the youth had previously fallen in love with the maid. His American fiancee, who might have caused trouble, agrees to listen to reason and the ending is conventionally satisfying.

"APHRODITE"

A romance of manners in ancient Egypt, by Pierre Frondaie and George C. Hazelton, from the novel of Pierre Louys, music by Henri Fevrier and Anselm Goetzl, produced by F. Ray Comstock and Morris Gest, at the Century Theater. New York, November 24, 1919.

Cast of characters —

Timon	Frederick Macklyn
Phrasilas	Richards Hale
Horatius	Mayne Linton
Naukrates	Etienne Girardot
Theoxenes	Robert Ayrton
Bubastic	William McNeill
Berenike	Hazel Alden
Officer of the Guard	Nikolai Glovatski
Demetrios	McKay Morris
Ampelis	Rita Gould
A Beggar	Renwick Roget
A Donkey Boy	Basil Smith
Fruit Peddler	Arnold Van Leer
Fish Peddler	Lester Sweyd
A Young Sailor	Richard Schwendler
A Snake Peddler	William McNeal
A Youth	Edward Howell
Harhingif Khyam	Mark Loebell
Myrtis	Annette Bade
Rhodocleia	Carolyn Nunder
Bacchys	Maude Odell
Chrysis	Dorothy Dalton
Aphrodite	Mildred Walker
Jester	Claude Forest
Chimeris	Clara T. Bracy
Touni	Nita Naldi
Melitta's Mother	Hazel Woodhull
Eunike	Genevieve Dolaro
Chief Butler	Clarence Redd
Aphrodasia	Mlle. Dazie
Old Sailor	William McNeal
Hight Priest	Guy Collins

Staged by E. Lyall Swete.

Demetrios, a sculptor of ancient Alexandria, has modelled a copy of the statue of Aphrodite, which he worships. In turn, he is much desired of Berenike, Queen of Egypt, to whose charms he is cold. Denying Berenike, Demetrios turns his attention to Chrysis, a famous courtesan of Galilee, who would test his love. If he will commit the crimes of theft, murder and sacrilege for her, she will accept him. Yet when Demetrios has done these things and won the love of Chrysis, Aphrodite appears to him in a dream and turns his love to loathing, whereupon Chrysis, the courtesan, leaps from a tower into the sea.   -

ELSIE JANIS AND HER GANG

In a bomb proof revue in two acts, book by Elsie Janis, songs by William Kernell, Richard Fechheimer, B. C. Hilliam and Elsie Janis, produced at the Geo. M. Cohan Theatre, New York, December 1, 1919.

The Gang —

Bill Kernell	Chick Deveau
Eddie Hay	Richard Hay
Bradley Knoche	Bill Reardon
Jerry Hoekstra	Henry Janswick
Jack Brant	Sam Burbank
Charles Lawrence	Frank Miller
Herbert Goff	

Cast of characters —

The Parisienne	Eva Le Gallienne
The Y. M. C. A. Girl	Ruth Wells
The K. of C. Girl	Henrietta Orville
The Ambulance Service Girl	Margaret Sousa
The Motor Transport Girl	Lillian Cullen
The Red Cross Nurse	Mary Balfour

THE JAZZ BAND

Ewart Allan	Harry Berger
Norman Merleton	Joe Wise
Howard Johnson	Nat Martin
Edward W. Reno	B. Romolo

Act I.— France and sections of Paris. Act II.— Coblenz and New York.

A series of episodes and specialties selected from

the entertainments given for the soldiers back of the lines in France.

"ONE NIGHT IN ROME"

A drama in three divisions by J. Hartley Manners, produced by George C. Tyler, at the Criterion Theatre, New York, December 2, 1919.

Cast of characters —

Richard Oak	Philip Mericale
Mr. Justice Millburne	H. Cooper Cliffe
Signor Diranda	George Majeroni
Denby Wragge	Barry Baxter
Gresham	Thomas Coffin Cooke
Bikra	John Davenport Seymour
Mrs. Oak	Mrs. Felix Morris
Mrs. Redlynch	Louise Beaudet
Zephyr	Helen Blair
Kiara	Olin Field
Iola	Greta Kemble Cooper
Aenea	Valentine Clemow
La Bambina	Marie Bianchi
" L'Enigme "	Laurette Taylor

Division I.—In the house of a Great City. Divisions II and III.—In the Heart of a Great Country.

" L'Enigme," an Italian fortune teller, who has become something of a society fad in London, reads the palms of an English house party. Among her clients is Richard Oak, back from the war. In him " L'Enigme " discovers a marked weakness of character. The young man lacks decision. He is wabbly and afraid in every crisis that he faces. Later, she meets him at a house party and when they find themselves in a compromising position, from which he would flee, she determines to force a decision upon him — to make him stand and truthfully explain why he is there. To do this she raises the house by deliberately smashing a jewel case, leaving herself open to the charge of intended theft. Young Oak, in order to protect the fortune teller, is forced to come forward and declare himself. Because of his declaration, his fiancee breaks their engagement. a climax that is not particularly displeasing to him as he had already acquired a sentimental interest in the fortune teller.   In the end " L'Enigme " confesses that she is an English girl who had married an Italian noble and was forced to assume the disguise to escape the consequences of a scandal attending her husband's death.

" MY LADY FRIENDS "

A farce in three acts by Emil Nyitray and Frank Mandel, produced by H. H. Frazee, at the Comedy Theatre, New York, December 3, 1919.

Cast of characters —

Catherine Smith	Mona Kingsley
Eva Johns	June Walker
Hilda	Rae Bowdin
Lucille Early	Theresa Maxwell Conover
Edward Early	Frank Morgan
James Smith	Clifton Crawford
Tom Trainor	Robert Fiske
Norah	Edith King
Gwendolyn	Jane Warrington
Julia	Jessie Nagle

Acts I and III.— Home of James Smith, New York.
Act II.— Chickadee Cottage, Atlantic City.

James Smith, who has made a fortune printing bibles, is desirous of spending a share of his money in having a good time. His economical wife opposes him so strenuously that he is forced to dissemble, so he adopts the habit of " spreading a little sunshine " wherever opportunity offers. Whenever he finds an attractive young woman lonesome and neglected it is his custom to set her up in a nice little apartment and provide her with enough change to keep the wolf from the dumb waiter. Mrs. Smith, growing suspicious, follows him to Atlantic City, where he has called a convention of his little sunshine girls. Here she is convinced that, while he may be innocent, the only sure way " to keep a husband good is to keep him broke." After that she will attend to the spending of the surplus family funds herself.

"THREE'S A CROWD"

A comedy by Earl Derr Biggers and Christopher Morley, produced by John Cort, at the Cort Theatre, New York, December 4, 1919.

Cast of characters —

Phoebe. ....Nesta Kerin
Boots................................Andre Aubry
Tims................................Harry Sothern
Josephine Vincent.....................Daisy Ruddo
Billy King.........................Charles Compton
Sir Alan Forbes...................Harold De Becker
Peter Whitney.........................Roy Gordon
Kathleen Kent.......................Phoebe Foster
Captain John Blair. A. E. F..........Allan Dinehart
Philip Kent........................Byron Beasley
Mrs. Kent........................Beatrice Moreland
Wadleigh...........................Douglas Ross
Rev. Joseph Tilleymoss.............Walter McEwen
    Act I.— The Blue Boar Inn, Stratford-on-Avon.
Act II.—Drawing room of Mr. Kent's home. Act III.— The Kents' kitchen.

Four ex-army officers, an Englishman, a Frenchman, an American and a Canadian, happening upon a letter in France that indicates a certain English girl is in trouble, severally decide to rescue her. They make their way to the English town in which she lives and smuggle themselves into her house by various means, each offering himself as the most logical of her protectors. Following numerous farcical complications she accepts one of them. The American, of course — in America.

"MISS MILLIONS"

A comedy with music, book by R. H. Burnside, music by Raymond Hubbell, produced by R. H. Burnside, at the Punch and Judy Theatre, New York, December 9, 1919.

Cast of characters —

Mary Hope	Valli Valli
Horace Honeydew	Rayley Holmes
Timothy Bond	Clayton White
Jack Honeydew	Vinton Freedley
Ephraim Tutt	William Burress
John J. Hawkins	John Hendricks
Mr. Sharpe	Harry Hermsen
Willie Lightfoot	Lewis Sloden
Bates	Frank Farrington
Waiter	Walter Coupe
Percy	Frank Slater
Reggie	Alfred Siegler
Ezra Tucker	George Stuart
Silas Dingley	B. J. Tieman
Tobias Wilkins	Harry Smith
Hiram Jones	William Duane
Mrs. Honeydew	Louise Mackintosh
Ethel Bradley Smith	Vera Rosander
Julia Joyce	Jessie Standish
Peggy	Cissie Sewell
Tabitha Tutt	Mrs. William Pruette
Aunt Miranda	Genevieve Tucker
Cynthia	Bonnie Murray
Matilda	Amy Scott
Martha	Gladys White

Act I.— A Tea Shop on Fifth Avenue. Act II.— Reception room of " Mary's " residence. Act III.— A Farm in New Jersey.

Mary Hope, a waitress in a Fifth Avenue tea shop, is engaged to marry Jack Honeydew, a young man of wealth and social position. Honeydew's uncle is convinced that Mary is a fortune hunter, to prove which he schemes to reverse the respective positions of the young people. He provides Mary with a richly furnished house, convinces her that she has inherited it from a distant relative, and at the same time announces to his young nephew the loss of his fortune. Mary is still true to Jack, however, until she learns of the uncle's scheme to test her. That makes her mad, and she runs away to New Jersey, forcing her lover to pursue her until the play's end.

"THE PHANTOM LEGION"

A fantasy in three acts by Anthony Paul Kelly, produced by the author at the Playhouse, New York, December 10, 1919.

Cast of characters —

Mrs. Weaver	Effie Ellsler
Jack Weaver	Raymond McKee
Dick Weaver	Edwin Strawbridge
George Weaver	Frederick Howard
Alice Craig	Miriam Sears
Tom Parker	William Williams
Peggy Carruthers	Hazel Turney
Ethan Leach	John Woodford
Chuck Leach, his son	Junius Matthews
Tip Turpin	Harry Sedley
Sergeant Bow-Bells	John M. Troughton
An English Corporal	J. W. Mason
Captain Croisset	Paul Gordon

Act I.— Living room of Mrs. Weaver's students' rooming house. Act II.— A bombproof shelter. Act III.— Lawn of the Weaver home.

Jack, Dick and George, the adopted sons of Mrs. Weaver, go to the war and are killed. As disembodied spirits they discover in spirit land an organization known as "The Phantom Legion," made up of those who die but never surrender. It is the legion that sang hopefully to the charging Frenchmen at the first Marne and held the stubborn Britishers in line when they were pushed back at Mons. The three Weaver spirits also re-visit the home of their foster mother and hover around there trying to get the message across to her that no spirit can be happy in heaven so long as relatives and friends continue to be sorrowful on earth. Their best work is to soften the steely heart of the village miser as he is about to foreclose mother's mortgage.

" MONSIEUR BEAUCAIRE "

A romantic opera in three acts by Andre Messager, produced by Gilbert Miller, at the New Amsterdam Theatre, New York, December 11, 1919.

Cast of characters —

Monsieur Beaucaire	Marion Green
Philip Molyneux	John Clarke
Frederick Bantison	Lennox Pawle
Rakell	Spencer Trevor
François	Yvan Servais
Duke of Winterset	Robert Parker
Beau Nash	Robert Cunningham
Townbrake	Andre Brouard
Captain Badger	Percy Carr
Joliffe	Harry Frankiss
Bicksitt	Eric Snowden
Marquis de Mirepoix	Yvan Servais
Lucy	Marjorie Burgess
Countess of Greenbury	Barbara Esme
A Girl (in Act I)	Ellen Grubb
Lady Mary Carlisle	Blanche Tomlin

Prologue.— Monsieur Beaucaire's lodgings in Bath. Act. I.— Lady Rellerton's ballroom. Act II.— At Mr. Bantison's park. Act III.— Assembly room at Bath.

An operatic version of Booth Tarkington's comedy, in which the adventurous Duc d'Orleans, in hiding as Beaucaire, the barber of Bath, forces his introduction to the beauties and gallants of Bath by the Duke of Winterset, whom he has caught cheating at cards and threatens to expose. His identity as the barber is discovered, following his successful wooing of the beauteous Lady Mary Carlisle, and he is ignominiously expelled from the pump room. He is grandly triumphant in the end, however, when his true rank as the Duc d'Orleans is established.

"ABRAHAM LINCOLN"

A drama in six scenes by John Drinkwater, produced by William Harris, Jr., at the Cort Theatre, December 15, 1919.

Cast of characters —

A Chronicler......................Leonard Mudie
Stone, a Farmer....................Thomas Irwin
Cuffney, a Store Keeper...........Thomas J. Keogh
Susan, a Maid in Lincoln Home......Florence Johns
Mrs. Lincoln.....................Winifred Hanley
Mr. Lincoln.......................Frank McGlynn
Tucker, Chairman of Delegation.......Forrest Davis
Hind, a Delegate...................Thomas Vaiden
Price, a Delegate..................Duncan Cherry
MacIntosh, a Delegate.............Penwood Batkins
White, of the Southern Commission..Charles Fleming
Seward...........................John S. O'Brien
Jennings, of the Southern Commission.........
.............................William R. Randall
Hawkins, First Clerk..............Conrad Cantzen
Hay..............................Paul Byron
Messenger.........................J. Philip Jerome
Salmon Chase....................Frank E. Jamison
Montgomery Blair..................Ernest Bostwick
Simon Cameron.....................Herbert Curtis
Caleb Smith.......................Joseph Reed
Burnet Hook.....................William A. Norton
Gideon Welles.....................Alfred Moore
Mrs. Goliath Blow............Mary Horne Morrison
Mrs. Otherly....................Jennie E. Eustace
William Custis...................Charles S. Gilpin
Stanton..........................David Landau
General Grant.....................Albert Phillips
Aide to General Grant............George Williams
Dennis, an Orderly................Charles P. Bates
William Scott....................Raymond Hackett
General Meade......................Frank Ginter
General Lee.......................James Durkin
John Wilkes Booth..................J. Paul Jones
Doctor...........................Charles Brill
  Scene I.— Lincoln's home at Springfield, 1860.
Scene II.— Seward's room at The White House,
Washington. Scene III.— Another room at The
White House. Scene IV.— The Cabinet Room at The
White House. Scene V.— General Grant's headquar-
ters near Appomattox. Scene VI.— A small lounge
back of the boxes in Ford's Theatre.

See page 14.

" CURIOSITY "

A comedy in three acts by H. Austin Adams, produced by J. S. Tepper, Inc., at the Greenwich Village Theater, New York, December 18, 1919.

Cast of characters —
```
Quong............................Arvid Paulsen
Tom North......  ........  -  --Ramsey Wallace
Mildred...........................Irene Fenwick -
Ethel.............................Merle Maddern
Hal Peabody.......................Cyril Keightley
    Act I.— The Living Room of the Norths' California
Ranch-house.  Act II.— The Same; a Few Hours
Later.  Act III.— The Same; the Next Morning.
Time — The Present.  Staged by Edgar Selwyn.
```

Mildred North, knowing that her husband had been guilty of a serious flirtation in Honolulu some years after they were married, determines that she has as much right as he to a similar adventure. Finding herself alone with a sweetheart of her youth, she confesses to him her willingness to be tempted, but, after a struggle, he succeeds in explaining to her that a single standard of morals is impossible — men and women being as they are. Her returning husband, though threateningly suspicious, is convinced finally by his inquisitive wife's confession that she has been cured of any desire for further experiments. Her curiosity has been satisfied.

" FOR THE DEFENSE "

A melodrama in three acts by Elmer L. Rice, produced by John D. Williams, at the Playhouse, New York, December 19, 1919.

Cast of characters —
```
Miss Brinton......................Virginia Jones
Miss Smith........  -  ....... .Louise Closser Hale
Margaret Cameron.................Frederica Going
Mrs. Reed........................Louise Sydmeth
```

```
Jennie  Dunn.......................Mary  Jeffery
Madame  Petrard................Georgette  Passedoit
Dr.  Kasimir.......................John  Sainpolis
Collins,  a  reporter..................Charles  Coghlan
Anne  Woodstock.................Winifred  Lenihan
Selma  Thorne...................Adrienne  Morrison
Dr.  William  Lloyd...............N.  St.  Clair  Hales
Christopher  Armstrong...  .........Richard  Bennett
Jane  .............................Angela  Ogden
Officer  McClellan....................Walter  Brown
Inspector  Austin.................William  A.  Crimans
Judge  Gray...........................George  Riddell
Act  I.— Dr.  Kasimir's  Apartment.  Act  II.— Scene
1 — Anne  Woodstock's  Apartment.  Scene  2 — Dr.
Kasimir's  Apartment.  Act  III.— Scene  1 — Judge
Gray's  Office.  Scene  2 — Dr.  Kassimir's  Apartment.
Scene  3 — Judge  Gray's  Office.
```

Anne Woodstock and Selma Thorne are patients of Dr. Kasimir, a psycho-hypnotist practicing in New York. The doctor is a wicked person and has aroused the suspicions of Christopher Armstrong, the young district attorney with whom Anne is in love. While the girls are in Kasimir's rooms he is shot and killed. Suspicion points to Anne. She is brought to trial for the murder and the district attorney is forced to prosecute her, believing her justifiably guilty. With the aid of a " flashback " scene, adopted from the movies, the real happenings in the Kasimir house the day of the murder are revealed, Anne is proved innocent and her ultimate marriage to Christopher Armstrong foreshadowed.

" THE SIGN ON THE DOOR "

A melodrama in three acts by Channing Pollock, produced by A. H. Woods, at the Republic Theatre, New York, December 19, 1919.

Cast of characters —

```
Hugh  ........................Elwood  Bostwick
Frank  Devereaux..................Lowell  Sherman
Ann  Hunniwell........      .  .....Mary  Ryan
```

Captain Burke........................Jules Ferrar
A Newspaper Photographer .....C. Bert Dunlop
Mrs. "Lafe" Regan..................Mary Ryan
Alan Churchill......................Neil Martin
Helen Regan......................Beatrice Allen
Marjorie Blake..................Mildred MacLeod
"Lafe" Regan.... . ...Lee Baker
Bates, a butler....................Kenneth Miner
Ferguson ....Robert Vivian
"Kick" Callahan................Herbert Broderick
Inspector Treffy....................Paul Everton
Officer McLoughlin.................Spencer Evans
The Prologue — A Private Supper Room at the
Cafe Mazarin, New York. Act I.— The Summer
Home of "Lafe" Regan, New Rochelle. Acts II
and III.— A Room at the Ritz — a Small Apart-
ment Hotel in the "Forties."

Anne Hunniwell, a stenographer, unacquainted with
the ways of New York, accepts the invitation of Frank
Devereaux, her employer's son, to dine with him at a
restaurant which, it transpires, is being watched by
the police. While they are there the place is raided
and a flashlight photo taken of the trapped couple.
They are arrested and jump their bail between acts.
Five years later Anne is married to "Lafe" Regan,
a widower with an attractive daughter of 18. Frank
Devereaux again appears on the scene, being this time
in pursuit of Anne's step-daughter. Hearing the girl
is in danger Anne goes to Devereaux's rooms to save
her. While she is there her husband is announced.
He has come to chastise Devereaux for having deceived the wife of a friend. The men scuffle and
Devereaux is killed. Regan, placing the gun in the
dead man's hand, hangs a sign on the door reading
"Do Not Disturb Me," and leaves, locking the door
on the outside and unknowingly locking his wife in
the room with the dead man. The police come, Mrs.
Regan is arrested and exposure seems imminent, when,
by a lucky melodramatic twist, she is saved and forgiven.

" FORBIDDEN "

A romantic play in three acts by Dorothy Donnelly, produced by George Mooser, at the Manhattan Opera House, New York, December 20, 1919.

Cast of characters —

Brigadier General Slocum.......William K Harcourt
Major Richard Flint................George Connor
Major Alexander Osgood..............Ben Taggart
Captain Tottenham Knowles.........John Rutherford
Captain William Bryant (" Snappy ").John McKenna
First Lieut John Booth Lawrence (" Boots ")....
                                        Richard Barbee
First Lieut. Edwin Brice...... - .Henry George
Second Lieut. Luke O'Keefe...........Nolan Leary -
Second Lieut. Vincent Moretti........Walter Abell .
Private Isaac Levy.................Harry Shutan
Private Darwin Bone................Harold Salter
Humboldt Feather....................Joseph Dunn
Anton Roonje.....................David Proctor
Count Robert von Eckdorf...........William Bailey
Kurt Schwartz........................John Burkell
An Orderly..........................Arden Page
Josef ....Herman Gerold
Countess Hildegarde Schoenweg von de Verde....
                                        Martha Hedman
Countess Ermintrude.............Claire Mersereau
Countess Wanda............Georgia Lucile Mooser ,
Carmen Flanagan.................Hermine Shone
Katchen ....Annette Westbay
    Act 1.— The Entry of the American Troops into the Coblenz Bridgehead. Act II and Act III.— Same Location. The action of the play takes place in the hall of the Schloss von der Verde. about thirty miles from Coblenz.

During the early days of the Allies' occupation of the German Rhineland, following the signing of the armistice, First Lieut. John Booth Lawrence finds himself billeted with a group of fellow officers in the Coblenz home of the Countess Hildegarde Schoenweg von der Verde, one of the most attractive of our late enemies. The lieutenant falls in love with the countess and she with him. They plan to marry, but are separated in the end, it may be for months and it may be forever, by Hildegarde's discovery that Lawrence is the very man who had shot her brother. a German

sniper, during the war, to revenge the sniper's killing
of the general's son and his (Lawrence's) best pal.

"NIGHT LODGING"

A drama in four acts by Maxim Gorki, produced by
Arthur Hopkins, at the Plymouth Theatre,
New York, December 22, 1919.

Cast of characters —

Michael Ivanov Kostiliov	William E. Hallman
Vassilisa Karpovna, his wife	Gilda Varesi
Natasha	Eva McDonald
Medviadev	Charles Kennedy
Vaska Pepel	Alan Dinehart
Klestch Andray Nitrich	Hans Robert
Anna	Rosalind Ivan
Bubnov	Cecil Yapp
Kvashnia	Lillian Kingsbury
Nastia	Pauline Lord
Satin	Edward G. Robinson
Actor	Edwin Nicander
Baron	Cecil Clovelly
Luka	W. H. Thompson
Aloyshka	E. J. Ballantine
Krivoi Zob	Louis Alter
Tartar	Alexis M. Polianov

A series of detached but arresting incidents in the
lives of Russia's submerged poor.

"THE FAMOUS MRS. FAIR"

A play in four acts by James Forbes, produced by
A. L. Erlanger, at Henry Miller's Theatre,
New York, December 22, 1919.

Cast of characters —

Sylvia Fair	Margalo Gillmore
Alan Fair	Jack Devereaux
Nora	Betty Hall
E. Dudley Gillette	Robert Strange
Angelica Brice	Virginia Hammond
Nancy Fair	Blanche Bates
Jeffrey Fair	Henry Miller
Mrs. Norman Wynne	Dallas Tyler
Mrs. Kellett Brown	Marian Lord
Mrs. Stuart Perrin	Maude Allen

Mrs. Leslie Converse...................Alice Baxter
Mrs. Gilbert Wells..............Florence Williams
Peggy Gibbs......................Kathleen Comegys
    Acts I and II.— The Fair Home on Long Island.
Acts III and IV.— The Fair Apartment in a New
York Hotel.

See page 65.

"THE WHIRLWIND"

A melodrama by George C. Hazelton and Ritter
Brown, produced by John Cort, at the Standard Theatre, New York, December
23, 1919.

Cast of characters —

Juan Ramson.....................Jacob Kingsberry
Rosita ....Marguerite Risser
Dona Fernandez.................. ....Helen Tracy
Padre Antonio.....................Frank Andrews
Dick Yankton.......................John C. King
Don Felipe Ramirez.................John Davidson
Chiquita ....Mme. Mimi Aguglia
Captain Forest.....................Orrin Johnson
Driver ....Chief Manabozho
Bessie Van Ashton..............Vivienne Osborne
Mrs. Forest.......................Rose Coghlan
Col. Van Ashton....................Oswald Yorke
Blanche Lennox.......................Paula Shay
Bob Carlton.......................Joseph Sweeney
Jim Blake........................John Harrington
Juana ....Jessie Villars
Mariquita ....Miriam Batista
White Cloud......................Dan Red Eagle
Poncho ....Hank Durnell
Tula ....Virginia Russell

Chiquita, a Mexican Indian maid, loves and is loved
by a brave American army officer. His high-toned
eastern family, however, discovering the situation while
touring Mexico, seek to break up the affair. Chiquita,
convinced that she should not marry the American, is
about to call everything off and marry a villain whom
she had, under threats, promised to accompany to the
altar. She keeps her word, and goes as far as the
altar, but there she spurns the villain and turns finally
to the American.

" CARNIVAL ".

A drama in three acts, translated from the Italian of
Mr. Pordes-Milo's play by H. C. M. Hardinge and
Matheson Lang, produced at the 44th Street
Theatre, New York, by Tearle. MacLeod
and Ephraim, December 24, 1919.

Cast of characters —

Silvio Steno	Godfrey Tearle
Simonetta	Margot Kelly
Nino	Bobby Clark
Lelio Di Cesari	Schuyler Ladd
Ottavia. Baroness Della Torre	Olive Oliver
Ettore, Baron Della Torre	Horace Pollack
Andrea, Count Scipione	A. E. Anson
Camilla	Harry Barfoot
Giuseppe	Idamae Oderlin
Dionigi	John P. Jendrek
Tommasso	Basil West
Sandro	Rupert Lumley
Colia	Mary Carroll
Clelia	Laura Alberta
Nella	Welba Lestina
Grazzo	Joseph Lothian
Porter	T. Whelan
Doctor	Edward Spalding

Act I.— A Room in the Steno Palace, on the
Grand Canal. Act II.— The Same. Carnival Night.
Act III.— The Alfieri Theatre. The Entire Action of
the Play Takes Place in Venice During Carnival Time.
Staged by Godfrey Tearle.

During the celebration of the carnival in Venice
Silvio Steno, leading actor of the Alfieri theater, is led
to believe that he has cause to be jealous of his wife,
who is also his leading woman. They are rehearsing
" Othello," and the night of the performance Silvio,
believing his suspicions have been confirmed, proceeds
to strangle his Desdemona in earnest. She is rescued
just in the nick of time to prove her innocence and
save a tragedy.

MORRIS GEST MIDNIGHT WHIRL

A revue in two parts, music by George Gershwin,
lyrics by Budd de Sylva and John Henry Mears,
produced by Morris Gest, at the Century
Grove, New York, December 27, 1919.

Principals engaged —

Helen Shipman
Bernard Granville
Annette Bade
James Watts
Rath Brothers — George,
Dick

Bessie   McCoy
Davis
Bennet and Rich-
ards
Margaret Morris
Gertrude Coates
Gladys Zelian

Staged by Julian Mitchell

" ANGEL FACE "

A musical play in three acts, music by Victor Herbert,
book by Harry B. Smith, lyrics by Robert B.
Smith, musical numbers staged by Julian Alfred, produced by George W. Lederer, at
the Knickerbocker Theatre, New
York, December 29, 1919.

Cast of characters —

Tom Larkins......................John E. Young
Arthur Griffin......................Tyler Brooke
Sandy Sharp........................Richard Pyle
Hugh Fairchild.....................John Reinhard
Rockwell Gibbs....................Howard Johnson
Professor Barlow...................George Schiller
Ira Mapes.........................Bernard Thornton
Slooch ....Jack Donahue
Irving ....Wm. Cameron
Mrs. Zenoba Wise...............Edna Von Buelow
Betty ....Marguerite Zender
Vera ....Minerva Grey
Paula ....Mary Milburn
Lily ....Marguerite St. Clair
Pearl ....Gertrude Wadelle
Mrs. Larkins......................Sarah McVicker
Tessie Blythe......................Emilie Lea
Moya ....May Thompson
     And Members of a Musical Comedy Company.
Act. I.— Bachelor Apartment Shared by Arthur Grif-
fin and Tom Larkins. Act II.-- The Same. Act
III.— The Hotel Lounge. Staged by George W.
Lederer.

A typical musical farce plot founded on the alleged discovery of Dr. Serge Voronoff that the grafting of monkey glands onto the aged will restore the vim and vigor of youth. Prof. Barlow, an eccentric scientist, has discovered an elixir of life, which he carelessly leaves on the table in the first act. It is sampled by various comic members of the cast and they are thereupon supposed to become more comic, and decidedly more agile.

"SMILIN' THROUGH"

A play in a prologue and three acts by Allan Langdon Martin, produced by the Selwyns, at the Broadhurst Theatre, New York, December 30, 1919.

Cast of characters —

THE PROLOGUE

Sarah Wayne...... ....Lalive Brownell
Mary Clare.........................Elaine Inescort

THE PLAY

John Carteret................ .....Henry Stephenson
Dr. Owen Harding..............Ethelbert D. Hales
Ellen ....Charlotte Granville
Kathleen Dungannon....................Jane Cowl
Willie Ainley.........................Philip Tong
Kenneth Wayne.....................Orme Caldara
Jeremiah Wayne.....................Orme Caldara
Moonyeen Clare.........................Jane Cowl
    Prologue — Outside the Gate. Act I.— The Carteret Garden. 1914. Act. II.— The Same. Fifty Years Before. Act III.— The Same. 1919. Staged by Priestly Morrison.

Kathleen Dungannon is in love with Kenneth Wayne, but her aging and stubborn uncle, John Cartaret, having taken an oath that no one of his line shall ever wed a Wayne, forbids their marriage. Pressed for an explanation of his seemingly unreasonable prejudice he begins the story of something that happened fifty years before. There is a "flashback" to the period in which Cartaret and one, Jeremiah Wayne, were in love with Moonyeen Clare. She selected Cartaret, and Wayne, becoming wildly jealous and quite drunk, forced his way into the house the night of the wedding and, shooting at Cartaret, accidentally killed Moonyeen when she jumped in front of her lover. Remembering this Cartaret continues firm in his opposition to the modern romance until the spirits of Moonyeen Clare and Sarah Wayne, mother of Kenneth, get a message across from the other world, softening his stubborn heart. Then he dies and joins his spirit bride and the lovers are free to marry.

" THE PURPLE MASK "

A romantic melodrama in four acts by Matheson Lang, freely adapted from " Le Chevalier au Masque " by Paul Armont and Jean Manoussi, produced by Lee Shubert, at the Booth Theater. New York, January 5, 1919.

Cast of characters —

The Duc de Chateaubriand	Burr Caruth
Armand, Comte de Trevieres	Leo Ditrichstein
The Marquis de Clamorgan	Stephen Wright
Monsieur de Morleve	Alfred Shirley
The Vicomte de Morsanne	George H. Frenger
The Baron de Vivonne	L'Estrange Millman
The Abbe Brochard	Walter Howe
Fouche	Eric Maxon
Brisquet	Brandon Tynan
Captain Lavernais	Orlando Daly
Lieutenant Roche	Earle Mitchell
Brigadier Maillard	Clyde Veaux
Brigadier Caron	Gustav Bowhan
A Sergeant of the Toll-Gate	M. A. Kelly
A Sergeant of Police	Robert A. Ranier
Germain	Burnie McDavitt
Bernard	William Nunn
Keeper of the Toll-Gate	Eldie P. Wood
First Dandy	Harold Seton
Second Dandy	Calvin Round
Laurette de Chateaubriand	Lily Cahill
Valentine de Crisolles	Ann MacDonald
Madame Anais	Margaret Sutherland
Sabine, Her Niece	Boots Wooster
A Customer	Josephine Hamner

Constance ....Violet Rendel
Irene ....Elsa Carroll
    Hussars, Gendarmes, Police Agents, Peasants, Etc.
Act I.— Majolin's Shop in Paris.   Act II.— The Pre-
fecture   at   Evreux.   Act   III.— A   Cellar   Below
Majolin's   Shop.   Act   IV.— Boudoir   at   the   Villa
Recamier at St. Cloud.   Act V.— Toll-House at North
Gate of Paris.   Time — 1803.   During the First Con-
sulate of Napoleon Bonaparte.

The Comte de Trevieres, a dashing royalist in Paris
during the early years of Napoleon's ascendency, is
the mysterious gentleman of the purple mask who has
been causing Fouchet's police much trouble.   During
the working out of one of many plots to halt the man
of destiny De Trevieres boldly challenges Fouchet's
men, helps abduct the prefect of Evreux from the pre-
fecture itself, though it is completely surrounded by
the soldiers of the republic, and later carries off successfully several other equally exciting coups, during
one of which he rescues Laurette de Chateaubriand
the heroine and later escapes with her, her family, and
his confederates to England.

"THE ACQUITTAL"

A Drama in Three Acts by Rita Weiman.   Produced
by Cohan and Harris at the Cohan and Harris
Theater, New York, January 5, 1910

Cast of characters —

Barton ....Franklin Hall
Nellie ....Barbara Milton
Madeline Winthrop.................Chrystal Herne
Dr. Hammand.......................William Walcott
Edith Craig............................Ann Mason
Joe Conway.....................William Harrigan
Kenneth Winthrop................Edward H. Robins
Robert Armstrong..................Morgan Wallace
Claflin ....Arthur V. Gibson
McCarthy ....Willard F. Barger
Ainsely ....Edward Geer
Wilson ....John Rowan
Hedges ....Harold Gwynn
Burke ....Norman Lane
    Act I.— Living Room.   Act II.— Madeline's Apart-
ments.   Act III.— Same as Act I.   Evening of Same
Day.   The Scenes of the Play Occur at the Winthrop
Home in an American City.   Staged by Sam For-
est.

Kenneth Winthrop has been acquitted of the murder of his aged benefactor, a philanthropist with a kind heart and a lot of money. Joe Conway is a San Francisco reporter detailed on the case, and one who is not satisfied with the verdict. Because the dead man was his friend Joe purposes to follow up the acquittal of Winthrop. Secreting himself in the Winthrop house he skillfully and patiently pieces together such bits of evidence as he is able to collect and finally extracts a confession from Winthrop that he did, in fact, commit the murder. Rather than face the facts, Winthrop commits suicide and Mrs. Winthrop, his young widow, who has some time since lost all affection for her husband, promises that after a decent interval, she will listen to the proposal of the young reporter, in whom she has acquired a sympathetic interest during the course of the trial and the events that followed.

" ALWAYS YOU "

A musical comedy in two acts, book and lyrics by Oscar Hammerstein 2nd, music by Herbert P. Stothart. Produced by Arthur Hammerstein at the Central Theatre, New York, January 5, 1920

Cast of characters —

```
Toinette Fontaine........ . ... ......Helen Ford
Bruce Nash.......................Walter Scanlan
An East Indian Peddlar..........Edouard Ciannelli
Julie Fontaine.......................Julia Kelety
Charlie Langford.....................Russell Mack
Montmorency Jones....................Ralph Herz
A Mysterious Conspirator...........Bernard Gorcey
Joan Summers.......................Anna Seymour
Thomas .........................Joseph Barton
A Waitress...........................Emily Russ
Dancers.......................Cortez and Peggy
    Prologue — Trouville, France, August, 1918. Act
I.— The Grounds of a Hotel in Trouville, August,
1919. Act II.— The Lounge of the Trouville Casino,
Late Evening of the Same Day.
```

Bruce Nash, when he was an A. E. F. captain in

France, assured Toinette Fontaine that she was indeed the only girl for him and always would be. Then he returned to America and became engaged to his regular girl.   Back in Trouville, however, he regrets his action, and after a variety of lyrical and dramatic complications, he is able to shift again, and is again successful in convincing Toinette that it has always been she.   This time she gets ready to marry him quick.

"THE LIGHT OF THE WORLD"

A drama in three acts by Pierre Saisson (Guy Bolton and George C. Middleton).   Produced at the Lyric Theatre by F. Ray Comstock and Morris Gest. New York. January 6. 1920

Cast of characters —
```
Mary Rendel........................Percy Haswell
Nathan ............................Fuller Mellish
Ruth le Doux.......................Jane Cooper
The Three Wise Men:
  Bert Adams.......................Wright Kramer
  Jan Van Veen.....................Fred Vogeding
  Arthur Brooks....................Leslie Palmer
Anton Rendel.......................Pedro de Cordoba
Simon Brock........................Ralph Kellard
Jonas Kurz.........................B. Wallis Clark
Agnes .............................Helen Chandler
Timothy ...........................Charles Crumpton
Pastor Saunders....................Arnold Lucy
Martin Gast........................Ernest A. Elton
James Mayre........................Burke Clarke
Paul Mayre.........................Gerald Rogers
Raymond Hott.......................Arthur Fitzgerald
Margot Haser.......................Philis Poyah
Marna Lynd.........................Clara Joel
```
Act I.— The Home of Anton Rendel. Act II.— Open Air Stage of the Passion Play Theatre, About Four Weeks Later. Act III.— Same as Act I. A Few Days Later. The Scenes of the Play Are Laid in a small Village in Switzerland Near the French Border.

Anton Rindel, a wood carver in a small village in Switzerland and a member of the amateur company that periodically produces " The Passion Play," is asked to give shelter to Marna Lynd, the village Magdalen, who has been betrayed by Simon Brock, and who returns to the village with Simon's child. Simon, though he is Rindel's best friend, denies his responsibility as the father of Marna's child, thus throwing the burden of suspicion upon Rindel. The villagers, shocked by the scandal, take the role of Christus away from the wood carver and threaten to stone the sinning Marna from the village. A happy ending, however, is provided for this particular adaptation of the Biblical story. Simon relents and confesses, his wife forgives him, and Rindel is restored to favor as the Christus and the prospective husband of Marna.

" NO MORE BLONDES "

A Farce in three acts by Otto Harbach. Produced by A. H. Woods at Maxine Elliott's Theatre, New York, January 7, 1920

Cast of characters —

May Merkel	Muriel Hope
George Harper	Leo Donnelly
Millicent Howells	Nancy Fair
James Howells	Ernest True...
Mrs. Stubbs	Alice Belmore Cliffe
Tanner	Dallas Welford
Cecile	Elizabeth Gergely
Eve Powell	Eileen Wilson
Battling Hogan	Frank Allworth
Thad Lynch	Edwin Walter
James Powell	Edward Douglas
Madge Saunders	Yvonne Gouraud

Act I.— Scene 1 — Harper's Real Estate Office. Scene 2 — Lounging Room on Third Floor of James Powell's Home. Scene 3 — The Same. The Next Morning. Act II.— Reception Room of the Same House. Act III.— The Same. Place — New York City.

James Howells, an automobile salesman, comes from Cohoes. N. Y., to the big city bringing his fiancée,

Millicent, with him. It is James' idea that they will
be married on the trip, thus permitting him to combine business with pleasure. They are married, but
the day of the wedding the young bridegroom, in
the interest of his business, takes a blonde to lunch.
This so angers the new Mrs. Howells that she is about
to star: back for Cohoes, when a mutual friend, thinking to patch up the quarrel, induces her to stay over
a day. That night the friend installs young Howells
in a furnished apartment. The wife of the owner
of the apartment returns unexpectedly and the following morning, when Mrs. Howells is sent to the apartment to meet and forgive her husband, she finds he
has spent the night under the same roof with another
woman and suspects the worst. Complications until
11 P. M., followed by general explanations.

" FRIVOLITIES OF 1920 "

A revue, in two acts and 21 scenes, music and lyrics by
William B. Friedlander, additional songs by Harry
Auracher and Tom Johnstone, scenes written
by Wm. Anthony McGuire. Produced
by G. M. Anderson at the 44th Street
Theatre, New York, Jan. 8,
1920

Principals engaged —

Henry Lewis	Doraldina
Moss and Fry	Colin Chase
Frank Davis	Fletcher Norton
Delle Darnell	Doris Lloyd
Nellie and Sara Kouns	Mabel Roberts
Zelda Santley	Victorine Voltaire
Edward Gallagher	Jeanne Voltaire
Dolly Best	Irene Delroy
Marie Grenville	Grace Lee
Merle Hartwell	Thelma Carlton

THE PASSION FLOWER

A drama in three acts by Jacinto Benavente, Translated from the Spanish by John Garret Underhill. Produced at the Greenwich Village Theatre, New York, Jan. 13, 1920

Raimunda .... Nance O'Neil
Acacia .... Edna Walton
Dona Isabel........................ Clara Bracey
Milagro .... Gertrude Gustin
Fidelia .... Alba Anchoriz
Engracia .... Helen Rapport
Bernabea ...,...................... Aldeah Wise
Gaspara .... Ridler Davies
Juliana .... Mrs. Charles G. Craig
Estaban .... Charles Waldron
Tio Eusebio........................ Robert Fisher
Faustino .... Edwin Beryl
Rubio .... Harold Hartsell
Bernabe .... Charles Angelo
Norbert .... J. Harper Macauley
  Act I.— Living Room in Raimunda's Home. Act II.
— Entrance Hall to Raimunda's Home. Act III.—
Same as Act II. The Scenes of the Play Are Laid
on the Outskirts of a Small Town in Spain.

Raimunda is the second wife of Esteban. Acacia is her daughter by her first marriage. Acacia is to be married, but the night of her betrothal her lover is shot and killed. A former lover is suspected, but gradually the suspicion shifts to Esteban, whose love for his step-daughter has long been a subject of gossip, though strenuously denied by the two. In the crisis following the accusation this love flares forth. Raimunda is bitterly jealous, but willing to forgive her husband. As she attempts to drag him away from Acacia, however, she is shot and killed.

"THE POWER OF DARKNESS"

A tragedy in four acts by Leo Tolstoi. Produced by The Theatre Guild at the Garrick Theatre, New York, Jan. 15, 1920

Cast of characters: —
Anisya .... Ida Rauh
Akoulina .... Marjorie Vonnegut

```
Peter .............................Henry Stillman
Nan ..............................Maud Brooks
Nikita ...........................Arthur Hohl
Akim .............................Fred G. Mories
Matryona .. . ...... .Helen Westley
Marina .......................Bertha Broad
Mitrich ..........................Erskine Sanford
Simon ........................ . .William Nelson
Bridegroom .......................Walter Geer
Ivan .............................Henry Travers
First Neighbour....................Mary Blair
Second Neighbour.................. .......Grace Ade
Driver ......................Robert Donaldson
Police Officer.....................Richard Abbott
Best Man..........................Michael Carr
Village Elder.......... ... .........Milton Pope
Matchmaker . .. . .Noel Leslie
First Girl................. .........Grace Knell
Second Girl........... .................Mary True
```

Act I.— The Interior of Peter's Hut. Act II.—
The Same Hut. Act III.— The Interior of a Court-
yard. Act IV.— In Front of a Barn.

Nikita, the godless son of old Akim, himself a godly man, assists Anisya in the murder of her husband, and later marries the widow. Heedless of his good father's advice he continues his descent into sin by abandoning his wife for the girl Akoulina, and later by strangling the child she bears him. "Sin fastens on sin," shouts old Akim; "when the claw is caught the bird is lost." In the end Nikita confesses his sins and Akim is happy in his son's regeneration, even though the officers of the law are waiting to lead him away.

"THE 'RUINED' LADY"

A comedy in two acts, by Frances Nordstrom. Produced at The Playhouse, New York,
January 19, 1920

Cast of characters —

```
Dorothy Mortimer....................Leila Frost
Dallis Mortimer....................Richard Farrell
Jack Torrence......................Freeman Wood
Julia .............................Helen Reimer
Bixby ........................Thomas Donnelly
" Bill " Bruce......................John Miltern
Mrs. Potts-Thompson. ... ..... ..Caroline Locke
```

Olive Gresham....................Carlotta Monterey
Ann Mortimer......................Grace George
Mayene Breslin.......................May Hopkins
"Cutie" Bird.......................Marie Bryar
    Act I.— At the Mortimers. Act II.— At "Bill's."
Act III.— The Same Place — Long Island. Time —
Spring.

Ann Mortimer has been engaged to Bill Bruce so
long she fears Bill has forgotten it. To refresh his
memory, and also to bring him again to the thought
of marrying her, she schemes to force him to "compromise" her. She will be found in his rooms at
night, and to save her good name he will have to
marry her. The scheme works, but not without many
amusing interruptions, including one that leads the
neighbors to believe that Ann really is a genuine village
vamp.

"PIETRO"

A comedy drama in a prologue and three acts by
Maud Skinner and Jules Eckert Goodman.
Produced by Charles Frohman at the
Criterion Theatre, New York,
January 19, 1920

Cast of characters —

IN THE PROLOGUE

The Court Interpreter................J. T. Chailee
The Bailiff.... .... .Walter F. Scott
Tomlinson ....Robert Smiley
Keith Oliphant.....................Thurlow Bergen
The Jail Matron....................Madalyn Kent
The Bambina........................Elizabeth
Pietro Barbano......................Otis Skinner

IN THE PLAY

Peter Barban........................Otis Skinner
Alfred Peyton.......................O. B. Clarence
Angela ....Ruth Rose
Keith Oliphant.... ....Thurlow Bergen
Keith Oliphant, Jr. ....Robert Ames
Clark ....William Bonelli
Padre Michetti......................Clarence Bellair
Jarrold ....George Harcourt

Miguel ....Joe Spurin
Teresa ....Mary Shaw
  Prologue — The Ante-room of the Court House at
West Durham, Pennsylvania. (Time — March, 1896.)
Act I.— California. Terrace of the Barban-Peyton
Estate, "Casa Esperanza." (May, 1914.) Act II.—
The Sun Room at "Casa Esperanza." Act III.—
Same as Act I. Evening.

Pietro Barbano, quarreling with his wife, Teresa, because she has abused their three-year-old bambina, suffers a momentary madness. When he recovers his wits his wife has disappeared and there are bloodstains all over the place. Pietro is tried for Teresa's murder, but the bloodstains are proved to be those of his pet dog, and he is released. He takes his child, and eighteen years later is discovered in California, his name changed to Peter Barban. He is now a rich man and has brought his girl up to believe that her mother was something of a saint and therefore desired in heaven. Teresa suddenly reappears on the scene, and Barbano's past threatens to spoil everything. A way to be rid of the mother is found, however, and the conclusion is sentimentally satisfying.

"MAMMA'S AFFAIR"

A comedy in three acts by Rachel Barton Butler. Produced by Oliver Morosco at the Little Theatre. New York, Jan, 19, 1920

Cast of characters —
Tommy Hooper.......................Little Billy
Henry Marchant...................George LeGuere
Eve Orrin..........................Ida St. Leon
Mrs. Marchant.................Katherine Kaelred
Mrs. Orrin..........................Effie Shannon
Dr. Brent Janson..................Robert Edeson
Mrs. Bundy.......................Amelia Bingham
  Act I.— "The Willows," a Hotel in the Hills of
Massachusetts. Act II.— A Private Sun Parlor on
the Top Floor of "The Willows." Act III.— Living
Room at Dr. Janson's Home. Time — The Present.

See page 215.

"BIG GAME"

A drama in three acts by Willard Robertson and
Kilbourn Gordon.   Produced by Mrs. Henry
B.   Harris   at   the   Fulton   Theatre
New York, January 20, 1920

Cast of characters —

```
Joe ..............................Charles Halton
Pigeon ...........................William Morran
White ............................Reginald Barlow
Lafontaine .....  ................William Maxson
Marine Smith.......................Pauline Lord
Larry Smith............  .....  .   Alan Dinehart
John St. John........................Paul Dickey
Lizard ...............................J. A. Curtis
```

Act   I.— The   Snow.   Act   II.— Snowbound.   Act
III.— The   Snow   Lifts.   The   Action   Takes   Place   in
a Trapper's Cabin Somewhere North of Quebec.

Larry and Marie Smith, he an American, she a
French Canadian, are adventuring north of Quebec.
They had been fellow employes in a department store
in the States.   Marie, accused of theft, was held in
jail; Larry stood by her, and when she was released
they were married.   In the woods Marie hopes her
rather anemic young husband will grow well and
strong.   But the life, the food, the people of the
north rather disgust Larry and Marie begins to doubt
his courage.   When John St. John, a fascinating
ladies' man, insults her she bids her husband avenge
the insult by shooting St. John.   Larry's refusal to
take a human life convinces Marie that he is a weakling, and she boldly agrees to run away with St. John.
Before they can start, however, Larry's courage returns and he plants three bullets in the person of
the handsome villain.

" AS YOU WERE "

A fantastic revue by Arthur Wimperis. Music by
Herman Darewski. Produced by E. Ray
Goetz at the Central Theatre, New
York, January 27, 1920

Cast of characters —
```
Chase Clews......................Hugh Cameron
Ethel Nutt.......................Ruth Donnelly
Pinkie Smith..........  . . .....Virginia Watson
Cuthbert ........................Stanley Harison
Wolfie Wafflestein...............Sam Bernard
Ki Ki............................Clifton Webb
Gervaise ........................Irene Bordoni
Professor Filbert................Frank Mayne
A Marquis........................Violet Starthmore
Louis, Comte de Belamy... .......Clifton Webb
Ninon de l'Esclos................Irene Bordoni
De La Reynie.....................Frank Mayne
Nicole ..........................Ruth Donnelly
Cleopatra .......................Irene Bordoni
Mark Antony......................Clifton Webb
```

Wolfie Wafflestein, a manufacturer of pies, driven
to desperation by Gervaise, his extravagant and flirtatious wife, embraces the offer of a scientist to feed
him pink pills that will turn time backward any suggested number of years. With the help of the pills
Wolfie goes back through the ages searching for a
loving, loyal and economical mate. He meets Ninon
de L'Enclos, Cleopatra, Helen of Troy, and finally a
primeval charmer — and satisfies himself that women
are all alike and always have been. Then he flies back
home, satisfied with the Gervaise he has married.

" BEYOND THE HORIZON "

An American tragedy in three acts by Eugene G. O'Neill
Produced by John D. Williams at the Mo-
rosco theater, New York, Feb. 2, 1920

Cast of characters —
```
Robert Mayo.........  ......... .Richard Bennett
Andrew Mayo......................Robert Kelly
```

```
Ruth Atkins...........................Elsie Rizer
Capt. Dick Scott.....................Sidney Macy
Mrs. Kate Mayo......................Mary Jeffery
James Mayo.......................Erville Alderson
Mrs. Atkins.................Louise Closser Hale
Mary ..............................Elfin Finn
Ben ...............................George Hadden
Dr. Fawcett......................George Riddell
    Act I.— Scene 1 — The Road. Sunset of a Day
in Spring. Scene 2 — The Farm House. The Same
Night. Act II.— Scene 1 — The Farm House. Noon
of a Summer Day. Several Years Later. Scene 2
— The Road. The Following Day. Act III.— The
Farm House Dawn of a Day in Late Fall. Five
Years Later. Staged Under the Direction of Homer
Saint-Gaudens.
```

See page 30.

" THE NIGHT BOAT "

A musical comedy in three acts, founded on a farce by
A. Bisson, libretto and lyrics by Anne Caldwell,
music by Jerome Kern.   Produced by Charles
Dillingham at the Liberty Theatre,
New York, February 2, 1920

Cast of characters —

```
Minnie ............................Marie Reagen
A Workman.....................Irving Carpenter
Mrs. Maxim........................Ada Lewis
Barbara .........................Louise Groody
Mrs. Hazel White....................Stella Hoban
Freddie Ides............................Hal Skelly
Inspector Dempsey..................John Scannell
Bob White.......................John E. Hazzard
Captain Robert Whilte..............Ernest Torrence
The Steward....................Hansford Wilson
Dora de Costa................Lillian Kemble Cooper
Little Miss Jazz....................Isabel Falconer
Betty....................................Arline Chase
Susan. ..............................Lois Leigh
Jane...............................Bunny Wendell
Alice.............................Patricia Clarke
Polly..............................Lydia Scott
Florence de Costa.....................Betty Hale
Mrs. Costa...................Mrs. John Findlay
    Act I.— At the White's.   Act II.— The Night Boat.
Act III.— At the De Costa's.
```

In order to enjoy an occasional week end holiday
Bob White has convinced his wife and his mother-in-
law that he is the captain of an Albany night boat.   Be-

coming suspicious the mother-in-law directs an investigation which brings Bob White's relatives down upon him during one of his trips. He borrows the real captain's uniform, but though it nearly covers it does not shield him for more than half an act. Exposure; explanations; finale.

" MY GOLDEN GIRL "

A comedy with music, book and lyrics by Frederic Arnold Kummer, music by Victor Herbert. Produced by Harry Wardell at the Nora Bayes Theatre, New York, Feb. 2, 1920.

Cast of characters —

```
Wilson ........................Robert O'Connor
Blanche ................. . .. ....Dorothy Tierney
Kitty Mason..................Evelyn Cavanaugh
Capt. Paul de Bazin.................Richard Dore
Arthur Mitchell......................Victor Morley
Peggy Mitchell....................... Marie Carroll
Martin ............. .... ........Raymond Barrett
Mr. Hanks........................Ned A. Sparks
Mr. Pullinger...... ......... ...........Edward See
Helen Randolph.....................Helen Bolton
Howard Pope.......................George Trabert
Mrs. Judson Mitchell.............Edna May Oliver
Mr. Clarence Swan.................Harold Vizard
 - Mildred Ray........... .......... ...Victoria White
Lois Booth...........................Adele Boulais
     Act I.— Scene  ɪ — Main  Hall — the  Mitchell's
Country  Home  on  Long  Island.  Act  II.— The
Mitchell's Private Bathing Beach.
```

Arthur and Peggy Mitchell, having each discovered an affinity, agree to divorce each other. They send for their lawyers, and their soul-mates, and proceed about the matter in a perfectly dignified, musical comedy way. Before the evening is over the affinities have fallen in love with each other and the Mitchells have become happily reconciled.

"TRIMMED IN SCARLET"

A comedy in four acts by William Hurlbut. Produced at Maxine Elliott's Theatre, New York, February 2, 1920.

Cast of characters—

Mrs. Todd (Mollie)	Peggie Payter
Nurse Maid	Luella Morey
Mrs. Kipp (Ruth)	Mrs. Katharine Stewart
Revere Wayne	Lumsden Hare
Sally Pierce	Elizabeth Bellairs
David Ebbing	Sidney Blackmer
Housemaid	Gwendolyn Valentine
Archer Kingston	Albert Gran
Cordelia, calling herself Mrs. Prudence	Maxine Elliott
Charles Knight	Stanley Warmington
Janitor	Biron Eagan
Blackburn	Charles Hanna
Benjamin Ebbing	Montague Ruthurford
Marie	Sylvia Newton

Act I.—Molly Todd's House. Act II.—David's Apartment. Act III.—Cordelia's Apartment. Act IV.—The Same Scene. The Next Morning. New York City.

Cordelia Ebbing has left her husband, and their two-year-old son, David, after an unhappy marital experience. Having departed with another man she creates a scandal which she does not consider sufficiently important to deny. Returning to her home city twenty years later she finds that her son has also left the home of his male parent, and is being blackmailed by the editor of a scandal sheet who threatens to reprint the story of his mother's past. To shield the son she promises to be kind to the man who holds David in his power, but in the end is saved that particular humiliation, wins the love of one who trusts her and is re-united with her boy.

Booth (Newton) Tarkington 1869 - 1946

" BREAKFAST IN BED "

A farce in three acts by George Feydeau. Adapted
for the American stage by Willard Mack and
Howard Booth. Produced by A. H. Woods
at the Eltinge Theatre, New York. February 3, 1920.

Cast of characters —

Raphael Bates	Harry Hanlon
Terry	Tommy Meade
Hugo Getsit	Vincent Dennis
Emily Duval Bates	Florence Moore
Benjamin Colby	Will Deming
Gloriana Gorgeous	Clara Verdera
Irene Anderson	Gladys Gilbert
Jack Marston	Leon Gordon
General Koschnoduff	C. Hooper Trask
Seth Latimor	Fred Strong
Prince Nicholas	Jules Epailly
Mazie	Anne Lorentz
Camera Man	J. O. Hewitt
Justice of the Peace	Waldo Whipple
Cecily	Blanche Clark
Police Officer	Wally Clark

Act I.— Emily's Apartment. Act II.— Jack Mar-
ston's Apartment. Act III.— Same as Act I.

Emily Duval Bates, a moving picture actress, seeking to help out a friend who must have a wife in order
to inherit a fortune, lets herself in for considerable
trouble. During one adventure her companion ab-
sorbs too much wine at a masquerade ball and she is
obliged to accompany him to his apartment. Next
morning she is discovered there by her fiance, having
breakfast in bed. Explanations and a blanket pardon
for the cast.

"HE AND SHE"

A domestic drama in three acts, by Rachel Crothers.
Produced by Lee and J. J. Shubert at the
Little Theatre, New York,
Feb. 12, 1920.

Cast of characters —

Keith McKenzie	Fleming Ward
Tom Herford	Cyril Keightley
Ann Herford	Rachel Crothers
Daisy Herford	Margaret Vivian Johnson
Millicent	Faire Binney
Ruth Creel	Ethel Cozzens
Dr. Remington	Arthur Elliott
Ellen	Frances Bryant

Act I.—Studio in the Herford House. Act II.—
Living Room in the Herford House. Act III.—
Same as Act II. New York — The Present Time.
Staged by Rachel Crothers.

For seventeen years Tom and Ann Herford have
lived a happy married life. Although they are both
artists they have been able to control and make the best
of their respective artistic temperaments. They are
equally devoted to their sixteen-year-old daughter,
Millicent. A prize of $100,000 has been offered for
the best design for a frieze. Tom Herford is to com-
pete, but Ann does not think his submitted design does
him justice. She tries to induce him to accept her
idea. He refuses, but urges her also to enter the competition. She does — and wins. Her victory is a
blow to her husband's pride and threatens to create a
domestic and artistic schism, which is avoided when
Ann discovers that through her interest in the frieze
competition she has neglected her daughter, who has
come perilously near to eloping with an unworthy
suitor. She decides that her first duty is to her child,
gives up the prize which thus goes to the husband, and
the family harmony is restored.

" SHAVINGS "

A comedy in three acts from Joseph C. Lincoln's novel,
dramatized by Pauline Phelps and Marion Short.
Produced by Henry W. Savage at the Knickerbocker Theatre, New York, Feb.
16, 1920.

Cast of characters —

J. Edward Winslow, " Shavings "	.Harry Beresford
Captain Sam Hunniwell	James Bradbury
Phineas Babbitt	Charles Dow Clark
Leander Babbitt	Douglas MacPherson
Major Leonard Grover	Mitchell Harris
Charles Phillips	Saxon Kling
Gabriel Bearse	George Neville
Roscoe Holway	Dudley Clements
Ruth Armstrong	Clara Moores
Barbara Armstrong	Lillian Roth
Maude Hunniwell	Vivian Tobin
Mrs. Powless	Eleanor Martin

Act I.— Interior of Jed's Windmill Shop. June.
Act II.— Yard Between Jed's Shop and Ruth's
Cottage. July. Act III.— Scene 1 — The Shop.
Early September. Scene 2 — The Same. One Day
Later.

J. Edward Winslow, a Cape Cod bachelor, is nick-
named " Shavings " because he makes a living whittl-
ing toy windmills for the children. He takes little
interest in life until a fascinating widow and her six-
year-old daughter rent a cottage from him for the
summer. The widow's brother is employed in the village bank, is wrongfully accused of misappropriating
funds, is defended by " Shavings " and finally proved
innocent. Then the widow marries an aviator and
" Shavings " philosophically returns to his windmills.

" THE CAT-BIRD "

A comedy in three acts by Rupert Hughes.   Produced
by Arthur Hopkins at Maxine Elliott's Theatre,
New York, February 16, 1920.

Cast of characters —
```
Martin Gloade.........................John Drew
James Brearley.....................Arthur Barry
Tom Forshay.....................William Raymond
Roy Morison.......................Sidney Mason
Ronald ........................William Williams
Parker .............................Albert Reed
Mullins ..........................Willard Bowman
Mrs. Fay Crosby...................Janet Beecher
Coralie Tippet.....................Ruth Findlay
Fanita Angevine..................Pauline Armitage
    Act I.— The Professor's Vivarium. That After-
noon. Act II.— The Hotel. That Evening. Act
III.— The Same as Act I. That Night.
```

Martin Gloade, a famous scientist, missed his chance
of marrying the young woman with whom he was in
love because he ran away in search of a particular
parasite.   When he returned the girl had married another.   Years later he meets her again.   She is a
widow with an attractive daughter whom she is having
some difficulty in managing.   The scientist, offering to
help her, falls again in love with the widow and in the
end his belated romance is crowned with success.

" THE TRAGEDY OF NAN "

A tragedy in three acts by John Masefield.   Produced
by Walter Hast and Morris Rose at the 39th
street theater, New York, Feb. 17, 1919.

Cast of characters —
```
Jenny Pargetter....................Beatrice Noyes
Mrs. Pargetter.....................Annie Hughes
William Pargetter..................Harry Ashford
Nan Hardwick..................Alexandra Carlisle
Dick Gurvil.......................Philip Merivale
Artie Pearce.......................Frank Gregory
Gaffer Pearce.....................John Harwood
Tommy Arker....................David Urquhart
```

Ellen................................Susan Given
Susan ....Mabel Hicks
The Rev Mr. Drew...............Walter Kingsford
Captain Dixon.....................Charles Francis
The Constable........................John Smith
Mary ....Jean May

Nan Hardwick, the daughter of a man hung for sheep stealing, is living with an aunt and uncle whose abuse of her is fiendish. Her love for Dick Gurvil. and his love for her, promises to take her away from her sordid surroundings, until the aunt, wanting Gurvil to marry her own daughter, tells him of the incident of Nan's father and his hanging. The lover can't overlook that and deserts Nan, only to return when he hears the government purposes paying Nan a sum of money to recompense her for the loss of her father, whose innocence has been belatedly established. The distraught heroine, having poisoned her cousin, kills her false lover and throws herself into the sea.

"THE WONDERFUL THING"

A comedy-drama in four acts by Mrs. Lillian Trimble Bradley, founded on a story by Forrest Halsey. Produced by George Broadhurst at The Playhouse, New York, February 17, 1920.

Cast of characters —

Donald Mannerby.....................Gordon Ash
Laurie Mannerby....................Henry Duffey
Captain Carser......................Fred L. Tiden
Thomas Fosdick....................Edward Lester
Bates ....George Schaeffer
Tabers ....Philip Dunning
Jacqueline Laurentie.................Jeanne Eagels
Mrs. Mannerby......................Olive Temple
Mrs. Truesdale.......................Gladys Maud
Angelica Mannerby..................Jane Marbury
Dulcie Fosdick....................Eva Leonard Boyne
     Act I.— A Room in the Home of the Mannerbys. Act II.— The Same as Act I. Act III.— The Same as Act II. Act IV.— The New House. Near Brighton, England. Time — The Present. Staged by Mrs. Bradley.

— Jacqueline Laurentie is an English girl reared in France. Her father was a seller of hams, and when she returns to England she is snubbed by the aristocrats. Misunderstanding their attitude, and being deeply in love with one of them, Donald Mannerby, she practically proposes to him, and he, being much in need of funds to assist a bad brother, accepts. After they are married the family continues snippy, and Jacqueline is finally led to believe that her husband does not love her and only married her for her money. She leaves him, but in the end discovers her error and they are reunited.

" SACRED AND PROFANE LOVE "

A drama in four acts by Arnold Bennett Produced by Charles Frohman at the Morosco Theatre, New York, Feb. 23, 1920.

Cast of characters —
```
Mrs. Joicey.... ................Augusta Haviland
Louisa Benbow......................Bertha Kent
Snape ....................A. Romaine Callender
Emilio Diaz..... .....................Jose Ruben
Carlotta Peel......................Elsie Ferguson
Jocelyn Sardis......................Peggy Harvey
Lord Francis Alcar...............J. Sebastian Smith
Marie Sardis.... ...................Maud Milton
Mary Ispenlove......................Olive Oliver
Frank Ispenlove...............Alexander Onslow
Emmeline Palmer.................Katharine Brook
Rosalie .........................Renee de Monvil
Leonie ...........................Denise Corday
A Parlor Maid......................Susan Given
```
Act I.— Mrs. Joicey's Sitting-room on the First Floor of Her House in the Five Towns. Act II.— Drawing-room of Carlotta's Flat in Bloomsbury. Act III.— The Salon of a Furnished Flat in a Dubious Street of Paris. Act IV.— Drawing-room of Carlotta's Flat in Bloomsbury. Staged by Iden Payne.

Carlotta of the Five Towns is fascinated by the celebrated pianist, Emilio Diaz. Meeting him at one of his recitals she accompanies him to his lodgings to talk art and listen to him play for her alone, and re-

mains the night. Next morning, horrified at the
thought of what she has done, she runs home. For
seven years Carlotta and Emilio hear nothing of each
other. Then Carlotta, now a successful novelist in
London, learns that Emilio is a failure and a drug ad-
dict in Paris. She gives up her career, hunts him out
and, though he tries to kill her, finally reclaims him.
Her reward is his profoundest gratitude, his love, and
his offer of honorable marriage, which she accepts.

"THE LETTER OF THE LAW"

A drama in four acts, adapted from "La Robe
Rouge" by Eugene Brieux. Produced by John
D. Williams at the Criterion Theatre, New
York, Feb. 23, 1920.

Cast of characters —

Madame Vagret	Zeffie Tilbury
Bertha	Leona Hogarth
Vagret	Russ Whytal
Cataliena	Josephine Wehn
Delorme	Goldwin Patton
Madame Bunerat	Maud Hosford
La Bouzule	Clarence Derwent
Bunerat	Charles N. Greene
Mouzon	Lionel Barrymore
Ardet	Charles Coghlan
Benoit	James P. Hagen
Janitor	Wallace Jackson
Mondoubleau	Frank Kingdon
Police Sergeant	Jacob Kingsberry
Policeman	Herbert Vance
Bridet	L. R. Wolheim
Etchepare	Charles White
Yanetta	Doris Rankin
Etchepare's Mother	Ada Boshell
Attorney General of France	Lionel Hogarth

Act I.— Vagret's Sitting Room. Mauleon, France.
Act II.— Mouzon's Office in the Courthouse. Act III.
— Magistrate's Office in the Courthouse. Act IV.—
Same as Act II.

Mouzon, a French magistrate, in an effort to swelll
his record of acquittals with the hope of advancing
his chances for promotion, attempts to brow-beat a
French peasant into a confession of murder. Prosecu-

tion becomes persecution and the poor and friendless prisoner is denied justice that the ambition of his judge may be served. In the crucial scene of third-degree examination the wife of the accused turns on the magistrate and berates him with tiggerish ferocity and later stabs him to his death by way of reprisal. The play is an adaptation of Brieux' "La Robe Rouge."

"JANE CLEGG"

A drama in three acts by St. John Ervine. Produced by The Theatre Guild at the Garrick Theatre, New York, February 23, 1920.

Cast of characters —

Jane Clegg.....................	Margaret Wycherly
Mrs. Clegg.....................	Helen Westley
Henry Clegg.....................	Dudley Digges
Mr. Munce.....................	Henry Travers
Mr. Morrison.....................	Erskine Sanford
Jennie	Jean Bailey
Johnny	Russell Hewitt

Act 1.— The Sitting Room of the Cleggs House. Evening. Act II.— The Same. Two Days Later. Act III.— The Same. The next Evening.

See page 120.

"TICK-TACK-TOE"

A revue in two acts and eleven scenes written, staged and produced by Herman Timberg at the Princess theater, New York, Feb. 23, 1919

Principals in the cast —

Flo Lewis	Billy Dreyer
Jay Gould	Pearl Eaton
Herman Timberg	George Mayo
Dora Hilton	Hattie Darling
C. Leland Marsh	J. Guilfoyle

"GEORGE WASHINGTON"

A " Ballad Play " in a prologue and three acts by Percy
Mackaye. Produced by Walter Hampden at the
Lyric Theater, New York, Mar. 1, 1920.

Cast of characters —

Quilloquon	George Marion
A Little Boy	Fred J. Verdi
A Little Girl	Phyllis Loughton
The Comic Mask	Albert Oswald
The Tragic Mask	James Whittaker
The Theatre	William Sauter
The Presence	J. Harry Irvine
Lawrence Washington	Frank Arundel
Lord Fairfax	Allen Thomas
Mammy Sal	Nellie Peck Saunders
Captain Van Bramm	Le Roi Operti
Mary Washington	Elsie Herndon Kearns
George Washington	Walter Hampden
Sally Fairfax	Beth Martin
Ann Spearing	Netta Sunderland
Elizabeth Dent	Beatrice Maude
Humphrey Knight	Ernest Rowan
Zekiel	G. F. Hannam-Clark
Colonel George Washington	Walter Hampden
Martha Washington	Beatrice Reinhardt
Leader of the Crowd	Ernest Rowan
Myles Cooper	William Sauter
Alexander Hamilton	Gerald Hamer
Jack Custis	Donald Foster
Billy	Coulter Gaines
Patrick Henry	Charles Webster
Chaplain Emerson	Jerome Colamor
Colonel Henry Knox	Frank Arundel
A Boston Girl	Katherine Haden
A Cambridge Girl	Elizabeth Milburn
A Virginia Soldier	Bernard Merrick
Leader of " Johnnies "	W. Donald DuTilly
Leader of " Jinnies "	Richard Abbott
General Washington	Walter Hampden
Billy	Coulter Gaines
Selectman	Le Roi Operti
Tom Paine	Maxwell Ryder
Lieut. James Monroe	William Sauter
A doctor	Jerome Colamor
Marquis de Lafayette	Paul Leyssae
Betsy Ross	Beatrice Maude
Colonel Nicola	Wm. Sauter

Act I.—Mt. Vernon, 1750. Act II.— New York,
1775. Act III.— Valley Forge, 1778.

A series of historic episodes concerning the life and
times of " the man who made us," showing Washington first as the young surveyor of Mount Vernon, in-

terested principally in scientific farming, and carrying on through his marriage to the widow Custis; Alexander Hamilton's defense of the Tory Cooper before King's (now Columbia) College in New York; Washington's departure from Mount Vernon for the war; the lonely night spent on the shore of the Delaware previous to the crossing at dawn; the arrival of Lafayette at Valley Forge; the victory of the Continentals at Yorktown and the return of Washington to the farm.

"THE HOTTENTOT"

A farce comedy in three acts by Victor Mapes and William Collier. Produced by Sam H. Harris at the George M. Cohan Theater, New York, March 1, 1920.

Cast of characters —

```
Swift ............................Donald  Meek
Mrs.  Ollie  Gilford..................Helen  Wolcott
Larry  Crawford.....................Calvin  Thomas
Alex  Fairfax....... ............ - -Arthur  Howard
Ollie  Gilford.......................Frederic  Karr
Peggy  Fairfax.....................Frances  Carson
Mrs.  Chadwick......................Ann  Andrews
Perkins  .........................Edwin  Taylor
Sam  Harrington...................William  Collier
Alice  ...............................Dorie  Sawyer
McKisson  .......................Claude  Cooper
Reggie  Townsend.............Howard  Hull  Gibson
    Act  I. — Living  Room  in  the  Gilford  Home.  Act
II. — The  Same.  Act  III— A  Hillside  Clearing.
```

Sam Harrington is in love with Peggy Fairfax. Peggy also loves horses and is much interested in a forthcoming steeplechase in which "The Hottentot," a swift, but vicious mount, is entered. Harrington, whose name is the same as that of a famous steeplechase jockey, is mistaken for the rider, and so praised by Peggy for all the wonderful things she has heard about him, he is reluctant to admit that not only is he not the rider, but that he hates horses. To win the girl he feels he must ride the Hottentot, even tho he perish. He works many schemes in an effort to have the horse withdrawn, but is finally forced to ride. He wins, finishing strong, seated just back of the animal's ears, and Peggy capitulates.

"LOOK WHO'S HERE"

A musical farce, book by Frank Mandel; lyrics by Edward Paulson; music by Silvio Hein; extra lyrics by Cecil Lean. Produced by Spiegels, Inc, at the 44th St. theater, New York, March 2, 1920.

Cast of characters —

James Saunders....................Geo. R. Lynch
May............... ....Madge Rush
Flo..............................Alicia McCarthy
Jo.............. ....Mary McCarthy
Caroline Holmes...................Louise Kelley
Carlos Del Monte..................Dave Quixano
Robert W. Holmes....................Cecil Lean
Rocamond Purcell..................Cleo Mayfield
Horace Bream.....................Georgie Mack
Dorothy Chase..................Sylvia de Frankie
Daniel V. Chase................John F. Morrissey
    Act I.— The Lobby of the Dreamer's Inn, Catskill Mountains. Early Evening. Act II.— Scene 1 — The Balcony Hallway. After Midnight. Scene 2 — Interior of Holmes' Room in the Hotel. 3 A. M Scene 3 — Same as Scene 1. Scene 4 — Same as Scene 2.

"SOPHIE"

A satirical comedy in three acts by Philip Moeller. Produced by George C. Tyler at the Greenwich Village Theater, March 2, 1909

Cast of characters —

Marie Guimard....................Marjorie Hollis
Mlle. Abigalette Heinel..............Daisy Vivian
Sophie's Third Lackey...............Basil West
Sophie's Second Lackey.... ....Paul V. Atherton
Sophie's First Lackey.................Sidney Toler
The Abbe de Voisenon...............Oswald Yorke
Sophie ....Emily Stevens
Rosalie Levasseur.................Jean Newcombe

Louis Leon Felicite de Brancas, Count de Lau-
raguais ....O. P. Heggie
Vivienne ....Claire Mersereau
Christoph Willibald Ritter Von Gluck...Hubert Wilke
Mercy D'Argenteau....................Adolf Link
Captain Etienne Mars..........Hubbard Kirkpatrick
The Count de Saint-Florentin..........John Webster
Soldiers
Act I.— Half-Past Seven, which Leaves Sophie in
a Quandary. Act II.— Half-Past Nine, which Leaves
Sophie in Danger. Act III.— Half-Past Eleven, which
Leave Sophie Almost Alone. The Scene is Sophie's
Little Drawing-Room Adjoining Her Boudoir in the
House of the Austrian Ambassador in Paris.

Sophie Arnould, a famous singer in Paris in the
17th century, is madly in love with the Count de
Lauraguais, a dreamy poet who has been imprisoned
for having indicted certain uncomplimentary verses to
the king. The night of his release Sophie is eagerly
awaiting his coming. She is somewhat troubled, however, because of a previous engagement she has made
with the Austrian Ambassador, in payment for the
influence that official has brought to bear in securing
for her the leading role in a forthcoming production of
Gluck's " Iphegenia." She finally gets the ambassador out of the way by forging an order for his arrest,
and welcomes her poet with open arms.

" THE TRAGEDY OF RICHARD III "

"As depicted by William Shakespeare." Produced by
Arthur Hopkins at the Plymouth Theater, New
York, March 6, 1920.

Cast of characters —

King Henry VI......................Arthur Row
Queen Margaret....................Rosalind Ivan
Edward, Prince of Wales.........Burford Hampden
Duke of York....................Marshall Vincent
Duchess of York................Mrs. Thomas Wise
Edward (Afterwards King Edward IV),...........
Reginald Denny
George (Afterwards Duke of Clarence),.........
E. J. Ballantine
Richard (Afterwards Duke of Gloucester and Rich-
ard III.)......................John Barrymore
Edward .... .Mary Hughes

Richard .... Helen Chandler
Children of Clarence.......... } Lois Bartlett
                                 Helen Chandler
Earl of Warwick......... .... ..Walter Ringham
Duke of Buckingham................Leslie Palmer
Duke of Norfolk.... . .. .Robert Whitehouse
Earl of Derby............ ....George De Winter
Lord Hastings................. ....Lewis Sealy
Cardinal Bourchier........ .Montague Rutherford
Earl of Westmoreland...........Robert Whitehouse
Lord Clifford...... ....Stanley Warmington
Lord Rivers....................William J. Keighley
Lord Grey........................ .....Denis Auburn
Sir James Tyrell................John M. Troughton
Sir Richard Ratcliff............Montague Rutherford
Sir William Catesby... .. ...Stanley Warmington
Sir James Blount.................. .Malcolm Barrett
Sir William Brackenbury.......William J. Keighley
The Lord Mayor of London.........Isadore Marcil
First Murderer.......................Tracy Barrow
Second Murderer....................Cecil Clovelly
Richmond ....Raymond Bloomer
Queen Elizabeth......... . ....Evelyn Walsh Hall
Lady Anne.................. ....Helen Robbins

The familiar acting version with four scenes from
" King Henry VI " added to clarify the preliminary
action.

" ZIEGFELD GIRLS OF 1920 "

A new " 9 O'Clock Revue " produced by Florenz Ziegfeld on the New Amsterdam Theater Roof, New
York, March 8, 1920.

Principals engaged —

Allyn King   Cameron Sisters
John Price Jones   Mary Hay
Kathleen Martyn   Thomas Handers
Sybil Carmen   Arthur Milliss
Lillian Lorraine   Princess Wha-Letka
Vanda Hoff   Prince Royle
Fannie Brice   Peggy Eleanore
W. C. Fields

" MUSK "

A drama in three acts by Leonie de Souny. Produced
by Dodge & Pogany at the Punch and Judy
Theater, New York, March 13, 1920.

Cast of characters —

Lars Larsson........ - .... .Henry Mortimer
Elizabeth ....Blanche Yurka

```
Olof ..............................Burnell  Lunbec
Thordis ..........................Natalja  Morley
Victor ............................Leah  Temple
Nils  Haglund......................Douglas  Garden
Antoinette  .......................Yvonne  Garrick
Aunt  Anna........................Marguerite  Rand
Samaroff  .........................Cecil  Owen
Erik  ............................Scott  Moore
Celeste ..........................Olga  Ziceva
```
      Act I.— Living Room in the Larsson Home. Act
II.— Antoinette's Boudoir. Act III.— The Same.
One Year Later. A Suburb of a Scandinavian Com-
mercial Centre.

Elizabeth makes the best of a bad matrimonial bargain until she discovers indisputable evidence of her husband's unfaithfulness. Then, disgustedly, in place of killing him she kills herself. The title refers to the scent affected by the lady who lured the husband away, and also to the heavy, sickening odors of city life as compared with the clear, fresh air of the country.

"THE BLUE FLAME"

A melodrama in four acts by George V. Hobart and John Willard, founded on a play of the same title by Leta Vance Nicholson. Produced by A. H. Woods at the Shubert Theater, New York, March 15, 1920.

Cast of characters —

```
John  Varnum. .  .     ........  .  .Alan  Dinehart
Ah  Foo...............................Jack  Gibson
La:ry  Winston....................Donald  Gallaher
Cicely  Varnum.....................Helen  Curry
Ned  Maddox.......................Kenneth  Hill
Clarissa  Archibald....................Thais  Lawton
Ruth  Gordon.........................Theda  Bara
The  Stranger.........................Earl  House
Nora  Macree.....................Tessie  Lawrence
Tom  Dorgan......................Harry  Minturn
Miller  ...........................Tom  O'Hara
Patterson  .........................Frank  Hughes
Inspector  Ryan................DeWitt  C.  Jennings
Quong  Toy.........................Henry  Herbert
Barnes  ...........................Joseph  Buckley
Grogan  ...........................Martin  Malloy
Wung  Ming.........................Robert  Lee
Ling  Foo ...  .        ..  .    --Royal  Stout
```

Act I.— The Laboratory in John Varnum's House, on a Side Street of the Gramercy Park Section, New York City. Act II.— Ruth's Boudoir. Act III.— Cherry Street, Near the Bowery and a Room in Quong Toy's Home in Pell Street. Act IV.— The Laboratory.

Ruth Gordon is engaged to marry a young scientist who does not believe in God. He, too, can create life. Give him the still warm body of a dead person and, with the help of an electrical invention, he will restore it to life. Ruth, being a gentle soul, is distressed at this attitude on the part of her intended and hopes in time to save him. At the end of the first act she is struck dead by lightning. Her atheistic lover thereupon places her body on his machine, and brings her back to life. She is as she was before — except that her soul has fled heavenward. Thereafter she is a heartless vampire on the trail of all men. She leads several to destruction, acquires the cocaine and murder habits, and is a generally uncomfortable person to have around — until the scientist weakens and discovers he has been dreaming. He promptly promises to reform.

"THE PIPER"

Poetic drama in four acts by Josephine Preston Peabody. Produced by the Shakespeare Playhouse at the Fulton Theater, New York, March 19, 1919.

Cast of characters —

The Piper	A. E. Anson
Michael-the-Sword-Eater	William Williams
Cheat-the-Devil	Joseph Allenton
Jacobus	Reginald Barlow
Kurt	Elmer Buffham
Peter	R. Henry Handon
Hans	Forrest Woods
Axel	W. J. Clark
Martin	Paul Hayes
Old Claus	Leigh Lovell
Veronika	Olive Oliver
Barbara	Mabel Taliaferro
Old Ursula	Elizabeth Patterson
Jan	George Walcott

A poetic fantasy founded on the legend of the pied piper of Hamelin.

"WHAT'S IN A NAME?"

A musical comedy in two parts, book and lyrics by John Murray Anderson, in collaboration with Anna Wynne O'Ryan and Jack Yellen, music by Milton Ager. Produced by John Murray Anderson, Inc. at Maxine Elliott's Theatre, New York, March 19, 1920.

Principals engaged —

Phil White
Herbert Williams
Alice Hegeman
Ed. E. Ford
Charles Derickson
Rosalind Fuller
Allyn Kearns
Mary Lane
Rex Dantzler
Sheila Courtney
Thomas Morgan

Ethel Sinclair
Marie Gaspar
Joe Burroughs
Beatrice Herford
Honey Kay
Vivian Connors
Olin Howland
Lane McLeod
Robert Manning
John Alexander
Thomas Morgan

"MEDEA"

The Gilbert Murray translation from the Greek of Euritides. Produced by Maurice Browne at the Garrick Theatre, New York, March 22, 1920.

Cast of characters —

Nurse of Medea.....................Janet Young
Two children of Jason and Medea................
　　　　　　　　　Dorian and Warner Anderson
Attendant on the children..........Byron Foulger
Leader of the Chorus...............Miriam Kiper
Chorus of Corinthian Women......................
　　　Dorothy Cheston, Margaret Fransioli, Marion
　　　McCrea, Leah-Marie Minard, Cornelia Ripley
Medea ....Ellen Van Volkenburg
Creon, ruler of Corinth.............Gordon Burby
Attendants on Creon..David Case and Irving Zechnoff
Jason, chief of the Argonauts..........Moroni Olsen
Aegeus, king of Athens.............Henry Stillman
A Messenger.......................Ralph Roeder
　　The Scene represents an open space before Medea's Palace in Corinth. The Medea was first presented in B. C. 431, in Athens.

"THE HOLE IN THE WALL"

A drama in three acts by Fred Jackson. Produced by
Alex. A. Aarons and George B. Seitz at the
Punch and Judy Theatre, New
York, March 26, 1920.

Cast of characters —

Limpy Jim	Charles Halton
Deagon	William Sampson
Margaret Lyons	Muriel Tindal
Danny MacKeaver	Vernon Steele
Gordon Grant	John Halliday
Jean Oliver	Martha Hedman
Nichols	Robert Stevens
Police Inspector	Leighton Stark
Mrs. Ramsay	Cordelia MacDonald
Donald Ramsay	Walter Lewis
Cora Thompson	Doris Moore

Act I.— At Madam Mystera's. Act II.— Office of
the Inspector of Police. Scene 2 — At Madam Mystera's. Act III.— Office of the Inspector of Police.
Staged by Ira Hards.

Jean Oliver, while acting as Mrs. Ramsay's companion, had the misfortune to attract the attention of
the son of the house. To cure the young man's infatuation his mother falsely accused Jean of theft, had
her arrested and later sent to Sing Sing. After serv-
ing a two-year sentence Jean returns to the city determined to be revenged upon Mrs. Ramsay. Falling
in with a gang of crooks, one of whom she had met
in prison, she agrees to help them with their " fake
medium graft," if they will help her with the abduc-
tion of Mrs. Ramsay's grandson. The bargain made,
the child is stolen. In following various clews Gordon
Grant, a young reporter-detective, comes upon Jean
Oliver, recognizes her and helps expose her. But because he loves her, he also saves her from arrest, proves
her innocent of Mrs. Ramsay's charge and asks her to
marry him.

"THE OUIJA BOARD"

A play of the Seen and the Unseen in Three Acts by Crane Wilbur. Produced by A. H. Woods at the Bijou Theater, New York, March 29, 1920.

Cast of characters —

Jules ....George Dannenborg
Richard Annixter.................Stewart E. Wilson
Winifred Annixter.................Regina Wallace
Kitty Kemp....... . . .. Ruth Hammond
Barney McCare.......................Crane Wilbur
Norman Kemp.......................George Gaul
Henry Annixter.................William Ingersoll
Rupe Gurney.......................Edward Ellis
Gabriel Mogador..... ....Howard Lang
Bartlett ....John Wray

Act I.— Library in Henry Annixter's House. Act II.— A Room in Gabriel Mogador's House. Act III. — Same as Act I.

The action of the play takes place in a large manufacturing town in the upper part of New York State. Staged by W. H. Gilmore.

Gabriel Mogador is a spiritualistic medium who specializes in automatic writing. His uncanny skill so impresses Henry Annixter, a rich merchant, that Annixter relies on the advice he gets from his dead wife, via Mogador, implicitly. Because of this advice he is urging his daughter Winifred to marry his adopted son, Richard, and planning to leave Richard a goodly share of his fortune. Seeking a final word of confirmation of this arrangement from his wife's spirit Annixter visits Mogador. During the writing of this message Mogador suddenly loses control of the situation. The message he is receiving is a real spirit message. It tells Annixter that Mogador is a charlatan; that he had betrayed and deserted Mrs. Annixter, and that he is now scheming to come into possession of Annixter's money through the boy, Richard. Annixter stabs the medium and hurries away. A moment later a friendly detective, investigating the case, notices the hand of the dead man move. Another message is coming through. It is a warning from the wife that

Annixter himself will be killed before aid can reach him. The detective hurries to the house and discovers the merchant has been shot through the heart while listening to a phonograph. Richard has attached an automatic revolver to the operating mechanism of the machine. The love story is carried by Winifred Annixter and Norman Kemp, who assists the detective.

"MRS. JIMMIE THOMPSON"

A comedy by Norman S. Rose and Edith Ellis in three acts. Produced by Joseph Klaw at the Princess Theatre, New York, March 29, 1920.

Cast of characters —

Dorothy Delmar	Minna Phillips
Julia	Sara Enright
Louise Clark	Peggy Boland
Edgar Blodgett	Warren W. Krech
Richard Ford	Richard Taber
Eleanor Warren	Gladys Hurlbut
Philip Bennett	George L. Spaulding
Remington Gilman	Gordon Johnstone
Katherine Summer	Anita Rothe
Mrs. Atwater	Gertrude Perry
James Thompson	Thomas A. Rolfe
Rev. William Woolley	John Clements

Acts I and II.— Parlor at Mrs. Delmar's Boarding House. Act III.—Eleanor's Room. Scene 2 — The Parlor. Time — The Present.

Eleanor Warren, discouraged with stenography, but hopeful of achieving matrimony, fails to attract men. One man in particular. She is advised by a wise little manicurist living in the same boarding house with her that young men are nowadays chiefly interested in married women, widows or divorcees. She thereupon conceives the idea of leaving the boarding house for two weeks and returning as a married woman, whose husband has been suddenly called to South America. The scheme works, and Eleanor soon is carrying on a violet flirtation with her favorite youth. There are complications, however, when she discovers the name she has selected, "Mrs. Jimmie Thompson," really belongs to another woman in the same boarding house who has concealed her secret marriage. When the real Mr. Jimmie Thompson arrives there is a farcial riot. Explanations made and engagements consummated.

"FLORADORA"

A musical play in two acts, book by Owen Hall, lyrics by E. Boyd Jones and Paul Rubens, music by Leslie Stuart. Produced by J. J. Shubert at the Century Theatre, New York, April 5, 1920.

Cast of characters —

Marquita	Marie Wells
Paquita	Perle Germonde
Leandro	Nace Bonville
Frank Abercoed	Walter Woolf
Pym	Minor McLain
Langdale	George Ellison
Symes	Lucius Metz
Allen	Lewis Christy
Scott	Allen C. Jenkins
Grogan	William Lillite
Anthony Tweedlepunch	George Hassell
Cyrus Gilfain	John T. Murray
Lady Hollyrood	Christie MacDonald
Angela Gilfain	Margot Kelly
Captain Arthur Donegal	Harry Fender
Claire	Dama Sykes
Bernice	Dorothy Leeds
Mabel	Fay Evelyn
Lucille	Beatrice Swanson
Alice	Marcella Swanson
Daisy	Muriel Lodge
Dolores	Eleanor Painter
Juanita	Isabelle Rodriguez
Valeda	Muriel de Forest

Act I.— The Island of Floradora. Act II.— The Garden at Abercoed Castle. Scene 2 — The Ball Room at Abercoed Castle. Staged by Lewis Morton.

"ED WYNN CARNIVAL"

A two-act entertainment. Dialogue and songs by **Ed** Wynn. Presented under the business direction of B. C. Whitney at the New Amsterdam Theatre. New York, April 5, 1920.

Principals engaged —

Ted Roberts	Ed. Wynn
Frank Ridge	The Meyakos
Richie Ling	Lillian Wood
Lillian Durkin	Fay West
Herbert Russell	Lillian Fitzgerald
Henry Regal	Marion Davies
Simeon Moore	Earl Benham

"THREE SHOWERS"

A comedy with music, book by William Cary Duncan, lyrics and music by Creamer & Layton. Produced by Mr. and Mrs. Coburn at the Harris Theatre, New York, Apr. 5, 1920.

Cast of characters —

Col. John White....................Walter Wilson
Anna Mobberly................. ....Vera Rose
Roberta Lee White ("Bob")........Anna Wheaton
Ray White.............................Edna Morn
Willie Mobberly..............Andrew J. Lawlor, Jr.
Peter Fitzhugh.......................Paul Frawley
Hudson Gatling............William Winter Jefferson
'Rastus Redmond Reynolds ("Red")..Lynn Starling
Riley ....Wilbur Cox
Bruce Payne.....................Norman Jefferson
"Worthless" Akers...................Wilbur Cox
    Act I.—"Longview," Col. White's Farm. Act
II.— Interior of Barn. Somewhere in Virginia.

"LASSIE"

A musical comedy in three acts, book and lyrics by Catherine Chisholm Cushing, music by Hugo Felix. Produced by Lassie, Inc. at the Nora Bayes Theatre, New York, April 6, 1920.

Cast of characters —

Lily ....Miriam Collins
Mrs. McNab........................Louie Emery
Winkie ....Colin O'Moore

```
Sandy ................................Ralph Nairn
Jean  MacGregor......................Alma  Mara
MacGregor  .........................Percival  Vivian
Meg  Duncan........................Molly  Pearson
Kitty  MacKay........................Tessa  Kosta
Lieut.  The  Hon.  David  Graham  of  the  Coldstream
    Guards  ....................Roland  Bottomley
Philip  Grayson.........................Carl  Hyson
Lady  Gwendolyn  Spencer-Hill.......Dorothy  Dickson
Lord  Inglehart....................David  Glassford
Mrs.  Grayson........................Ada  Sinclair
Robbins  ..........................Robert  Smythe
    Act  I.— Juniper  Green,  on  the  Banks  of  the  Waters
of  Leith.    Act  II.— Lord  Inglehart's  Town  House  in
Berkley  Square,  London.    Act  III.— Juniper  Green.
Place — Scotland  and  London  in  the  60's.    Directed
by  Edward  Royce.
```

A musicalized version of "Kitty MacKaye." The heroine, having been brought up obscurely by poor people in Juniper Green, on the banks of the River Leith, is sent for by those who had abandoned her as a baby and taken up to London town. There she lives in luxury and falls in love with the son of the family, only to learn that she cannot marry him because he is her half brother. Back to Juniper Green and poverty she goes, broken hearted, later to learn that she is not the girl she was thought to be after all. The original baby had died and Kitty had been substituted, that her foster parents could go on collecting the allowance for her care. Thus she is able to marry her true love after all.

" THE BONEHEAD "

A satirical comedy in three acts by Frederic Arnold Kummer. Produced by Claude Beerbohn at the Fulton Theatre, New York, April 12, 1920.

Cast of characters —

```
Jean  Brent.......................Vivienne  Osborne
Robert  Campbell...................Edwin  Nicander
James  Griggs.......................Leonard  Doyle
Betty  Campbell....................Myrtle  Tannehill
Horace  Frothingham..............Claude  Beerbohm
Clarence  Potts...................William  St.  James
Mrs.  Violet  Bacon-Boyle.................Nita  Naldi
Mrs.  St  Claire................. .Beatrice  Moreland
```

Ethelbert St. Claire..............John Daly Murphy
Serge Levinsky.......................Paton Gibbs
Paul Popemoff......................David M. Callis
    Acts I., II. and III.— The Studio Room of the
Campbells' Apartment in Greenwich Village, New
York City. Time — The Present. Staged by Frank
McCormack.

Robert Campbell's wife has heard the call of the
" free " Greenwich Village life. She surrounds herself with a collection of village freaks. To cure her
Robert pretends he, too, has received the great message. He becomes more freakish than any of them,
and is particularly enthusiastic about acquiring a soul
mate. Mrs. Campbell soon decides she had rather go
back to Flatbush and the simple, normal life of the
Brooklyn suburbs.

" MARTINQUE "

A romance in three acts by Laurence Eyre. Produced
by Walter Hast at the Eltinge Theatre, New
York, April 26, 1920.

Cast of characters —

Dede ....Elsa Roem
Youte ... .Liane Byron
Ye ....Charles Kraus
Rufz Quembo.....................Arthur Hohl
Marie-Clemence De Chauvalons.......Helen Blair
Madame De Chauvalons.............Ida Waterman
Pere Benedict... .. .. Emmett Corrigan
Stephane Seguineau...............Vincent Coleman
Paul Vauclin......................Fleming Ward
Zabette De Chauvalons...........Josephine Victor
Nini ....Mary Laura Moore
Azaline ....Maidel Turner
Maximilien Bezart..................Frank Dawson
The Pastry Seller...................Stewart Evans
Cendrine ....Juliette Crosby
Yzore ....Margaret Bird
Pierre Girotte......................Donald Coll
Fabien Larides......................Edwin Hensley
Loulouze ....Marion Dyer
Diogenes ....Roy Hunt
Dr. Arnauld....................Robert Heyworth
Sister of Mercy...................Mercides Lee
    Act I.— Time — 1842. Gateway of the de Chauva-
lons' Residence in St. Pierre. Two Weeks Elapse.
Act II.— Zabette's House in the Quarter. Six
Weeks Elapse. Act III.— The Court-yard of Stephane
Seguineau's House on the Outskirts of St. Pierre.

Zabette de Chauvalons, reared in a French convent, has been kept in ignorance of the facts of her birth. Following the death of her mother, the beautiful La Belle Carolie, Zabette pawns her jewels and goes in search of her father, who had but recently returned to his ancestral home in the French West Indies. Arrived in Martinique Zabette learns that her father also is dead, and that she has no legitimate standing in the De Chauvalons household. She is advised to find a place in the "quarter," with others of her class. She does so, but not until after she has met and charmed the handsome Stephanne Seguineau, who is being forced to marry the proud Marie de Chauvalons, her half sister, that there may be an heir for the De Chauvalons lands. The night of his wedding Stephanne runs away from Marie to be with Zabette, and some weeks later, though he dies as a result of wounds inflicted by a jealous rival, he dies content because Zabette is able to assure him the De Chauvalons lands will have an heir, while she, its mother, will seek consolation at the nearby convent.

"THE GIRL FROM HOME"

A musicalized version of Richard Harding Davis farce, "The Dictator;" libretto and lyrics by Frank Craven; music by Silvio Hein. Produced by Charles B. Dillingham at the Globe theater, New York. May 3, 1920.

Cast of characters —

Brook Travers, alias "Steve Hill"	Frank Craven
Simpson, alias "Jim Dodd"	Jed Prouty
Charles Hyne	Russell Mack
Col. John T. Bowie	John Parks
Duffy	Charles Mitchell
General Santos Campos	William Burress
Rev. Arthur Bostick	Walter Coupe
Lieut. Victor	Sam Burbank
Dr. Vasquez	George E. Mack
Jose Dravo	John Hendricks
Senor Hoakumo	Jose Vallhonrat
Lucy Sheridan	Gladys Caldwell

```
Merci Hope......................Marion Sunshine
Senora Juanita Arguilla..............Flora Zabelle
Sister Agnes......................Virginia Shelby
Sister Eleanor....................Eleanor Masters
Sister May........................Sophie Brenner
Sister Marie.......................Marie Sewell
Sister Isabelle   ........  .  . ... .Edna Fenton
Sister Helen.......................Kathryn Yates
Sister Mabel.......................Janet Megrew
Sister Clara.......................Clara Carroll
```
    Act I.— Deck of the Steamship Bolivar, Harbor
of Porto Banos. Republic of San Manana, Central
America. Act II.— The Exterior of the Hotel Del
Prado, and Consulate of the United States at Porto
Banos. Act III.— The Interior of the Consulate.
Staged by R. H. Burnside.

Brook Travers, running away to South America to
escape arrest after he thinks he will be held for an
assault upon a taxi-cab driver, plunges into a revolution in the fictitious country of San Manana. Posing
as the American consul, he becomes more and more involved until the only thing that saves him is a wireless
call for help that reaches an American warship cruising
in the vicinity. His efforts to convince Lucy Sheri-
dan, an attractive ingenue he met on the boat, that he
is worthy her abiding trust, in spite of appearances,
provides the romance.

" HONEY GIRL "

A musicalized version of Henry Blossom's comedy
" Checkers." Book by Edward Clark, lyrics by
Neville Fleeson, music by Albert von Tilzer.
Produced by Sam H. Harris at the Cohan
and Harris theater, New York,
May 3, 1920.

Cast of characters —
```
Judge Martin...................... .Peter Lang
Cynthia ..:...........................Rene Riano
Honora (Honey) Parker..............Edna Bates
Lucy Martin........................Louise Meyers
David (Checkers) Graham...........Lynne Overman
Orville Bryan................... Robert Armstrong
Timothy (Tip) Smiley..............George McKay
G. W. Parker.....................Dodson Mitchell
Sol Frankenstein.................William Mortimer
Carmencita ......................Sidonie Espero
```

```
Jim Hayward.......................Edmund Elton
Charles Hawkins.................Mercer Templeton
Marion Rose.........................Cissie Sewell
Thomas Lyons....................Charlie Yorkshire
Esther Blake.........................Ottie Ardine
          CHARACTERS IN BLUE-BIRD NUMBER
Good Fairy.........................Sidonie Espero
Berylune .........................Lucretia Craig
Fire  .  . . . . . . . .  . . . . . . . . . . . . .  . . .Harriet Gustin
Water  ............................Grace Elliott
Light ...........................Catherine Wilson
Night ..............................Helen Trainer
(Bluebird) ..........................Cissie Sewell
Tyltil  .............................Mercer Templeton
   Act I.— Parkerstown, La. Act II.— At New
Orleans, La. Act III.— G. W. Parker's Home.
Staged by Bert French and Sam Forrest.
```

David ("Checkers") Graham, trying to reform after years spent in following the races, drifts into the small Louisiana village of Parkerstown, and falls in love with Honora (Honey) Parker, the daughter of the village banker. The girl's father insists David can not have his daughter until he can produce $25,000 cash. The boy leaves Parkerstown in search of the $25,000, after promising "Honey" that whatever else he does he will not return to racing. A year later he is still drifting and out of funds. "Honey" meets him at the races and suspects the worst, when Dave, in a last desperate effort to gather the $25,000, breaks his promise, pledges "Honey's" ring with a book-maker, and bets $1,000 on a horse named "Honey Girl" at 25 to 1. He wins the money, returns to Parkerstown in time to save his future father-in-law's bank from a threatened run and wins the girl.

"NOT SO LONG AGO"

A romantic comedy in three acts by Arthur Richman. Produced by Lee and J. J. Shubert at the Booth theater, New York, May 4, 1920.

Cast of characters —

```
A Lamplighter....................... ...John Gray
Sylvia .........................Margaret Mosier
Mary .........................Leatta Miller
```

Elsie Dover......................Eva Le Gallienne
Sam Robinson...................Thomas Mitchell
Michael Dover...................George H. Trader
Mrs. Ballard......................Esther Lyon
Ursula Ballard......................Beth Martin
Agnes ....Mollie Adams
Rosamond Gill...................Mary Kennedy
Billy Ballard.....................Sidney Blackmer
Rupert Hancock..................Gilbert Douglas
    Prologue — A Street in New York. Act I.— The
Ballards'. Act II.— The Dovers'. Act III.— The
Ballards'. Epilogue — A Street in New York. Time
— The Early '70's. Staged by Edward Elsner.

A romance of the '70s in which Elsie Dover, the
romantic daughter of a visionary inventor, " pretends "
that she is having a desperate love affair with " Billy "
Ballard, the aristocratic son of the house in which she
is employed as a seamstress.   She tells all the neighbor
girls about it.   Word reaches her father through one
of Elsie's jealous beaux of her " affair " with
" Billy; " and the old gentleman takes steps to warn
young "Billy " off.   Thus is Elsie's game of pretense
exposed, but not until " Billy " has decided that she
is altogether a charming person and makes love to her
in earnest.   Thus her dream comes true in the last
act.

" BETTY BE GOOD "

A musical farce in three acts adapted from a French
vaudeville by Scribe.   Book and lyrics by Harry
B. Smith; music by Hugo Reisenfeld.   Produced by Stewart and Morrison at the
Casino Theater, New York, May
4, 1920.

Cast of characters —

First Bridesmaid...................Grace Hallam
First Guest.......................Gladys Elliott
Second Guest.....................Louise Hersey
Page ....Frances Grant
Somers Short...................Raymond Oswald
Philip Fuller.................Worthington Romaine
Maggie ....Jeannette Wilson
Bernice ....Thy Daly
Col. Ichabod Starkweather.............Eddie Garvie
Mrs. Starkweather.................Josie Intropodi
Tom Price........................Irving Beebee

```
Amy Starkweather..................Georgia Hewitt
Sam Kirby.      ......  ...........Frank Crumit
Betty Lee.....................Josephine Whittell
Marion Love...................Vivienne Oakland
Madame O'Toole.................Lucille Manion
Guy .........................Raymond Oswald
Percy ...............................Peter Mott
    Act I.— Exterior Bon Ton Hotel, Lenox, Mass.  Act
II.— Living Room of Betty's Apartment, New York
City.  Act III.— Exterior Betty's Country Home,
Kew Gardens, Long Island.  Staged by David Ben-
nett.
```

Betty Lee, a flirtatious actress, discovers an old sweetheart in Lenox, Mass., the day of his wedding. He seeks to keep her from knowing he is to be married, by pretending to be only the best man. The deception would have worked very well if the real best man had not rented the actress's New York apartment for the use of the bride and groom. There all parties meet, seek and dodge each other for two more acts.

"OH, HENRY"

A farce comedy in three acts by Bide Dudley. Produced by Theodore C. Deitrich at the Fulton Theater, New York, May 5, 1920.

Cast of characters —

```
John Carson........................Edwin Walter
Mrs. Carson.......................Jane Wheatley
Jennie Carson................. ........... ....Clay Carroll
Harley West.......................Roland Hogue
Aunt Annabelle Carson...............Eva Condon
The Stranger....................Spencer Charters
Henry Boswell....................Dallas Welford
Lizzie O'Malley...................Florence Carrette
    Acts I, II and III.— The Living-Room of the Carson
Summer House at Long Beach.  Staged by Tom Wise.
```

A stranger, unmistakably under the influence of liquor, the eighteenth amendment notwithstanding, drifts into a Long Beach house and insists upon remaining. The new butler suspects he may be the master he has never seen and attempts to hide him. The family, fearful lest the inebriated one be discovered by a prohibitionist aunt, aids in keeping the stranger out of sight until deception is no longer of any use.   Then it transpires that the stranger is the newly acquired husband of the prohibitionist aunt, and is indulging his last spree.

" FOOTLOOSE "

A drama in three acts by Zoe Akins, adapted from " For-get-me-not," by Herman Merivale and F. C. Grove.   Produced by George C. Tyler at the Greenwich Village Theater, New York, May 10, 1919.

Cast of characters —

Prince Malleotti	Robert Casadesus
Alice Verney	Elizabeth Risdon
Rose de Brissac	Tallulah Bankhead
Pietro	John Webster
Barrato	O. P. Heggie
Sir Horace Welby	Norman Trevor
Stephanie, Marquis de Mohrivart	Emily Stevens
Lady Phyllis Nelson	Lillian Brennard

Act I.— The Late Afternoon of a Day in Early Spring.   Act II.— The Next Afternoon.   Act III.— After Dinner, That Evening.   The Action of the Play Occurs in Mrs. Verney's Apartment in a Palazzo in Rome   Staged by O. P. Heggie.

Stephanie, Marquise de Mohrivart, socially declassee, determined to enjoy six weeks of respectability, forces Alice Verney, head of an exclusive English family, to accept her as a guest.   Her hold upon the Verneys is gained through her threat to prove that her son was under age when he married Alice's sister, Rose.   The marquise's conspiracy is highly successful until there arises in her path one Barrato, a Corsican whom she had on one occasion ordered thrown out of her husband's gambling parlor in Paris.   The presence of Barrato so frightens Stephanie she is glad to scamper back to London and leave the Verneys in peace.

"RESPECT FOR RICHES"

A comedy in four acts by William Devereaux. Produced at the Harris Theater, New York, May 11, 1920.

Cast of characters —

Sir Robert Chesleigh............William Devereux
Sir Guy Brampton.................George Giddens
Louis Hirsch.........................Fred Tiden
John Ricker......................Hamilton Christy
Lady Brampton.......................Julia Stuart
Mrs. Kenyon...................Alexandra Carlisle
Mrs. Warrington...................Lucile Watson
Clara Warrington............Muriel Martin Harvey
Muriel ....Florence Malone
Patridge ....Nancy Lewis Waller
Jules ....Louis La Bey
Henry ....Frank Bixby
    Acts I and II.— Room in Sir Guy Brampton's
Country Home on the Thames. Act III.— Room in
Crozier Inn   Act IV.— Same as Act I. Morning.
Time — The Present

Mrs. Kenyon, supposedly a wealthy widow, knows that she is facing bankruptcy, and that the moment her real financial condition is made public the friends who have fawned upon her out of respect for her money will desert her. In order to help a brother who is in trouble, it is necessary that she should maintain her position until she can charm a rich youth into marriage. Her conspiracy is discovered by a philosophical bachelor who long has loved her, and though he is partly responsible for the exposure of her schemes he makes honorable and sentimental amends by marrying her himself.

"ALL SOUL'S EVE"

A domestic drama in three acts by Anne Crawford Flexner. Produced by John D. Williams at the Maxine Elliott's Theater, New York, May 12, 1920.

Cast of characters —

Alison Heath.......................Lola Fisher
Peter ....Leland Chandler
Katy ....Eleanor Hutchinson

Oliva Larkin........................Anne Faystone
Jim Heath..........................Cyril Keightley
Dr. Sandy McAlister.............Clifford Dempsey
Edward Knox, Jr... .... . .Walter Kingsford
Norah ....Lola Fisher
Tom Larkin.........................John Thorn
Rua ....Manabozho
    Act I.— Jim Heath's Study. Act II.—The Nursery.
All Souls' Eve. Two Years Later. Scene 2 — Jim
Heath's Study. Scene 3 — The Nursery. Act III.
— The Lanai of Jim's Home on Mt. Tantalus Outside
Honolulu. Place — Any Little Suburban Home.
Time — Always. Staged Under the Direction of
Homer Saint-Gaudens.

Alison Heath, devoted to her husband and their infant son. is killed suddenly in an automobile accident.
Norah, an Irish girl but recently landed in America,
having wandered into the Heath home the day before
the accident, is retained as the child's nurse. A year
later, on All Soul's Eve, when, according to an Irish
superstition, the souls of dead mothers return to the
earth to see if their children are being well cared for,
the soul of Alison Heath returns to find her baby
dangerously ill with the croup and her husband a
spiritless, drink-befuddled failure. She tries to get a
spirit message across to them, but only the child
recognizes her. This recognition, however, makes the
" miracle " possible; the soul of the mother is then
permitted to inhabit the body of Norah, the nurse, and
remain on earth. Two years later the neighbors have
remarked Norah's likeness to the dead Mrs. Heath,
but the reformed husband does not recognize it until
the Irish girl threatens to leave. Then he asks her to
stay on as his wife.

" HIS CHINESE WIFE "

A domestic drama in three acts by Forrest Halsey and
Clara Beranger. Produced at the Belmont
Theater, New York, May 17, 1920

Cast of characters —
    Mrs. Alaide Barring...............Frances Neilson
    Mrs. Corinne Sturgis.. . ...Leah Winslow

Elise .... .Vernon Brown
Cecelia Sturgis.....................Doris Fellows
Livingston Sturgis...................Ethel Wright
Rodney Sturgis.....................Forrest Winant
Mrs. Rodney Sturgis (Tea Flower)..Madeline Delmar
Wan Ti Ti........ ....Laura Clairon
Mrs. Maria Victoria Sturgis.............Mabel Burt
Mrs. Caroline Stockton.............Jane Meredith
Inspector Immigration Bureau.....George L. Brown
Jane ....Frederica Going
   Act I.—At the Old Sturgis Home, on Sturgis
Street. Act II.—At the New House on Lorilard
Boulevard. Act III.— Same as Act II. Small City
in New Jersey. Staged by Hal Briggs and Jack
White.

Rodney Sturgis, member of an old and proud New
Jersey family, is sent to the far east in the hope he
will mend his dissipated ways. In China he is reformed by a princess who finds him sleeping by the
roadside. He marries the princess and brings her to
America, where the Sturgises not only refuse to receive her, but seek to force Rodney to divorce her.
Their conspiracy, in which a former sweetheart of
Rodney's takes the lead, is threatened with success,
until the young man suddenly awakes and, with the
aid of his most loyal grandmother, saves his Chinese
wife from committing hari kari and decides to return
with her to China, where there is more happiness and
less Christianity.

" AN INNOCENT IDEA "

A farce in three acts by Martin Brown. Produced by
Charles Emerson Cook at the Fulton Theater,
New York, May 25, 1919

Cast of characters —
Henry Bird.................Robert Emmett Keane
Ernest Geer............ - ....Russell Fillmore
Philomena Rose.....................Miriam Doyle
Myrtilla Marne.....................Helen Barnes
Lily Dell.......................Antoinette Walker
Bonnie Wing.....................Claire Whitney
Mrs. Lord................Edna Archer Crawford

Mrs. Case...........................Florence Gerald
Fannie Fish...........................Rose Mintz
Chambermaid ....Amy Ongley
Mrs. Coyle...........................Sadie Duff
Mrs. Lee........................Elizabeth Alexander
Mrs. Turk..........................Renee Johnson
Henderson Wing......................Loral Lake
Hector Home......................Harold Howard
Waiter ....Arthur Villars
Bell Boy...........................Teddy Hart
Act I.— The Parlor of Ernest Geer's Suite in the
Battle Rapids Hotel. Act II.— Same as Act I.
Act III.— The Corridor Outside of Ernest's Door.
Staged by Max Figman.

Henry Bird, known as the wickedest man in Michigan, seeks to prove to certain delegates to the Bed trust convention, that reports of his wild ways are greatly exaggerated. He moves out of his own hotel apartment, where anything might happen, and takes lodgings with a highly respectable friend across the way. The experiences he has there, trying to escape the wild folk of farce, are even more incriminating than any he had had at home. But the soubrette believes him when he promises her to reform.

"SCANDALS OF 1920"

A revue in two acts and sixteen scenes, book by Andy Rice and George White, music by George Gershwin, lyrics by Arthur Jackson. Produced by George White at the Globe Theater, New York, June 7, 1920

Principals engaged —

Ann Pennington	Lou Holtz
'a Sylphe	Lester Allen
Frances Arms	George Bickel
Ethel Delmar	Jack Rose
Ruth Savoy	George Rockwell
Myra Cullen	Lloyd Garrett
Peggy Dolan	James Miller
Christine Welford	Lester O'Keefe
Darry Welford	Al Fox
Sascha Beaumont	Yerkes Happy Six
James Steiger	

"FALL AND RISE OF SUSAN LENOX"

A melodramatic "pilgrimage" in three acts and ten
scenes, by George V. Hobart. Produced at
the 44th Street Theater, New York by
Lee and J. J. Shubert, June 9, 1919

Cast of characters —

George Warham	Walter Walker
Mrs. Warham	Anne Sutherland
Ruth Warham	Charline Thomas
Betty	Marie Vernon
Maud	Jane Williams
Belle	Gladys Dale
Lula	Justine Braun
Mary	Eleanor Pendelton
Susan Lenox	Alma Tell
Sam Wright	Harry Southard
Thomas Wright	Albert Sackett
Kesiah Ferguson	Grace Hampton
Jeb Ferguson	Robert T. Haines
Robert Burlingham	Philip Lord
Gregory Tempest	John W Cowell
Jess	Henry Lyons
Elbert Eshwell	Douglas Cosgrove
Violet Anstruther	Georginna Such
Mabel Connomora	Anna Straton
Samuel Greenbrier	Louis Mountjoy
Roderick Spencer	Perce Benton
Rufus Small	Adin Wilson
Gladys	Beatrice Noyes
Victoria	Clara Burton
Etta Brashear	Marie Jepp
Marie	Irene Matthews
Elliot Ray	James Wolf
"Fish Hawk" Morris	Paul Stewart
Barney	John Abbot
Cora	Isabel Grey
Mr. Gideon	Edward Talbot
A Maid	Milicent Sharpe

Act I.— Geo. Warham's Home, Sutherland, Ind.
Act II.— Jeb Ferguson's Farm.   Act III.— A "Show
Boat" on the Ohio River; at the Entrance to a
Park in Cincinnati; in Mrs. Marshall's Boarding
House; in the Park; the Display Room in Spencer's
Department Store.   Act IV.— Drawing Room in
Roderick Spencer's Home.

Susan Lenox, a "child of sin" brought up by the
George Warhams, trusts Sam Wright and is deceived.
Her foster father, thinking to save her honor, forces
her to marry Jeb Ferguson, a hard-drinking farmer.
Susan runs away, joins a theatrical troupe on a Missis-

sippi river " show boat," later makes her way to Cincinnati, where she suffers poverty until her true worth is recognized by Roderick Spencer, the rich proprietor of a department store.   Marrying Roderick she is in a position to tell the Warhams, and the world, to go hang.

WHERE AND WHEN THEY WERE BORN

Adams, Maude.........Salt Lake City, Utah..1872
Adelaide, Le Petite......Cohoes, N. Y.........1890
Allen, Viola.. ....Alabama 1869
Anglin, Margaret.......Ottawa, Canada 1876
Arbuckle, Maclyn.......Texas 1867
Arliss, George. ....London, England 1868
Atwell, Roy...........Syracuse, N. Y........1880
Arthur, Julia..........Hamilton, Ont. 1869
Bainter, Fay.. ....Los Angeles, Calif. ...1893
Bacon, Frank.........California 1865
Barrymore, John........Philadelphia, Pa. 1883
Barrymore, Ethel. .. ..Philadelphia, Pa. 1880
Barrymore, Lionel......London, England 1878
Bates, Blanche........Portland, Ore. 1873
Barbee, Richard........
Beban, George.........San Francisco, Calif. ..1873
Bayes, Nora...........Milwaukee, Wis. 1880
Belasco, David........San Francisco, Calif. ..1862
Beecher, Janet.........Chicago, Ill. 1884
Bennett, Richard.......Cass County, Ind. 1872
Bennett, Wilda........Asbury Park, N. J.....1899
Bernard, Sam.........Birmingham, England..1863
Binney, Constance......Philadelphia, Pa. .....
Bingham, Amelia.......Hickville, Ohio 1869
Blinn, Holbrook.......San Francisco, Calif. ..1872
Brady, William A.......San Francisco, Calif. .1865
Brady, Alice...........New York 1896
Brian, Donald.........St. John's Newfound-
                        land .... .1880
Brooks, Virginia Fox...New York 1893
Burke, Billie..........Washington 1886

Cantor, Eddie.........New York ....
Carlisle, Alexandra.... ..Yorkshire, England ..
Carle, Richard.........Somerville, Mass. ...1871
Cawthorn, Joseph......New York 1868
Claire, Ina............Washington, D. C.....1897
Clarke, Marguerite.....Cincinnati 1887
Chatterton, Ruth.......New York City 1893
Coghlan, Rose.........Petersboro, England ..1850
Cohan, George M......Providence, R. I.....1878
Collier, Constance......Windsor, England 1882
Collier, William.......New York City 1866
Collinge, Patricia......Dublin, Ireland 1894
Conroy, Frank........London, England ....
Corthell, Herbert.......Boston, Mass.........1875
Courtenay, William....Worcester, Mass. 1875
Courtleigh, William.....Guelph, Ont. 1867
Cowl, Jane...........Boston, Mass. 1890
Crane, William H......Leicester, Mass. 1845
Crothers, Rachel.......Bloomington, Ill. .....
Crosman, Henrietta.....Wheeling, W. Va. 1865
Daly, Arnold......... .New York 1875
Dawn, Hazel..........Ogden, Utah 1891
Day, Edith...........:.Minneapolis, Minn. 1899
De Angelis, Jefferson.. .San Francisco ..... .1859
Dean, Julia...........St. Paul, Minn. 1880
De Belleville, Frederic..Belgium 1857
De Cordaba...........New York 1881
Dickson, Dorothy......Chicago, Ill. ....
Dinehart, Alan........Missoula, Mont. 1889
Ditrichstein, Leo.......Temesbar, Hungary ..1865
Dixey, Henry E........Boston, Mass. 1859
Dodson, John E........London .... .1857
Donnelly, Dorothy Agnes.New York 1880
Dressler, Marie........Canada 1869
Drew, Louise..........New York 1884
Drew, John...........Philadelphia, Pa. 1853
Dunn, Emma.........England 1875

PROMINENT STAGE PEOPLE WHO HAVE DIED

(June 15, 1919–June 15, 1920)

George Primrose, minstrel, 68. Died San Diego, Cal., July 23, 1919.

Oscar Hammerstein, impresario, 67. Born Berlin, Germany; died New York, Aug. 1, 1919.

R. Leoncavallo, composer, 64. Died Rome, Italy, Aug. 9, 1919.

Harry A. Lee, old-time manager, 76. Born San Francisco; died Atlantic City, N. J., Aug. 2, 1919.

Adalina Patti, prima donna, 77. Died Craig-y-nos, Wales, Sept. 27, 1919.

A. T. Ringling, circus man, 57. Died Oak Ridge, N. J., Oct. 21.

H. B. Irving, eldest son the late Sir Henry Irving, 50. Died London, Oct. 17, 1919.

Effie Ellsler, actress, 97. Played in support of Charlotte Cushman, Edwin Forrest and Clara Morris. Died Nutley, N. J., Dec. 12, 1919.

Ethan M. Robinson, vaudeville manager, 47. Died New York, Dec. 3, 1919.

Cleofonte Campanini, impresario, 60. Director Chicago Opera Company. Born Parma, Italy; died Chicago, Ill., Dec. 19, 1919.

Pauline Hall, comic opera star, 60. Died Yonkers, New York, Dec. 29, 1919.

Frank Pixley, composer, 53. Born Richfield, O.; died San Diego, Cal., Dec. 31, 1919.

Nat C. Goodwin, actor, 63. Born Boston, Mass.; died New York, Jan. 31, 1920.

Shelley Hull, actor, 35. Born Louisville, Ky.; died
    New York, Jan. 14, 1920.
Ermeti Novelli, Italian tragedian, 69. Died Rome,
    Italy, Jan. 30, 1920.
Reginald De Koven, composer. Born Middletown,
    Conn,; died Chicago, Ill., Jan. 16, 1920.
Hiram ("Hi") Henry, minstrel, 76. Died New York,
    Jan. 30, 1920.
Maude Powell, violinist, 51. Died Uniontown, Pa.,
    Jan. 8, 1920.
Deshler Welch, dramatic critic and founder Theater
    Magazine, 65. Died Buffalo, N. Y., Jan. 7, 1920.
Anson Phelps Pond, playwright, 71. Died New
    York, Jan. 22, 1920.
Bessie Abbott, prima donna, 42. Died New York,
    Feb. 9, 1920.
Rudolph Aronson, composer, 62. Died New York,
    Feb. 4, 1920.
Lew Benedict, minstrel, 80. Born Buffalo, N. Y.,
    died New York, Feb. 13, 1920.
Gaby Deslys, French comedienne, 36. Born Mar-
    seilles, France; died Paris, Feb. 11. 1920.
Frederick Hallam, comedian, 60. Of the team of
    Hallam and Hart. Born Montreal, Canada; died
    New York, Feb. 29, 1920.
Walter N. Lawrence, manager, 62. Died Bronxville,
    N. Y., Feb. 28, 1920.
Richard Harlow, comedian. Famed as a female im-
    personator in Rice's "Evangeline," "1492," etc.
    Died New York, Feb. 19, 1920.
William E. Meehan, comedian, 35. Born New York;
    died New York, March 23, 1920.
Bonnie Thornton, vaudeville comedienne, 47. Born
    New York; died New York, March 13, 1920.
Charles H. Yale, manager, 64. Produced "The
    Devil's Auction," etc. Died Rochester, N. Y.,
    March 23, 1920.

Sam Sothern, actor, 55. Brother of E. H. Sothern. Born England; died Los Angeles, March 21, 1920.

Sidney Drew, comedian, 55. Brother of John Drew. Died New York, April 9, 1920.

Imre Kiralfy, producer, 75. Famed as the producer of spectacles. Died London, April 27, 1920.

Marjorie Benton Cooke, writer and monologist, 44. Died Manila, P. I., April 26, 1920.

Lillie E. Wilkinson, comedienne, 79. Gained fame as the most successful of the Topsies in " Uncle Tom's Cabin." Born England; died Worcester, Mass., April 10, 1920.

George P. Goodale, dramatic critic, 77. Died Detroit, May 7, 1920.

Frank Carter, comedian, 32. Died in automobile accident near Grantville, Md., May 9, 1920.

David Kessler, Jewish tragedian, 61. Born Russia; died New York, May 14, 1920.

Hal Reid, playwright, 60. Died Red Bank, N. J., May 22, 1920.

Clifton Crawford, comedian, 45. Born Edinburgh, Scotland; died London, June 3, 1920.

Gabrielle Rajane, French comedienne, 63. Born Paris; died Paris, June 14, 1920.

LONG RUNS ON BROADWAY

	Performances
" Lightnin' " (to June 15, 1920)...	763
" East is West "	680
" A Trip to Chinatown "	657
" Peg o' My Heart "	604
" Adonis "	603
" The Music Master "	540
" The Boomerang "	522
" Hazel Kirke "	486

THE SEASON IN PARIS

By Leon Stolz
Paris Dramatic Correspondent, *Chicago Tribune*

According to one French dramatic critic no one could reasonably expect good plays to be produced in Paris this year with the world's greatest play being acted daily in opposition.

He was referring to the Peace Conference as the opposition. There is no denying that the Conference has had its moments and there is also no denying that the Paris stage has from an artistic standpoint had a sorry season indeed. Yet if you ask the manager of any one of Paris' sixty theaters he will assure you that seldom has his theater enjoyed a more prosperous years, despite a doubling in prices. The best theaters now get from 18 to 25 francs for their orchestra seats, which, at the rate of exchange latterly prevailing, amounts to about $1.50 to $2.

There were two brief interruptions in the season resulting from strikes, both of which ended in compromises. The coal shortage also interfered somewhat with playgoing but the interference was not serious.

From this rather dreary summary I turn to the plays themselves. Of these probably the one of widest interest to Americans as such was Eugene Brieux' new work " Les Americains Chez Nous " (" The Americans in Our Midst "), which, I am told, is to be produced by Leo Ditrichstein in New York. During the winter it has occupied a prominent place in the repertoire of the Odeon, the subsidized theater of the Latin Quarter. A young American officer is stationed during the war on the run-down estate of an old French family. His American sense of business management is placed at the service of his hosts, among whom is his fiancée. There are troubles with the hired hands which the American adjusts rather ruthlessly, but all goes on more or less serenely until the son of the family announces he is going to America to marry a Red Cross girl, whom he met during the war.

Indeed, he is not, replies the family. This can never be. Here he was born and here he must remain to carry on the traditions of his race.

There is a deal of talk and it is ended by the American captain taking his French fiancée to America and the Red Cross girl and the son remaining on the somewhat mouldy French estate. The detail of the play develops the thesis that the French are a conservative, beauty-loving people, whereas the Americans are a restless, forceful people.

The American soldier has also appeared frequently on other stages, especially, as might be expected, in the revues, where he has been everything from a model of dashing ball-room propriety to an instructor of apaches in American methods of highway robbery. It is interesting to contrast this new stage American with the old one seen somewhat earlier in the season in the revival of "The Hawk" under its French title, "L'Epervieu." This pre-war American was simply a brisk Yankee, full of money and hard, rather too hard, common sense, but the newer Yank is a man of infinite resource — and little soul.

Paris theater-goes have not forgotten the Yanks, though they will persist in calling them Sammies. Nor has the war been forgotten. The play which probably was the most sensational of the year was "La Captive," produced at the Theatre Antoine, which is Paris' art theater, under Gemier's direction. "La Captive" is by Charles Méry and it is frankly an anti-war play. No higher tribute to the French sense of artistic liberty could be paid than to record that this production, which I am convinced, would have been refused a permit in any American city, ran for three months in Paris at the very time when the Peace Conference was holding its daily meetings at the Quai D'Orsay.

"La Captive" is the story of a mother who lives in an imaginary neutral country between two equally imaginary states at war. The play opens as war is declared. Now this woman has been twice married, once to a citizen of one of the belligerent nations and the second time to a citizen of the other. By each of her marriages she has had two children. The son of her first marriage has already joined the colors, and the first act presents the conflict between the mother and the two sons of her second marriage, both of whom are eager to volunteer. She pleads earnestly with them. What is there for them to gain? What cause are they fighting for worth the risk? How can their little contribution do any good? They belong to her, not to their father's country. Did she bear them in pain that they should go out to kill other men's sons and be killed themselves?

The sons pay as little attention to the mother's pleas as sons usually do in war time, and rush out to join the somewhat theatrical drums beating in the distance. "Oh, the madness of men!" cries the tortured mother and the curtain falls.

What I cannot convey by this bare recital is the simulated physical suffering of the captive, the mother, as she sees the arguments she knows to be the very truth — whatever we may think of them — utterly ignored by those sons of hers, obsessed by notions of duty and glory.

The play doesn't end there, though it might. As they story proceeds, we see the daughter, the only child remaining, also answering the call of patriotism. She leaves not only her mother, but her fiancèe as well, to return to her father's land. But before she goes the French audience gets what it came for, a debate. The girl's uncle, a white-whiskered patriot, has come to claim her for his country's service as a nurse. He meets at her home a professor, the father of her fiancèe. Now this professor is a Sermon-on-the-Mount, if not a League-of-Nations internationalist and he has it out with the uncle who, as noted above, is a good deal of a chauvinist. It is the clash of ideas that the books on French drama tell you about; and the audience has a party. It is all to M. Méry's credit that he has played fair in the debate and stated each man's case as well as he could. That enables about two-thirds of the orchestra and a fraction of the galleries to applaud the uncle to the echo; and two-thirds of the galleries and one-third of orchestra to shout and stamp as the professor scores for internationalism. The cheering fairly broke up the play on the opening nights and I have no doubt accounted in a measure for the play's success.

As the debate improved, the drama almost went to pieces, but it recovered for a moment in the last act,

when the war was over and the two surviving sons
who had fought on opposite sides, return home, one
crippled, the other blinded. There is a terrific and
pathetic scene when they meet and the blind one sinks
into a chair as the lame one stumbles out. He has
almost reached the door when the hobbling noise of
his going pentrates the mind of the blind boy.

"Where," he asks listlessly, "did you get it?"

"At Hill 102," the lame lad responds. They had
both been there and suffered the same tortures. The
common experience reconciles them, and the final curtain descends on the hope, if, alas, not the dawn, of
universal brotherhood.

M. Méry who wrote "La Captive" has written a
number of pieces which have been acted at the Grand
Guignol, Paris' theatrical chamber of horrors. I do
not at the moment recall any of his plays which were
done there this year where much the best productions
have been revived adaptations from Poe. "The Fall
of the House of Usher" left a good deal to be desired
to one who had the original in mind; but for horror,
physical horror, I commend you to the Grand Guignol
version of "The System of Dr. Goudron."

Of lighter plays we have, of course, had any number, some of which will be sent overseas sooner or
later, though they will have to be cleaned up considerably. I doubt if New York's chaste policemen will
permit three women to undress and climb into bed
right in front of everybody in the course of one evening's entertainment, as they do in one of our revues,
and I know they won't stand idly by while the companions of these three undress and climb in alongside,
especially when it is recalled that Frenchmen persist,
even on the stage, in wearing blue underwear and sus-
penders.

Rare among the lighter plays, partly because there
was no undressing in it but especially because it was

in the best French comedy tradition, was " Le Denseur
de Madame " by M. Armont and Jacques Bousquet.
It is a comedy trifle built about the theme that the
devotees of the " new " dances are true devotees and
therefore have no time for another love, be it husband,
lover or friend. The central character is Huguette
Chavelin who has all three, but time for none of them.
She spends her afternoons and evenings and some of
her mornings with her dancing partner, a professional.
Here is the dancing man to the life. He is by no
means pretty and, except when dancing, he is awkward. Always he is stupid. Huguette dances with
him until the pleasures of dancing, despite her pro-
ficiency, begin to be exhausted and there is a suspicion
that the home life is calling her. The play ends as
she announces that she is giving up dancing forever
and agreeing to an engagement with her lover for 5
o'clock the next afternoon. She has broken dozens of
such appointments in the interest of the fox-trot before; but this one she is going to keep.

So much for the story. It gains much by the ex-
pertness of its handling by its author. I believe there
is a future for " Le Danseur de Madame " in America, provided the interest in dancing holds out until
it can be worked over. Its title, by the way, is an
echo of the title of the preceding success " Le Bon-
heur de ma Femme," at the same smart little theater.

Toward the close of the season, Paris saw a new
Arabian Nights play presented under Gemier's direction at the Champs Elysees. This theater may be
remember by the A. E. F. as the Y. M. C. A.'s magnificent playhouse on the Avenue Montaigne. Gemier
is to France what Max Reinhardt is to Germany but
" Les Mille et Une Nuits " is not to be considered with
" Sumurun." The story is built around the Sheerazade
incident. The sultan finds moral lessons in her tales
of Ali-Baba and Sinbad and retracts his order of

execution. Whatever the Arabian Nights are, they are not Æsop's Fables. The play failed, but not in its pictures. The dancing and the costuming were beyond praise.

The revues this year have been far more daring than even Paris has known. The game is simply to shock and there are no rules. Thus Act I of the present piece at the Folies Bergere, " L'Amour en Folie! " concludes with — I give you my word — the crucifixion of three of the chorus girls. In the second act the smoking-room story which begins, " A traveling man went into a farm house one night because there was no place else to go in the rain " is enacted with more detail than humor and the finale is built around three naked women. I didn't see even the traditional beads.

An interesting novelty for Paris is to be staged during the summer months at the Antoine. It is a French version of " Male and Female " which, quaintly enough, is entitled " L'Admirable Crichton! "

INDEX OF PLAYS AND CASTS

CPSIA information can be obtained at www.ICGtesting.com
Printed in the USA
LVOW04s2134240814

400731LV00012B/127/P